Taking into account the long history and wide range of Confucian studies, this book introduces Confucianism – initiated in China by Confucius (c. 552–c. 479 BC) – primarily as a philosophical and religious tradition. It pays attention to Confucianism in both the West and the East, focusing not only on the tradition's doctrines, schools, rituals, sacred places and terminology, but also stressing the adaptations, transformations and new thinking taking place in modern times.

While previous introductions have offered a linear account of Confucian intellectual history, Xinzhong Yao presents Confucianism as a tradition with many dimensions and as an ancient tradition with contemporary appeal. This gives the reader a richer and clearer view of how Confucianism functioned in the past and of what it means in the present.

There are important differences in the ways Confucianism has been presented in the hands of different scholars. This problem is caused by, and also increases, the gap between western and eastern perceptions of Confucianism. Written by a Chinese scholar based in the West, this book uses both traditional and contemporary scholarship and draws together the many strands of Confucianism in a style accessible to students, teachers, and general readers interested in one of the world's major religious traditions.

XINZHONG YAO is Senior Lecturer in and Chair of the Department of Theology and Religious Studies at the University of Wales, Lampeter. He has doctorates from the People's University of China, Beijing, and from the University of Wales, Lampeter. Dr Yao has published widely in the area of philosophy and religious studies and is the author of five monographs including *Confucianism and Christianity* (1996) and *Daode Huodong Lun* (*On Moral Activities*; 1990), four translations (from English to Chinese), and about fifty academic papers. He is a Fellow of the Royal Society of Arts.

D1212071

儒家・儒學・儒教

An introduction to Confucianism

XINZHONG YAO
University of Wales, Lampeter

CAMBRIDGE
UNIVERSITY PRESS

PUBLISHED BY THE PRESS SYNDICATE OF THE UNIVERSITY OF CAMBRIDGE
The Pitt Building, Trumpington Street, Cambridge, United Kingdom

CAMBRIDGE UNIVERSITY PRESS
The Edinburgh Building, Cambridge CB2 2RU, UK   http://www.cup.cam.ac.uk
40 West 20th Street, New York NY 10011–4211, USA   http://www.cup.org
10 Stamford Road, Oakleigh, Melbourne 3166, Australia
Ruiz de Alarcón 13, 28014 Madrid, Spain

First published 2000

Printed in the United Kingdom at the University Press, Cambridge

Typeface Sabon (*The Monotype Corporation*) 10/13.5pt
System QuarkXPress™   [GC]

A catalogue record for this book is available from the British Library

Library of Congress cataloguing in publication data

Yao, Hsin-chung.
An introduction to Confucianism / Xinzhong Yao.
    p.   cm.
Added t.p. title in Chinese characters.
Includes bibliographical references and index.
Added title page title: (Ru jia, ru xue, ru jiao)
ISBN 0 521 64312 0
1. Confucianism.   I. Title.   II. Title: Ru jia, ru xue, ru jiao
BL 1852.Y36   2000
181'.112–dc21   99-21094 CIP

ISBN 0 521 64312 0 hardback
ISBN 0 521 64430 5 paperback

Contents

List of illustrations

An inscribed portrait of Confucius travelling around to teach, supposedly painted by Wu Daozi, a famous painter in the Tang Dynasty (618–906) **frontispiece**

(Located between pages 138 and 139)

1 The statue of Confucius at the main hall of the Temple of Confucius, Qufu, the home town of Confucius
2 The Apricot Platform where Confucius is said to have taught, in the Temple of Confucius, Qufu, Confucius' home town
3 The Sacred Path leading to the tomb of Confucius, the number of trees at one side symbolising his seventy-two disciples and at the other his life of seventy-three years
4 The tablet of Confucius in front of his tomb
5 The tablet and tomb of Zisi (483?–402? BCE), the grandson of Confucius
6 People meditating in front of the hut at the side of the tomb of Confucius where Zigong (502?–? BCE), a disciple of Confucius, is said to have stayed for six years mourning the death of his master
7 The tablet and statue of a Former Worthy (*xian xian*), Master Yue Zheng (?–?) who is traditionally regarded as a transmitter of the Confucian doctrine of filial piety, in the Temple of Confucius at Qufu

Preface

As a schoolboy I read an Indian story about four blind men and an elephant: each of these men gave a different and highly amusing account of the elephant after touching only a specific part of the animal, and, of course, not one of them was able to describe the animal correctly. To my young mind, they couldn't do so because they weren't able to touch the whole of the elephant in one go. In other words, I believed that if any of them had had an opportunity to do this, then he would certainly have been able to generate a correct image of it. As I grew up, and had an opportunity to read more on philosophy and religion, I realised that it was perhaps not as simple as this. Could a blind man, who had never seen or heard about such an animal as an elephant, tell us what it is, even if we suppose that he could have physical contact with ALL the parts of the animal? Besides the limitation of sense experience, there are many other factors that would hinder us from acquiring full knowledge of such an object, and in addition to intellectual inability, there are many other elements that would distort our image.

Having fully understood the problem arising from the intellectual process of knowing things, Zhuangzi, a Daoist philosopher of around the fourth century BCE, argues that our vision has been blurred by our own perceptions when coming to grasp things, and that true knowledge is possible only if we take all things and ourselves to be a unity, in which no differentiation of 'this' and 'that' or of 'I' and 'non-I' is made. Shao Yong, a Confucian scholar of the eleventh century CE, approached this problem from a similar perspective. For him, error in human knowledge is due to the fact that we observe things from our own experience. He therefore proposed that we must view things, not with our physical eyes, but with our mind, and not even with our mind, but with the principle inherent in things. When the boundary between subject and object disappears, we will be able to see things as they are.

The majority of scholars who have been trained in the West, however, find it difficult to accept the underlying philosophy of the Chinese methodology proposed above. A much appreciated intellectual tradition in the West maintains that an investigation must start from a separation of subject and object, and that experience along with a critical examination of experience is the only guarantee of the 'objectivity' of the investigation. According to this view, a differentiation of values from facts is therefore central to any presentation of a religious and philosophical system.

Neither of these two seemingly different and even contradictory methodologies alone can assure us of a true knowledge of religion and philosophy. More and more people are coming to appreciate that we would benefit from a combination of these two approaches in our investigation of religious and philosophical traditions. Although this is a topic far beyond the parameters of a short preface, suffice it to say, that the inquiry into religious phenomena should involve empathy to some degree, and that an inquirer should be able to enter into the doctrine and practice of a religion almost as an 'insider', as well as to step outside as a critical observer. Indeed this methodology underlies the structure and contents of my introduction to Confucianism, and readers may easily see that the nature and image of the Confucian tradition as revealed in this book have been the result of a 'double' investigation, with the author being both a 'bearer' of the values examined and a 'critic' of the doctrine presented.

The formation of the book took place whilst lecturing on Confucianism in the University of Wales, Lampeter. I have run this course for a number of years, and the last time I did it was during the first term of the 1998/9 academic year, when I had just completed the first draft of this book. Conveniently, I took the manuscript as the textbook for the course, and I was pleased to know that it functioned well in this capacity both in and outside the class. Looking back at the writing process, I realise how much I have benefited from teaching and from the questions asked and suggestions made by the students.

I am grateful to Clare Hall, University of Cambridge for awarding me a Visiting Fellowship in 1998, which, supported also by the Pantyfedwen Fund and the Spalding Trust, made a significant contribution to the completion of the first draft of the book. Intellectually, I benefited from conversations and discussions with colleagues both at Lampeter and at Clare Hall, whose knowledge and insight added much value to the formation and reshaping of my original presentation. A number of colleagues, friends and students read various parts of the book. I would especially like to thank Oliver Davies, Gavin Flood and Todd Thucker, for their comments and advice, which have enabled me to avoid errors and oversights and to correct infelicities of English style throughout the book. Any that remain are, of course, my own responsibility.

Various sections of this book originally appeared as papers in academic journals or as part of research projects. Among them, 'Peace and Reconciliation in the Confucian Tradition' (*Reconciliation Project*, Gresham College) becomes the basis of the third section in chapter 3, and 'Confucianism and its Modern Values' (*Journal of Beliefs and Values*, no. 1, 1999) has been incorporated into the third section of chapter 5. I wish to thank the editors for allowing me to reuse the materials in this book. I would also like to thank the editors of Cambridge University Press, especially Mr Kevin Taylor, for their efforts in nurturing the project and bringing this book to the readers.

Confucianism in history: chronological table

In the world	Chinese history	Confucianism
	Legendary ages	Sage–kings: Yao, Shun, Yu the Great
	Xia Dynasty (2205?–1600? BCE)	Jie, the last king, a condemned tyrant
	Shang or Yin Dynasty (1600?–1100? BCE)	Tang, the founding father Zhou, the last king, a condemned tyrant

	Zhou Dynasty (1100?–249 BCE)
	Western Zhou (1100?–771 BCE)
	Eastern Zhou (770–256 BCE)
	Spring and Autumn period (770–476 BCE)
	Warring States period (475–221 BCE)
		King Wen, King Wu, Duke of Zhou, the three Zhou sages;
		Confucius (551–479 BCE)
		  The Confucian classics
		School of Zisi (483?–402 BCE)
		  The *Great Learning* and the *Doctrine of the Mean*
		Mengzi (372–289 BCE)
		Xunzi (313?–238? BCE)

In the world	Chinese history	Confucianism
	Qin Dynasty (221–206 BCE) First emperor (r. 221–210 BCE)	Burning of books and the killing of Confucian scholars
Confucianism was introduced to Vietnam, Korea and Japan Indian Buddhism was introduced to China and interacted with Confucianism	Han Dynasty (206 BCE–220 CE) Former Han (206 BCE–8 CE) Liu Bang (r. 206–195) Emperor Wu (r. 140–87) Xin Dynasty (9–23) Later Han (25–220)	Confucianism became the state orthodoxy Classics annotated Grand Academy established Old Text School Dong Zhongshu (179?–104 BCE) New Text School Yang Xiong (53 BCE–18CE) Liu Xin (?–23 CE) Huan Tan (23 BCE–50 CE) Wang Chong (27–100?) Ma Rong (79–166) Zheng Xuan (127–200) Chenwei Literature
National Academy in Korea established (372) *The Analects* were brought to Japan in 405(?) by a Korean scholar Wang In.	Wei–Jin Dynasties (220–420) Wei (220–265) Western Jin (265–316) Eastern Jin (317–420)	Mysterious Learning Wang Bi (226–249) He Yan (d. 249) Xiang Xiu (223–300) 'Pure Conversation' Ruan Ji (210–263) Ji Kang (223–262) Daoist Religion incorporated Confucian ethics
	Southern and Northern Dynasties (386–581)	Buddhism flourished and debates between Confucianism and Buddhism intensified

Confucianism in history: chronological table

In the world	Chinese history	Confucianism
Nestorians came to China (635) Korean Silla Kingdom (365–935) established Confucian Studies First Japanese Constitution (604) incorporated Confucian ideas	Sui-Tang Dynasties (581–907) Sui (581–618) Tang (618–906)	Confucianism gradually regained its prestige; civil service examination system established Han Yu (768–824) Li Ao (772–841) Liu Zongyuan (733–819)
Korean Koryo Dynasty (918–1392): civil service examination system; national university	Song Dynasties (960–1279) Northern Song (960–1126) Southern Song (127–1279)	Renaissance of Neo-Confucianism Zhou Dunyi (1017–1073) Zhang Zai (1020–1077) Rationalistic School Zhu Xi (1130–1200) Idealistic School Lu Jiuyuan (1139–1193) Practical School Chen Liang (1143–1194)
	Yuan Dynasty (1260–1368)	Harmonising Rationalism and Idealism Wu Cheng (1249–1333) Zhu Xi's annotated *Four Books* as standard version for civil service examinations (1313)

In the world	Chinese history	Confucianism
Korean Yi Dynasty (1392–1910): Neo-Confucianism Yi Hwang (1501–1570) Yi I (1536–1584) Japanese *bakufu* system Fujiwara Seika (1561–1619) Hayashi Razan (1583–1657) Japanese *Shushigaku* Yamazaki Ansai (1618–1682) Kaibara Ekken (1630–1714) Japanese *Yômeigaku* Nakae Tôju (1608–1648)	Ming Dynasty (1368–1644)	Chen Xianzhang (1428–1500) Wang Yangming (1472–1529) Schools of Wang Yangming Li Zhi (1527–1602) Donglin School Gao Panlong (1562–1626) Liu Zongzhou (1578–1654)
Korean Practical Learning Korean Eastern Learning Japanese *Kogaku* Itô Jinsai (1627–1705) Ogyû Sorai (1666–1728) James Legge (1815–1897) translated the Confucian classics into English	Qing Dynasty (1644–1911)	Learning of the Han School of Evidential Research Gu Yanwu (1613–1682) Wang Fuzhi (1619–1692) Huang Zongxi (1610–1695) Dai Zhen (1724–1777) New Learning Kang Youwei (1858–1927)

Confucianism in history: chronological table

In the world	Chinese history	Confucianism
Wing-tsit Chan (1901–1994) W. T. de Bary Okada Takehiko Cheng Chung-yin Tu Wei-ming	Republic of China (1911–) People's Republic of China (1949–)	Modern New Confucianism Xiong Shili (1885–1968) Fung Yu-lan (1895–1990) Tang Junyi (1909–1978) Mou Zongsan (1909–1995)

Introduction
Confucian studies East and West

> If we were to characterize in one word the Chinese way of life
> for the last two thousand years, the word could be 'Confucian'.
> No other individual in Chinese history has so deeply influenced
> the life and thought of his people, as a transmitter, teacher
> and creative interpreter of the ancient culture and literature
> and as a moulder of the Chinese mind and character.
>
> (de Bary, *et al.*, 1960, vol. 1: 15)

At the end of the sixteenth century, an Italian Jesuit Matteo Ricci (1552–1610) arrived in China. Ricci soon realised that the first task for him should not be to win over a great number of people to conversion and baptism, but instead to try to secure a stable and respectable position for himself within Chinese society. So Ricci and his fellow missionaries strenuously attempted to integrate themselves into the community. The Jesuits saw a similarity between Christianity and Buddhism – both were religions from the West – and therefore they presented themselves as 'Monks from the West', shaving their heads and changing their clothes to Buddhist robes in order to win the support from the Chinese, just as they thought the Buddhists had done a thousand years before. However, it was not too long before the missionaries realised that the Buddhists were not so highly regarded as they had at first imagined. They discovered that in fact it was Confucian scholars who were the true social elite of Chinese society. Accordingly the Jesuits changed their habits once more, wearing Confucian clothes and growing their hair long. In this way they created a new image of 'Scholars of the West'. Ricci continued with his Chinese studies, paying great attention to Confucian texts, and began to be regarded as a highly respected western scholar (*xi shi*). Rule says:

> The decisive change from the dress and role of Buddhist monks to
> those of Confucian literati was accomplished in May 1595 when
> Ricci left Shao-chou for Nanking, but it had been in preparation
> for a considerable time . . . Matteo Ricci first discovered and then

adapted himself to Confucianism in the course of his thirty-odd years
in China. (Rule, 1986: 15, 26)

Ricci became friends with a number of Chinese scholars and officials
who introduced him to the court. He and his fellow missionaries sent
back hundreds of letters, travel reports, treatises and translations to
Europe which made a major contribution to the introduction of Confucius and Confucianism to the West. Although there had been some
knowledge of China and the Chinese, until Ricci and other Christian
missionaries began their work, Confucianism had hardly been studied in
Europe. The serious way in which the missionaries treated Confucian
doctrines suggested that as Christianity was to the Europeans, so Confucianism was to the Chinese.

Ricci and his fellow missionaries clearly studied Confucian classics as
part of their missionary strategy and their presentation of the Confucian
tradition may indeed be taken as a 'Jesuit creation' (Rule, 1986). However, by introducing Confucianism to Europe, Ricci became one of the
pioneers of Confucian Studies in the West. The Jesuit version of Confucianism played a key role in generating Sinophilism among the learned
community in Europe and some Enlightenment thinkers and philosophers,
such as Voltaire and François Quesnay in France, Leibniz and Christian
Wolff in Germany, and Matthew Tindal in England thereby became
fascinated by Confucian ethical and social doctrines. For some of them, the
Confucian political blueprint that the state was ruled 'in accordance with
moral and political maxims enshrined in the Confucian classics' appeared
to provide an ideal prototype for a modern state (Dawson, 1964: 9). Since
then, Christian missionaries and those influenced by Christian images
of the eastern tradition have continuously played an important role
in the introduction of Confucianism to the West and in promoting the
interpretation of Confucian doctrine within a Christian or European
framework. 'In the nineteenth and twentieth centuries', according to Karl
Jaspers, 'it was not rare for Protestant missionaries in China to be so overwhelmed by the profundity of Chinese thought that they would reverse
their role and return to the West, so to speak, as "Chinese missionaries"'
(Jaspers, 1962: 143–4). The twentieth century has seen a rise in the
number of sinologists, philosophers, anthropologists and historians
taking part in Confucian Studies. As a result, Confucian Studies has
gradually become a discrete discipline and is now an established subject

not only within the subject of Asian Studies but also in the areas of philosophy and religious studies.

Modern scholars from West and East introduce and examine the Confucian tradition from the standpoints both of insiders and of outsiders. More recent examples of preeminent scholars in the West who take their points of view roughly from within Confucianism but also critically examine the tradition include, to name but a few, Wing-tsit Chan (1901–94), Wm. T. de Bary, Tu Wei-ming, Cheng Chung-ying, Roger T. Ames and Rodney L. Taylor. These scholars have not only introduced Confucian Studies to western students and readers, but have also developed and enriched the Confucian tradition itself. In their hands, Confucianism is not merely treated as an old political ideology or a socio-economic system, but primarily as a religious or philosophic tradition, open both to the modern world and to the future. These scholars have striven to establish a strong link between the past and the present, a healthy interaction between the Chinese tradition and other great traditions in the world. Their influence on western students of China and Confucianism is enormous, and some of them have created a new image of Confucian masters. This can be seen from Sommer's testimony in relation to Wing-tsit Chan, a prominent translator and researcher of Confucian Learning, that 'some of us students secretly suspected that, in some mysterious way, Professor Chan *was* Chu Hsi [a great Neo-Confucian master]' (Sommer, 1995: ix).

Two main problems engage Confucian Studies in the West. The first problem is that after about 400 years of study and research, Confucianism in the West is still a subject which only involves a small group of scholars. This situation is due in part to highly scholarly Confucian works being less accessible to students pursuing general philosophical and religious studies. This problem is one of the major factors in the slow development and expansion of Confucian Studies in the West. The second problem arises from methodology and the ways in which Confucianism is introduced and studied. Confucianism has been presented variously in the hands of different scholars, which causes further confusion among readers. These two problems are both caused by, and also increase, the gap between Confucianism as it is perceived in the West and the Confucianism understood in the East. More and more scholars have realised the extent of these problems and have sought to solve them in one way or another. For example, in a book entitled *Thinking Through*

3

Confucius, David L. Hall and Roger T. Ames attempt to return to the pre-
suppositions that sustain the Confucian tradition through reinterpreting
Confucius. They comment that

> The primary defect of the majority of Confucius' interpreters – those ·
> writing from within the Anglo-European tradition as well as those
> on the Chinese side who appeal to Western philosophic categories
> – has been the failure to search out and articulate those distinctive
> presuppositions which have dominated the Chinese tradition.
>
> (Hall & Ames, 1987: 1)

Much of East Asia was once under the influence of Confucianism, but
this has waned, and Confucianism has clearly lost its dominant position
there. Even so, despite all criticism, Confucianism still has an important
role to play in East Asian philosophy, religion, politics, ethics and culture.
Consequently, one of the major tasks facing all scholars of Confucian
studies is how to communicate between traditional values and modern
applications, between eastern and western Confucian scholarship.

Stages of the Confucian evolution

Confucianism is primarily a Chinese, or more precisely, East Asian, tradition. To understand Confucianism as a way of life or as a traditional
system of values, we have to go to its homeland and find out how it came
into being and how it was transformed. A popular method that is used in
presenting the Chinese Confucian tradition is to divide its history into as
many periods as there are Chinese dynasties. In this way Confucianism
becomes part of a much more complicated history and the Confucian progress is mixed up with the general changes in political, social, economic,
religious and cultural life. On many occasions Confucianism gained
strength and positive influence from these changes, yet on other occasions
it suffered from the breakdown of the social fabric and responded by
becoming either more flexible or more dogmatic. Throughout the history of the Chinese dynasties, Confucianism changed and adapted itself
to new political and social demands, and these changes and adaptations
are as important as the teachings of the early Confucian masters.

It can be said in general that the advance of Confucian Learning
was directly related to the replacement of one dynasty with another. The
link between Confucianism and dynastic government was formally forged
during the Former Han Dynasty (206 BCE–8 CE) when it was promoted as

the state ideology. Since then, right up until the beginning of the twentieth century, Confucian scholar–officials were influential in laying down the basis for government, and the amount of influence exerted by Confucian scholars more or less depended on the patronage of those people who were in a position to implement the teachings. None the less it does not follow that Confucianism was always a shadow of political change. Much of the development of Confucian Learning was largely independent of imperial patronage and many of its schools remained outside the political milieu and presented a direct challenge to the establishment. Confucianism was not merely a passive tool of government. Rather, it functioned, to a considerable extent, as a watchdog for ruling activities, endeavouring to apply its principles to shaping and reshaping the political structure. There were doctrinal elements that sustained the development of Confucian schools and there were also spiritual reasons for Confucian masters to direct their learning away from the current actions and politics of those in power. In this sense de Bary is right when he points out that

> It is probably to the Confucian ethos and Confucian scholarship that the Chinese dynastic state owed much of its stability and bureaucratic continuity . . . Yet the reverse was not equally true; Confucianism was less dependent on the state for survival than the state on it. Even though affected by the rise and fall of dynasties, Confucianism found ways to survive. (de Bary, 1988: 110)

If Confucianism is not simply a shadow of dynastic change, then how should we present a historical perspective of it? When discussing the history of Chinese philosophy as a whole, Fung Yu-lan (1895–1990), one of the great Modern New Confucians, divided this history into two ages, the creative and the interpretative. He calls the creative age, from Confucius to the Prince of Huainan (d. 122 BCE), the Period of the Philosophers (*zi xue*); and names the interpretative age, from Dong Zhongshu (179–104 BCE) to Kang Youwei (1858–1927 CE), the Period of Classical Learning (*jing xue*) (Fung, 1953: 2). This two-part division reveals some essential characteristics of the development of the Confucian tradition. The creative period represents the initial formulation of the early teachings into a cohesive tradition while the interpretative period illustrates the expansion of the tradition in line with social and political developments that necessarily take place over the centuries. However, if we simply apply this two-fold pattern to the history of Confucianism, then our perspective would be seriously limited. By merely singling out the methodological features of Confucian Learning, this division under-emphasises the distinctive contributions made by distinguished masters and overlooks the multidimensionality of various Confucian schools. More importantly, this approach does not take sufficient account of the interplay between Confucianism and the many other traditions that also existed through its long history and development.

Focusing on the development of modern Confucianism, Mou Zongsan (1908–95), another modern New Confucian master, formulated a different pattern for the history of Confucianism, dividing it into three periods or 'epochs' (Fang & Li, 1996: 486–95). His disciples, among whom Tu Wei-ming presents a most persuasive argument, have developed this theory further. According to this three-period theory, Confucianism thus far has gone through three epochs. The first epoch from Confucius (551–479 BCE), Mengzi (371–289 BCE) and Xunzi (310?–211? BCE) to Dong Zhongshu represents the origin of Confucianism and the accept-ance of the tradition as the mainstream ideology, which corresponds to the period from the Spring and Autumn period (770–476 BCE) to the end of the Later Han Dynasty (25–220 CE). The second epoch starts from the renaissance of Neo-Confucianism and its spread to other parts of East Asia and ends with the abolition of the dominance of Confucianism in China and East Asia, corresponding to the era from the Song Dynasty (960–1279) to the beginning of the twentieth century. The third epoch takes place in the twentieth century, beginning with the critical reflection on the tradition initiated in the May Fourth Movement (1919) and which is still an ongoing process. A significant feature of the third epoch is that modern Confucian scholars propagate and reinterpret Confucian doctrines in the light of Western traditions, in which Confucianism is being brought into the world and the world into Confucianism (Tu, 1993: 141–60; 1996a: 418). The primary question behind the three-epoch theory is whether or not Confucianism is able to develop so that it can become part of a global spirituality and culture. In search for answers to this question the emphasis must be on the Confucian expansion of its geographical area in relation to its self-transformation in response to external challenges. The three-epoch theory implies that the further development of Confucianism depends upon whether or not it can re-spond appropriately and successfully to industrialisation, modernisation, democracy and the 'global village'. Commendable as the three-epoch theory is, it is nevertheless inadequate for us to use this theory to present the historical perspective of the Confucian tradition. As a highly abstract formula, the theory inevitably pays less attention to many significant parts or periods of Confucian evolution which have made important contributions to sustaining and innovating Confucian Learning. Therefore, if we use it as a paradigm for the history of Confucianism, it would be too general to reveal what characterises the Confucian tradition as a constantly growing and changing tradition. If using it to highlight Confucian history, we would overlook the fact that Confucianism draws its energy and vitality both from within and from the interaction between itself and many other traditions, and between the past and the present.

This introduction is not intended as a thorough study of Confucian history. We nevertheless need to present a brief account of how Confucianism evolved and how it was transformed. In our historical perspective, Confucianism has gone through five stages, or in other words, it has presented itself in five dimensions. In each of these stages or dimensions, Confucian doctrines gained new characteristics, the contents of Confucian practices were enriched and the range of Confucian teaching was widened.

Confucianism in formation

In this first stage, Confucianism acquires a 'classical' form. The classic presentation of Confucianism (*ruxue* or *rujia*) took shape during the so-called Spring and Autumn period (770–476 BCE). Confucius and his faithful followers made the first efforts to formulate a new philosophy based on the old tradition and propagated it as the path to peace and harmony. Much modification of, elaboration and clarification on classical Confucianism were added by brilliant scholars in the Warring States period (475–221 BCE), among whom Mengzi and Xunzi became preeminent in the later Confucian tradition, and due to their efforts Confucianism became one of the major schools with many different presentations.

Confucianism in adaptation

In the second stage, Confucianism is reformed and renewed in the interaction between Confucian schools and the schools of Legalism, Yin–Yang and the Five Elements, Moism and Daoism. Following the replacement of the Qin Dynasty (221–206 BCE) by the Han Dynasty, Confucianism recovered gradually from the setback under the Qin persecution and the Legalist discrimination. Having clearly realised that they were in an eclectic culture, Han Confucians started a long process of adapting their doctrines to the need of the empire. During the process of adaptation, classical Confucianism was transformed, elaborated and extended. A theological and metaphysical doctrine of interaction between Heaven and humans was established and consequently became the cornerstone of the revived Confucianism. There were two prominent schools of the time: the New Text and the Old Text Schools. Debates between them resulted in new interpretations of Confucius and the Confucian classics. This led to what is known as 'Classical Learning', or more accurately, 'scholastic studies of the classics' (*jing xue*). Attention focused on close interpretation of words and sentences in the classics and by the end of the Later Han Dynasty the extensive exegesis had nearly exhausted all the life energy of Confucian scholars. To counter this stagnation, scholars of the Wei–Jin Dynasties (220–420) adopted one of two courses. Some introduced Daoist philosophy into Confucianism while others adapted Confucian world-views to Daoist principles. In each way Daoism and Confucianism came together in what is known as Dark Learning or Mysterious Learning (*xuan xue*). This was to have a lasting influence upon the later development of Chinese thought.

Confucianism in transformation

In this stage, Confucianism responds to the challenges from Buddhism and Daoism by 'creating' a new form of Confucian Learning. Confucianism of the Song–Ming Dynasties (960–1279, 1368–1644) regained its authority over all aspects of social and religious life. Inspired by Buddhist philosophy and Daoist spirituality, Confucian scholars re-formulated the Confucian view of the universe, society and the self on the one hand, and endeavoured to strip Confucian Learning of the elements they considered to be Buddhist–Daoist superstitions on the other. The result of their efforts was a comprehensive system of new Confucian Learning called *Dao Xue* (the Learning of the Way) or *Li Xue* (the Learning of the Principle/Reason), which as such is normally translated in the West as Neo-Confucianism.

Confucianism in variation

The fourth period sees Chinese Confucianism being introduced to other East Asian countries, and combined with local culture and tradition to acquire new forms of presentation. China is the homeland of

Confucianism, but Confucianism is not confined to China. The history of Confucianism can be characterised as a process of radiation. From its origins in the north, it spread to the whole of China and then to other countries of East Asia. More recently it has spread to North America, Europe and the rest of the world. According to historical records, Confucian doctrines and institutions were introduced to Vietnam, Korea and Japan as early as the Former Han Dynasty. In the beginning, scholars in these countries simply replicated the Chinese system but gradually, eminent native scholars emerged who, taking the Chinese masters as their guides, reinterpreted the Confucian classics and commentaries in the light of their own understanding, experience and insight. In this way, they successfully recreated a new scholarship by introducing new forms and contents into Confucian Learning to satisfy the social and political needs of their own countries. Thus, Chinese Confucianism acquired additional manifestations, where the common sources of Confucian Learning and practices were transformed into different and yet related streams flowing into the twentieth century.

Confucianism in renovation

Confucianism is further transformed during this last period and develops in the light of other world philosophies, especially European philosophical tradition and Christian spirituality in the modern age. Prominent scholars of the twentieth century such as Xiong Shili (1885–1968), Liang Suming (1893–1988), Fung Yu-lan (1895–1990), Qian Mu (1895–1990), Tang Junyi (1909–78) and Mou Zongsan (1909–95), devoted the whole of their lives to the revival of Confucian values and the transformation of Confucian doctrines. Their contributions have rejuvenated Confucianism and constitute a significant part of 'modern new Confucianism' (*xiandai xin ruxue*).

While intending to give a brief but clear account of Confucian history, we recognise that it is not possible in this work to take full account of all the Confucian schools and sub-schools. Therefore we will have to single out the most influential masters and examine their contributions to the development of the Confucian tradition. In so doing, we will especially emphasise the epoch-making innovations and transformations achieved and highlight the crucial stages in its development, while leaving many great Confucians and their teachings unexamined, or less closely examined than they might otherwise deserve.

Methodological focuses

Taking into account the long history and wide range of Confucian studies engaged in the East and the West, and the great contributions made by modern scholars during the last few decades, I will present Confucianism primarily as a philosophical and religious tradition, with a special focus on its intellectual creativity and its modern relevance. I intend summarily to highlight, and critically examine, what has been achieved both in the West and in the East. I will also pay special attention to what has been understood as 'Confucianism' with regard to its doctrines, schools, rituals, sacred places and terminology presented in history, while at the same time stressing the significance of the adaptations, transformations and 'new thinking' taking place in modern times.

One way to write an introductory book about Confucianism is to follow its historical development, beginning with the pre-Confucius age down to modern times. This is the basic structure of a few books of this kind, and James Legge (1815–97), Herrlee Creel, and more recently John Berthrong have done it in this way. While giving the reader a linear account of Confucian intellectualism, these scholars are less successful in their presentation of Confucianism as a philosophical and religious spirit penetrating all strata of society. In contrast to them, I will introduce Confucianism as a single tradition with many facets and as an ancient tradition with contemporary appeal. I hope to give the reader a multidimensional view of the Confucian tradition by investigating how Confucianism functioned in the past and how it is applied in the present.

To examine the Confucian tradition, we need to explore its original sources, not solely relying on second-hand materials available in the West. By original sources we mean two kinds of texts. Firstly, original texts in Chinese either in the form of ancient classics, annotations and commentaries or in modern deliberation and presentation. Secondly, interpretative books and articles in other languages, both highly specialist materials including translations and annotations, and theme studies and original research. These two kinds of material are equally important and cross-references between them will be made throughout the chapters. A select bibliography containing both categories is appended for further reference.

Whether or not Confucianism is religious is a question of debate, and this will be closely examined in chapter 1. Here, suffice it to say that

Confucianism is a tradition open to religious values. There are two approaches to religious traditions in China adopted by prominent sinologists; in one, a religion is studied as it was presented in the sacred writings, while in the other, it is studied as it is applied in the way of life. At an earlier stage these two methodologies were represented respectively by James Legge and J. J. M. de Groot. W. E. Soothill points out the deficiency of each of them and believes that any religious tradition must be studied in both dimensions. This comment is of insight, and will be useful for our present study of Confucianism:

> A study of a religion which limits itself to the teachings of the early
> founders, and which ignores the present condition of its development,
> will give a very imperfect presentation of the religion as a whole. On
> the other hand, a study which is limited to its expression in practice,
> without doing justice to the ideals of the founders, equally fails to do
> justice to the religion as a whole, for the religious ideals of a people,
> while they may be written on the tablets of their hearts and conscience,
> often find very imperfect expression in their lives.
>
> (Soothill, 1973: 21)

The Confucian tradition is both a tradition of literature and a way of life. These two dimensions are related to and supplement each other. To introduce Confucianism as a living tradition flowing from the past to the present, we must look into how these two dimensions function together, i.e., how the Confucian doctrine underlies the life of the people and how the practice, political or religious, reflects as well as refreshes Confucian Learning. To examine in detail the complicated relation between the Confucian Way and Chinese practices is beyond the reach of this introductory book. How Confucian doctrine was used in East Asian politics, religions, literature, arts and daily life are topics for different kinds of thematic research. Nevertheless we insist that relevant to our study are not only the Confucian doctrines of Heaven, humanity and harmony, but also how these doctrines are put into practice; not only the philosophic discussion of human nature, but also devoted self-transformation in relation to one's spiritual and cultural destiny.

Similar to studies of any other philosophical and religious tradition where numerous and various interpretations create both depth and confusion, a study of Confucianism is also an area full of differences. As an introduction, this book has to be content with what has been generally recognised in Confucian studies. While taking into account newly found evidence, it does not argue for a specific theory, and while discussing the most important issues concerning Confucian studies, it does not fully engage in all the current debates. What is intended throughout the book is to present a phenomenological investigation of what Confucianism was and is, and to generate a seamless interpretation and presentation of its religious and philosophical doctrines. Having done this, I will supplement a number of questions to each chapter for further discussion, to stimulate students and readers in general to think about the questions to which there are no straightforward answers.

Structure and contents

This book comprises five chapters apart from this introduction. Chapter 1 is a thematic presentation of what Confucianism is and what characteristics it has. The focus of this chapter is on Confucius and his contribution to the Confucian tradition, but attention is also given to the origin and nature of what is called 'Confucianism' in the West. Chapter 2 presents a historical view of how Confucianism evolved, focusing on major Confucian schools and their leaders, from the early records to the time when Confucianism was stepping into the modern age. It investigates the common heritage of various schools and also highlights the distinctiveness of each of them, treating them as necessary links in the whole process of Confucian transformation and evolution. In terms of geographical location, it concentrates on the unique contributions made by Confucian masters and scholars in China, Korea and Japan, while leaving Confucianism in other areas such as Vietnam and Southeast Asia to future studies.

Chapter 3 discusses the key elements of Confucian doctrine, and presents them in the form of the Three Ways: the Way of Heaven, the Way of Humans and the Way of Harmony. The Way of Heaven is central to the Confucian view of the transcendental, the metaphysical, the natural, the ethical, the political and the religious. The Way of Humans deals with the human correspondence with, and implementation of, the Way of Heaven, as manifested in human nature, moral virtues, social integration, political order, and personal destiny. Central to Confucian belief is that the Way of Heaven cannot be fulfilled, unless it has been understood and consciously carried out by humans in our life. The Way of Harmony is concerned with how harmony can be achieved between humans and Heaven, between conscious activities and the environment, between individuals, between family members, as well as in society and the world. It is argued that harmony is not only a central concept, but also the spirit manifesting the life and power of Confucianism; it is both the Confucian reality and the ideal that Confucian believers endeavour to realise. Confucian harmony is primarily about the unity between Heaven and humanity. According to Confucian understanding, this unity indicates a harmonious state of the world in which humans live and behave, which provides humanity with enjoyment, peace and order. It also indicates a continuous relationship between the spiritual and the human, the mind and the body, form and matter, and the traditional and the present, which gives individuals the sense of continuity, eternity and security. It indicates once more the mutual transformation of the eternal and the temporal, the infinite and the finite, and the sacred and the secular, which can be observed in the proper performance of ritual, and must be carried out in human engagement in conscientious and industrious activity.

Chapter 4 concentrates on religious ritual and practices fostered and upheld in the Confucian tradition. It demonstrates how Confucian values have penetrated the lives of the Chinese, Koreans and Japanese, and that people in these countries inevitably come under the influence of Confucianism, and that their thinking is underpinned or shaped by Confucian values, whether or not they have studied the Confucian classics. It starts with an investigation of how Confucian doctrines are used to transform religious rituals and practices and how these rituals and practices reflect the rational and humanistic ideals propagated by Confucian masters. Confucian practices exist not only in the form of religious worship and cults, but also in the unique way that Confucianism takes learning and self-improvement as a spiritual path. Confucian spirituality is influenced by the interaction between Confucianism and other religious traditions, notably Daoism, Buddhism and Christianity. It is in this interaction that Confucianism has transformed itself and has caused transformations in other traditions as well.

The modern development of Confucianism and the problems facing modern Confucian scholars are dealt with in chapter 5, in which the so-called 'three generations of modern new Confucians' are examined, and fresh challenges to Confucian theories and practices and Confucian responses to these challenges are investigated. Confucianism has survived the impact of western culture and Communist revolution and is being revived as a motivating force for modernisation. We are repeatedly reminded that behind economic, political and social life in East Asia are the values fostered in the Confucian tradition. Some scholars even claim that 'the new patterns of behaviour in these rapidly modernizing societies are undergoing modification that can only be understood with reference to the ancient Confucian heritage' (Küng & Ching, 1989: 95). In view of the influence and the revitalised image of Confucianism in the last few decades, some scholars argue that Confucianism is moving towards a 'new age'. It is also suggested that the new creativity of Confucianism is not simply confined to East Asia; it has offered a positive response to universal and perennial human problems and concerns. In critically examining these suggestions and taking into account the efforts to accentuate Confucianism made by modern scholars in the West and the East, the book reaches a conclusion that Confucianism is by no means only a tradition of the past, and that a revived Confucianism is able to offer positive values conducive to a healthy life in the modern age.

Translation and transliteration

Most of the original texts quoted in this book have been translated into English. As a matter of fact, there are perhaps few books from other non-western traditions that have been rendered into western languages as often as the key Confucian classics have been. This leads to one of the problems with which most students of Confucianism are often faced, namely, the differences between various renderings of the same book. Similar to the rendering of the scriptures of other religious/philosophic traditions, translation of the Confucian classics often reflects a personal involvement in re-experiencing the philosophy behind the texts. Different translators have different understandings of the philosophy, and their renderings inevitably differ. In order to present the Confucian tradition in the best way, we cannot possibly adopt single translations exclusively. As far as the key sources are concerned, especially in the case of *Lunyu* or the *Analects of Confucius* and *Mengzi* or the *Book of Mengzi*, I will make selective use of the translations rendered respectively by James Legge, Arthur Waley, D. C. Lau and Wing-tsit Chan. When necessary, I will select the translations I judge most accurate. As these texts are numbered in the order of chapters and paragraphs, it is reasonably easy for the reader to match our quotations with any of the available translations. On some occasions when no translation is satisfactory, I will rerender what is quoted, while on other occasions when there is no translation available for a Confucian text, I will be responsible for rendering the quoted passages directly from the original source. The references to the original sources and to their English translators are given in the first and second parts of the select bibliography.

The second problem facing a student is how to understand Chinese terms and characters through translations. Some of the Confucian terms and phrases are so complicated in meaning and application that it would be impossible to find English equivalents for them, while others have so wide a range of references that none of the English terms or phrases is sufficient to denote its meanings. In this case, I will give a number of English words that are close to the original meanings of a Chinese character, while if possible choosing one of them in the following pages.

The third problem most students find difficult to handle, is the romanisation of Chinese words or characters. There are two major systems currently in use for transliterating Chinese characters into English. The first is the Wade–Giles or modified Wade–Giles system, which used to be the dominant system for romanising Chinese characters among western sinologists and the scholars from Taiwan and Hong Kong. The second is the *pinyin* system prevailing in Mainland China, Singapore and Malaysia, which although a newcomer, has recently been adopted by many western sinologists and Chinese specialists, partly due to the fact that more and more materials are being published in Mainland China. Although there are good arguments for either system, this book will primarily use the *pinyin* system, only retaining the Wade–Giles transcription for some well-known names, for example, Fung Yu-lan or Tu Wei-ming, which are so familiar in the West that it would cause misunderstanding or unnecessary difficulty if I were to retransliterate them into *pinyin* spellings. I have not changed the Wade–Giles spellings or other systems of transliteration used in book titles or in quoted passages. To make it convenient for readers, I have provided a glossary of Chinese, Japanese and Korean characters, with their *pinyin*, Wade–Giles or other transliterations used in this book.

Confucianism, Confucius and Confucian classics

About 2,500 years ago, a man was born to a once aristocratic family in a small state called Lu in East China. During his lifetime, the man endeavoured to work 'towards a goal the realisation of which he knows to be hopeless' (*Lunyu*, 14: 38), carrying forward the old tradition in a chaotic environment and opening up a new horizon in a dark age. By the time he died at the age of seventy-three, his teachings had spread throughout the state and beyond. His disciples and students compared him to the sun and moon, while his rivals considered him a man 'who does not work with his arms and legs and who does not know how to distinguish between different kinds of grain' (*Lunyu*, 18: 7). But there was one thing that neither side knew: that Chinese culture, and to some extent, East Asian culture, would be forever linked with his name, and that the tradition he loved and transmitted would rank with the greatest in the world. This tradition is known in the West as 'Confucianism'.

'Confucianism' and *ru*

The origin of the English word 'Confucianism' may be traced back to the Jesuits of the sixteenth century:

> Until Nicholas Trigault published his version of Ricci's journals
> in 1615, there was hardly any knowledge of, not to say debate about,
> Confucianism . . . The Jesuits were virtually the first Europeans to
> discover Confucius and Confucianism, 'the sect of the literati' as they
> not inaccurately called it . . . The Jesuits, representatives of European
> values and intellectual methods, attempted . . . to understand Chinese

intellectual life in terms of systems, and transmuted the tradition of
the Ju or Chinese 'scholars' into an '-ism', Confucianism.

(Rule, 1986: 2, 195)

Since then 'Confucianism' or its equivalents in other European languages has been taken in the West as a proper name for the East Asian
tradition with Confucius as its fountainhead. In fact, what is meant by
'Confucianism' is more a tradition generally rooted in Chinese culture
and nurtured by Confucius and Confucians rather than a new religion
created, or a new value system initiated, by Confucius himself alone. It is
true that as a distinctive 'school' Confucianism began with Confucius.
It was Confucius who explored deeply and elaborated extensively on
the basic principles of what was to become Confucianism, and it was
Confucius and his disciples who succeeded in transmitting and transforming their ancient culture. But it would go too far to suggest that
Confucianism was 'created' solely by Confucius and Confucianism was
sustained exclusively by the faith in Confucius. In this sense, the word
'Confucianism' is a misnomer for the tradition that is normally referred
to as *ru jia, ru jiao, ru xue* or simply as *ru* in China and other East Asian
countries. Confucius played a key role in the development of the tradition which had originated long before his time. He is usually regarded
as a 'sage–teacher' for the people or as the Sage for Confucians, but
seldom as the Saviour, and never as the Lord. Confucius functioned as
'the founder' of the Confucian tradition in a way quite different from the
founders of other religious traditions.

RU AND THE RU TRADITION

Ru jia, ru jiao or *ru xue* may be translated roughly as 'the doctrine,
or tradition, of scholars'. To understand the nature of this doctrine or
tradition, we have first to explore its root in *ru*. A prominent scholar
of the Han Dynasty (206 BCE–220 CE), Liu Xin (?–23 CE), located the
formation of *ru* as a profession in the early years of the Zhou Dynasty
(1100?–256 BCE) and asserted that *ru* was characteristic of its devotion
to the 'six classics' (the *Book of Poetry*, the *Book of History*, the *Book
of Rites*, the *Book of Music*, the *Book of Changes*, and the *Spring and
Autumn Annals*), and that as a social group and a distinctive school,
ru emphasised the virtues of humaneness (*ren*) and righteousness (*yi*),
followed the ancient sage–kings, and took Confucius as their master
(*Hanshu*, 1997: 1728). However, the identification of *ru* with Confucian

scholars was not recognised until a much later time, when Confucianism had been recognised as a prominent school with its scholars engaging with the classics and the Way of ancient Sages. What then is the original meaning of the *ru*?

Among ancient texts, the character *ru* first occurs in the *Analects*, where Confucius taught his disciples to be a *ru* of virtuous gentlemen (*junzi ru*), and not a morally deficient man or a vulgar *ru* (*xiaoren ru*) (*Lunyu*, 6: 13). Some scholars, both Chinese and Western, argue that although groups of men professionally skilled in ceremonial practice existed prior to Confucius' time, the character *ru* post-dated Confucius' time and was in fact coined as a name for the followers of Confucius (Eno, 1993: 192). While we cannot engage in this debate, suffice it now to say that there is no reason for us to disregard what is implied by the reference to the two kinds of *ru* in the *Analects*, and we have grounds for believing that as a profession or distinctive group in society, *ru* must have predated the time of Confucius.

As mentioned above, Liu Xin gave a clear explanation to the origin of *ru*. He traced the origin of *ru* to a government office (*situ zhi guan*, Ministry of Education) whose function was to 'assist the ruler to follow the way of the yin–yang and to enlighten [the people] by education' (*zhu renjun, shun yinyang, ming jiaohua*, in *Hanshu*, 1998: 1728). There seem to have been few debates concerning the meaning of *ru* before the twentieth century, and people generally accepted Liu Xin's explanation. Following the introduction of a western scientific methodology at the beginning of the twentieth century, however, Chinese scholars started to rethink the character *ru* and reassess its meanings and connotations. A group of scholars followed Liu Xin to confirm that *ru* was indeed from a government office. Zhang Binglin (1869–1936), for example, argued that all the schools which came into being during the period of Spring and Autumn (771–476 BCE) and the period of Warring Sates (475–221 BCE) originated from the imperial offices (*wang guan*) of the Zhou Dynasty. In his article *Yuan Ru* ('Exploring the Origin of *Ru*'), Zhang pointed out that in ancient times *ru* was a general term with a range of references, and that there were three kinds of *ru* in the Zhou Dynasty: *ru* as a distinguished title for intellectuals or gentlemen who were equipped with skills and expertise in one or more areas of social life (*shu shi*); *ru* as a classification for those who were professionals in the six arts (rites, music, archery, carriage driving, history and mathematics); and *ru* as an official title for those who assisted the ruler to follow the way of yin–yang and to enlighten the people by education. Zhang believed that the three kinds of *ru* were later disregarded and *ru* as a general term became a specific name for those who taught and transmitted the Confucian classics (Zhang, 1909: 56).

Other modern scholars such as Kang Youwei (1858–1927) and Hu Shi (1891–1962) disagreed with Liu and Zhang with regard to the origin of *ru*. For them, *ru* did not originate in a government office of the Zhou Dynasty. Based on the records that Confucius usually wore a special cap (*zhangfu zhi guan*), Hu Shi claimed that *ru* referred to the adherents (*yimin*) of the Shang Dynasty (c. 1600–c. 1100 BCE) who because of their expertise in religious rituals were employed as priests by the Zhou Dynasty. When the Western Zhou Dynasty (1100?–770 BCE) declined shortly before the time of Confucius, these professionals lost their privilege and social status, and became a group of people who lived on their knowledge and skills in rituals and ceremonies (Hu, 1953: vol. 4). In his *Yuan Ru Mo (On the Origins of the Ru and Moists)* Fung Yulan argued against this assumption that wearing the Shang cap did not mean that these people were adherents of the Shang. Fung further separated *ru* and *rujia*, the former being a professional group who lived on education and performing rituals, the latter being a distinctive school established in the Spring and Autumn period (Chen, 1996: 334).

Most of the debates were concentrated on the immediate predecessors of *ru* that later tradition knew as Confucian scholars. Whether or not it was associated with a government office, the members of *ru* were certainly associated with learning and education. But what was their original profession? Recently, a number of Chinese scholars have returned to the question. Some conclude that as a profession *ru* refers originally to dancers and musicians in religious ceremonies of the Shang Dynasty when the worship of spirits and gods dominated the life of the people. A *ru* would perform various dances and play music as imprecation for a good harvest and as offerings to gods or ancestors, and would lead ceremonies for the coming of rain during the seasons of drought. To fulfil their duties *ru* had to study not only the rituals proper, but also other relevant subjects such as astronomy/astrology to predict rain or drought. The character *ru* (儒) is said to come from the character *xu* (需). *Xu* was composed of two parts, 'cloud' (雨) above sky (而) (Yan, 1995: 50), which reveals the relation of *ru* to ritual dance in rain-praying. In the oracle bone inscriptions, *xu* was rendered as a man who is in a shower (🙊), suggesting a ritual ablution before a *ru* went about his responsibilities. In chapter 38 'The Conducts of Scholars' of the *Book of Rites*, we can see the importance of bathing for a Confucian scholar: 'The scholar keeps his person free from stain, and continually bathes (and refreshes) his virtue' (Legge, 1968, vol. 27: 407).

Other etymological connections also suggest that *ru* were related to ritual dance, music and religious ceremonies. The character *ru* shares the same root with those for 'weaklings' and 'cowards', indicating that the members of *ru* were characterised by their softness, suppleness and flexibility. Probably for this reason, Xu Shen (58?–147?), the first Chinese philologist, defined it as such: '*Ru* means "soft." It is the title for [Confucian] scholars (*shu shi*) who educated the people with the six arts' (*Shuowen Jiezi Zhu*, 1981: 366). Therefore, a *ru* was gentle and yielding rather than competitive and commanding, in contrast to a warrior who was known for his vigour in war and competition. As a master of music and dance, a *ru* was clearly aware of his own refinement and manners, and believed his own worth to reside in his cultivated and noble etiquette; it was this which served to distinguish the *ru* from common people, such as farmers, craftsmen and merchants.

To summarise and assess what has been presented above, we may hypothesise that the different explanations of the origins of *ru* might actually refer to the different periods in the evolution of the groups of men who were called *ru*. The *ru* went through a number of stages before the time of Confucius. Firstly, *ru* referred to dancers and musicians in religious rituals, who were characterised by their softness and flexibility. At this stage, *ru* was a special group in society whose members were roughly equivalent to what we mean by shamans, magicians and sorcerers. Secondly, *ru* were masters of rituals and ceremonies, who performed, or assisted the performance of, various rituals. At this stage, *ru* referred to professionals expert in religious rituals, rites and ceremonies. Thirdly, ritual masters became teachers in official education. To be able to look after rituals, *ru* must have mastered history, poetry, music, astrology, archery and mathematics which were closely related to rituals in ancient times. As experts in these areas they exercised responsibility for training young dancers, musicians and performers, and for teaching on rituals and ritual-related subjects, which earned them the title of *shi* (師): 'Masters/Teachers', although they were still employed as professional priests or assistants at official or non-official ceremonies.

Along with the decline of cultic practices and the rise of rationalism during the Spring and Autumn period, a large number of *ru* departed from the officially assigned profession, and entered various areas of social life. The *ru* became distinctive for their skills in state rituals and in official and private education. The character *ru* was also gradually extended to become a specific term for those who had skills of ritual, history, poetry, music, mathematics and archery, and who lived off their knowledge of all kinds of ceremonies and of many other subjects (Chen, 1996: 350). Among the teachers of these disciplines Confucius stood out as an outstanding *ru* of his time, and opened up a new course by developing and transforming the *ru* tradition. By the time of the Warring States period, Confucius had been recognised as the highest figure in the *ru* tradition, as indicated by Han Fei (280?–233 BCE), a leading Legalist philosopher and a well-known critic of Confucianism, 'In the present age, the celebrities for learning are the literati [*ru*] and the Mohists. The highest figure of the Literati was K'ung Ch'iu [Kong Qiu]; the highest figure of the Mohists was Mo Ti' (Liao, 1960, vol. 2: 298). Not long after that, the tradition of *ru* was totally identified with the doctrines clarified, elaborated and propagated by Confucius, and 'the rituals of the *ru*' and 'the Way of Confucius' became interchangeable in a collection of the Former Han Dynasty (*Huainanzi Yizhu*, 1990: 501). One way or another, Confucius' transmission and interpretation of the ancient culture and his practices of education played a major part in shaping and reshaping the *ru* tradition. The process involved in this transformation must be taken into account when we discuss the relationship between Confucius and *ru*. Therefore, whatever method one may employ in tracing the origin of Confucianism, one must take into account both the cultural heritage on which Confucius worked and the transformation Confucius made to the *ru* tradition. In this sense it is misleading to simply 'characterize Confucius and his followers through their role as masters of dance' (Eno, 1990: 2–3). As we have pointed out above, by the time of Confucius, the *ru* had fundamentally changed their social and cultural functions, and therefore, should not be treated in the same way as the earlier masters of dance and music.

CONFUCIUS

'Confucius' is a Latinised form of the Chinese name Kong Fuzi, Master Kong, which is in turn a reverent title for Kong Qiu or Kong Zhongni

(551–479 BCE). Confucius was born and lived in the Spring and Autumn period of the Zhou Dynasty. The Zhou Dynasty was established on the system of feudalism: under the central government the empire was divided into many feudal states, either headed by the members of the royal house or awarded to those who had rendered outstanding service to the state. There were about 124 states shortly before Confucius' birth and around 70 during his life. Initially the system worked well. The princes and dukes of the states took the king as the 'Son of Heaven' and as their chief commander. When the grasp of Zhou Kings over the states weakened, however, the administrative system began to collapse. The heads of individual states ignored the command and order from the central government, and competed with one another for a bigger share of land and property. This led to military conflict between states and power struggles within a state. The old order of social life was being destroyed and a new one was advancing, while the people were left in endless suffering and misery, husband being torn from wife, and wife being forced to leave husband; the rich enjoying their luxury, while the poor had nothing to rely on (Legge, 1992, vol. 4: 117, 320, 423, 424).

Many thinkers explored the cause of chaos and disorder, and expanded upon their ways of solving the problems. Some became pioneers of different schools, and Confucius was one of them, probably the most famous one of his time. He believed that chaos and disorder developed from the misuse and abuse of ritual/propriety (*li*) and music (*yue*). He described these as a situation of *li huai yue beng* – 'the decay of ritual/propriety (*li*) and the collapse of music'. Unable to endure this state of affairs, Confucius embarked upon a life-long enterprise to restore the value of rituals and to propagate the rules of propriety. For him chaos and disorder could not be corrected under a bad government, in which neither ruler nor minister acted in accordance with the true values of their roles. To establish a righteous government, the ruler and his ministers must act according to what was established in ancient rites, because what made a government good was the power of moral virtues rather than the power of cruel and punitive laws. Moral virtues could produce trust and faith in the people, while punitive measures might stop wrongdoing only for a moment. A ruler 'who governs the state through his virtue is like the pole star which stays put while the other stars revolve around it' (*Lunyu*, 2: 1). An efficient way to secure 'governing by virtue' was to perform rituals and play music correctly, which would enable performers to remain in a state of sincerity and loyalty and to set up good examples for the common people so that they knew what was right and what was wrong. In this sense, Confucian Learning, performing rituals and playing music were not merely a matter of ceremonies. Either at a personal level or at a social level, 'flourishing comes from [learning of] poetry; establishing results from [properly performing] ritual; and completing is to be achieved by means of music' (*Lunyu*, 8: 8). In order to set up guidelines for good family and social life, Confucius reinterpreted the meaning and methods of learning and education of the *ru* tradition, and believed that the promotion of the tradition had great leverage on improving the quality of social life, was the key to overcoming present problems, and would lead the people to a refined and redefined world of goodness and harmony. As his objective was the restoration of social and moral excellence, and the cultivation of purity within the heart of individuals, so that society and humanity at large could function harmoniously, Confucius took on the task of reforming the government through revitalising the ancient ways which was believed to have been established at the beginning of the Zhou Dynasty and carried out effectively and efficiently during the first half of the dynasty: 'The Zhou is resplendent in culture, having before it the example of the two previous dynasties. I am for the Zhou' (*Lunyu*, 3: 14).

The political ambition and moral strength with which Confucius strove to realise his ideal came in part from his ancestral background and aristocratic origins. Confucius is believed to have been a descendant of the royal house of the Shang Dynasty and his family lived in the state of Song until his grandfather was forced to move to the state of Lu. His father died when Confucius was three years old and it was his mother who raised him and had him properly educated. The passing away of his father led to the further decline of the family, and Confucius once described himself as 'being of humble station when young so that I was able to handle many menial things' (*Lunyu*, 9: 6). The humbleness of his living conditions and the nobility of his ancestry were probably two main factors which encouraged him to learn. The road to the final achievement was long but gradual, as we find in his poetic self-description which records that he set his heart firmly on learning at the age of fifteen, and by thirty he had achieved some success; ten years later, he had reached a higher step, when he was no longer perplexed with world affairs; at fifty, he believed that he had understood the Mandate of Heaven; at sixty his ears were docile, and at seventy, he had reached the peak of human transformation so that he could do everything following his own heart's desire without transgressing the norm (*Lunyu*, 2: 4).

In his public career, however, the progress was much less obvious. He was a private educator and a well-known master for most of his life. Although Confucius was keen to transform government, he himself seemed to be more interested in practising virtues at home than in holding office. When asked why he was not involved in government, Confucius replied, 'What does the *Book of History* say? "Simply by being a good son and friendly to his brothers, a man can exert an influence upon government." In so doing a man is, in fact, taking part in government. How can there be any question of his having actively to "take part in government?"' (*Lunyu*, 2: 21). Confucius held office for only a few years, the first significant post assigned to him being that of magistrate of the district Zhongdu when he was nearly fifty-one years old (501 BCE). Due to the success of his administration in this district, he was promoted to Minister for Construction (500 BCE) and the Chief Justice, possibly even serving as acting Prime Minister for a short period (499 BCE). Seeing that he was unable to turn his doctrines into practice, Confucius left his home state of Lu for other states in 497 BCE, hoping that his words would be heeded, his politics carried out and his ideal realised in other parts of the world. For thirteen years (497–484 BCE), he and a group of his disciples travelled from one state to another, frequently encountering failure and despair. However, he never lost his faith in the Way of Heaven *(tian)* and his mission in the world. Confucius believed that Heaven is the Ultimate, the source of faith from which he drew his optimism and wisdom in dealing with human affairs.

When Confucius realised that the situation was hopeless and when the political climate in the state of Lu changed, he returned home, devoting the rest of his life to teaching disciples and editing ancient classics, in the expectation that the disciples would carry on his work and pass his teachings on to later generations. Confucius died in the fourth month of 479 BCE, and it was said that Duke Ai of Lu (r. 494–467 BCE) came to pay his condolences: 'Alas! Heaven has no mercy on me, and has not spared me the Grand Old Man, leaving me unprotected and in deep regret. Alas! Father Ni (Confucius' name)! Great is my sorrow!' (Lin. 1994: 153; Legge, 1992, vol. 5: 846). A few hundred years later, when Sima Qian (145?–86? BCE), the greatest Chinese historian, wrote a biography of Confucius, he concluded with the following paragraph:

When I read the works of Confucius, I try to see the man himself. In Lu I visited his temple and saw his carriage, clothes and sacrificial vessels. Scholars go regularly to study ceremony there, and I found it hard to tear myself away. The world has known innumerable princes and worthies who enjoyed fame and honour in their days but were forgotten after death, while Confucius, a commoner, has been looked up to by scholars for ten generations and more. From the emperor, princes and barons downwards, all in China who study the Six Arts take the master as their final authority. Well is he called the Supreme Sage!

(*Shiji*, 1997: 1947; Yang & Yang, 1974: 27)

It is commonly agreed that as a distinctive school Confucianism took shape in the hands of Confucius and he was responsible for the formation of the basics of Confucianism. His commanding personality and profundity of knowledge attracted many followers and he himself became the centre of gravity and the embodiment of Confucian virtues. His understanding of the world and religious matters led the Confucian tradition to the direction of rationalism and humanism, which characterises Confucian practices, either secular or religious. He deliberated on many important concepts, which laid down the very foundation for Confucian doctrines. He virtually instituted a pedagogic tradition which transcended the class distinctions. And he painted a picture of the gentleman/virtuous man (*junzi*) as an attainable ideal. All these become the backbone of the Confucian Way, illustrating how a Confucian follower should behave, how he should lead his life and what he must do for an ideal society. It is believed that following this Way, a Confucian will be able not only to manifest the Principle of Heaven and Earth, but also to continually 'make' the Principle out of his own practices.

With all his contributions clearly recognised, however, there is no agreed evaluation of Confucius and his works, and opinions on him among western scholars vary dramatically. For example, in his history of philosophy, Hegel looked down upon Confucius as merely a moral educationalist and his teachings as a collection of moral proverbs, which represents the primitive stage of the progression of the Absolute Spirit. For Karl Jaspers, the image is different. Confucius is said to be one of the FOUR 'paradigmatic individuals – It would be difficult to find a fifth of equal historical stature' – who 'by being what they were did more than other men to determine the history of man. Their influence extended through two millennia down to our own day' (Jaspers, 1962: 6). As regard to his contribution to religion, Herbert Fingarette emphasises the sacredness of his secular teaching, while Julia Ching would rather consider him 'a seminal thinker' (Ching, 1993: 52).

The main concern of Confucius was with humans and with the fundamental principles of humanity. Confucius believed that these principles were the root of social relationships, the foundation of the stability, peace and prosperity of the state, the family and individuals. He developed his ethics around two central theses; that goodness can be taught and learned, and that society can only be in harmony and at peace under the guidance of wisdom. He further developed a system of concepts to expound the central theses. Of these concepts four became the underlying ideas of the Confucian tradition, namely, the Way (*dao*), ritual/propriety (*li*), humaneness (*ren*) and virtue (*de*), and later the backbone of the ideological structure of a Confucian state. Devoting himself wholeheartedly to solving human problems, Confucius propagated the value of education, virtue and self-cultivation. On the one hand Confucius kept a distance from religious matters such as serving 'spirits and ghosts', and would rather talk about this life than the life after (*Lunyu*, 11: 12); on the other hand, he held a deep faith in Heaven and destiny (*ming*), and preserved religious ritual strictly. Although he believed in his mission that was endowed by Heaven, he never saw himself as the leader or founder of a religious tradition; what he did was merely to transmit the ancient culture, which in his mind was the model for the present and the guarantee for the future. However, in the transmission he 'innovated' the old tradition, as asserted by Schwarts that 'in his focus on the concept of *jen* [humaneness] Confucius is an innovator rather than a transmitter' (Schwarts, 1985: 76). According to Fung Yu-lan, 'in transmitting, he originated something new' (Fung, 1961: 41), while in the words of Jaspers, 'in the philosophy of Confucius, the new expressed itself in the form of the old' (Jaspers, 1962: 54).

CONFUCIANISM AS A 'FAMILY' (*JIA*)

It was said that Confucius had three thousand students, among whom 72 were intimate disciples – the number of his disciples varying in different books, for example, 70 in *Mengzi* 2A:3, 77 in *Shiji*, 76 in *Kongzi Jiayu*, and 72 in *Hou Hanshu*, and the number of 72 becoming widely accepted probably under the influence of the Five Elements School's numerological configuration of the perfect number 360 divided by 5. After three years' mourning (in one case six years') for their master, these disciples and students went to different areas, either engaging in administration of a state, or setting up schools to teach the principles of the *ru* tradition. Confucius was recognised as the symbol of the *ru*, and the *ru* gradually became a specific term for those who followed Confucius to interpret, and teach, the classics, and who engaged themselves in administration, education and the preservation of ancient rituals and music. The multidimensional themes raised in Confucius' conversations and the rich resources of his teaching made it possible for the members of the *ru* to develop different understandings and interpretations of Confucius and his philosophy. The differences in the methods of learning and practice led to a variety of sections within the broad category of the *ru*. According to Han Fei, during this period there were eight prominent sections of the *ru* (Watson, 1970: 119). Although these sections developed Confucian doctrines in manifestly different directions, all of them considered themselves faithful followers of Confucius, devoted to studying, editing and interpreting the classics as well as producing a considerable amount of new literature in the *ru* tradition, and thus receiving recognition as distinguished scholars (*ru*) on the ancient classics. All these sections together were known as *ru jia*, one of the *bai jia* (a hundred schools).

Jia means a structure of family home, being extended to refer to a group of people who are devoted to the same ideal and who form among themselves relationships which are like those of a large family. By *ru jia* it is meant the school or tradition of *literati* or scholars who have committed themselves to the tradition of the *ru*. As a school, *ru jia* sought to make the Way of ancient sage–kings prevail again in the present world. The Way of the ancients was understood as multidimensional in its contents, including the vision of harmony, the rules of propriety, the values of rituals and rites, virtues and methods of a benevolent government. All these were believed to have been well illustrated in the classics that *ru* scholars held Confucius to have edited and interpreted. *Ru jia* propagated the study and learning of these classics to correct disorder and to transform the society, and strove to bring order to the state and peace to the world. Like many other schools, the *ru* transmitted these teachings and principles through forging a seemingly unbroken chain of master–disciples. Its practices were characterised by untiring study of, and instruction on ancient writings, and by performing rituals and playing music properly under the guidance of masters.

CONFUCIANISM AS A CULT (*JIAO*)

For a long time after the death of Confucius, Confucianism remained only one of many schools. Although its teaching was considered prominent and its followers were numerous, it did not enjoy any privilege throughout the Warring States period. On the contrary, it was frequently mocked and attacked by the followers of other schools, as it had been during the lifetime of Confucius. In the eyes of its rivals, Confucianism did not provide adequate answers to the problems of life, nor did it show any advantage over other schools. In a passage from a Daoist work, the *Book of Zhuang Zi*, Confucianism is treated the same as other schools, having its strong and weak points: 'The various skills of the hundred schools [*bai jia*] all have their strong points, and at times each may be of use. But none is wholly sufficient, none is universal' (Watson, 1964: 364).

The First Emperor of the Qin Dynasty (221–206 BCE) relied on Legalism (*fa jia*) to unify and govern the empire. As Legalism was one of the chief rivals of Confucianism, Confucianism was humiliated and suffered from suppression and persecution. With a gradual recovery in the first few decades of the Former Han Dynasty (206 BCE–8 CE), Confucianism became a dominant school and an orthodox ideology during the reign of Emperor Wu (r. 141–87 BCE). Closely related to the religious sacrifices of the state, Confucianism was given another name, *jiao*, and later became one of the three *jiaos*, Confucianism, Daoism and Buddhism. In *Shiji* or the *Records of the Historian ru* and *jiao* are first linked together. However, the meaning here is perhaps no more than the teaching of the *ru* (*Shiji*, 1997: 3184; Watson, 1961, vol. 2: 455.) One of the early references to Confucianism as a religious doctrine is made in the *History of the Jin Dynasty* (*Jinshu*, 1997: 1). When Kang Youwei of the late Qing Dynasty (1644–1911) launched a reform movement to transform the Confucian tradition into a state religion, he confected the story that Confucius created the *ru jiao*, the religion or religious doctrine of *literati*.

The original form of '*jiao*' (𡥈) is a pictograph, consisting of 'a hand holding a stick (|)' and 'beating (𝖝) a child (𝖞)'. The later form of the character (教) consists of 'teaching (educating, 攵)' and 'filial piety (孝)', meaning that a child is rigorously brought into a filial relation. This meaning was broadened to include the doctrines that a group of people endeavoured to transmit and spread. A *jiao* also implies a system of observance of rituals, disciplines of behaviour and faith in the teachings of the founders of a tradition, which are regarded as three of the most important factors in maintaining the unity and transmission of a *jiao*. Therefore, what is meant by *ru jiao* is the cult of the learned or cultured, the continuous tradition of the scholars who followed Confucius to take part in the interpretation and application of the doctrines explored in the classics, and who emphasised the importance and significance of rituals and ceremonies for the realisation of their ideal. As Confucianism was promoted to be the state ideology, the reverence and worship of Confucius became part of state religious activities. Confucius was given the title of Perfect Sage and Ancient Teacher; religious ceremonies were performed on his birthday and other festivals, and sacrifices were offered to his spiritual tablet in temples dedicated to Confucius. Along with the rising of Confucius' status and with the dogmatic application of his teachings, two more names were invented to refer to Confucianism. *Kong jiao* ('the cult of Confucius') emphasises that the teaching and figure of Confucius are central to the tradition, and recognises that Confucianism as a distinctive school, a glorious tradition and an orthodox doctrine was promoted, explored, transmitted and interpreted by Confucius, while *li Jiao* ('the ritual religion') reveals the overemphasis of Confucianism on *li*, the rules of propriety, the rites, rituals and ceremonies.

CONFUCIANISM AS A FORM OF LEARNING (*XUE*)

One of the features that serves to distinguish Confucianism from many other traditions is its commitment to the study and transmission of ancient classics. Confucius is said to be the great editor and commentator of the classics, and his reputation as the sage is based on the fact that he embodies ancient culture. Following him, each generation of Confucian masters and scholars made a contribution to learning, and the doctrines of Confucianism were gradually enriched and extended in numerous writings, treatises and discussions. The Confucian tradition has gathered around its classics an unparalleled abundance of annotations and commentaries. As the tradition of *literati*, Confucianism is steeped in the spirit of scholarship. Confucianism is thus known by the name *ru xue*, meaning the learning of scholars, and the term is first used in the *Records of History* (*Shiji*, 1997: 3118). It is agreed that Confucianism has been able to outlive its status as state religion, and has survived persecution, suppression and revolution, because it is sustained not by its social and religious privilege, but by its unflagging efforts to further learning. It is also contended that Confucian temples may be demolished, devotion to its sages abolished and Confucian followers may be stripped of their social privileges, but Confucianism can still survive and thrive as long as learning is permitted, and the classic texts are available. For this reason, most modern East Asian intellectuals prefer to name Confucianism as *ru xue* rather than *ru jia* or *ru jiao*, in recognition of the fact that the life and spirit of Confucianism lies in its learning.

It is generally recognised that either as a school of thought or as the state orthodoxy, the vitality of Confucianism can be generated through learning and education, and renewed in practising what has been learnt. Confucian Learning differs significantly from what we mean today by 'learning'. For a Confucian, Learning is first of all a process of reading, understanding and deliberating, but it is more than a purely academic subject. Confucian Learning is the study of the Way of Heaven both in the inner self and in external practices. The only purpose of learning is the promotion of virtuous action and the cultivation of a moral character, as Confucius made it clear that 'A person of virtue studies the Way in order to love people' (*Lunyu*, 17: 4). Confucian Learning is also closely related to human nature and destiny. Learning is to transform one's self and retain what is virtuous. It is in this sense that Mengzi, the second sage in the Confucian tradition, understood the way of learning to be nothing other than 'going after the lost heart' (*Mengzi*, 6A: 11).

As a particular kind of learning, the Confucian tradition is known for three characteristics (1) that its members are mostly learned people or civilised intellectuals in a broad sense, which reveals that in Confucian Learning preference is always given to the virtuous way of life (2) that they commit themselves to expanding upon, and interpreting, the classics, which indicates that the value of Confucianism lies in a continuous process of transmitting and furthering the ancient tradition; and (3) that they endeavour to carry out, politically and ethically, collectively and individually, the principles embodied in the classics, which implies that the intention and goal of Confucian Learning is to transform the world in the world.

Ethics, politics and religion in the Confucian tradition

The seven-dimension theory of religion put forward by Ninian Smart has become a useful tool for scholars in Religious Studies to explore the richness and depth of a particular tradition. Smart believes that although it is difficult to define a religion, we can examine it usefully in its different aspects or dimensions, such as the practical and ritual dimension, the experiential and emotional dimension, the narrative or mystic dimension, the doctrinal and political dimension, the ethical and legal dimension, the social and institutional dimension, and the material dimension (Smart, 1989: 12–21).

'Confucianism' literally means the tradition and doctrine of *literati/* scholars. In fact, it is more than the values of a group of people. It contains a socio-political programme, an ethical system, and a religious tradition. It functions as an underlying ideology and a guiding principle permeating the way of life in China and informing the cultures of many other East Asian countries.

Confucian doctrines are primarily explored and illustrated in the Confucian classics, and are also enriched, transformed and extended at the hands of many generations of Confucian masters and students. The interpretation of Confucian principles changes with the times, and we can therefore observe a number of distinct phases or stages in the process of Confucian evolution. Confucianism was the dominant school of thought and orthodox ideology for the most part of two thousand years, exercising both dogmatic and dynamic functions. It was dogmatic in maintaining and strengthening its dominance, but it was also flexible enough to adapt to different environments and situations, shaping and reshaping itself constantly and synthesising new ideas from other schools. It is essentially a Chinese tradition, primarily reflecting the Chinese attitude towards life and the world, although of course it has spread also to other East Asian nations, flourishing in both a distinctively Korean and Japanese form.

Any adequate understanding of Confucianism, past and present, will depend upon a thorough examination of all its dimensions, phases and forms as well as the interplay between it and its social environment. Each of these dimensions is in itself a miniature of the whole tradition, embodying the fundamental principles of Confucianism and at the same time reflecting other dimensions in its own distinctive way. Can we single out from the many dimensions the one which is more important than the others and by which Confucianism may be defined? Many modern scholars and students in Confucian Studies have attempted to answer this question, yet Confucianism demonstrates an ability to cross the boundaries of the traditionally defined subjects in the West, therefore the variety of its presentations has made it almost impossible to be clearly defined. Even so, some of them still argued that Confucianism must have some essential characteristics that serve to set it apart from other traditions and to preserve its distinctiveness, and that it should be possible to define Confucianism in its relation either to ethics, politics or religion.

AN ETHICAL SYSTEM?

Morality has been characteristic of Confucian theory and practice. It was on the foundation of Confucianism that various codes of moral life, rules of propriety, patterns of behaviour and guidelines for social and daily life were produced and enhanced. Confucianism underlined, and perhaps to a smaller extent continues to underline, the basic structure of society and community, to orient the life of the people and to define their moral standards and ethical ideal in most parts of East Asia.

Considering the central position of morality in Confucianism and the significance of Confucian ethics for society, some Western scholars have concluded that the moral dimension is so essential for Confucianism that Confucianism itself can be defined as a form of ethics. A number of prominent scholars hold this position. For them, 'Confucianism . . . was essentially a system of ethics' (Needham, 1970: 24–5); 'What is called in the West "Confucianism" is . . . the traditional view of life and code of manner of the Chinese gentry' (Zaehner, 1988: 370); and Confucianism should be viewed only as 'a set of behavioural patterns' (Tu *et al.*, 1992: 40).

As a moral tradition, Confucianism demonstrates many features in common with other moral systems in the world. For example, Confucian ethics emphasises that both inner motive and its external results must be taken into account when we evaluate a person or his/her conduct. In this sense, it is both deontological and consequentialistic. Confucius repeatedly taught that while it was important to observe ancient rituals strictly, it was even more important to have a sincere heart and a devoted spirit: 'For if a person lacks humaneness (*ren*) within, then what is the value of performing rituals? For if a person lacks humaneness within, what is the use of performing music?' (*Lunyu*, 3: 3). Confucius took a holistic view of a person and believed that if we looked at how a person acted, examined his motives and his tastes, then it would be impossible for the person to conceal his real character from us (*Lunyu*, 2: 10).

Confucian morality revolves around family relationships, especially around the relationships between parents and children, between elder and younger brothers, and between husband and wife. In these relationships, the primary emphasis is put on fulfilling responsibilities to each other with a sincere and conscientious heart. However, Confucian ethics is not confined to the family. It takes family virtues as the cornerstone of social order and world peace. Its logic is that the family is the basic unit of the human community and that harmonious family relationships will inevitably lead to a harmonious society and a peaceful state: 'If only everyone loved his parents and treated his elders with deference, the Empire would be at peace' (*Mengzi*, 4A: 11). For those who are members of the ruling class, their virtues in family affairs are even more significant for the whole country: 'When a ruler feels profound affection for his parents, the common people will naturally become humane' (*Lunyu*, 8: 2).

In the light of such points, some modern philosophers believe that the way by which the Confucian moral system was established is similar to that of virtue ethics. Moral instruction and ethical persuasion employed by Confucius and Mengzi are even said to be able to 'provide a radical alternative to the Aristotelian and Thomistic paradigms most often involved' in the West (Nivison, 1996: 2). As a system of virtue ethics, Confucianism is said to point to a solution for social problems arising from the lack of virtues and from the lack of will to practise virtues. With respect to the lack of virtues, the Confucian solution is a sort of persuasion enforced by rules of ritual/propriety, while for so-called 'weakness of will' it follows the path of self-cultivation and education.

Even if we agree with all these arguments, the question still remains: are these arguments enough for Confucianism to be defined as a system of ethics? There is no question that Confucianism is oriented towards morality and that ethics is the central part of its theory and practice. But what is meant by 'morality' in Confucianism is in fact quite different from that defined in Western ethics. In this respect, Henri Maspero's comments are to the point:

> The central problem of the Doctrine of *Literati* in all ages was one of ethics; and that is probably what has so often led to the judgement that Confucianism was above all a morality, which is far from accurate ... It is indeed a matter of a very particular ethics, quite different from what we generally understand by this word, and that is probably why it is so often omitted from Western accounts of Confucianism. In reality, the problem is the effect which the good or bad acts of man (and especially the governmental acts of the sovereign, representing humanity) have

> upon the orderly progress of natural phenomena (the progress of
> stars, eclipses, earthquakes, floods, etc.) and upon human affairs
> (the deaths of sovereigns, revolts, overthrow of dynasties, etc.).
>
> (Maspero, 1981: 71)

Indeed, Confucian ethics are not only about what we mean by 'moral
issues', but also about politics, religion, education, psychology and metaphysics. All these aspects are integral to Confucian ethics. As morality
is integrated with religion and politics, moral virtues become essential
both for governing and for religious activities. As religion and metaphysics are part of morality, religious ritual and practice are a way of
moral improvement. Taking these into account, we have to say that since
Confucianism contains a special kind of morality, and since Confucian
ethics cover a much wider area than in the West, it would be misleading
simply to define Confucianism as a moral system.

AN OFFICIAL ORTHODOXY?

As the tradition of *literati*, Confucianism is characterised by its deep
involvement in politics, aspired to by its ambition to bring order and
peace to the world. After Confucianism gained predominance over all
other schools, Confucian ethics gradually became a universal yardstick
for behaviour and ideas, an orthodoxy that oriented conduct, thought
and relationship. The moral and political requirements of Confucianism
were crystallised as 'Three Guiding Principles' (*san gang*) and 'Five
Constant Regulations' (*wu chang*), on which Confucian states were
established. Among the three principles maintained and propagated
by Confucianism, the first and foremost one is the subordination of a
subject or minister to his ruler, which is followed by that of a son to his
father and of a wife to her husband. The Five Regulations are actually
five Confucian virtues, humaneness (*ren*), righteousness (*yi*), ritual/pro-
priety (*li*), wisdom (*zhi*) and faithfulness (*xin*), which are believed to be
as constant and unchanging as natural laws, remaining the same for all
time and guiding/ordering all other virtues. These principles and regulations are taken as the essence of life and the bonds of society. In this way,
Confucianism extended the boundaries of moral codes from individual
matters to social and political areas, not only providing the state with an
ideological format, but also equipping the authority with the standards
to judge behaviour and thoughts.

To emphasise the function and value of Confucianism in shaping and reshaping society and politics, some scholars argue that Confucianism was none other than an official state orthodoxy. In posing the question 'What was the Confucianism that concerned society at large in late imperial China?', for example, Kwang-Ching Liu and his companions obviously have in mind the answer of 'an official state orthodoxy' (Liu, 1990: 1, 53–100).

Confucius was seriously concerned with political irregularities. In order to bring peace to states and to restore the brilliant Way of the ancients in his time, he paid great attention to the rules of propriety. One of his concerns was about the discrepancy between names and reality, between language and action, and between rights and duties:

> If names be not correct (*zheng*), language could not be fluently used.
> If language be not fluently used, affairs could not be carried on to
> success . . . ritual/propriety (*li*) and music could not be flourishing
> . . . the punishments could not be properly made . . . then the people
> would not know how to behave. (*Lunyu*, 13: 3)

What Confucius tried to argue here is that if a ruler, a subject, a father and a son do not fulfil their duties, they abuse their titles and violate the names by which they are defined. For Confucius, this is the beginning of the collapse of ritual/propriety and music, and is one of the causes which bring about social disorder and political chaos.

Having given preeminence to the role of a ruler in restoring the Way of the ancients, Confucius seldom emphasised the one-way loyalty of the subject or minister to the ruler. Rather, he insisted that the relationship must be reciprocal: 'The ruler should employ his subject–ministers according to the rule of propriety/ritual (*li*), while subject–ministers should serve their ruler with loyalty (*zhong*)' (*Lunyu*, 3: 19). However, to serve the purpose of imperial government, this theory of 'rectification of names' was, especially in the latter part of history, extended and interpreted as a conservative bulwark for an authoritarian regime in which absolute subordination of subject–minister to ruler guaranteed an effective administration. In this way, Confucianism became more than a system of morality or a school of thought, and it was the core of the state orthodoxy that every person, every event and every affair must be in accordance with what was required from them.

For a long period in the past, government bureaucracy and Confucian scholarship were almost identical: the officials of the state were chosen either by examining a candidate's learning of the Confucian classics or by recognising his achievements in practising Confucian virtues. A systematic way of selecting officials in accordance with Confucian principles was already put into use in the Han Dynasty, and this system later developed into a network of civil servant examinations at county, provincial and national levels. On the one hand, Confucianism gained its energy from the scholars who took the Confucian Way as the Truth and Confucian Learning as an efficient and effective means to transform society and to bring peace to the world. Within an ideal Confucian context, a scholar is a Confucian whether or not he is in office, and he can do what is expected of him whether he is an official or not. On the other hand, as Confucian Learning was identified with the contents of examination, many scholars took it as their greatest duty to gain success in civil examinations and to be part of government bureaucracy. To some extent, whether achievement in Confucian Learning could be recognised or not depended upon success in examination, as depicted in a proverb: 'All other careers are inferior, while only [Confucian] Learning is superior [*wanban jie xiapin, weiyou dushu gao*].' It was perhaps true that for many men over a long period of history, Confucian Learning was no more than a stepping-stone to success in an individual's career. Confucianism was eventually transmuted from a resourceful doctrine into an authentic scheme, not only binding the performance and thinking of a social elite, but also defining how to lead a life for every individual.

There is no doubt that Confucianism acted as an official state orthodoxy during the latter part of East Asian history; but our inquiries into the nature of Confucianism as an orthodoxy lead to a number of other questions. What kind of function did the state orthodoxy exert on the life of the people? Wm. Theodore de Bary believes that as the orthodox tradition, Confucianism was 'a life-style, an attitude of mind, a type of character formation, and a spiritual ideal that eluded precise definition' (de Bary, 1975: 24). In order to elucidate its social functions, he analyses the four types of orthodoxy assumed by Neo-Confucianism in late imperial China, educational orthodoxy, bureaucratic orthodoxy, philosophical orthodoxy, and 'liberal' orthodoxy (de Bary, 1981: 50–7, 188–94). The quartet presentation of Confucian orthodoxy draws a clear picture of how Confucianism functioned in history. But as these four are very different by nature and in function, it would not make our task any easier to define Confucianism, even if we agreed that it was a socio-political orthodoxy.

A more serious question would arise if we defined Confucianism as the state orthodoxy: What was or is Confucianism when it either was not yet, or no longer is, the state orthodoxy? Confucianism was not always a dominant ideology, nor has it been the state orthodoxy since the beginning of the twentieth century. From Confucius until the middle of the Former Han Dynasty, Confucianism was not orthodox at all. It was subject to attack, criticism and persecution. From the collapse of the Later Han Dynasty (25–220 CE) to the Song Dynasty (960–1162) Confucianism maintained the name of the state ideology but in reality its control over the state and over social life was limited to a very small area, thanks to the popularity of Daoism and Buddhism. From the beginning of the twentieth century until the 1980s, Confucianism lost its grasp over the state and over people's life and thinking. It was criticised and attacked as a reactionary and conservative force by many liberals and Communist intellectuals alike. Nevertheless, Confucianism still existed and developed during all these periods. The fact that Confucianism has outlived its status as the state orthodoxy demonstrates that 'orthodoxy' is not the essential quality of Confucianism.

The third question in relation to the definition of Confucianism as the state orthodoxy is this: was Confucianism an orthodoxy manipulated by a small group of social elite, or a culture shared by a large portion of people? From a historical perspective Confucianism existed both as an official orthodoxy and as a popular culture, being at once a tradition for scholars–officials and a common system of values for peasants, artisans and merchants. On the one hand, Confucianism evolved out of the *ru* tradition, and Confucius educated his students to be true gentlemen, to devote themselves to learning and practising the principles of the ancient classics. A great number of Confucian masters were prominent philo-sophers (*zi*) who loved wisdom and endeavoured to make plain the secret of human and natural life, although 'the Chinese word corresponding to philosopher denoted group attachment to tradition rather than individual love of wisdom' (Dawson, 1963: 10). For these reasons, Confucianism is said to be 'a circle of academics' and the way of life for a small group of social elite. On the other hand, Confucianism does have its ordinary character, appealing to the people of all ranks. Its theories and practices were initially the new products of freethinking and private education. All but two of Confucius' disciples came from the families of a lower social status, and Confucius was a very 'common' person whose early life was spent in poverty, and whose knowledge was gained through hard learning. Most of his conversations were humorous and many of his attitudes to life were typical of the Chinese. Many Confucian scholars of later generations could even be said to be half-Confucian and half-Daoist: in office they engaged themselves in administration, while out of office they concentrated on self-cultivation, either through learning, cultivation and education, or on enjoying natural and social pleasures.

It is thus clear that Confucianism is not merely an official orthodoxy. Otherwise, we would not be able to explain properly why Confucianism is said to be both conservative and radical, retrogressive and progressive. Measured by modern values, it did indeed have its 'good' as well as its 'bad' side. Some modern scholars have only seen or emphasised the one side or the other by which they label Confucianism. Having examined the long history of Confucianism, for example, Shryock commented that 'Confucianism is one of the major achievements of the human mind, and its noble code of ethics makes it worthy of the deepest respect' (Shryock, 1966: 226). This view, however, is not shared by others. For the latter, Confucian orthodoxy was a product of history, and has become completely obsolete and is an obstacle for forward progress. An early example of the latter opinion was provided by James Legge, an outstanding translator and interpreter of Confucian classics, who saw the teachings of Confucius as the cause of the backwardness of China. According to Legge, 'There has been a tendency to advance, and Confucius has all along been trying to carry the nation back', and because Confucius and his followers had no sympathy with progress, Legge believed that the influence of Confucianism 'will henceforth wane' (Legge, 1991, vol. 1: 108, 113). The divergence of their views itself demonstrates that the definition of Confucianism as an official orthodoxy can lead only to a partial evaluation of the tradition.

A RELIGIOUS TRADITION?

'For the historian or phenomenologist of religion, Confucianism presents a kind of extreme or limiting case in which the religious or sacred elements are elusive and challenge many of the accepted generalisations' (Rule, 1986: xiii). One problem regarding an overview of Confucianism is whether or not Confucianism should be considered a religious tradition, and if we are to take it as a religion, then what can we say are its distinctive features? The western interpreters of Confucianism disagree greatly on this issue, partly because of a terminological ambiguity arising from applying western terms of religion, philosophy and ethics to an eastern tradition, and partly because of a phenomenological confusion coming from restructuring Confucianism in light of these scholars' own religious or non-religious convictions.

Whether Confucianism is religious or not is directly related to the question of how to define the Confucian tradition. Under the influence of a Christian definition of religion, earlier generations of western scholars judged it on the basis of the Christian doctrine, so that Confucianism swings between religious and agnostic or between good and evil. For example, 'Confucianism, which for the Jesuits had seemed a wonderful preparation for the Gospel, was, even for Legge the great interpreter of it, an evil which had to be swept away' (Dawson, 1964: 25). In general, contemporary western scholars have extended their concept of religion, but this has not yet reached an agreement about the religious elements of the Confucian tradition. A number of contemporary western scholars avoid involvement in any kind of questions on the religious nature of Confucianism, while others attempt to argue for their own views. However, their views have by no means converged. For the sake of convenience, we can classify their opinions into two groups. The first group holds an opinion diametrically different from the second group and attempts to establish that Confucianism was and is a religion. For example, Rodney Taylor argued

> those interpretations that have sought to define Confucianism as a
> form of humanism devoid of religious character have failed to realise
> the central feature that persists throughout the tradition. I argue
> that a single thread runs throughout the tradition, and this thread is
> religious . . . Let us make no mistake, Confucianism is an ethical system
> and humanistic teaching. It is also, however, a tradition that bears a
> deep and profound sense of the religious, and any interpretation that
> ignores this quality has missed its quintessential feature.
>
> (Taylor, 1986b: 1–2)

The character of Confucianism as a religion is examined on varying grounds. With respect to traditional function and cultural heritage, Confucianism is considered a religion because it 'has played a central role in the cultures of China, Korea and Japan as the major moral and religious teaching at the very heart of each of these cultures' (Taylor, 1986a: 1). With respect to the content of the tradition, it is believed to be religious because it has a strong ritual dimension: offerings and sacrifices to ancestors, for example, have been central to Confucian beliefs (Smart, 1989: 110). With respect to its metaphysical ultimate, Confucianism is considered to be a religion due to its understanding of Heaven and to 'the relationship of humankind to heaven' that functions as a religious core from which all that flows 'is part of religious meaning' (Taylor, 1986b: 2).

The opinions of the second group are marked as much, if not more, by disagreement. For some, Confucianism is not a religion because it focuses on interpersonal relationships, rather than on a human relationship to God or a supernatural Being. For others, it is because Confucius is mostly a teacher of morals and 'it is considered wrong therefore to class his doctrine as a religion' (Giles, 1915: 67). For some again, it is because Confucianism lacked a supernatural element and 'depended on no supernatural sanctions' (Needham, 1970: 24–5). Max Weber concluded that 'Confucianism was indifferent to religion', and that 'Completely absent in Confucian ethic was any tension between nature and deity, between ethical demand and human shortcoming, consciousness of sin and need for salvation' (Weber, 1968: 146, 235). Much unsatisfied with Weber's evaluation that Confucianism is so rationalistic that it has eradicated 'all the residues of religious anchorage', Creel remarked sharply that 'it would be pleasant to be able to say that Weber's comments on Confucius and Confucianism were all equally penetrating, but unfortunately this is not the case' (Creel, 1960: 310).

Eastern scholars in Confucian Studies do not perform much better than their western counterparts, although their divisions are due to reasons quite different from those in the West. One of the many difficulties in defining Confucianism as a religion is that the term 'religion (*zong jiao*)' has quite a different resonance in Chinese than in a western language. If in English, the term 'religion' often carries, along with its descriptive meanings, a commendatory implication of 'devotion, fidelity or faithfulness, conscientiousness, pious, affection or attachment' (*The Oxford English Dictionary*, 2nd edition, vol. 13: 569), in Chinese, the word that refers to religion is primarily suggestive of superstitions. A religion is usually regarded as a superstructure which consists of superstitions, dogmas, rituals and institutions (Fung, 1961: 3). For this reason 'the things of religion were not greatly appreciated' in China, as Matteo Ricci observed a long time ago (Gernet, 1985: 16).

Historically it was believed in the West that human knowledge about the world and about ourselves would be much better served by maintaining a division between the secular and the religious (initiated by Plato), and by the compartmentalisation of human sciences such as philosophy, ethics, politics, economics, education and religion (probably starting with Aristotle). To the ancient Chinese, however, these divisions are inappropriate. Their religious view of the world is not intentionally distinguished from their philosophical or political view. The terms which were used to refer to their views of the world, such as *dao* (the Way), *jiao* (doctrine or the tradition) and *li* (principles or laws) are all, without exception, suitable to denote philosophical thinking, political ideal, ethical norms and religious practices. The distinction between different traditions is seldom categorically emphasised and an individual is normally able to commit himself to more than one doctrine. With this fact in mind, Eric Sharpe argues that 'to talk of syncretism of religious thoughts or threads, and particularly in any discussion about the "three religions of China", any scholar had to admit that it was possible for a Chinese to belong to all three systems at the same time' (Sharpe, 1994: 82).

The modern Chinese use a term coined by combining two characters, *zong* and *jiao*, which originally meant 'ancestral' and 'teaching/doctrine'. In the mind of the ancient Confucians, there were two kinds of teaching. Those transmitted from ancient times by sages are considered to be noble and orthodox, encouraging people to be good and sincere, to be filial to their ancestors and parents. When these teachings are corrupted or misused, they become associated with superstitions, involving belief in miracles, strange powers, reincarnation and so forth. They believe that noble doctrines are those by great sages like Confucius, Lao Zi and Sakyamuni the Buddha, while the depraved teachings were evident in popular Daoism, popular Buddhism and folk cults. When 'religion' is identified with the theories and practices of the latter, it enjoys the respect of few scholars. This perhaps explains why in the modern age only a handful of scholars such as Kang Youwei (1858–1927) would enthusiastically argue for establishing Confucianism as the state religion, and this effort met a strong reaction and harsh criticism from other Confucians. Liang Qichao (1873–1929), for example, opposed any attempt to label Confucianism a religion because he believed that 'religion' was incompatible with Confucius' own views and was contrary to rationalism (cited in Yang, 1961: 5).

Here we encounter that definitions of Confucianism turn on definitions of religion in general. 'Religion is difficult to define in a way that satisfies everyone . . . It is always a part of the general culture of the people who hold it, and at the same time it is an interpretation of that culture' (Shryock, 1966: 223). Many modern scholars in the West have gone beyond the old and ultimately Christian definitions of religion so that many different traditions and cultures can now be comfortably drawn under its umbrella. Durkheim rejected various definitions of 'religion' popular in his time. Among these definitions, one defined religion by the supernatural and the mysterious, and the other defined religion in relation to God or a spiritual being. Durkheim believed that 'A religion is a unified system of beliefs and practices relative to sacred things, that is to say, things set apart and forbidden – beliefs and practices which unite into one single moral community called a Church, all those who adhere to them' (Durkheim, 1961: 21–44). Paul Tillich took religion as the 'state of being grasped by ultimate concern' (Tillich, 1963: 4). John Bowker examined religions in their sociological and anthropological functions so that a religion is a way of breaking 'through limitation' or is expressive of 'route-finding activities' (Bowker, 1973: viii). Frederick Streng defines religion as 'a means towards ultimate transformation' (Streng, 1985: 1–8). John Hinnels emphasises specifically that there are inherent dangers in assuming that there will always be a definable and separate phenomenon recognisable as a 'religion', since 'the religion of the majority is often expressed mainly through custom and practice', which leads him to believe that the nature of a religion is in its custom and practice (Hinnels, 1991: 12–13).

In the light of this expansion of the understanding of religion, more and more western scholars tend to think of Confucianism in terms of a religion. In Mainland China, where the Confucian tradition is in general defined as a feudal ethical system, the perception of Confucianism has also started to change, as indicated by a group of recently published articles in which a number of prominent intellectuals confirm the close link between Confucianism and religion in one way or another (*Xinhua Wenzhai*, no. 10, 1998, pp. 37–42). It is clear that these new attempts are different from those made by the Sinologists of old generations who took Confucianism as a religion because of its similarities to Christianity. Contemporary scholars attempt to establish that Confucianism is religious, a tradition of a unique character that is distinctive from other religions in one way or another. Inquiries into the religious nature of Confucianism thus focus on its distinctiveness.

It is agreed that the difficulty in defining Confucianism as a religion does not lie much in its practices, and the practices Confucianism cherishes such as ancestral worship, patronage of Confucian sages and sacrifices offered to Heaven do not differ greatly from the religious practices of many other traditions in the world. The nub of the difficulty lies in its humanistic teachings and rational understanding of the world and life. Even W. E. Soothill who listed Confucianism as one of the three religions in China had to resort to the complementary unity of the three religions in China to make up for 'the deficiency of Confucianism in making little or no provision, beyond a calm stoicism, for the spiritual demands of human beings' (Soothill, 1973: xi–xix). Is there ever any religious spirit and value in the Confucian doctrines on philosophic, ethical and social matters, so that a distinct type of religiosity can be identified?

Hans Küng believes that Confucianism is a religion, a religion of wisdom, distinguishable and yet related to two other types of religion in the world. According to him, there exist three Great River Systems of world religions. The first river system is of Semitic origin in the Near East, which is of prophetic character and is composed of 'three Abrahamic religions', Judaism, Christianity and Islam. From the Near East to the Indus Valley, we encounter the second great river system of religion. It is of Indian origin and has a mystical character. It originated in the Indian tradition (Upanishads). As a reformation or adaptation of this, there emerged three further religions: the reform movement of mahavira, called Jina, the 'victor', founder of Jainism; the reform movement of Gautama Buddha which gave birth to Buddhism; and the more recent Hindu religions, whether monotheistic or polytheistic. The third great river system of religion is of Chinese origin and is associated with the figure of the sage; it is therefore labelled a religion of wisdom, and includes Confucianism, Daoism and part of Chinese Buddhism. In the third system of religion, it is the wisdom of the sages, Confucius, Lao Zi and the Buddha, that leads the people to their salvation (Küng & Ching, 1989: xi–xix).

Julia Ching defines Chinese religions as 'religions of harmony', because they are all based on the theme that 'Heaven and human are one (*tianren heyi*)'. For her, there are two kinds of religion of harmony, the first one intending for 'a greater harmony between God and man', while the second seeking 'a greater harmony between the divine and the human orders, such as in Taoist philosophy, in the humanism of Mencius, of Neo-Confucianism, as well as Chinese Mahayana Buddhist philosophy, especially of Ch'an (or Zen)'. Taking these two sides into account, Ching believes that Confucianism is 'a humanism that is open to religious values'. Recognising that the main concern of Confucius and Confucianism is with social and moral affairs, Ching does not agree that all humanists are 'secularists or at least religious agnostics', and insists that Confucius is a humanist of a special kind and that there is a profound spirituality in his moral teachings which are the foundation of Confucianism (Ching, 1993: 6, 51, 52).

Confucianism covers a wide range of doctrinal deliberations from pure humanism to ultimate spiritualism but a spiritual concern over human destiny runs through it. Some people therefore concentrate on the distinctiveness of the religious dimension of Confucianism rather than on whether or not Confucianism is a religious tradition (Tu, 1989a). In a recently published book entitled *Confucianism and Christianity*, this author argues that the distinctiveness of Confucianism as a religion lies in its humanistic approaches to religious matters, such as beliefs, rituals and institutions, and in its religious concerns with secular affairs, individual growth, family relationships and social harmony (Yao, 1996a). There is more than one type of religion in the world. Different understandings of transcendence, imminence, immortality and the ways to eternity, manifest different religious values, which underlie the variety of religions, either theistic, humanistic or naturalistic. One of the ways in which some writers have failed to recognise Confucian spirituality is that Confucianism has been examined and judged with the yardsticks of a theistic system. Within a theo-centric framework, Confucianism is said to be definitely *not* a religion, since 'It has no priesthood, no church, no bible, no creed, no conversion, and no fixed system of gods. It has no interest in either theology or mythology' (Ferm, 1976: 150). However, if one recognises that different types of human religiosity exist, it would not be so difficult for us to see that there are Confucian counterparts to the Christian 'priests, church, bible, creed, theology and mythology'. For example, Confucian academies functioned in much the same way as churches of Christianity. Matteo Ricci first noticed that these Confucian Academies (*shu yuan*) were equivalent to Christian preaching houses and the Confucians were also 'impressed by the resemblances between the [Jesuit] preaching houses and their own traditional academies' (*shu yuan*). E. Zürcher also observed that 'the atmosphere of *shu yuan* did have something solemn and almost holy': each meeting began with a ceremony in honour of the founder and Confucius; the rules of conduct were codified according to a convention, which often included pious hymns sung by choirs of young boys (Gernet, 1985: 17–18).

The different approaches discussed above lay the ground for our own view of the distinctiveness of religious Confucianism. As a religion, Confucianism is indeed of special character. The backbone of Confucian doctrines is composed of three principles: harmony and unity between humanity and Heaven, harmony and unity between descendants and ancestors, and harmony and unity between the secular and the sacred (Yao, 1996a: 31–3). In analysing, and expanding on, these three dimensions of harmony, Confucianism develops a systematic and unique doctrine of human religiosity. This is a kind of humanism, because it concentrates on solving secular problems and insists on human perfectibility. However, Confucianism is not humanistic in the normal sense of this term, because it does not end with the material satisfaction of human needs, nor does it reject pursuing the spiritual Absolute. Although it holds a different conception of what can be counted as the 'spiritual', Confucianism does have a common sense of the ultimacy of a personal experience of the sacred and a personal commitment to the Ultimate. It is thus a humanistic religion, a humanistic tradition manifesting spiritual longing and discipline in its classics, creed, practices and institutions, and leading to a religious destination that answers human ultimate concerns. These concerns are expressed through individual and communal commitments and revealed by the desires to transform self and society according to their moral and political vision. Confucianism is a kind of humanism that seeks sacredness in an ordinary and yet disciplined life; or in Paul Rule's words, it is a 'secular religion, this-worldly in emphasis yet appealing to transcendent values embodied in the concept of "heaven" ' (Rule, 1986: 31). By relating the secular to the sacred, the humanistic to the religious, Confucianism demonstrates a unique understanding of the Ultimate and of transcendence, and opens a distinctive path to human eternity.

Confucianism is a humanistic religion because the Confucian understanding and conception of the Ultimate, of the imminent power, of the
transcendent, of the world, life and death are all related to, and based
on, its exploration of human nature and human destiny. Human life is
meaningful and invaluable, not only because it is a way of fulfilling human
destiny, but also because it is the only way of bridging this life and the
beyond, the limited and the infinite, the temporal and the eternal, which
is well illustrated by Confucius in his reply to the questions of how to
serve spiritual beings and how to understand death: 'If you are not yet
able to serve humans, how can you possibly serve spiritual beings? If you
do not yet understand life, how can you possibly understand death?'
(*Lunyu*, 11: 12).

As a religious humanism, Confucianism is characterised by its faith
in Heaven (*tian*) and the Mandate of Heaven (*tian ming*), and by its
belief that humanity can achieve perfection and live up to heavenly principles. It insists that humans have their mission in the world. But it also
insists that this mission cannot be fulfilled unless men and women have
done their best to fulfil their ethical and moral duties, from which there
develops a unique understanding of the moral as the transcendental
and the secular as the sacred. Confucianism stresses the importance
of self-consciousness and self-cultivation as the pathway leading to
'transcendence'. Self-transformation is never meant to be a matter of
isolation of the self from others and from society. Rather, it is closely
related to human and natural orders, conscientiously exercised in the form
of social and political action, and optimistically aimed at harmonising
the world through changes. It is in this sense that Tu Wei-ming points out
that 'The question of being religious is crucial for our appreciation of the
inner dimension of the Neo-Confucian project', and that the religiousness of Neo-Confucianism should be defined in terms of the individuals'
efforts in engaging in 'ultimate self-transformation as a communal act'
(Tu, 1985: 135).

As a humanistic religion, Confucianism is also distinctive in its rationalism. According to Max Weber, 'To judge the level of rationalization a
religion represents we may use two primary yardsticks which are in many
ways interrelated. One is the degree to which the religion has divested
itself of magic; the other is the degree to which it has systematically unified
the relation between God and the world and therewith its own ethical
relationships to the world' (Weber, 1968: 226). By the first measure,

Confucianism is almost devoid of any belief in magic, which is demonstrated by Confucius who was recorded as seldom talking about 'prodigies, magic powers, disorder and spirits' (*Lunyu*, 7: 21). By the second measure, Confucian rationalism is revealed in its insistence that Heaven is the ultimate source of human virtues, that the Mandate of Heaven can be known through one's conscious search in one's nature and/or in the natural and human world, and that fulfilment of Heaven's Mandate is nothing other than undertaking self-cultivation and extending one's virtues to others and to the world.

And as a rationalistic religion, Confucianism does not emphasise transcendence as a delivery from without. It is concerned with human destiny, but this concern is based on, and in turn supported by, the belief in the possibility of sagehood or the perfectibility of every individual, visible in daily improvement in terms of moral quality and social progress. Confucianism does not hand out a blank cheque for those who are eager to embrace an eternal hope. It is fully aware of the imperfection of human individuals and the limitation of social reality. Therefore, it repeatedly warns that perfectibility will remain merely a possibility unless each individual engages in a life-long process of learning and practising, and is constantly under self-discipline and education. For Confucianism, life is indeed a process of continuous self-cultivation and self-transformation leading to self-transcendence, the realisation of one's authentic nature in which the all-pervasive principles of Heaven are fully manifested. It is in this process, engaged in by so many people in so many generations, that Confucianism gains its power, energy and vitality.

Confucian classics
As the doctrine of *literati*, Confucianism may well be called a tradition of books, in the sense that it takes the sacred writings of the ancients as the source of values and ideals. It has been agreed that the Confucian classics contains the core of Confucian doctrines, the root of the late Confucian schools and sub-schools, and the fountain-head of all the Confucian streams. Indeed, without a proper knowledge of Confucian classics, it would be impossible for us to draw a full picture of Confucianism.

The image of Confucianism in the West has always been closely related to how these classics are evaluated. For some of the early Christian missionaries, the Confucian classics represented the holy past of China when it had not yet been corrupted by later rationalism and by Buddhist superstitions. For example, seeing a relation between elements in the Confucian classics and Christian belief, Matteo Ricci (1552–1610) remarked that,

> Of all the pagan sects known to Europe, I know of no people who fell into fewer errors in the early ages of their antiquity than did the Chinese. From the very beginning of their history it is recorded in their writings that they recognized and worshipped one supreme being whom they called the King of Heaven.   (Dawson, 1964: 9)

The fundamentally appreciative view of the Confucian classics changed as the function of these classics in East Asian society and history was fully revealed, and as radical Chinese and Korean intellectuals began to denigrate the classics in their desire to demolish Confucianism. Some western historians took a radical view of the Confucian classics. For them, China is 'the oldest state and yet no past, but a state which exists today as we know it to have been in ancient times' (Dawson, 1964: 15). One of the reasons why China was not a progressive state is said to be that it had been held back by the Confucian classics: 'This stereotyping of their books has caused the stereotyping of their ideas' (Dawson, 1964: 6). The classics were therefore deemed to be obstacles for the further development of Chinese culture, constantly drawing China back to the past. In this sense it is said that Confucianism as 'a scriptural tradition' does not have a future.

Neither that the Confucian classics are the embodiment of human civilisation nor that they are completely useless and oppressive would do justice to them. For a long time the classics have been considered the sacred writings and the source of supreme values. They are indeed the foundation on which Confucian thinking was formulated and behaviour guided. As the source of values they stimulate Confucian students to follow and to create. Therefore, it is not very far from the truth to say that the Confucian classics are, to a great extent, identifiable with Confucianism, and that to be a Confucian is to dedicate oneself to the classics or more precisely, to the values embodied in the classics. On the one hand, these classics were the products of history, contingent upon time and space. This would inevitably make them dogmatic and stereotyped if their words and sentences were to be applied absolutely and universally to communal and personal life. Unfortunately, this was the case during a long period in the later part of East Asian history. On the other hand, it is argued that what we know as the Confucian classics did not remain unchanged for two thousand years. Rather, they have been constantly renewed, extended and deepened in the form of annotation, interpretation and reinterpretation made by each generation of Confucian scholars. The religious and political visions projected in the classics have always been subject to development, and the directions of that development have always been a topic of debate between the different Confucian schools.

ANCIENT RECORDS AND THE CLASSICS

Long before Confucius a well-developed tradition of official learning (*guan xue*) had existed and thrived. Following the collapse of the Shang Dynasty, the newly founded Zhou Dynasty felt a strong need for an official system of learning and education that could provide the state with ideological ideas and administrative skills. The Duke of the Zhou, a great sage for Confucius, was said to be the first person who consciously implanted such a system into the imperial institution, and who, with the help of *ru*, intellectuals of a wide range of knowledge, transformed the sophisticated ritual system of earlier ages to institute a new system of 'ritual and music' with a clearly new moral and political orientation. The learning of the new system was transmitted partly through education in local and state colleges and partly through written materials (bronze inscriptions and inscriptions on bamboo/wooden strips). In order to preserve and carry on this learning, various kinds of records gradually accumulated and became official versions of ancient culture.

Confucianism emerged when the unified ideology began to fragment and the official learning was torn apart by semi-independent states and was gradually replaced by private learning or education (*si xue*). Confucius was one of the earliest teachers to start private education and to extend learning to the poor and to the masses. He was said to have taught as many as three thousand students, among whom only one or two are known definitely to come from aristocratic families. As the head of the group, Confucius himself was keen to learn and grasp what had been achieved in previous times. One of his life-long aims was to preserve, edit and transmit the recordings of the culture of the ancients. Edited and interpreted, these records then became known as the classics (*jing*), sacred books believed to be the work of ancient sages. Having been established as the state orthodoxy, these classics were revered both in China and in all other countries where Confucianism was influential.

Confucianism cherishes the classics as the truthful records of ancient culture, value-added by Confucius' editing and commentaries. The customs and events of the past are believed to serve as a mirror of the present and the guide to the future. As far as the Confucian doctrine is concerned, Confucians believe that in the classics, heavenly principles are revealed to them and that by studying these classics and books they will be able to understand the Way of Heaven and by applying it to human life they can establish the Way of humanity.

The Confucian classics played four primary roles in the transmission of the Confucian tradition. Firstly, they were the key textbooks for students. Either as one of many schools or as the official ideology, Confucianism was celebrated for its reverence for the classics. Confucian followers were required to learn the texts by heart, and most students would indeed be able to extract 'significant meanings and implications' from seemingly abstract texts. When Confucianism became the 'official learning' sponsored and supervised by the government during the Han Dynasty, Confucian classics were taken as basic textbooks for state education. It is recorded that in 124 BCE, the Grand Academy of the state (*tai xue*) was established at the capital, and learned masters of the five classics were appointed as imperial academicians (*bo shi*). By 130 CE, the academy had grown so big that 240 buildings were built with 1850 rooms to accommodate students. The academy was under the control of a rector, *tai chang*, a minister of the rites who took care to see that the instruction was consistent with the tradition. Students took the course of two of the classics during the first two years, and were examined at the end of this period. Those who passed the exam received a title and a stipend, and those who failed had to start again. Those who wished to carry on their learning would study the other three classics, each for two years, and they would be examined at the end of that period (Shryock, 1966: 21). When the civil examination was decreed to be based on the Confucian writings, the classics and their standard commentaries became compulsory for all candidates and schoolboys in the empire.

Secondly, the classics were considered to be the source of the Confucian way of life. For Confucian believers, the Confucian classics were, to a great extent, the blueprint of an ideal life. Political instructions recorded in the classics were taken to be the guidelines for governmental activities. Rituals observed by the ancients became necessary rites of passage. Poems and music were believed to be essential for cultivating a good character. Even daily conversations recorded in the books became the mottoes and proverbs to be taken by heart. Poetry, history, rites, the principles of change and the melody of music thus became something to live by and to act on. Confucius devoted most of his later years to editing and arranging the *Spring and Autumn Annals*. For him, the *Annals* were not merely a historical chronicle; they communicated values, both recommending and prohibiting various paths of action. Confucius invested so much in the work that he remarked on it with great confidence: 'The future generations shall understand me through the *Spring and Autumn Annals* and shall also judge me on the basis of the *Spring and Autumn Annals*' (*Mengzi*, 3B: 9).

Thirdly, the classics were the root from which numerous Confucian branches developed. Due to the richness of their materials and complexity of their contents, the classics became the area where controversies and debates between different Confucian sections frequently took place. Creative scholars would read different meanings out of the classics, which led to the establishment of different schools. Masters of these schools often gave their own interpretations to the texts. Full of personal insights and unique experience, the annotations and commentaries of school masters inspired further speculation and expansion. Some of the Confucian schools were directly generated from the different versions of the same classics. For example, there appeared to be three schools of the *Book of Poetry* at the beginning of the second century BCE, based on three different versions of the text available at that time. There were also three schools for the *Book of History*, and four for the *Book of Changes*. Although some of these schools came to an end when their versions became unpopular or when different versions were integrated into one, they nevertheless left a deep impression on, and provided a heritage of learning for, later generations, who in due time would produce or reproduce new interpretations and new controversies.

Fourthly, the Confucian classics were appreciated primarily for their political functions and applications. Confucius was recorded to have intended all the six arts to help establish a good government:

> All Six Arts help to govern. The *Book of Rites* helps to regulate men, the *Book of Music* brings about harmony, the *Book of History* records incidents, the *Book of Poetry* expresses emotions, the *Book of Changes* reveals supernatural influence, and the *Spring and Autumn Annals* shows what is right. (*Shiji*, 1997: 3197)

Deeply involved in politics, the Confucian classics were also taken as an easy tool for various political purposes. On the one hand, mastery of the classics was necessary for a good reputation which in turn earned a scholar a successful career. On the other, changes of dynasties and rulers often led to the promotion or demotion of this or that classic. The fortune of a particular school depended upon whether or not its understanding of the Confucian classics would be accepted by the authority of the day, and adoption of one rather than another version directly pointed to the failure of one school and the triumph of another. The Confucian classics became the central arena again for political debates at the end of the nineteenth century and the beginning of the twentieth century, when different 'political parties' made use of them to justify their own political programmes. Thus, on some occasions the Confucian classics were said to be reformative by nature, while on other occasions they were rebuked as conservative. In one way or another, the Confucian classics were simply used as a means for various political ends and were closely related to the process of political changes.

CONFUCIUS AND THE CONFUCIAN CLASSICS

There are good reasons for holding that the Confucian classics took their shape in the hands of Confucius. However, nothing can be taken for granted in the matter of the early versions of the classics, and debates and arguments concerning what are original texts and how much Confucius did to them have erupted time and again.

Confucius is believed to be the Sage primarily for what he did with the ancient recordings. At least since the Former Han Dynasty, the majority of Confucian scholars have come to believe that there were no 'classics' proper before Confucius, and that Confucius established what is known as the classics. Before his time there might have been some writings recording early political speeches, court or popular poems, philosophical and religious deliberations, various rites and rituals, as well as historical and natural events. However, these writings had either been corrupted or were virtually lost by the time of Confucius. Confucius recollected and edited them by rearranging the orders of the chapters and by commentating on passages. In this way, Confucius 'fixed' the versions of the ancient writings and established their value as classical textbooks. The *Records of the Historian* of the second century BCE related how this had happened:

In the time of Confucius, the power of the Chou Emperors had declined, the forms of worship and social intercourse ('ritual and music') had degenerated, and learning and scholarship had fallen into decay. Confucius studied the religious or ceremonial order and historical records of the three dynasties (Hsia, Shang and Chou), and he traced the events from the times of Emperors Yao and Shun down to the times of Duke Mu of Ch'in and arranged them in chronological order . . . Therefore, Confucius handed down a tradition of historic records and various records of ancient customs and ethnology . . . Confucius taught poetry, history, ceremonies and music to 3,000 pupils of whom 72 had mastered 'the six arts' (probably referring to the Six Classics).

(Lin, 1994: 127–35)

This tradition became an orthodox story about how the Confucian classics came into being and was adopted by almost all the royal houses after the Han as the truth of the classics. Many Chinese scholars still hold to this tradition. Lifu Chen, for example, believes that 'Confucius edited the *Book of Songs*, and the *Book of History*, compiled the *Book of Rites*, and the *Book of Music*, annotated the *Book of Changes*, and wrote the *Spring and Autumn Annals*. These were called the "Six Classics"' (Chen, 1972: 2). And Xiong Shili believes that 'the [existent] six classics were the final version fixed up by Confucius at his late years' (Xiong, 1996: 406–42).

However, there is also a different account of this. For some scholars, especially those of the Old Text School – a Confucian school based on the version of the classics written in the scripts of pre-Han times – the classics originated in the early years of the Zhou Dynasty. What Confucius did was no more than rearrange the early writings so that he could take them as textbooks for his students. Confucius was a preserver of early writings and transmitted them to later generations. By this account it is therefore wrong to say that Confucius 'created' or 'initiated' the classics. Some scholars of this century fall into line with the Old Text School and put forward an even stronger argument that Confucius had nothing to do with the Confucian classics. The Five Classics are said to be five unrelated books, which were put together as the Five Classics during the end of the Warring States period (Gu, 1926: 40–82). This debate continues among modern western scholars. Some of them have lent their firm support to the tradition that the classics were the work of Confucius, while others dispute it. H. G. Creel, for example, came to an overall negative conclusion:

> Our examination of the various books Confucius is supposed to have written. . . . leaves us with the conclusion that we have no convincing evidence that he wrote or even edited anything at all. This is not an original verdict; an increasing number of scholars have reached this same conclusion in recent years. (Creel, 1960: 106)

In contrast to these factions, many other scholars hold a pragmatic view of the relation between Confucius and the Confucian classics. They believe that the history of the Confucian classics is a long one, and that Confucius and his immediate followers contributed to their formation. These scholars neither accept nor reject the traditional story that Confucius was responsible for the formation of the classics. They work instead to establish which sections of the classics took shape during the time of Confucius and his disciples, and which were edited or added or re-written much later (Loewe, 1993). It would be an exaggeration to say that Confucius purposely created a system of the classics by editing the early writings. From the testimonies given by his disciples and contemporaries, however, it would also be misleading to deny that Confucius did make a great contribution to the transmission of the ancient writings, classifying and rearranging the earlier records and employing them as textbooks for his students, whether or not the versions of the classics we have today come directly from his work. It is of no importance to this introduction to examine in detail the historical accuracy of authorship for each classic. Suffice it is to say that these classics have formed a body of literature which has gained great importance in the Confucian world, as works inspired by Confucius' aims and ideals.

CONFUCIAN CLASSICS IN HISTORY

The earliest known reference to the Confucian classics is made in the *Book of Zhuangzi*, a Daoist book compiled during the Warring States period. In this book the *Book of Poetry*, the *Book of History*, the *Book of Rites*, the *Book of Music*, the *Book of Changes*, and the *Spring and Autumn Annals* are grouped as the classics (Watson, 1964: 363). This means that at least by the middle of this period, the status of the classics within and without the Confucian tradition had been recognised. After that, three important 'events' were decisive for what we know today as the Confucian classics. The first was the 'burning of books' during the Qin Dynasty. Having brought separate states into a unity by war, the First Emperor of the Qin (r. 221–210 BCE) turned his attention to ideology, to unify people's minds by submitting different schools to one voice. Encouraged by Legalists who were the chief rivals of the Confucians at that time, the Emperor decreed in 213 BCE that 'heretical books' must be handed over to the government and burnt. The Confucian classics were probably the first, if not the sole, target of this policy. It is said that among all literature only that on medicine, agriculture, divination and the official history of the Qin, and those possessed by the state academicians who taught in the imperial college and who advised the government escaped this catastrophe. Whether or not these events were purposely aimed at eradicating Confucianism is an open question; but they caused a heavy blow to Confucianism as its tradition was preserved in the books and its appeal and value depended upon learning of the classics. The Confucian classics were not fully recovered until several decades later when Confucianism re-emerged from the destruction and consolidated its position during the early years of the Han Dynasty.

The second 'event' was the rediscovery or re-editing of the Confucian writings during the Former Han Dynasty. The Confucian classics were devastated by the anti-Confucian policies of the Qin Dynasty and by the wars that brought down the tyrannical government of the Qin. Consequently no complete version of the classics was available during the early years of the Han. In order to overcome the difficulties caused by the lack of reliable materials in their transmission of the tradition and to satisfy the urgent needs of the new Empire for administrative skills, Confucians laboured hard to discover, reconstruct, re-edit and even rewrite some or a large portion of the lost classics. Most of what we know today as the Confucian classics were in fact 'formatted' during this period, and the different versions put forward as 'true Confucian classics' laid the ground for many of the Confucian controversies and contrasting schools of thought which developed then and thereafter. It took a long time for the Confucian classics to assume their definitive shape, and it is the royal decree of 175 CE to engrave the five classics in stone that symbolises the final establishment of the orthodox version of the Han classics.

The third 'event' was the 'renaissance' of Confucianism in the Song Dynasty (960–1279 CE). Confucianism was adopted as the state orthodoxy in the Han Dynasty, but from that time on it suffered greatly from the advance of Daoism and especially of Buddhism. For a long time, from the collapse of the Later Han Dynasty to the end of the Tang Dynasty (618–907), it was Buddhism or Daoism rather than Confucianism that commanded the secular and religious life of the Chinese. The decline of Confucianism was substantially reversed only in the Song, when a new type of Confucianism, *dao xue* (the Learning of the Way), or *li xue* (the Learning of the Principle) and *xin xue* (the Learning of the Heart/Mind), known together as Neo-Confucianism in the West, regained the upper hand over all other religious and non-religious traditions. Neo-Confucians launched a new movement to reinterpret, reannotate and re-edit the ancient classics. Most of these new interpretations and annotations were strongly under the influence of Daoism and Buddhism, and the newly constructed doctrines were syncretic by nature. Nevertheless, they were established as the official interpretations of the Confucian classics, and were taken as standard texts for education, state examination and official learning. Due to the supreme status of Confucianism as the state-cult, Neo-Confucian philosophy was not only cherished and venerated by Confucian scholars, officials and students, but also absorbed by Daoism and redeployed by Buddhism. Neo-Confucian classics were taken to other East Asian countries where they found new audiences and adherents, and underwent a further process of syncretisation with the cultures of these nations.

THE THIRTEEN CLASSICS

In the Confucian tradition, there are two kinds of sacred writing: one is called *jing* (經), referring to ancient scriptures or classics, which, it was believed, had the same function for society as did the warp for fabrics, since the Chinese character *jing* originally means the warp of cloth, from which it is extended to mean the constant principles that guide life and history. The other is called *shu* (書, 𢓓), which is a combination of 'holding a writing brush (𦘔)' and 'mouth (ㅂ)', meaning the 'records of sayings' and thus refers to 'books'. There used to be a difference between a *jing* and a *shu*, a *jing* being earlier and more fundamental than a *shu*. Indeed, with only one exception (*Xiao Jing* or the *Book of Filial Piety*), all those that are known as *jing* have their origins in the ages before Confucius. However, in their later usage in a Confucian context, the meaning of these two characters fused, both referring to the sacred writings.

Historically, Confucian classics and books were combined in variously sized groups. The earliest known number of Confucian classics is six: the *Book of Poetry*, the *Book of History*, the *Book of Rites*, the *Book of Music*, the *Book of Changes* and the *Spring and Autumn Annals*, which are named variously as the 'Six Classics' (*liu jing*), 'the Six Arts' (*liu yi*), and 'the Six Forms of Learning' (*liu xue*). One of them, the *Book of Music*, was completely lost probably in the 'burning of books', and so the Six Classics became the Five. When Emperor Wu (r. 156–87 BCE) of the Former Han Dynasty (206 BCE–8 CE) proscribed all non-Confucian schools of thought and espoused Confucianism as the orthodox state ideology, the Five Classics became the official learning and the standard for selecting civil servants. To the Five Classics were added the *Analects of Confucius*, and *the Book of Filial Piety* in the Later Han Dynasty and thus the Seven Classics came into being. Taken as the textbooks in the Tang Dynasty (618–906 CE), the 'Nine Classics' were inscribed on stone tablets, namely, the *Book of Changes*, the *Book of History*, the *Book of Poetry*, the three commentaries on the *Spring and Autumn Annals*, the *Rites of the Zhou*, the *Rites of Etiquette and Ceremonial*, and the *Book of Rites*. The Nine Classics later became the Twelve Classics by taking in three more books, namely, the *Book of Filial Piety*, the *Analects of Confucius* and *Er Ya* (The earliest Chinese dictionary, the meaning of the title is something like 'approaching "what is correct, proper and refined" '). In the Song Dynasty (960–1279 CE), the *Book of Mengzi* was added to the Twelve Classics so that the 'Thirteen Classics' was finally established, which has been used as the standard collection of the Confucian classics ever since.

THE FIVE CLASSICS

In all these groups, the 'Five Classics' are the basic component, and have been treated as the faithful records of ancient culture, touching on its every aspect: politics, philosophy, legend, history, poetry and religion, and as the primary source of the Confucian Learning which unfolds interrelated visions for human life: poetic, historic, politic, metaphysical and ethical.

From the Han Dynasty on, the *Book of Changes* or *Yi Jing* or *Zhou Yi* (the *Yi* of the Zhou) has been listed as the first of the Five Classics. It is singled out to be the 'origin of the six arts' in *Han Shu* (the *History of the Former Han Dynasty*), while in earlier literature it is normally given the fifth position in the Six Classics. *Yi* means 'change'; hence *yi jing* the *Book of Changes*. *Yi* also refers to 'easy', which indicates the nature of the book, a handbook for divination and for understanding the world. Although the book has been highly regarded for its metaphysical and moral implications in the Confucian tradition, it was originally used as a primary manual of divination, being consulted for an oracle message by following a process of manipulating yarrow sticks, and to a great extent it is still used in this way today.

The *Book of Changes* is composed of two parts, the text and the commentaries. The text (*jing*) is a much earlier part, the product of ancient practices in relation to divination. Central to the text are the patterns of six lines, which are known as hexagrams. The hexagrams are composed of six broken lines (- -) and/or unbroken lines (—), which are well known today as yin and yang lines. Recent studies of ancient Shang–Zhou oracle bones and bronze inscriptions have caused much conjecture about curious groupings of recurring six-part symbols. Modern scholarship has shown that the current form of yin and yang lines was not used in the oracles until a later period. They may have been represented previously by numerals. Excavated oracle bones and ceramic pieces display a number of identifiable numerical hexagrams, for example, ┼𝄁┼∧∧∧ (757666), —┼∧┼)〈∧ (176786). When converting their odd numbers into yang lines and even numbers into yin lines, we have in front of us two patterns, ☰☷ and ☶☴, which are respectively Hexagram 12 and Hexagram 53 of the existing text of the *Book of Changes* (Rutt, 1996: 99). In the silk manuscript of the *Zhouyi* found in the Han Tomb, dated at the beginning of the second century BCE, yang and yin lines are presented as —,〉〈, which appear to be similar to the old forms of two numerals — (1), 〉〈(8) (Zhang, 1992: 8). This further indicates a continuity of the gradual formation of the hexagrams from odd/even numerals to yin–yang lines. Traditionally, it was held that trigrams were invented and functioned well before the existence of hexagrams, and that hexagrams were formed by adding two trigrams together. James Legge and Richard Wilhelm (1873–1930), for example, give much emphasis to the constituent and nuclear trigrams as paths leading to the comprehension of hexagrams. Today's scholarship recognises that there is little evidence for the use of nuclear trigrams before the Han Dynasty. Further discoveries that trigrams of three numerals and hexagrams of six numerals co-existed in the earliest dated records indicate that there might not be a clear sequence of development from trigrams to hexagrams. Ancient diviners may have consulted their deities by directly forming a hexagram or a trigram (*ibid.*: 13–14). Both trigrams and hexagrams might well have been tools for divination and other religious rituals, either independent from each other or being linked in a two-way flow.

Early western translators of the book partly accepted the Confucian tradition that the texts and commentaries were the work of ancient Sages such as Fu Xi, a legendary sage, King Wen, the founding father of the Zhou Dynasty, and the Duke of Zhou, a Confucian sage. It is perhaps in this sense that Soothill suggested that the importance of the book be found as 'the first signs of humanity moving away from primitive barbarism to civilised conditions' (Soothill, 1973: 152). The majority of modern scholars do not consider the traditional belief to be an authentic narrative of the origins of the *Book of Changes*. An agreed opinion on the text is that this part of the book was produced over a long period and materials from various sources were collected together to become a more or less recognised manual by an unknown number of learned diviners, probably during the early period of the Zhou Dynasty.

The second part of the book is ten pieces of commentaries, also called the Ten Wings. Traditionally these commentaries are credited to Confucius, who not only edited the book but also transmitted the book with his commentaries to his disciples. Confucius was said to be so fond of the book that he wore out the leather bindings of his copy three times. It is also believed that a sentence in the *Analects* means to the effect that 'Grant me a few more years so that I would have studied the *Book of Changes* (*yi*) at fifty years of age, then I should be free from major errors' (*Lunyu*, 7: 17), although there is an argument that *yi* in this sentence does not refer to the book (Lau, 1979: 88). The Confucian tradition holds that Confucius delivered a copy of the *Book of Changes* with his own commentaries to one of his disciples, Shang Ju (522–? BCE), who was especially faithful to the book and from whom the book was transmitted (*Shiji*, 1997: 2211; Watters, 1879: 45). This tradition has again been refuted by modern scholars. It is agreed that the commentaries were actually added to the text probably towards the end of the Warring States period or probably even as late as the time of the Qin–Han Dynasties, although there are surely some elements that come from Confucius or his school (Lynn, 1994: 3).

The second of the Five Classics, *shijing*, is translated variously as the *Book of Poetry* or the *Book of Songs*, or the *Book of Odes*. The *Book of Poetry* is a collection of poems, written during the 500 years between the beginning of the Zhou Dynasty and the middle of the Spring and Autumn period. It is believed that Confucius selected 305 from more than 3,000 pieces and edited them into a book to be used for education.

However, modern scholars such as Arthur Waley have expressed their doubts about this tradition. One thing that is clear, is that Confucius did use the *Book of Poetry* to teach his followers and said that all the 300 poems could be summarised by one phrase: 'Having no depraved thought' (*Lunyu*, 2: 2). The poems are primarily used to reveal the internal resonance of the human community, in which 'the interaction among the people is like the natural flow of sympathetic response to familiar tunes and dance forms' (de Bary & Chaffe, 1989: 142). Like other Confucian classics, the *Book of Poetry* suffered dearly during the Qin Dynasty and by the beginning of the Han it was no longer available. Three academicians had to transmit the *Book of Poetry* orally, from which the 'Three Official Versions of *the Poetry*' became known. The first version was handed down by a learned master named Han Ying (the *Poetry of the Han*), the second was derived from the teachings of a learned master from the State of Qi (the *Poetry of the Qi*), and the third was modelled on the lessons given by a master from the State of Lu (the *Poetry of the Lu*). A scholar with the surname of Mao also taught on the *Book of Poetry*, and the version with his commentaries is thus called the *Poetry of Mao*. The three official versions were lost after the Han Dynasty, while the version of Mao survives, becoming the only available version of the classic.

Of the 305 poems, each is usually known by its title that is drawn from phrases that are usually found in its opening words. Each poem is also preceded by a short passage, a preface, which explains or summarises its content or main points. The 305 poems may be conveniently classified into four parts: firstly, 160 poems are about local customs, festivals and daily life in thirteen different states or regions; secondly, 74 minor odes are concerned with the courts of local states, their festivals and complaints about life; thirdly, 31 major odes are about the Kingdom of the Zhou, some concerning its overthrow of the Shang Dynasty, and some recording historical or legendary figures from ancient times; and fourthly, 40 hymns of praise or liturgies, divided into sections for the Zhou, the State of Lu and the Shang Dynasty, describing various rites, feasts, or musical performances.

Following the *Book of Poetry* is the *Book of History*, or the *Book of Documents*, translated from the original Chinese title *Shang Shu*, or *Shu Jing*, or simply *Shu*. *Shang* means 'above' or 'ancient' and *shu* means a book, which together reveal the literary meaning of the title: the venerated ancient book, or the book about the ancients. It is the earliest book of history and has served for more than two thousand years as the foundation of Confucian historiography, politics and philosophy. The contents of the book mainly concern historic and political events of the Three Dynasties (*sandai*, the Xia, the Shang and the Zhou), in the form of addresses and conversations of the kings and their ministers. The central part of the book can be conveniently divided into five types: consultations (*mo*), namely, dialogues between a king and his ministers; instructions (*xun*), ministers' advice for a king; announcements (*gao*) by a king to the people at large; declarations (*shi*), battlefield speeches made by a king; and commands (*ming*), entitlements of royal responsibilities and privileges for a single individual.

It is said that the *Book of History* was used both by Confucius and by Mozi (479?–381? BCE) as a textbook for their schools. It is also believed that at the time of Confucius the book was composed of 100 chapters. This version, if ever existed, had been lost by the time of the Han Dynasty. What we have today is a book comprising of two kinds of texts. The 28 or 29 chapters of the 'New Text' (chapters written in the new script of the Qin and Han period) were 'rediscovered' from memory after the fall of the Qin Dynasty, but 'recently scholarship has shown that even many of these chapters were composed "well after the events they purport to record"' (Loewe, 1993: 377). The chapters of the 'Old Text' (written in the 'tadpole script' that was current before the script-reform of the Qin Dynasty) were said to be found at the old house of Confucius but were subsequently lost again. It was said that the newly discovered chapters of the Old Text were presented to an Emperor of the Jin Dynasty (265–420). These chapters became part of the book and were deemed as the true historical documents until the Qing Dynasty (1644–1911) when they were definitely shown to be forgeries dating from the Jin Dynasty.

Nevertheless, the *Book of History* was for a long time considered the most important classic for Confucians, not only because it was believed that Confucius arranged the texts chronologically and added prefaces to each chapter, but also because many of its ideas were regarded as the original source of Confucian philosophy, ethics, religion and politics. Confucians took it as the mirror of their own times and derived moral or religious teachings from the historical records.

The fourth classic is a book called *Li Ji*, normally translated as the *Book of Rites*, 'a ritualist's anthology of ancient usages, prescriptions, definitions and anecdotes', although the 'date of each section and its provenance are subjects of considerable disputes, just as the date and origin of the *Li Ji* as a whole have proved to be controversial throughout Chinese intellectual history' (Loewe, 1993: 293). On various occasions, the *Book of Rites* was mentioned by Confucius, Mengzi and others. However, it suffered the same fate as other classics and the original version was probably lost in the fire of the Qin Emperor. During the Former Han Dynasty, when a number of sections were obtained from various sources, two versions of the *Book of Rites* became available, edited respectively by two Confucian scholars, Dai De and his nephew Dai Sheng. The first version is composed of 85 chapters but most of them are lost, and the latter is of 49 chapters and has become the standard version of the book (*Liji Jijie*, 1989: 1–3). Although these 49 chapters are all said to be about rituals of the Zhou Dynasty and to have been interpreted by Confucius and recorded by his disciples, most of them are now believed to have been produced only between the Warring States period and the Former Han Dynasty.

For convenience, the contents of the book can be divided into five categories (1) comprehensive discourses on ritual, rites and learning, such as *Da Xue* (the *Great Learning*), *Zhong Yong* (the *Doctrine of Mean*), and *Li Yun* (the *Evolution of Rites*) (2) interpretations on ancient rites recorded in *Yi Li* (the *Rites of Etiquette and Ceremonial*) such as *Guan Yi* ('Meaning of the Capping'), *Hun Yi* ('Meaning of the Nuptial Rites for a Common Officer'), and *Yan Yi* ('The Meaning of the Rites of Banquet') (3) Recordings of the sayings and affairs attributed to Confucius and his disciples (4) Ancient ritual or ceremonies, and (5) Ancient Proverbs, maxims and aphorisms.

The last of the Five Classics is *Chun Qiu* or the *Spring and Autumn Annals*, a historical work recording political, economic, natural and diplomatic events for a period of 242 years from 722 BCE to 481 BCE. It follows the chronicle of the State of Lu, the home state of Confucius. The name of this book reflects the tradition of giving the year, month, day and season before each recorded event. Since spring then included summer, and autumn included winter, the entries are all preceded by one of these two terms, with a resulting profusion of 'Spring and Autumn'. Since the time of Mengzi, the Confucian tradition has considered Confucius to be the author of the *Annals* and the *Annals* to have embodied matters of the most profound significance: Confucius edited or composed (*zuo*) the *Annals* in order to pass judgement on the violence, lawlessness and corruption of his age (*Mengzi*, 3B: 9). This traditional belief was not much challenged until the beginning of the twentieth century, when a number of critical scholars gave various evidence to prove that Confucius was not possibly involved in writing up the *Annals* (*Chunqiu Zuozhuan Zhu*, 1981: 8–16).

As the texts of the *Annals* are extremely terse, three major annotations by scholars with surnames of Zuo, Gongyang and Guliang appeared at the beginning of the Han Dynasty or perhaps earlier, to help readers to understand what a particular passage meant, to add information concerning the context of particular events and to interpret the purpose of using a particular phrase. As in the case of the *Book of History*, the three annotations on the *Annals* together with the texts were also divided into two groups: the one was based on an older version of the *Annals* written in the pre-Qin 'ancient script', the other two were based on the version written in the 'new script' current in the Han time. Which of these two versions was true to history became a constant debate between the Old Text School and the New Text School. For most Confucians, the *Annals* are the mirror of history, a tool for setting up the good government, putting usurping princes in their proper place and condemning misbehaving ministers, so that the cause of peace and unity of the world might be upheld.

THE FOUR BOOKS

From the Han to the Tang Dynasty, the Five Classics were the key textbooks for Confucian Learning and for state examination. Of other Confucian writings, only the *Analects of Confucius* was occasionally accepted as one of the official textbooks. However, this situation changed during the Song Dynasty, when great Neo-Confucians, especially Zhu Xi (1130–1200), paid more attention to the *Analects of Confucius*, the two chapters from the *Book of Rites*, the *Great Learning* and the *Doctrine of the Mean*, and the *Book of Mengzi*. Zhu's annotations and commentaries on them were published as a book entitled *Sishu Jizhu*, the *Collected Annotations on the Four Books*. Zhu believed that the Four Books were a necessary ladder for scholars who wanted to learn the Way of Sages, and that a scholar would only be able to read other classics, investigate fundamental principles and deal with social and personal affairs, if he had thoroughly studied the Four Books. If he was able to read through and thoroughly understand these, then there would be no book that he would not understand, no principle (*li*) that he could not investigate, and no affair that he could not deal with. Since then, the status of the Four

Books rose quickly, and in 1313 the Imperial court of the Yuan Dynasty (1260–1370) decreed that the questions of state civil examinations had to be taken from the Four Books and all the answers had to be based on Zhu Xi's annotations and commentaries. This decree effectively promoted the Four Books to a position above the Five Classics. From then until the beginning of the twentieth century, a majority of Confucian scholars concentrated on the Four Books rather than the Five Classics, and every schoolboy had to learn them by heart before he reached adolescence.

As the Four Books are the basic textbooks, they are ordered according to their length and depth. Thus, the shortest of the four, the *Great Learning*, is the first, and study of this text is believed to enable one to have a good foundation of learning: 'the *Great Learning* is the first stage where the learning of the Sage must be explored' (*Songyuan Xuean*, 1992, vol. 4: 882). It is followed by the *Doctrine of the Mean*, and then by the *Analects*. The longest book, and more difficult to apprehend *Book of Mengzi* comes last. The Four Books are also arranged according to their contents. Thus, the *Great Learning* is given the first position, which is followed by the *Analects*, the *Book of Mengzi* and finally the *Doctrine of the Mean*. Zhu Xi suggested that the reason why the *Doctrine of the Mean* was listed the last was because the Way of the Mean was the peak of the learning and without it one would be unable to 'read the book of the world and to discuss the world affairs' (*ibid.*: 918).

The *Great Learning* is a translation of *Da Xue*, literally meaning the learning for adults or the learning for those who wish to be great, which is in contrast and yet related to 'small learning' (*Xiao Xue*), the textbook for primary schools. The *Great Learning* is believed to be a work of one of Confucius' disciples, Zengzi (Zeng Shen, 505–432 BCE). It purports to teach people how to learn and practise 'the Great Way'. In this book, the author explains what a person should do if he wants to govern the whole world well. The goal cannot be achieved by arms, nor by power or law, but only by moral strength and moral virtues. The core of the book is thus concerned with how to cultivate moral virtues within and how to exert moral influence without: manifesting the illustrious virtues, loving the people and abiding in the highest good. To this end, the book provides the so-called Eight Items or Steps for the beginner to follow, namely, investigating things, extending knowledge, making the will sincere, rectifying the heart/mind, cultivating the character, regulating the family, governing the state, and bringing peace to the world.

The *Doctrine of the Mean* (*Zhong Yong*) is believed to have been composed around the fifth century BCE, and re-edited during the time of the Qin and Han Dynasties. It is probably the first Confucian writing that introduces the idea of the Five Elements into Confucianism and extends it to explain moral and social affairs. If the *Great Learning* is a search for the Way of governing the world, the *Doctrine of the Mean* is an exploration of the Way of cultivating one's character and becoming a sage. This Way is called the Middle Way, the way of centrality and harmony. The Middle Way does not mean simply pursuing a middle course. It is said to be a course following the harmonious process of the universe. In order to follow the 'Way of the Mean', one has to keep one's mind sincere. Sincerity (*cheng*) enables people to extend and develop their nature: those who possess sincerity achieve what is right without effort, understand without thinking, and can naturally and easily embody the Way. Sages are those who, by their sincerity, stand between Heaven and Earth and with them form a triad. This theory was later accepted as orthodox Confucianism, and the goal of the 'triad' became the supreme ideal for many Confucians.

Listed as the third of the Four Books is the *Analects*, which is a translation from the Chinese title *lun yu*, literally meaning 'discussion or conversations and sayings', and implying 'a compilation of the words' by Confucius and his students.

> The *Lun Yu* contains the replies made by Master Kong to his disciples and contemporaries, and the discussions between the disciples or the words that they heard from the Master. At that time each disciple held his own records, so that when the Master died, his followers put their notes together to make a compilation, thus called the *Lun Yu*.
>
> (*Han Shu*, 1997: 1717)

This is the primary source by which we know Confucius and his teaching. This book comprises 20 sections or books, around 500 chapters or paragraphs. It took about one hundred years after the death of Confucius to compile the records of his disciples as a book. Japanese Scholar Yamashita Toraji, in his *The Chronology of Editions of 'Lun Yu'*, takes the date of its edition between the death of Confucius (479 BCE) and the death of Confucius' grandson, Zisi (d. 402 BCE). The Chinese scholar Yang Bojun sees the students of Zengzi, the youngest disciple of Confucius as responsible for the edition. He also argues that the editing started at the end of the Spring and Autumn period and was completed around the beginning of the Warring States period (*Lunyu Yizhu*, 1980: 26–30). The version of the book as we have it today did not come into being until the third century CE (Lau, 1979: 221). Therefore, how much of the *Analects* is authentic in the sense of representing the original Confucius faithfully becomes a matter of debate. Arthur Waley, for example, in the introduction to his translation of the *Lun Yu*, cautions that 'I use the term "Confucius" throughout this book in a conventional sense, simply meaning the particular early Confucians whose ideas are embodied in the sayings' (Waley, 1938: 21). It has become accepted that the different chapters of the *Analects* are of very different dates and proceed from very different sources: for example, Books 3–9 are believed to represent the oldest stratum, Books 16–17 are not from a source close to the earliest Confucian students, and Book 18 and parts of Book 14 are even later, because they contain many anti-Confucian stories, similar to those prevalent in Daoist works (*ibid.*). While this scrutiny has some academic credentials, it would not do justice to Confucianism if it is meant to cut the connection between Confucian wisdom as revealed in the book and Confucius himself.

The fourth book is *Mengzi* or the *Book of Mengzi*, possibly edited by his disciples. Mengzi (Meng Ke, 371–289 BCE) was a great Confucian thinker during the Warring States period. But from the fact that his writings are listed in the part of philosophical writings (*zi bu*) in the *History of the Former Han Dynasty*, we can assume that he was not particularly prominent in the Confucian tradition in the Qin–Han period. The *Book of Mengzi* was probably not a key textbook in classical learning throughout the Han Dynasty. Although Zhao Qi (108?–201, the author of the earliest existent commentary on the *Book of Mengzi*) mentioned about a Han official post of academicians on the learning of the book, and this might indicate that the book had been listed among the Confucian classics, his reference has not been verified in other sources. As a matter of fact, the book bearing his name was not listed among the Confucian classics until the Song Dynasty. Only then was Mengzi himself regarded as the second sage in Confucianism next to Confucius himself. The book comprises seven sections, each of which has two parts. In this book, Mengzi, by arguing with representatives of other schools, expounds his own theories, such as the original goodness of human nature, the unity of humans with Heaven, the possibility for everybody to become a sage, the humane government and so on.

Besides the Five Classics and the Four Books, there are other writings which also hold an important position in the Confucian canon and have exerted a great influence on Confucian doctrines and on the Confucian spiritual practice. Among them, two are of particular significance, namely, the *Book of Music* and the *Classic of Filial Piety*, although for one reason or another they were not listed among the major Confucian classics.

Questions for discussion

1. Is Confucianism identical to the *ru* tradition? How did Confucius transform the *ru* tradition into a distinctive school of thought?
2. Looking at the three Chinese characters, *jia*, *xue*, and *jiao* which are used for 'Confucianism', consider what is revealed about the East Asian understanding of the Confucian tradition.
3. Why is it said that Confucianism is a system of morality?
4. Can we define Confucianism as a religious tradition? If we can, what kind of religious characteristics does this tradition have in comparison with other world religions?
5. Why is Confucianism sometimes called a tradition of books? What is meant by the Confucian classics? How did these books function in a Confucian society?

2

Evolution and transformation – a historical perspective

Confucianism has been in a continuous state of development, from the past to the present and onward into the future. To introduce Confucianism as a tradition we need a historic perspective. In this perspective, Confucianism consists of several main 'stages', which together forge the links of a long chain; each link of the chain shares common features with, yet differs from, others, which enables us to appreciate the continuous evolution and development of the whole tradition.

CONFUCIANISM AND THREE OPTIONS

The Spring and Autumn period and the Warring States period were times when the old order was breaking up and the new one was not yet established. Many thinkers 'pondered' about just how to save the world from collapse and about how to lead a meaningful life in such a chaotic environment. Various proposals and opinions were thus put forward. These proposals and theories can be conveniently classified into three central groups, each pointing in a different direction.

The first group proposed that all social conventions and institutions must be abolished in order to have a peaceful and harmonious life: 'Abandon sageliness and discard wisdom; then the people will benefit a hundredfold. Abandon humaneness (*ren*) and discard righteousness (*yi*), then the people will return to filial piety (*xiao*) and fraternal love (*ti*)' (*Dao De Jing*, 19). Authors of some passages in the *Dao De Jing*, a collection of Daoist aphorisms attributed to Laozi (?–?), may be deemed as the chief representatives of this group, and by calling for the return to the primitive life of the ancient times they advocated a quasi-anarchism. The second group consists of the pessimists who had given up all hope of saving the world from chaos and destruction. They advocated either complete withdrawal from the world or a kind of apathy that was contrary to any positive intervention. The representatives of this group are those mentioned in the *Analects*, namely, the Keeper of the Stone Gate (14: 38), the Mad Carriage Driver of Chu (18: 5), and the Farmers at the Ford (18: 6). The third group consisted of those who intended to change the world. The differences in the approach of the last group led to the development of three major schools, namely, Confucianism, Moism and Legalism. Each school had its own understanding of the steps necessary for 'straightening the crooked system' and proposed positive ways to bring this about.

Confucius championed a humanistic outlook. He argued against those who determined to abandon the world by saying that 'One cannot consort with birds and beasts. If I do not associate with humankind, with whom shall I associate? If the Way prevailed in the world, there would be no need for me to change it' (*Lunyu*, 18: 6). Confucius believed that the prevalent problems of his time could be 'sorted out' if the traditional values were revived. His investigation into the cause of the chaos and his solution to the resulting disorder opened the way for the development of the tradition that was to change political courses in East Asia.

The second option was proposed by Mo Di or Mozi (Master Mo, 479?–381? BCE). This developed into the Moist School. In a sense, the Moist proposal directly opposed that of the Confucians, although Mozi was once a student within the Confucian tradition. Confucianism presented a humanistic system that defined and redefined the moral–political–religious code by way of a 'virtue ethic'. Moism opted for a utilitarian way to improve people's material welfare, to install the social order of justice and to reform political structure. The Moists maintained that a good government was one that could bring benefits to the people, order to the society and an increase in population to the state. Confucians treasured ritual/propriety (*li*) and music for their value in cultivating virtues, while the Moists dismissed ritual and music as useless. Instead, Moism proposed a shamanistic belief in spirits and sought a solution for social and spiritual problems by making offerings to Heaven (*tian*) and faithfully carrying out the Mandate or Will of Heaven (*tianming*). As regard to how to attain peace and harmony, the major differences between Confucianism and Moism were manifest when the Moists emphasised utilitarian love and universal equality, while Confucianism stressed the supreme importance of personal character and the extension of family affection.

The third option was propagated by a group of people who claimed that the only way to save the world was to govern it by laws and restrain it with a clearly defined criminal code. Thus, they were labelled the School of Law or Legalism (*fa jia*). This is a very special school and quite different from all other schools that appeared in this period:

> The men who composed the School of Law were not united by loyalty to a master, nor by organisation, nor because they were contemporaries, nor did they have the relation of pupils to teacher in the clear-cut way of the Confucians. The list of men included in the group varies, and the classification itself was not made until their epoch had closed.
>
> (Shryock, 1966: 16)

There are many fundamental differences between Confucianism and Legalism but by far the most important are their views concerning how to govern the state. Within the application of Legalism, universal laws punish anyone who violates them to maintain social order; for Confucianism, universal virtues lead anyone who learns and practises them to goodness. Legalists attacked Confucian education and learning as a path to vulnerability and weaknesses, as pointed out by a later leading Legalist, Shang Yang (390?–338 BCE): 'Eminent men all change their occupations, to apply themselves to the study of the *Book of Poetry* and the *Book of History*, and to follow improper standards . . . When the people are given to such teachings, it is certain that such a country will be dismembered' (*Shangjun Shu*, 1959: 5).

The Legalist policies proved to be an efficient way for the government to accumulate wealth and increase the power of the state. Legalism reached its peak at the end of the Warring States period and overwhelmed all other schools by helping the First Emperor of the Qin Dynasty (221–206 BCE) to unify the whole of China.

From the struggle against these unfavourable circumstances emerged a number of Confucian masters whose contributions are recognised as the most important constituent elements in the formation of Confucianism. Four of them gained preeminence, and later were revered as the Four Associates (*sipei*) of Confucius. Yan Hui (Yan Yuan, 511–480 BCE) was a favourite disciple of Confucius. The Master's praises of Yan Hui's virtues and talents are found in many chapters of the *Analects*. He was the first among the disciples to receive sacrifices alongside the Master. Zengzi (Zeng Shen, 505–435 BCE) was famous not only as a disciple of Confucius and for his filial piety towards his cruel and violent father, but also for being credited as the transmitter of the *Great Learning* and the author of the *Book of Filial Piety*, two of the most popular Confucian classics in late imperial China (Watters, 1879: 5–6). Zisi (Kong Ji, d. 402 BCE), the grandson of Confucius and a pupil of Zengzi, was considered the compiler of the *Doctrine of the Mean* and the pioneer of the school that bears his name. A recent excavation of a tomb dated to the Warring States period reveals some of the Confucian writings characteristic of the Zisi School. The Confucian treatises inscribed on bamboo strips in the tomb fill up the gap of our knowledge of the Confucian tradition between Confucius and Mengzi, because these writings are now recognised as the predecessor proper of Mengzi's theory on human heart/mind and human nature (*People's Daily*, 16 June 1998). Mengzi (Meng Ke, 372–289 BCE), a follower of Zisi, developed the Confucian tradition further in the direction of moral humanism. Recognising the great contribution Mengzi made to the transmission of Confucian teaching, the Confucian scholars of the Song Dynasty included the work attributed to him in the Four Books.

Alongside these four, we must include Xunzi (Xun Qing, 313?–238 BCE) who represents a line of the Confucian tradition that points in a different direction. Xunzi developed the naturalistic dimension of Confucianism that regarded human nature as evil and Heaven as an impersonal power or natural principle. He emphasised law (*fa*) and ritual/propriety (*li*) rather than humaneness (*ren*) and righteousness (*yi*). Two of his disciples, Han Fei (d. 233 BCE) and Li Si (d. 208 BCE), became the most celebrated representatives of Legalism and were instrumental in having Confucianism suppressed during the Qin Dynasty. Mainly because of these two reasons, Xunzi was no longer considered a legitimate transmitter of Confucianism after the Tang Dynasty (618–960).

MENGZI AND HIS DEVELOPMENT OF IDEALISTIC CONFUCIANISM

Among all the prominent Confucian scholars before the Qin Dynasty, idealistic Mengzi and rationalistic Xunzi stood out as the two greatest. Mengzi believed in the religious, ethical, and political vision contained in the Confucian classics, and developed the Confucian doctrine in a religio-ethical direction, whilst Xunzi was inclined towards the naturalistic and ritualistic vision and cultivated it in the spirit of humanistic rationalism. They both honoured Confucius but they differed dramatically in their views on human nature. Xunzi exerted a great influence on Han Confucianism, and Mengzi gained preeminence during and after the Song Dynasty when he came to be regarded as the only orthodox transmitter of the ancient culture after Confucius himself, and was revered as the Second Sage (*yasheng*).

Very little is known about the life of Mengzi. He was born in the small State of Zou which is close to the State of Lu, the birthplace of Confucius. His father is believed to have died when Mengzi was very young and he was brought up single-handedly by his mother. Mengzi took Confucius as his ideal and believed that his mission was to glorify the doctrines of the great Sage. The social and political conditions were even worse in the time of the Warring States than in the time of Confucius. Yet like Confucius, Mengzi attempted to teach his ethical ideal as a way to alter the political situation and to alleviate social problems. He visited many states and made painstaking efforts to persuade the ruling Dukes and Princes to adopt his ideal and to implement his political philosophy of the humane government (*renzheng*). According to Mengzi, a humane government abandons war and governs not by power or force, nor by cruel rules or punitive laws but by the moral power and good character of the ruler, which is presented as a good example for the people to follow. As a moralistic pacifist, Mengzi strongly opposed war, conquest and killing, and sincerely believed that 'If only everyone loved his parents and treated his elders with deference, the Empire would be at peace' (*Mengzi*, 4A: 11). Obviously, his political and moral arguments appealed to few rulers in that war-ravaged period. The state of Qin in the west adopted the advice of the Legalist, Shang Yang, as the way to enrich the state and empower the military force; the state of Chu in the south made use of the military strategies of Wu Qi (?–381 BCE) to subdue its adversaries, and the state of Qi in the east followed the policies of Sun Bin (?–? BCE) and overwhelmed all other neighbouring states. In this atmosphere, the moral teachings of Mengzi appeared to be of little value for any state. Realising that he could not succeed, Mengzi retired from the courts and devoted himself to interpreting the Confucian classics and transmitting the doctrines of Confucius.

Mengzi admired Confucius and proclaimed him the greatest sage (2A: 2; 3B: 9; 7B: 38). He followed Zisi and continued to develop the religio-ethical discourse of the Confucian classics. He believed that Confucianism was a tradition that originated in the works and lives of the ancient sage–kings and that this tradition was exemplified in the teachings of Confucius and thereby transmitted to future generations. He lamented that 'From Confucius to the present it is over a hundred years. In time we are so near to the age of the sage while in place we are so close to his home, yet if there is no one who had anything of the sage, well then, there is no one who has anything to transmit of the sage' (7B: 38).

Throughout his life, Mengzi engaged in a struggle on two fronts; on the one side against the misuse of political power by dukes and princes (*zhuhou fangzi*), on the other against 'the pervasive doctrines' of non-Confucian scholars (*chushi hengyi*). Mengzi travelled for over forty years, offering advice to dukes and princes on the way of 'Kingly Government' (*wang dao*) and in opposition to the 'way of a despot' (*ba dao*). He took the 'way of a despot' to be the rule by force, with harsh punishment and killings and therefore the way to lose the empire (*tianxia*, literally meaning 'under the sky'), because it would lose the hearts of the people and not gain their support. A kingly government is the way to win and keep the empire: to win the empire, one has first to win the people; to win the people, one has first to win their hearts (*Mengzi*, 4A: 9). As the empire has its basis in the state, the state in the family, and the family in one's own self, then in order to win the people's hearts, there is no need for the ruler to use force or power. Being correct in one's self, a ruler would bring the whole empire to himself. Peace and harmony are the natural results of moral cultivation and ethical correction. By practising virtues, Mengzi promises, one will become a humane person or a person of humaneness (*ren zhe*), who is unbeatable because of his moral power (*Mengzi*, 2A; 5; 7B: 3). He said that a humane ruler had no match in the world. If a ruler was not fond of killing, he would easily become the legitimate king of the empire and the people would turn to him like water flowing downwards (*Mengzi*, 1A: 6).

Mengzi tried hard to persuade the ruler to adopt his humane policies on the one hand, and was wholeheartedly engaged in debates with scholars and in attacking his opponents on the other: 'Driving away the doctrines of Yang Zhu and Mo Di and banishing excessive views so that the advocates of heresies will not be able to rise' (3B: 9). Mo Di or Mozi and Yang Zhu (440?–360? BCE) were two of the most influential scholars of the day and their teachings presented a direct challenge to the followers of Confucius. According to Mengzi, Yang Zhu advocated a selfish doctrine of 'everyone for himself' (*wei wo*), which Mengzi believed to be a denial of one's sovereign, while Mozi advocated 'mutually equal love' between the people (*jian ai*, Graham, 1991: 41; Yao, 1995: 189), which Mengzi claimed amounted to a denial of the special relationship one had with one's father. Mengzi believed that both, in one way or another, stripped morality from human relationships and made men no better than beasts. Opposing these doctrines Mengzi taught the Confucian understanding of individuals as members and participants in the wider society of family and state. He called for all human relations to be based on family affections and believed that the world would naturally be at peace if only everyone respected the old people in their own family as they should be respected, and extending this respect to the old of other people's families; and cared for the young people in their own family as they should be cared for, and extending this care to the young of other people's families (*Mengzi*, 1A: 7).

Along with Confucius, Mengzi emphasised the virtue of humaneness (*ren*) which he equated with humanity: 'Humaneness is what a human is *(ren zhe ren ye)*' (7B: 16). Mengzi differed from Confucius by closely relating humaneness to righteousness (*yi*), and was the first Confucian scholar to raise 'righteousness' to the level of a cardinal virtue. Mengzi took both humaneness and righteousness to be essential ingredients of true humanity: 'Humaneness is the heart/mind (*xin*) of a human and righteousness is his path'; or 'Humaneness is the peaceful abode of a human, while righteousness is his right path' (4A: 10). Dwelling in the abode and following the path is to fulfil one's nature. As an idealist, Mengzi indicated that the root of humaneness is within the human heart, a heart that makes one unable to bear seeing the sufferings of others. This he believes is the beginning of all virtues, and by extending this heart one will become humane and righteous (7B: 31). With such a heart the government will find it as easy to make peace in the Empire as rolling it in the palm of one's hand (2A: 6).

Mengzi's view of humaneness and righteousness comes from his profound understanding of human nature. Confucius believed that humans were similar by nature but separated by practice, while Mengzi affirmed that human nature was originally good, that people were born with good potential, and that if this potential was cultivated like a shoot then they would grow up to be a beautiful blossoming tree, full of expressed virtues. Mengzi developed this thesis in his arguments against Gaozi. Gaozi (?–?) was supposed to have proclaimed that human nature was initially neutral. Firstly, he claimed that human nature was like a willow tree, while goodness, like humaneness and righteousness, was like a wooden bowl. A bowl is made from the tree, but is not the same as the tree. Mengzi totally rejected this view as simply inappropriate. 'In making a bowl out of a tree, we have to cut it down and deprive the tree of its natural life' (6A: 1), while in cultivating goodness we simply developed what we already had. Secondly, Gaozi argued that human nature was like running water that could flow either to the east or to the west and that human nature did not make a distinction between good and evil just as the water made no distinction between the east and the west. To rebuke this, Mengzi argued: 'Water will indeed flow indifferently to the east or the west, but will it flow indifferently up or down? Human nature is disposed to goodness just as water tends to flow downward. There is no water but that which flows downward, and no man but he who shows tendency to be good' (6A: 2). Thirdly, some people argued that human nature might be good or bad, as demonstrated by the fact that under the rule of a virtuous king, the people loved what was good, whereas under the rule of a cruel king, the people loved what was cruel. For Mengzi, however, the reverse is the case. Under good government, the goodness of human nature is protected and developed and the people are given to goodness, while under bad government the goodness of human nature is destroyed and corrupted so that the people are given to cruelty (6A: 6).

Mengzi's claim that human nature is good does not imply that humans are always entirely good. His teaching maintains that humans have within them the inclination to the good and the innate capacities for goodness. At the psycho-ethical level, all humans have a heart/mind that cannot bear to see the sufferings of others, and this shows that humans are born with innate feelings of goodness. Mengzi argued that the virtues of humaneness (*ren*), righteousness (*yi*), propriety (*li*) and wisdom (*zhi*) were not drilled into us from without; we already had their beginnings (*duan*) as soon as we were born. Virtues are the result of developing what we already have in the heart, the sense of compassion, of shame, of respect, and of right and wrong. In developing and cultivating these innate senses, we will be able to express the virtues in the following manner: compassion becoming the virtue of humaneness, the feeling of shame becoming the virtue of righteousness, respect becoming the virtue of propriety, and the sense of right and wrong becoming the virtue of wisdom (6A: 6).

From psycho-ethical arguments concerning human nature, Mengzi developed three metaphysical–religious theses, which would prove to have a profound effect on Confucian spirituality. Firstly, his view of human nature confirms that Heaven (*tian*), which instilled such good nature to human beings, must itself be good or the source of goodness. As the source of goodness, Heaven is the supreme judge and sanction of human behaviour. Secondly, he sees the way of learning as a process of self-cultivation which extends one's moral senses and accumulates righteousness. Self-cultivation not only preserves one's innate good nature, but is also the way to serve Heaven. According to Mengzi, having given full realisation to one's heart, one is able to understand one's own nature; having understood one's own nature one is able to know Heaven; and by retaining one's heart and nurturing one's nature, one is serving Heaven (7A: 1). Thirdly, if one develops one's heart to its utmost, then one will be able to fulfil one's own destiny and become a Great Man (*da zhangfu*). A Great Man dwells in the wide house, stands in the correct station and walks in the great path of the world. He practises virtues along with the people if successful, and practises the Way alone if not. His heart would not be dissipated by wealth and honours, his integrity would not be disrupted by poverty and humble situation, and his will would not be altered by force and might (3B: 2). With self-cultivation, one achieves the greatness and complete transformation which would allow one to be called a sage. In this way, Mengzi expresses his optimistic view of human destiny by saying that everyone has potential sagehood within his nature, and that 'sages like Yao and Shun are the same as everyone else' (4B: 32).

XUNZI: A GREAT CONFUCIAN SYNTHESISER

Xunzi, whose personal name is Kuang, is also known as Xun Qing, Minister Xun after the office he once held. A native of the State of Zhao, Xunzi went to the State of Qi to pursue his studies, where he was three times the leader of the Jixia Academy, the intellectual centre of the period. At the invitation of a number of princes or kings, Xunzi went to offer his advice on politics, military affairs, education, and ritual/rites. He wrote a large number of treatises, which were compiled and edited by a Han scholar named Liu Xiang (77–6 BCE), the work being known as *The Book of Xunzi*.

Towards the end of the Warring States period, there existed an academically free environment which enabled the many schools to be fully developed. The pre-eminent schools of the time were Confucianism, Daoism, Legalism, Moism, the School of Logicians (*mingjia*), and the School of Yin and Yang. Within Confucianism many sub-schools developed, the influence of Zisi and Mengzi being most prominent. Xunzi was deeply dissatisfied with these teachings and critically examined all their doctrines and social effects; this led him to attempt to correct what he perceived to be derivations from the true tenets of Confucius himself. He attacked the prevailing Confucian doctrines as 'following the model of the ancient kings in a fragmentary way', because 'being mysterious and enigmatic, they lack a satisfactory theoretical basis'; and he criticised these scholars as 'stupid and delusive Confucians (*goumao ru*)' or as 'base and mean Confucians (*jian ru*)' (*Xunzi Jijie* 1959: 59, 66; Knoblock, 1988: 224, 229). Taking the extensive critiques as his basis Xunzi synthesised all previous teachings of the Confucian schools and established a comprehensive Confucian system that represented the highest development of the rational doctrine in the pre-Qin age (before 221 BCE). Xunzi's comprehensive and inclusive system contains elements from many other sources. For example, his discussion of Heaven as Nature shows a clear understanding of Daoist metaphysics, and his interest in logic shows familiarity with the School of Logicians, while his views on education indicate an affinity with *The Great Learning* which is supposed to have been composed by Zengzi. Xunzi placed his greatest emphasis on ritual/propriety (*li*) rather than humaneness (*ren*, Confucius) or righteousness (*yi*, Mengzi), and this naturally prompted him to give more attention to penal laws rather than moral models, which made him akin to the ideas of Legalism.

It is not without reason that when writing his great book on history, Sima Qian put Mengzi and Xunzi in the same chapter. Both Mengzi and Xunzi regarded themselves as true followers of Confucius, and both were indeed the same as far as their underlying commitment was concerned. But they differed greatly in their interpretation of their spiritual master. Xunzi presents the other side of Mengzi's doctrine and on occasion is wholly contradictory or simply complementary. Unlike Mengzi's idealism and moralism, for example, Xunzi is characterised by his naturalism and rationalism, as is evident in his deliberation on Heaven (*tian*), human nature (*xing*), morality, knowledge, education and ritual. As a naturalistic philosopher, Xunzi is fundamentally humanistic, and his concern is with human affairs rather than with metaphysical queries. His naturalism, realism, emphasis on logic, belief in progress, appreciation of law and his sound criticisms of various philosophical schools make him unmatchable both in Chinese intellectual history and in the Confucian tradition. He played an important part in the formation of Confucianism. These essential contributions established his dominant position during the Qin–Han Dynasties. Indeed three sections of the *Book of Rites*, a Han compilation, are identical to passages from the *Book of Xunzi*. His realistic political vision set him apart from earlier idealist Confucians and marked a significant step towards the adoption of authoritarianism in Chinese politics. His emphasis on education as the means for correcting the inherent evil nature of humans inspired the development of the Confucian Academies established by the Han Emperors (Shryock, 1966: 14). Despite his great influence in the Qin–Han times and despite his many innovations, he was eventually eclipsed by Mengzi who gradually became the accepted transmitter of the true Confucian tradition. To understand the reasons for this change, we have to look at Xunzi's theories, especially those on Heaven (*tian*, or Nature), human nature, propriety/ritual, education and learning.

Two fundamental beliefs are central to Zisi-Mengzi's understanding of Heaven. Firstly, Heaven provides humans with principles and with supreme moral sanctions which in turn demand respect and service. Secondly, Heaven and human beings establish a responsive relationship, namely, that circumstances in Heaven correspondingly affect how humans lead their lives, and what takes place in human society also elicits responses from Heaven. In the *Book of Xunzi*, 'Heaven' is used in an entirely different sense. Although Xunzi emphasised the ultimate significance of harmony between Heaven and humans, he does not present Heaven as a religious and moral reality. For him, Heaven is none other than Nature, Natural Law or the principle of the cosmic evolution. He therefore denies a responsive relationship between Heaven and human behaviour, between cosmic movement and political change, and between the natural and the moral. Whatever humans do will not have any effect on the laws of Nature, because Nature (Heaven) does not change its course in response to human action. Regardless of whether the government is good or bad, Nature remains the same and does not get better or worse: 'The course of Heaven is constant: it does not exist for Sage Yao; nor does it perish because of Evil Jie' (17: 1; Knoblock, 1994: 14). Consequently, humans should not be frightened by natural changes, nor should they look for good or evil omens in Nature. Nature functions in a different way from human action. Fortune or misfortune and order or disorder are the results of human actions which Nature cannot change.

Born of naturalistic Heaven, Xunzi argues, humans are innately inclined to satisfaction of physical desires and thereby to competition, which in turn cause disorder and chaos, if not restrained and guided properly. He regards this as evidence that human nature is innately evil rather than good. Despite his view of human nature as evil, Xunzi does not hold an unduly pessimistic view of human destiny. Rather, he insists that human nature can be transformed and that peace, harmony and goodness can prevail in the world. Xunzi puts forward two arguments to support his view. Firstly, he argues that as propriety/ritual and righteousness have been created by the sages as the guidelines for human behaviour, then education is of primary importance for ordering the state and transforming human nature. Education means a wide range of social learning and moral training, enforced by law and guided by moral codes. Central to this programme is the concept of ritual/propriety, which in Xunzi prescribes correct behaviour in all situations. He argues that the sages instituted ritual/propriety to bring order to society. Natural desires lead humans to seek satisfaction without measure and to compete for gains without limits, which is the way to disorder and poverty. 'The Ancient Kings abhorred such disorder, so they established the principles of propriety and righteousness to apportion things, to nurture human desires, and to supply the means for their satisfaction' (Knoblock, 1994: 55). These principles are not merely man-made rules; they originated in Heaven and Earth, are formulated in the hands of ancestors, and practised by sovereigns and teachers. In their highest perfection they are that by which 'Heaven and Earth are conjoined, the sun and moon shine brightly, the four seasons observe their natural precedence, the stars and planets move in ranks, the rivers and streams flow; and the myriad things prosper' (*ibid.*: 60).

Secondly, Xunzi argues that although humans are born without moral virtues, they do have the ability to learn how to be virtuous. Learning is thereby a necessity and of supreme importance if humans are to become good. Humans are all born with the same nature and it is learning that sets them apart. 'Those who undertake learning become men; those who neglect it become as wild beasts' (Knoblock, 1988: 139). For Xunzi, learning should begin with reciting the Classics and conclude with reading the *Book of Rites*, the purpose being first to create a scholar and in the end a sage. To become a sage, one must constantly accumulate wisdom and virtues 'to make whole one's inner power', 'to acquire a divine clarity of intelligence' and 'to fully realise a sagelike mind'. Xunzi's learning does not solely consist of reading and memorising as he teaches the importance of cultivating one's character (*xiu shen*): when seeing the good one must preserve it within oneself; when seeing what is not good, one must search one's inner self to see if it has already existed there (*Xunzi*, 2: 1; Knoblock, 1988: 151). He considers self-cultivation a multidimensional process which includes controlling the vital breath (*zhiqi*), nourishing life (*yangsheng*), cultivating one's character and strengthening one's self (*xiushen ziqiang*), etc. (Knoblock, 1988: 152). If one engages properly in these activities one is able to establish a reputation equal to the ancient sage–kings. Xunzi emphasises that self-cultivation must be guided by the principles of ritual/propriety and faithfulness (*xin*). If one follows the requirements of ritual/propriety and measures one's behaviour by faithfulness, then 'good order penetrates every aspect of one's activity'. If not, 'then one's actions become unreasonable and disorderly, dilatory and negligent'. Xunzi's discourse on learning and self-cultivation emphasises his view of the importance of ritual/propriety: 'a man without ritual will not live; an undertaking lacking ritual will not be completed; and a nation without ritual will not be tranquil' (Knoblock, 1988: 153).

Through learning and self-cultivation one can understand the teaching of sages, and become capable of restraining selfish desires and transforming one's nature. One's natural desires can be satisfied according to principles, while one's activities, when regulated by ritual/propriety, can fulfil one's life. At this point, according to Xunzi, one is not much different from a sage: 'A man in the street can become a Yu (sage–king)', because what makes Yu a sage is his 'use of humaneness, righteousness, the model of law and rectitude' (Knoblock, 1994: 158). Since all people can know the four principles and all are capable of putting them into practice, it naturally follows that everyone is able to become as great and virtuous as a sage.

THE VICTORY OF CONFUCIANISM AND ITS SYNCRETISM

Confucianism suffered greatly during the short-lived Qin Dynasty. With the advent of the Han Dynasty, Confucianism found itself at a turning point facing new opportunities, challenges and problems. Classical Confucianism needed to adapt to this new environment and to change in order to satisfy cultural, social and spiritual needs. The Han Confucians took these challenges seriously and Confucianism entered a new era. Those who could not or did not adapt to the new circumstances were rebuked as 'despicable Confucians' (*bi ru*), while those who did it successfully gained a high reputation.

The story of how Confucianism adapted itself to the new age is part of the Confucian victory over all other schools. There were many causes for this final triumph. One of these was certainly that Confucians preserved and reintroduced religious ritual and court ceremonies, which were enjoyed and highly valued by the new rulers. The Confucian advance into politics was seen in 200 BCE when Emperor Gao Zu permitted Shusun Tong to arrange a well-ordered court ceremonial in the manner of the Zhou Kings. A further reason for the rise of Confucianism was the scholars' knowledge of the skills necessary for state administration. The founder of the Han Dynasty (Gao Zu, r. 206–195 BCE) was not greatly in favour of Confucianism, yet he appears to have been impressed by some of the advice he received from these scholars. For example, Shusun Tong (?–? BCE) advised him that 'Confucianism may not be enough in making progress, but it does suffice in preserving' (*Hanshu*, 1997: 2116), and Lu Jia (240?–170? BCE) reminded him that 'An empire can be conquered but cannot be administered on horseback' (*Hanshu*, 1997: 2113). Encouraged by prominent officials, the Emperor issued an edict in 196 BCE to regulate the recruitment of able men (*xianren*) for government service (*Hanshu*, 1997: 68). Thus Confucianism, with its knowledge of ceremonies alongside its understanding of the needs for state administration, proved itself to be a strong candidate to provide the new minders of the Empire with the skills necessary to manage the state.

The first battle Confucianism had to win was against the Legalists. The Qin Dynasty adopted Legalism, and under the guidance of Legalist policies the state of Qin consolidated its power and by 221 BCE had subdued all the warring parties, thus unifying China. It ruled this vast land by imposing harsh penal laws and ruthlessly putting down rebellions.

This brutality and disregard for the dignity of human life contributed to the overthrow of the dynasty following the death of the First Emperor (259–210 BCE). Confucians argued that history thus demonstrated that while Legalism was useful in a time of war, it was unsuitable as the basis of a permanent government; and that if the Han rulers were not about to make the same mistake, an alternative to Legalism was imperative.

The second battle the Confucian scholars engaged in was with Daoist doctrines. The early Han emperors took heed of the failure of the Qin and initially favoured a 'naturalistic and liberal' ideology provided by the doctrines of Huang (the Yellow Emperor) and Lao (Laozi). Huang–Lao were believed to have taught something similar to *laissez-faire* and proposed little or no governmental interference. As a result, the economy began to recover and the state was becoming richer. However, there was a fundamental weakness in the Huang–Lao doctrine which diametrically opposed Legalistic extremes with *de trop* individualism. Such a doctrine could not satisfy the needs of a strong and growing empire, and failed to provide any coherent administrative policies.

Confucianism was, at that time, the best option, but it needed to adapt in order to secure its position. Han culture was comprised of an eclectic variety of elements. Under the Huang–Lao banner Daoism was popular and shamanistic practitioners *(fang shi)* flourished. The concepts of yin–yang and the Five Elements *(wuxing*, Five Activities, Five Phases or Five Material Forces) which had been systematised by Zou Yan (305–240 BCE) now penetrated to all levels of society. Moism gained followers among lower classes. Legalism was entrenched in the practices of the court and nobility. The most dynamic and inclusive of the doctrines was Confucianism, which was ready to adapt to the new order. Not only did it draw on the traditions of the past, but it was also open to the best ideas from other schools and integrated them into its own doctrines. Many scholars who became prominent in the Confucian tradition had actually been adherents of other schools. When they were converted to Confucianism, they carried with them their old beliefs and theories into Confucian learning. A new form of Confucianism took shape in the flow of eclecticism and inclusiveness. It accepted the cosmic view of the Yin–Yang School and partly adopted the Daoist view of life. It made some use of Legalist policies to strengthen the power of the rulers and took advantage of the Five Elements theory to explain the cyclical nature of history and the change of dynasties. It integrated some apocryphal writings (*chenwei*) to enhance its appeal in a more or less superstitious society. What emerged was an eclectic Confucianism which appealed to all levels of Han society and which met with approval from its rulers. Confucian scholars became more and more confident in the power of their doctrines to satisfy all the needs of the empire. It was against this background that Dong Zhongshu (179?–104 BCE) made it clear in his memorial to the Emperor that 'All not within the field of the six disciplines/arts of Confucius should be cut short and not be allowed to progress further' (*Hanshu*, 1997: 2523). Thus the Confucians of the Han on the one hand were open and flexible, syncretic and inclusive, and on the other hand they retained power from unifying the thought by controlling and containing other doctrines. Together these two dimensions contributed to the success of Confucianism. Emperor Wu (r. 140–87 BCE) took the final step and established the Confucian classics as the state orthodoxy and the worship of Confucius as the state cult.

DONG ZHONGSHU AND THE ESTABLISHMENT OF HAN CONFUCIANISM

In adapting Confucianism to the new culture of the Han and in the transition of Confucianism from a moralistic system to 'a universalistic and holistic view providing inescapable sanctions for the deeds of men and the ordering of society, and a place in the cosmos for the imperial system' (Twichett & Loewe, 1986: 754), Dong Zhongshu took a leading role and developed a comprehensive Confucian doctrine based on the conception of mutual responsiveness between Heaven and humans.

When young Emperor Wu took control of the state, he consulted officials and academicians to hear their advice on good government and their remedies to cure the ills besetting the nation. Dong submitted three memorials in response to the Emperor's inquiries proposing new ways to reform the government and to unify governmental rules and regulations. He recommended the establishment of a Grand Academy (*taixue*) to train scholars for official administrative positions and he urged that these officials be selected on the basis of their talents and virtues. Dong encouraged the Emperor himself to practise the ideas contained in the Confucian classics as he claimed that the classics demonstrated the constant principles of Heaven and Earth, and manifested the guidelines both for the ancient times and for the present (*Hanshu*, 1997: 2523). These recommendations deeply impressed the young Emperor, and proved

instrumental in the establishment of Confucianism as the state orthodoxy. Dong became the most famous scholar of the period and his writings dominated Confucian Learning throughout the Former Han Dynasty.
Apart from these memorials, Dong wrote numerous treatises, most of
which are preserved in the book entitled *Luxuriant Gems of the Spring
and Autumn Annals* (*Chunqiu Fanlu*) (Queen, 1996: 5). In these writings
Dong continued the tradition of Confucius–Mengzi–Xunzi which emphasised virtues, education, humane government, etc. on the one hand,
while attaching more importance to the sanction of a supernatural Heaven
on the other. His preference marked a return to an earlier tradition recorded in the *Book of History* and the *Book of Poetry*, and as such Dong
sought to 'subject the people to the ruler and the ruler to Heaven' and to
provide a 'theological' foundation for the imperial government.

Dong believed that all the Confucian classics had profound meanings
and implications, but he favoured the *Spring and Autumn Annals* as he
believed that in the *Annals* the heavenly norms governing the universe
were successfully applied to the process of human history. He believed
that Confucius had examined Heaven above and humans below, the past
and the present, in order to compose the *Spring and Autumn Annals*.
There exists a mutually responsive communication between Heaven and
humans and this is the principle of human life and the guideline for human
behaviour. What is condemned in the *Annals* must be heeded, as failure
to do this would bring about nothing but misfortune, calamities and
abnormalities (*Hanshu*, 1997: 2515). There were three major commentaries on the *Annals* available in the Han time, but the one by Gongyang
Gao (*Chunqiu Gongyang Zhuan*) was said to be the most suited to the
new age, as it contained the ideal of Great Unity (*da yi tong*, in *Hanshu*,
1997: 2523) and illustrated the matters that were profoundly significant.
Drawing on ideas in Gongyang's commentary, Dong developed a comprehensive system to cover metaphysical, theological, social, moral and
psychological dimensions of Confucianism.

This system starts with a cosmology in which the unity of heaven, earth
and humans forms the foundation of peace and harmony, while the interaction between yin and yang is the motive force, and the right orders
among the Five Elements represent the laws of change. For the first time
in an unequivocal language, Dong developed a systematic Confucian
'theology', discussing the mutual responsiveness of Heaven and humans,
in which Heaven is the transcendental reality and the source of human

life, and humans must faithfully follow the principles of Heaven and fulfil Heaven's mandate. In this relation, Heaven is the spiritual power and the great grandfather (*zeng zufu*) of humans, and Heaven alone can reward the good and punish the bad. Not only are humans considered to be physically shaped by Heaven but their moral and political ways are similarly determined. Human qualities are endowed and animated by Heaven. Insofar as Heaven loves people they should be humane (*ren*); Heaven acts regularly in the progression of the four seasons and day and night, so people should observe the principles of propriety (*li*); Heaven has authority over Earth so the Sovereign has authority over his subjects, a father over his son and a husband over his wife. Human behaviour must model the operating forces of Heaven, yang and yin. Yang signifies virtue and is associated with spring thus symbolising the giving of life and education; yin completes yang and is thus associated with autumn, the season of destruction, and symbolises death and punishment. To carry out the will of Heaven, a ruler must rely on education and the propagation of virtue, and not on punishments and killing. Violation of these principles would bring about disturbances in both the natural and the spiritual world. For example, if the ruler and the people do not agree, the harmony of yin and yang will be disrupted, thereby leading to evil, famine and chaos which are warnings and punishments from Heaven. If the ruler and the people are in accord and upright, evil will not appear, yin and yang will be in harmony, the wind and rain will come at the right seasons, life will be peaceful, the harvest plentiful, the grass and trees flourish, and the whole world will be nourished. These are blessings and rewards from Heaven and the Spirits (Shryock, 1966: 50–1).

In accordance with the principles of Confucius, Dong offered his advice to the ruler on how to reform the old mechanism of government and how to restore the ways of the ancient kings who sincerely practised the five virtues of humaneness, righteousness, ritual/propriety, wisdom and faithfulness. However, his advice constitutes not only moral admonitions, for it contains theological understanding, educational strategy and legal policies. Dong says that a good ruler must first carry out the will of Heaven and follow Heaven's decree, which includes issuing a new calendar and changing the colour of clothes and banners in accordance with the order of the Five Elements (*Hanshu*, 1997: 2510). Dong argued for a kind of authoritarianism in his ideas concerning state administration. In his attempt to strengthen the power of the ruler, however, Dong did not give the ruler free reign to do as the ruler pleased. He emphasised that the ruler must submit himself to the principles of Heaven and manifest this in his practice of Confucian virtues. Education is foremost on Dong's agenda and he sees the first duty of the king as ensuring the proper education of the people. It is education that makes the people upright and virtuous, and only when education is well established will the state prosper. Dong is concerned with the method as well as the content of education. The study of the classics, accumulating good merits and practising virtues are the essential content of education. The method of delivering that education as proposed by Dong consisted of a system of colleges and schools. Dong was anxious to have the Grand Academy established because 'Among the important ways to nurture scholars none is greater then the Grand Academy . . . The Grand Academy . . . is the root and source of educational transformation' (*Hanshu*, 1997: 2512). As the third measure, Dong urges the emperor to uphold the law to maintain the distinctions of the social order and to prevent the resultant excesses of human desires. Dong does not see human nature as either good or bad. He insists that as Heaven has its dual manifestations of yin and yang so humans likewise have the dual qualities of covetousness and humaneness. Both qualities are born within humans and humaneness is the outward expression of human nature (*xing*) while covetousness is the outward expression of human feelings (Chan, 1963a: 275). Humans harbour the good within their nature, but it is only through education that this goodness can be manifested: 'nature needs to be trained before becoming good' (*ibid.*: 276). Humans also possess feelings that can prevent human nature from being wholly good and it is these feelings that can lead to wickedness. This is why social order must be maintained through law and regulations.

Dong sees these three measures as being equally important and thus advises that 'A real ruler sincerely listens to Heaven and follows its decree. He educates the people to complete their nature and upholds the law to maintain the social order and check the desires . . . Having carried out these three measures, the ruler will have a solid foundation for his empire' (*Hanshu*, 1997: 2515–16; Shryock, 1966: 57).

CLASSICAL LEARNING: CONTROVERSIES AND DEBATES

The institution of Confucianism as the state orthodoxy during the reign of Emperor Wu made Confucian Learning the only legitimate content of state education (*guan xue*). A new education system was established to explore and propagate Confucian principles. The official curriculum was restricted to the Five Classics, and on each of them a number of academic posts were created and highly respected scholars representing the approved traditions of interpretation were appointed as chairs. A system of examination and recommendation was then formally institutionalised, and officials were appointed for their achievement either in Confucian Learning or in the practices of Confucian virtues. An intense interest in the Confucian texts and commentaries arose and these texts and commentaries attracted talented scholars who produced further interpretations and annotations. During this time, the dogmatism of Confucian Learning greatly increased; annotation and interpretation followed strict transmission from master to disciple; and Classical Learning was confined to a very narrow area in which attention was given exclusively to the minute interpretation of words, sentences and paragraphs (*zhang ju*). Classical Learning created an immense number of intense commentaries. For example, commentaries and interpretations on a five-word text could be as long as 30,000 words (*Hanshu*, 1997: 1723). This academic method was criticised by many independent scholars as the act of petty-minded scholars (*xiaoru*), which could only result in the destruction of the great Way of Confucianism (*ibid.*: 3159).

Another problem facing Han Confucians was how to read the classics. A majority of them firmly believed that the Confucian classics could provide the standards that enabled humans to arrange their lives and the ruler to govern the empire. They maintained that in reading these works one must first be able to understand the profound significance of the terse texts (*weiyan dayi*), so that the meaning acquired provided a clue to understanding the secrecy of the cosmos, society and human psychology. Secondly, they insisted that scholars must be able to relate the signs of the times to the words of the classics and be able to interpret various kinds of derivations from the norms of nature, thus determining a connection between natural phenomena and human actions. These two methods of learning contributed to the rise of a type of literature known as *chenwei*, which used a mystical language to 'reveal' the so-called oracular predictions of the classics. Pieces of *chenwei* writings were deliberately attached and affiliated to individual classics, some of which were even deemed to be the work of Confucius himself and as such were to be treated with the same reverence as the classics. Being of such an oracular nature, they could be used for many different purposes, guiding the ruler to predict rebellion and dynastic change (*Weishu Jicheng*, 1994: 1290). At the same time, various stories about the divinity of Confucius became popular. Prophetic messages are common in these stories, and literature and stories of this kind were deliberately used in political struggles for the establishment of the Later Han Dynasty (25–220 CE). However, its superstition, mysticism and superficial understanding of the relationship between Heaven and humanity eroded the spirit of Confucianism. *Chenwei* literature also led Confucian Learning further into scholasticism, and corrupted the transmission of the Confucian tradition. It was no surprise therefore that independent-minded thinkers like Yang Xiong (53 BCE–18 CE), Huan Tan (23 BCE–50 CE), and Wang Chong (27–100? CE) as well as orthodox scholars aimed their attack at this pseudo-Confucianism. It was gradually recognised that *chenwei* literature was harmful to the state and therefore had to be phased out. *Chenwei* was forbidden in the fifth century and by the beginning of the seventh century most of its texts had been destroyed.

Different versions of the Confucian classics, especially those of the *Spring and Autumn Annals* and their commentaries, led to different understandings, different methodologies, and ultimately to different schools. Of these schools the most well known are the New Text and the Old Text Schools. The New Text School was pioneered by Dong Zhongshu. Consequently, the New Text School became the orthodoxy, and its scholars were appointed as state academicians and their transmissions were deemed the official learning for most of the Former Han Dynasty. Liu Xin (?–23 CE) and Yang Xiong (53 BCE–18 CE) strove to establish the authenticity of the texts written in the old script. Central to the debate between these two schools is how to interpret the classics. The New Text School explores the philosophic and metaphysical meaning and implications contained in the subtle and brief texts, while the Old Text School reads the classics from a historical perspective. The New Text School in general, favours the apocryphal and prognostic approach to the ancient writings, and is thus rebuked as superstitious by the leading Old Text scholars. These two schools present different pictures of Confucius. The New Text followers presented him as the 'Saviour' of the world, without whom humanity would have remained in darkness and the world in chaos. To these scholars Confucius was not only a sage, but also an 'Uncrowned King' (*su wang*, in *Hanshu*, 1997: 2509).

As opposed to the above view, the followers of the Old Text School took Confucius as essentially an ancient teacher who transmitted the wisdom of the past.

In 51 BCE and 79 CE two conferences sponsored by the imperial court were convened to examine the true meaning of the classics and to moderate the differences between these two schools. The record of the second conference, the *Comprehensive Discussion of the White Tiger Hall* (*Baihu Tong*), summarises the different interpretations put forward by the members of different schools and sects, and stands as a monument to Han Confucianism. Towards the end of the Later Han Dynasty, both schools indulged in minute and detailed study of the classics, and turned the dynamic and realistic Confucian thought into nothing more than pedantic scholasticism. The controversies of the two schools were brought to a temporary resolution only by a number of prominent scholars, Ma Rong (79–166) and Zheng Xuan (127–200), who strove to harmonise the various schools of interpretation in their own commentaries. The commentaries of Zheng Xuan in particular incorporated the achievements of the two schools and clarified various interpretations and annotations of the classics, which thus stood as the more or less standard versions for a long period (Makeham, 1997).

THE CONFUCIAN DIMENSION OF 'MYSTERIOUS LEARNING'

Classical Learning in the main had become so scholastic by the end of the Later Han Dynasty that it no longer reflected reality; consequently the influence of Confucianism over the state and society diminished dramatically. Young, creative thinkers were increasingly impatient with the established scholarship, and Confucian scholars had to find a way out of their difficulties by adapting Confucian doctrines to the psychological and spiritual needs of the people. Gradually their interests turned to Daoist writings or the books with a strong Daoist tendency. This led them to focus their attention on the *Book of Changes*. The naturalistic world-view of Han scholars like Yang Xiong and Wang Chong was reflected in their writings and in effect pioneered a new form of Confucianism. In this way, scholars of the Wei–Jing Dynasties (220–420) reinterpreted the Confucian classics in Daoist language and carried the Daoist spirit into the heart of Confucian Learning. Brilliant scholars such as Wang Bi (226–49), He Yan (d. 249), Xiang Xiu (223?–300), Guo Xiang (d. 312) and Pei Wei (267–300) led Confucian Learning towards a new philosophic direction. The move was carried forward in the manner of 'pure conversation' (*qing tan*) led by the Seven Worthies of the Bamboo Grove (*zulin qixian*), amongst whom the best known were Ruan Ji (210–63) and Ji Kang (223–62). It became fashionable in intellectual circles to mock, be indifferent to, or abandon totally, the scholastic ways of Classical Learning. A new series of commentaries and annotations on the Confucian classics were produced, declaring the end of Han scholasticism and leading Confucianism to a new stage: Mysterious Learning (*xuan xue*).

Many people in the West see only the Daoist character of Mysterious Learning and therefore translate it as Neo-Daoism. It is true that the character, *xuan*, has its origin in Daoism, and that the fundamental principles of the learning are characteristic to Daoist philosophy. The central issues and boundaries of this learning are also defined by Daoist terminology. However, Mysterious Learning has a Confucian dimension. It does not negate Confucian Learning; rather it expands and develops Confucianism in new ways by reinterpreting the social and moral understanding of Confucianism in terms of Daoist philosophy. As a result Mysterious Learning is an essential link in the chain of Confucian evolution and transformation.

Mysterious Learning is the first serious attempt to synthesise Confucian and Daoist philosophies. It infuses Daoism into Confucianism and adapts Confucianism to Daoist metaphysics. Thus even such brilliant scholars as Wang Bi, He Yan, Guo Xiang etc. are very unlikely to be ranked along with the Confucian masters before or after them. This may explain why there is so little material available to western readers which would reveal the Confucian character of Mysterious Learning. Fung Yu-lan's *A History of Chinese Philosophy* and Wing-tsit Chan's *A Source Book in Chinese Philosophy*, two of the most widely used source books on Chinese philosophy, make little mention of the Confucian dimension of Mysterious Learning. Instead, they focus their attention almost exclusively on how Mysterious Learning transformed the 'old' Daoism into a new form (Neo-Daoism). When discussing the Confucian tradition from the Classical Learning of the Han to the advent of Neo-Confucianism in the Song, Jacques Gernet comments that although there were a few famous commentators during this period, they were isolated scholars who simply 'carried on the Han traditions and did not radically change either methods of textual interpretation or the philosophy implicit in them' (Gernet, 1996: 204). What Gernet does not take into account are the contributions made by the scholars of the Wei–Jing Dynasties to the transformation of Han Confucianism. Contrary to this opinion, Paul Demieville notices that although Confucianism suffered from philosophic and religious sterility in this period, 'it had one last period of philosophical brilliance, owing to its association with Taoism', not least because their commentaries on the classics are 'permeated throughout with the spirit of compromise between Taoism and Confucianism, the stress being carefully placed on Confucianism' (Twitchett & Loewe, 1986: 828, 834).

Mysterious Learning is indeed an important stage in the development of Confucianism and this is appreciated within the Confucian tradition and is evidenced by the fact that although it has clear Daoist tendencies, many of its commentaries on the Confucian classics, in particular the *Analects of Confucius* and the *Book of Changes*, were considered standard commentaries as early as the Tang Dynasty (618–907). Mysterious Learning exerted a great influence on the mutual transformations between Confucianism, Buddhism and Daoism in the following centuries. To a great extent, its debates, terminology and principles underlay all subsequent intellectual works and it provided the Neo-Confucians of the Song–Ming Dynasties with the philosophic tools and the metaphysical mind to establish their new system. This system was constructed on the discussions of such relations as those between substance (*ti*) and function (*yong*), one (*yi*) and many (*duo*), nature (*xing*) and emotion (*qing*), metaphysic principle (*li*) and material force (*qi*), most of which had been either explicitly or implicitly discussed in Mysterious Learning.

Although most scholars from the Wei–Jing period were deeply dissatisfied with Han Confucianism, they still acknowledged Confucius to be superior, deeming him to be the sage *par excellence*. In this sense they were carrying on the Han tradition in which Confucianism was regarded as the state orthodoxy and Confucius as the supreme ideal of virtue and wisdom. What makes them distinct is that they incorporated Daoist qualities into the Confucian notion of virtue and wisdom, and thereby made the conception of sagehood a semi-Daoist ideal. Wang Bi and He Yan believed that Confucius demonstrated the highest truth within human society, and was thus a sage unparalleled in the world. Confucius transmitted wisdom without writing anything (*shuer buzuo, Lunyu,* 7: 1) and devoted his life to 'remembering silently (*moer shizhi, Lunyu,* 7: 2), a feat which is far beyond the reach of Laozi, the so-called founder of Daoism. Although emphasising that the sage educated [the people] without words, Laozi nevertheless wrote down his wisdom in a work of 5,000 words, the famous *Dao De Jing.* Wang Bi contrasted Confucius with Laozi and Zhuangzi: 'The Sage [Confucius] embodied Non-Actuality (*wuwei*). Furthermore, Non-Actuality may not be the subject of instruction. Therefore of necessity his words applied to Actuality (*yu*). Lao-tzu and Chuang-tzu, not yet free of Actuality, were continually giving instruction about that in which they felt a deficiency' (Mather, 1976: 96). A similar argument was also made by Guo Xiang, who compared Confucius to the Daoist Spiritual Man (*shenren*) and praised the Confucian sages for 'their staying in the midst of government but their mind was transcendent'. For Guo, a sage is one who has perfectly harmonised the secular and the sacred, roamed 'in the transcendental world in order to enlarge the mundane world', in contrast to Laozi and Zhuangzi who travelled over 'the transcendent world to the utmost and yet were not silently in harmony with the mundane world' (Chan, 1963a: 327, 333).

A question directly related to and constantly debated about sagehood is whether the sage should or should not be influenced by his emotions. For He Yan, the sage is a sage because he 'lacks either joy, or anger, sorrow or pleasure' (Fung, 1953: 188). In this sense, the sage is like a perfect Daoist who has neither desire nor contention. Wang Bi puts forward the antithesis that 'where the sage is vitally superior to other men is in his spirit-like intelligence, but where he is like other men is in having the five emotions' (Fung, 1953: 188). In this way, Wang argued for Confucius, as when Confucius felt joyful in seeing a good man and grief at the death of his disciples, he fully expressed his emotions and reacted naturally. The sage has emotions but does not allow himself to be 'ensnared' by such emotions. This opened up a long discourse in which Buddhism, Daoism and Confucianism explored human destiny, and was illuminating for the Neo-Confucians of the Song Dynasty when they considered the problems concerning human nature and emotions.

Han scholasticism had made Confucianism irrelevant to social and political life, and created tension between Confucianism as official learning and the real needs of society. Hypocritical politicians made immoral use of Confucian virtues and used the Confucian code of ethics simply to restrict individual freedom and creativity. Mysterious Learning set out to overcome the problems created by the scholastic learning of the Han and to do away with the false and hypocritical applications of Confucian ethics. They sought to establish a new system of learning in which the true spirit of Classical Confucianism could be revived. For the scholars of the Wei–Jin Dynasties this could not happen unless Daoist principles were introduced into Confucianism, thus ridding Confucianism of trivial exegetical analyses in order to reveal its philosophic meaning and rationalistic value. This is what makes Mysterious Learning a distinct stage in the history of Confucian philosophical evolution and transformation.

The scholars of Mysterious Learning sought urgently to solve the problems created by the perceived tension between moral codes/social institutions (*mingjiao*) and the natural tendencies of human beings (*ziran*). In general, Confucianism is believed to emphasise the former and Daoism the latter. Central to the debates was whether these two sides should be separated or be related, and how to interpret their similarities and differences. Three theses were put forward and each implied a different attitude towards Confucian Learning and Confucian virtues. Paul Demieville sees Mysterious Learning as the 'halfway between Confucianism and Taoism' (Twitchett & Loewe, 1986: 829), but he stops short of pointing out the variety of positions adopted by different individuals and groups, with some being closer to Confucianism and others to Daoism. An examination of these three theses concerning the relationship between the moral and the natural will enable us to see where the different groups stood.

The first thesis is that 'Moral codes come from nature (*mingjiao chuyu ziran*).' In this thesis, scholars like He Yan, Wang Bi and Guo Xiang maintained that there was a fundamental consistency between institutionalised morality and nature. The logic of this thesis leads to the conclusion that being derived from nature, moral codes and ethical rites must not contradict the law of spontaneity. In order to illustrate how this worked, they examined the more metaphysical issue of 'being (*you*)' and 'non-being (*wu*)', with moral codes being identified with 'being' and nature with 'non-being'. Some insisted that 'being' was nameable, diverse and subject to change while 'non-being' as the source of 'being' was unnameable, unchanging and unified. In order to understand the moral thoroughly, one must first understand the natural. Others argued the opposite, saying that being and non-being, moral codes and nature could not be separated, that the natural was manifest in moral codes, and that things existed and transformed themselves spontaneously. Whatever arguments they employed, these scholars attempted to establish that nature was the source or root of social institutions and that any moral codes that did not fit [human] nature must be abandoned.

The second thesis developed from the first. Scholars such as Ruan Ji and Ji Kang went one step further and argued that since moral codes come from nature, then it is natural and moral for us to go beyond these codes to follow our own nature (*yue mingjiao er ren ziran*). Classical Confucianism contends that morality is one of the most important paths leading to the fulfilment of one's nature. Indeed, the institutionalisation of Confucianism in the Han as the official learning made the moral dimension of Confucianism an academic subject. Scholars looked closely at the system of moral codes as it related to the needs of the state and government. Moral virtues and rituals became the means by which the state constrained 'humanity' rather than the method by which one developed one's own nature. Defiant scholars such as Ruan Ji and Ji Kang opposed this misuse of Confucian ethics and argued that we should follow our nature, especially physical desires, rather than being constrained by moral codes that opposed nature. Ruan and Ji directed their attack at the application of Confucian doctrines, but not at Confucian Learning itself. Their thesis is individualist in essence and, to some extent, hedonistic in practice. Their behaviour can be explained, of course, by their social circumstance – that military dictatorship emerged from social chaos and it in turn pushed the chaos to the extreme, which not only 'killed' academic freedom traditionally enjoyed by intellectuals but also caused life to be nothing but miserable and insecure. But the implications of their challenges to social and moral codes brought about an unintended crisis in Confucianism. The notion that moral requirements could be brushed aside as mere dogma and forms of social constraint, clearly appalled many scholars and was held responsible for the degenerated moral situation typical of the times. It was indeed that Ruan Ji, Ji Kang and their followers went to the extreme of ignoring all social conventions and moral principles, and lived a totally 'natural life': 'Juan Chi [Ruan Ji] in his fondness for wine let himself go completely . . . After him his disciples who valued "free wandering" . . . all carried on the tradition . . . claiming that they had attained the root of the Great Way.

So they doffed kerchief and cap, stripped off their clothes and exposed their foul ugliness like so many birds or beasts' (Mather, 1976: 12).

The third thesis argued against the first two, stating that 'Moral codes and social institutions are themselves natural (*mingjiao ji ziran*).' Confucianism was in a real crisis. Prominent scholars saw a danger of bringing down the entire social structure in the midst of much 'empty talk' (*kong tan*) and absurdity stemming from the hippie lifestyle. The weakness and corruption of Confucian Learning must be overcome, and the rationality of Confucian doctrines must be re-established too. It was believed that the former could not be done unless Daoist philosophy was used to supplement Confucian Learning, and that the latter could not be carried out unless the tendency to Daoist non-being (*wu*) was checked. Xiang Xiu and Guo Xiang thus made a third attempt to synthesise the moral and the natural by insisting that Confucianism and Daoism were one (*ru dao wei yi*, quoted by Xie Lingyun (385–433), Zhong, 1985: 58). As the conception of non-being (*wu*) underlay the empty talk and unconventional ways of life proposed by scholars like Ruan Ji, a new theory that prioritised being (*you*) was proposed. Pei Wei (267–300) wrote a treatise entitled 'Justification of Being' (*chong you lun*), attacking those who extolled non-being and thereby corrupted Confucian Learning. Pei argues that Nature (*ziran*) is what is so (*ran*) by itself (*zi*), and that Nature is in 'being' rather than 'non-being', because 'non-being' cannot create by itself. The logic of the argument for 'being' demonstrates that what is natural is not the mysterious 'non-being' that Wang Bi and He Yan propagated, neither was it the physical desires as proposed by Ruan Ji and Ji Kang. By denying that 'non-being' is the foundation and beginning of all things, Pei's argument aims at destroying the root of 'mysterious philosophy', getting rid of 'empty-talking', and restoring the nobility of Confucian ethics. Insisting that 'humaneness and righteousness are the principles of human nature', Pei Wei, Xiang Xiu and Guo Xiang guarded Confucian Learning from going further in the direction of Daoism. For them, the dogmatism, prejudice and hypocrisy that had arisen in the Confucian tradition had to be opposed, but its moral codes and applications had to be protected.

In summary, Confucian Learning of the Wei–Jing Dynasties acquired a mystical character in general, as a result of Daoist learning's domination of culture and scholarship. The dominance of Daoism in the circles of scholars did not overwhelm Confucianism. Rather, it led to a new type

95

of learning by which Confucianism developed through incorporation of Daoist understanding and methodology. On the surface, Mysterious Learning is a form of Neo-Daoism, but in its essence and to a great extent in its form, it is a Confucian endeavour to adapt its philosophy and thus rescue Confucianism from sheer scholasticism of the Later Han Dynasty. Mysterious Learning revitalised Confucian Learning by introducing Daoist philosophy into Confucian scholarship. This one-way flow from Daoism to Confucianism would soon be compensated when Daoist religion came to appreciate and borrow the codes of Confucian ethics, thereby giving it a useful social and moral tool to enhance its religious appeal and to pave the way for its adoption as the state religion.

THE EMERGENCE OF NEO-CONFUCIANISM

Despite the efforts of some brilliant scholars in the Wei–Jin period they were unsuccessful in reviving Confucianism as a philosophy guiding personal and social life. Confucian Learning lost its supremacy under the rapid spread of Daoism and the new doctrines of Buddhism. Confucianism could only maintain superficial values in the state administration and had to fight to preserve its position against the religious currents of spiritualistic Daoism and Buddhism. Confucianism gradually regained some of its power and position of dominance when China was once again unified during the Sui and Tang Dynasties (581–907). Buddhism and Daoism were still popular, both with ordinary people and in the courts. Nonetheless, executive responsibilities for government and administration were firmly back in the hands of the Confucian scholars. Confucians of the Tang consolidated their position and prepared the way for the dawn of yet another new age. They increased their influence by means of the education system and civil service examinations. Efforts were made to restore the Confucian teachings of humane government and self-cultivation, with an emphasis on the regulation of the family and social responsibility. Among Tang scholars, Han Yu (768–824) was the most famous. A forerunner of Neo-Confucianism, Han took human nature as his starting point and attempted to establish the orthodox transmission of the Confucian tradition. He argued that there had been a fine tradition in China, transmitted from the ancient sage–kings, Yao, Shun, Yu, Tang, King Wen, King Wu and the Duke of Zhou to Confucius and Mengzi. But after Mengzi, the transmission of the Way stopped, because Xunzi and Yang Xiong were not regarded as links in the orthodox transmission. Han believed that if we had succeeded in the transmission, people would have enjoyed peace and harmony, and the state flourished. With indignation over the cult of the Buddha's relic, he presented a memorial in 819 and petitioned the Emperor to forbid the superstitious practice. To stand against the tide, Han argued that Buddhism was the source and cause of social disruption and called for a burning of the Buddhist sutras and for monks and nuns to return to their homes (Han, 1987: 18, 616).

The new interpretation explored by Tang Confucians was expanded and deepened by the scholars of the Song–Ming Dynasties, leading to a full renaissance of humanistic and rationalistic Confucianism which differed from the Han understanding of Confucian doctrines. This was a monumental period in the history of Confucianism. Great scholars such as Zhang Zai (1020–1077), Zhu Xi (1130–1200), Lu Jiuyuan (1139–1193) and Wang Shouren (1472–1529) were stimulated by Buddhist teachings and by arguments with each other, and they sought to systematically answer the questions raised by Buddhism and Daoism. They successfully traced the sources of their answers to the ancient classics, and found an ideal and a vision in the Four Books and in the metaphysical views explored in the *Book of Changes*. The real value of Neo-Confucianism is not only in its 'return' to classical Confucianism, but in its fundamental transformation of Confucian doctrines which thereby enabled Neo-Confucians to construct a comprehensive and complicated doctrinal system containing an evolutionary cosmology, a humanistic ethics and a rationalistic epistemology. This system is built upon the influence of Buddhism: 'Without the introduction of Buddhism into China there would have been no Neo-Confucianism' (Chang, 1958: 43). Indeed most of the Neo-Confucian masters spent either an extended or somewhat shorter period studying Buddhism and Daoism. Yet their system is by nature anti-Buddhist and its underlying theme is to present a powerful argument against Buddhism. Confucianism is portrayed as righteous and public-spirited, in contrast to the selfish and 'desiring profit' nature of Buddhism (Chan, 1963a: 576). Neo-Confucianism vigorously supports the understanding of life in this world in opposition to the Buddhist doctrines of impermanence, *anataman* and other-worldliness; stressing the value of family and community and rebuking the life in Buddhist and Daoist monasteries as corrupt and disordered. Neo-Confucianism opts for the Confucian rites of passage in which tradition, human relations, social responsibilities and personal commitment replace 'superstitious' (Pure Land) Buddhist worship of their 'messiah' the Buddha, Bodhisattvas and gods. As a fully developed humanistic and rational doctrine, Neo-Confucianism greatly contributed to the absolute dominance of Confucianism in the politics, ethics, literature and culture of China for the next eight hundred years. By reshaping and redefining Confucian Learning, it also encouraged the adoption of Confucianism by other East Asian countries.

FIVE MASTERS OF EARLY NEO-CONFUCIANISM

The establishment of the Song Dynasty ended the disunity that followed the collapse of the Tang Dynasty and created a favourable environment for Confucian Learning. A critical spirit was cultivated among the scholars, in which the entire development of the tradition since the Han Dynasty was re-examined. The focus moved from exegetical studies typical of the Han Learning to the study of the classical themes of body–mind and nature–destiny (*shenxin xingming*), and thus gave Confucianism a new direction.

This move was pioneered by the early Neo-Confucian masters, especially Zhou Dunyi (1017–73), Shao Yong (1011–77), Zhang Zai (1020–77), Cheng Hao (1032–85) and Cheng Yi (1033–1107), who are together alternatively called the Five Masters of the early Song period.

Zhou Dunyi is known as the first of the Neo-Confucian philosophers and is considered by some historians to be the founder of the Song Learning (*song xue*). There were a number of thinkers before him who had contemplated the new themes of Confucian Learning; yet it was Zhou who completed the change of focus to the study of the heart/mind (*xin*), human nature (*xing*) and philosophic principles (*li*). Like many of his contemporaries, Zhou was a low-rank official but a prominent scholar. As an official, he practised the Confucian virtue of being just in making a decision, and thus became known as a man who would criticise higher officials at the expense of his own career. As a scholar, he taught students and wrote moral theses, in which he successfully established a new Confucian world-view. In his two major writings, a short essay of little more than 250 characters, *An Explanation of the Diagram of the Supreme Ultimate* (*taijitu shuo*), and a longer essay entitled *Tong Shu* (*A Comprehensive Understanding of the Book of Change*), Zhou explored the origin, movement, and principles of the universe and attempted to establish a universal view that all things and human beings were one body. He used the *Book of Changes* as the foundation for his cosmological, religious and ethical system, and adopted the Daoist diagram of the supreme ultimate and transformed it into the Neo-Confucian world-view. Zhou argues that the origin of the universe (*wuji*, the Ultimate of Non-Existence) manifests itself as the origin of the existence (*taiji*, the Supreme Ultimate), and that the activity and tranquillity of the Supreme Ultimate generate yang and yin, two forms of the cosmic power from which the Five Elements arise. With the integration of the Supreme Ultimate, yin–yang and the Five Elements, the Way of Heaven and the Way of Earth, feminine and masculine forces come into being and the interaction be-tween these two forces engenders the myriad things. The myriad things produce and reproduce, resulting in an unending transformation (Chan, 1963a: 463).

This is a holistic world-view covering all dimensions of existence and non-existence, and incorporating cosmic principles into human life and destiny. It confirms the Confucian belief that humans are the highest crea-ture in the universe with intelligence and consciousness to comprehend the universal principles. There are problems in the human world, and the sages resolved these problem by setting up the principles of the Mean (*zhong*), sincerity (*cheng*), humaneness (*ren*) and righteousness (*yi*). 'The sage is the one who is in the state of sincerity, spirit, and subtle incipient activation' and 'establishes himself as the ultimate standard for man' (*ibid.*: 467). In this sense, the sage represents the perfection of the world and hope for the future, as illustrated in the *Book of Changes* where the character of the sage is 'identical with that of Heaven and Earth; his bril-liancy is identical with that of the sun and moon; his order is identical with that of the four seasons; and his good and evil fortunes are identical with those of spiritual beings' (*ibid.*: 463–4).

This world-view presents an idealistic cosmological-ethical system and sees human moral qualities as responsible for the order and harmony of the universe. The focus is on tranquillity rather than activity, taking the extinction of desires as necessary for the attainment of tranquillity. The absence of desires induces tranquillity in the heart/mind and sincerity (*cheng*) is thus manifest. A mind of sincerity leads to enlightenment, com-prehension, impartiality and universality. It is both the mind of the sage and the mind of the universe. In the *Doctrine of the Mean* sincerity is the necessary quality for sagehood. Zhou greatly enhances the conception of sincerity so that sincerity is considered not only an inner principle, but also the substance of the universe. As the substance of the universe, sincerity is regarded as the essence of sagehood, the source of all virtues and the origin of all beings, and above all as the power that unifies humanity and the universe.

Shao Yong was a controversial character among the Neo-Confucians. He was regarded as a hermit, fond of Daoism and Buddhism, a fact which is frequently taken by orthodox scholars as an excuse to exclude him from the mainstream of Confucian scholarship. He did not explicitly engage in the discussion of humaneness and righteousness, which in turn is used to disqualify him as a prominent master of Neo-Confucianism. Thus the *History of the Song Dynasty* lists him after Zhang Zai, even though he was nine years senior to Zhang (*Songshi*, 1997: 12710).

Shao was content with a simple life naming himself *anle xianshen* 'Mr Happiness' and his house *anle wo* 'Happy Nest' (*Songyuan Xuean*, 1996, vol. 3: 564). His teaching and thinking were famous but he declined the offers of official posts. He was welcome everywhere he went, but he perceived himself to be a 'Mr Nameless', because for him the source of everything – the Supreme Ultimate (*taiji*) – meant none other than the 'Nameless' (Chang, 1962, vol. 1: 161–3). Among his essays, the one of lasting influence both in Confucianism and in Daoism is a short essay entitled the *Cosmic Chronology of the Great Ultimate* (*Huangji Jingshi*).

Along with Zhou Dunyi, Shao insisted that all things in the cosmos came from a single origin, the Supreme Ultimate. Yet Shao differed from Zhou and his contemporaries by identifying the Supreme Ultimate with the heart/mind. He concluded that all things originated in the heart/mind and that the laws/principles of the universe were also the laws/principles of the heart/mind. As all existences came from the same source, the same principles must be embedded in all creatures. Shao believed that we would thoroughly comprehend the world if these principles were revealed. To understand these cosmic laws, he studied the *Book of Changes*, in which he found a numeral pattern that illustrated the process of cosmic evolution. This is a number sequence in which one divides to make two, two four, four eight, eight sixteen, sixteen thirty-two, and thirty-two sixty-four, which is the number of hexagrams in the *Book of Changes*. The Supreme Ultimate, being one and unmoving, is the inner nature or essence of all things. It manifests itself in two modes, movement and quiescence or activity and tranquillity, which being supra-mundane and not concrete, are known as 'spirit' (Fung, 1953: 458). Yin (- -) and yang (—) together form the four emblems (☰, ☲, ☳, ☷), which give the basic pattern for all phenomena in the cosmos. There are four heavenly bodies: the Sun (Greater Yang), the Moon (Greater Yin), the stars (Lesser Yang) and zodiac space (Lesser Yin). There are also four earthly substances: water, fire, soil and stone. Humans have four sense organs: eye, ear, nose and mouth. Human history has gone through four major periods: the spring (The period of the Three Sovereigns, *sanhuang*, who founded the cultural institutions), the summer (that of the Five Emperors, *wudi*, which was a period of growth), the autumn (the Three Dynasties, *sandai*, Xia, Shang and Zhou, the period of maturity) and the winter (that of Five Despots, *wuba*, the period of decline). From Four Emblems come Eight Trigrams, which represent eight phenomena fundamental to the universe: heaven, earth, mountain, lake, fire, water, wind and thunder. And from these eight come the sixty-four hexagrams, which cover all things and phenomena as well as events in the universe and human history.

Shao argued that since the universe has a numerical structure and its evolution follows a numerical sequence, then by mathematical calculation, the nature of things, their changes and their future can be predicted and known. However, to understand and predict the changes in the universe, one needs to gain objective knowledge, and the ability to view things from the viewpoint of things:

> By viewing things is not meant viewing them with one's physical eyes but with one's mind. Nay, not with one's mind but with the principle, nature, and destiny . . . [Things] can be known only when principle has been investigated to the utmost, when nature is completely developed, and when destiny is fulfilled. The knowledge of these three is true knowledge.
> (Chan, 1963a: 487)

Shao maintains that due to his ability to observe objectively, the sage is able to use the eyes, ears, mouth and mind of the entire world as his own eyes, ears, mouth and mind. Thus, for the sage, there is nothing that is not observed, nothing that is not heard, nothing that is not spoken, and nothing that is not deliberated upon (Fung, 1953: 466–7).

Zhang Zai is normally considered the founding father of Neo-Confucianism. Inspired by the study of the *Book of Changes*, Zhang constructed a doctrinal system based on the concept of *qi* (originally meaning air, vapour, breath and then the vital force of life, translated variously as material force, primary energy, ether or matter), *li* (principle or reason), *xin* (the heart/mind) and *xing* (nature or human nature). Many of his writings are regarded as great masterpieces of the Neo-Confucian tradition. In the *Western Inscription* (*Xi Ming*), and the *Correcting Youthful Ignorance* (*Zheng Meng*) he presents a new picture of the Confucian ideal and constructs a new system of the Confucian world-view. His ideas and illustrations greatly inspired later Confucian scholars.

Zhang maintains that the universe originates in *qi*, and *qi* is both the Supreme Ultimate – the source of the universe – and the driving force of endless changes. In the beginning, *qi* exists without form and is called the Great Void. This void *qi* then begins to contract and consolidate with the light part rising to become Heaven (yang) and the heavy part descending to become Earth (yin). The interaction between the *qi* of Heaven and the *qi* of Earth creates different forms and things. Consolidated *qi* has various shapes and is visible, while on the other hand unconsolidated or dissolved *qi* has no shape and is invisible. All things, creatures and humans are made of consolidated *qi* and return to dissolved *qi*. Thus all things have their own individual characteristics differing from each other, but in essence they are all equally of one substance and at one with the principles of the universe. From this cosmological unity, Zhang proposes a universal ethics with Heaven and Earth, human beings and the myriad things being members of the same cosmological family. He declares thereafter that

> Heaven is my father and Earth is my mother, and even such a small creature as I finds an intimate place in their midst. That which fills the universe I regard as my body and that which directs the universe I consider as my nature. All people are my brothers and sisters, and all things are my companions. (Chan, 1963a: 497)

Zhang uses his theory of *qi* to explain human nature and destiny. The nature of *qi* is the nature of humans. *Qi* has two forms, the void and the solid, and human nature has two aspects, the good and the bad. Good nature comes from the Great Void which is the same as the nature of Heaven and Earth and exists before one's physical body is formed. An individual possesses his physical nature that is composed of the contracted (solid) *qi*. The nature of Heaven and Earth (*tiandi zhi xing*) as the source of goodness is composed of universal principles, while physical nature (*qizhi zhi xing*) varies from one person to another according to the composition of *qi*, be it either light or heavy, pure or mixed. The composition of one's individual *qi* is given as the reason why some people incline towards goodness while others do not. The dual nature of humanity forms the basis of Zhang's thesis on moral cultivation and sagehood. Human nature can be manifest in two ways, good or bad. Physical nature relates to bodily desires, and therefore the reduction of these desires will purify our heart/mind and enable us to return to our original and essential nature (*benran zhi xing*). Our behaviour can thus be in accordance with propriety and in avoidance of extremes, and our action is naturally in agreement with the Middle Way. This is the way to gradually change our physical nature and develop our nature of Heaven and Earth.

Like all other great Confucian masters, Zhang believes that life is the process of manifesting the supreme principles of Heaven and Earth. Unlike the Daoists who value and seek physical immortality, Zhang proposes that a good Confucian will seek neither to destroy nor to prolong existence; rather, he will cede himself to the will of Heaven, model himself on Heaven and Earth, and do nothing to violate virtue or humaneness. For Zhang, a Confucian scholar should make untiring efforts to nourish his heart/mind and nature, and regard wealth, honour, blessing and benefits as the enrichment of his life, while poverty, humble station and sorrow as a means to help him fulfil his destiny. Zhang sees it as his mission and the mission of all Confucians 'to set up a universal mind for Heaven and Earth, to give new life to humans, to continue the learning of the former sages which has been interrupted, and to give peace to future generations for 100,000 years' (Chang, 1958: 170). A good Confucian follows and serves Heaven and Earth during his life, and is thus fulfilled so that when death comes he is at peace.

Zhang Zai's nephews, Cheng Hao and Cheng Yi, spent one year studying with Zhou Dunyi. In the orthodox transmission of Song Learning, the Cheng brothers are listed after Zhou but before Zhang (*Songshi*, 1997: 12713), for they were the ones who completed the separation of Confucianism from Daoism and Buddhism and who presented Confucianism as a totally 'new' system. Cheng Hao held a number of official positions and was devoted to studying and teaching the Confucian classics. Cheng Yi took the Four Books as his guide and delved into the classics, composing commentaries on the *Book of Changes* and the *Spring and Autumn Annals*. They mutually developed their doctrines around a number of common themes, namely human nature, Heavenly Principle, heart/mind and self-cultivation. They attempted to solve all social and moral problems by way of overcoming the tension between heavenly principle (*tian li*, Natural Law) and human desires (*ren yu*). They saw life and learning as pursuing the same goal, i.e., to preserve heavenly principle and to reduce and even extinguish human desires so that every action and feeling would manifest moral virtues. They believed that to achieve this, one must cultivate one's heart/mind in the mood of sincerity (*cheng*) and earnestness/seriousness (*jing*) and in the process, accumulate good deeds. They proposed three ways in which one could successfully cultivate one's heart/mind: studying principle exhaustively, developing one's nature completely, and attending to the decree of Heaven (Fung, 1953: 527).

The teachings of the two Chengs have formed a single school, *Luo Xue*. However, the two Chengs have discernable differences in their deliberations on Confucian doctrines, each establishing a different school. Cheng Hao made the concept of humaneness the centre of his teaching and believed that learning was not merely a matter of knowledge. For him the universal principle exists in the human heart/mind and by extending one's heart/mind one comes to know Heaven, and a person of humaneness forms a unity with the myriad things – one body of the universe. Cheng Yi paid more attention to principle (*li*), which he understood as the logic and reason for the pattern in all things and all events. He believed that each individual thing had its own principle, a principle of all things, for the simple reason that there was only one principle in the universe. According to Cheng Yi, principle exists eternally and is unchanging through time and space; thus, understanding principle is the first step in one's spiritual cultivation, something which can be done only through investigating things thoroughly and extending one's knowledge to its utmost. The different emphases of the Cheng brothers foretold the two streams in the later development of Neo-Confucianism. Cheng Hao exerted an influence on the Learning of the Heart/Mind (*xin xue*, subjective idealism or idealistic learning) which was fully developed by Lu Jiuyuan and Wang Yangming, while Cheng Yi led the way for the Learning of Principle (*li xue*, objective idealism or rationalistic learning) which was systematised by Zhu Xi, henceforth known as the School of Cheng–Zhu.

ZHU XI AND HIS SYSTEMATIC CONFUCIANISM

Zhu Xi's thought represents the culmination of Neo-Confucianism. He made a great effort to propagate the teachings of the earlier Neo-Confucian masters, editing and publishing the writings and conversations of the Cheng brothers, and writing insightful commentaries on the works of Zhang Zai and Zhou Dunyi. He established the orthodox line of transmission from Confucius and Mengzi to Zhou Dunyi, Zhang Zai and the Cheng brothers. Zhu learned from all his predecessors but was especially fond of Cheng Yi, and contributed to the final formation of the Learning of Principle (*li xue*) by creating a systematic doctrine around the concepts of the Supreme Ultimate (*taiji*), principle (*li*), material force (*qi*), [human] nature (*xing*), the investigation of things (*gewu*), and humaneness (*ren*). Zhu summarised and synthesised the achievements of Song scholarship in Classical Learning, and inaugurated new tendencies in textual criticisms. He edited, and commented on, most of the Confucian classics especially the *Book of Changes*, the *Spring and Autumn Annals* and the Four Books. In this sense, Zhu completed the transformation of the Classical Learning of the Han Dynasty to the Learning of Principle, and established a syncretic system of Neo-Confucianism based on the teachings of the *Book of Mengzi*, the *Great Learning* and the *Doctrine of the Mean*. He also incorporated into his system the ideas from the *Book of Xunzi*, the *Book of Changes*, the School of Yin–Yang and Five Elements, Buddhism and Daoism.

In his career as a civil servant Zhu demonstrated scholarly integrity and determination to carry out the Confucian ideal in everyday life. He did not gain honours during his life and his works were even labelled as heretical (*wei xue*, 'false learning', *Songshi*, 1997: 12768), yet after his death, he was ennobled as a duke. In 1313 during the Mongolian Yuan Dynasty (1279–1368), Zhu's version of the classics and commentaries were adopted as the official textbooks for civil service examinations. His orthodox credentials were established and his tablet was placed alongside eleven of the close disciples and followers of Confucius in Confucian Temples. His edition and commentary on the Four Books became the official version of the Confucian classics and mainly due to his efforts, the Four Books were for the first time put ahead of the Five Classics (*wu jing*). Zhu Xi dominated Confucian scholarship over the next eight hundred years, and this dominance in the orthodox tradition gained him the honour of being addressed as Zhu Fuzi, Master Zhu. Only two before him (Confucius and Mengzi), and none after, were given this title.

In Zhu's systematic doctrine, *li* (Principle, 理) occupies a central position. Originally meaning the lines on a piece of stone or wood, *li* becomes a concept that refers to something similar to the principle of existence, the constitution of all things, or Natural Law. Zhu identifies Principle with Heaven (*tian*), with the Way (*Dao*) and with the Supreme Ultimate (*taiji*), thus affirming that Principle is the origin of the world, the final sanction of life, the inner nature of all things, and the power and source of evolution. In other words Principle is that by which the world comes into being and that by which the world runs its course. Principle exists before the myriad things, and without Principle nothing could come into being and neither movement nor tranquillity would be possible. As the source and the pattern of the world, Principle is both universal and particular. Although everything has its own principle, this is only a reflection of the universal Principle. The principle of an individual thing is not different from the principle of other things, as all things come from, or partake in, the same universal Principle. If we say that the Principle is the Supreme Ultimate, then everything has the Supreme Ultimate within; and yet the Principle or the Supreme Ultimate is not divided, because everything has been endowed with it in its entirety. Zhu takes the moon as his example and says that there is only *one* moon in the sky but moonlight is scattered upon rivers and lakes and can be seen everywhere. It seems that each river or mountain has its own moon and has its special moonlight, but in the final analysis all moonlight comes from the same and single moon (Chan, 1963a: 638). Principle is the pattern of existence and the law by which everything comes and goes, so we need to know nothing but Principle. The highest knowledge is the knowledge of the oneness of Principle, and the realisation that there is only one Principle in the universe is the finest achievement of learning. Zhu also maintains that in order to understand this universality, we must begin by studying particular principles, and that without a thorough study of the many, it is impossible to understand the *one*.

The world is not composed only of principle, for material force (*qi*) is also necessary. In dealing with the relationship between principle and material force, Zhu synthesises what has been argued by his predecessors, in particular the views of Zhou Dunyi, Zhang Zai and the Cheng brothers.

Firstly he establishes a monistic theory of principle by arguing that although material force produces a variety of things, this is only so because there is principle already, and that the ability of material force to produce comes entirely from the inherent principle. In this sense he takes principle to exist prior to material force. Secondly, he argues that principle and material force are complementary and interdependent, with material force being the carrier of principle and that by which principle is materialised, substantialised, differentiated and individualised. Principle has no form, while material force operates in forms, nourishes and develops forms. Therefore, there is no principle without material force, and no material force without principle. Material force is like the seed of a plant, while principle is its potential for growth and development. A seed without principle is like a dead seed and growth of a plant must start with a seed. Thirdly, Zhu argues that principle and material force are not only interdependent, but also have mutual effects on each other. Material force can fully manifest principle and it can also limit or distort principle by way of its own existence in purity or turbidity or in fineness or coarseness. Principle is like a pearl, and material force like water. Whereas in pure and clear water the pearl shines, in muddy water it is obscured.

The discussion of principle and material force paves the way for Zhu Xi to deal with human nature and moral cultivation. 'The [human] nature is the same as principle . . . In relation to the mind, it is called the nature. In relation to events, it is called principle' (Chan, 1963a: 614). As principle, human nature is endowed with filial piety, loyalty, humaneness, righteousness, propriety and wisdom, which is the heart/mind of the Way (*dao xin*). Humans are also born of material force, endowing their physical nature and the 'human heart/mind' (*ren xin*) with feelings and desires. Zhu quoted a passage from the *Book of History* to the effect that 'The heart/mind of humans is full of danger. The heart/mind of the Way is subtle and delicate. In proficiency and unity keep to the proper Mean' (*Sishu Zhangju Jizhu*, 1983: 14). The difference between the heart/mind of humans and the heart/mind of the Way is the difference between particular material force and universal Principle. Principle, with which all things are endowed, is fundamentally complete; but due to the imperfection and impediments of the material force, principle is unable to manifest its completeness, appearing incomplete. The same follows with humans. Human endowment is different according to the opaqueness or clarity, purity or turbidity of the material force received. If one receives material force in its purity one may become a sage or a virtuous person (*xianren*), but if one receives it in impurity one may become ignorant and wicked (Fung, 1953: 553–4).

Zhu is not pessimistic with regard to human destiny, since human nature has within it virtues, principle and the Supreme Ultimate. What we have to do is to remove those things that obscure our nature. A sage is one who has achieved this and ordinary people are those who have not yet succeeded in manifesting their virtuous nature. To manifest the brightness of human nature and bring Heavenly Principle (*tian li*) within to light, we have to cleanse it of dirty water, that is, to get rid of selfish desires and feelings and let the good nature shine. This is what Zhu called 'moral cultivation'.

Moral cultivation must start with the investigation of things as taught in the *Great Learning*. All things embody principle and to gain knowledge of principle one must investigate things to extend one's knowledge. By extending one's knowledge of things one extends the knowledge of one's nature. Without an exhaustive investigation of things, there is no possibility of our being able to grasp the Supreme Ultimate, to attain enlightenment or to manifest the heart/mind of the Way. If we continue our efforts in investigating things and realise that the principle of things is also the principle of our nature, then 'there will be thorough comprehension of all the multitude of things, external or internal, fine or coarse, and every exercise of the mind will be marked by complete enlightenment' (Fung, 1953: 562).

Despite his systematic and comprehensive deliberation of Confucian doctrines, Zhu was attacked on two fronts. Firstly, he was criticised by the Practical Learning led by Chen Liang (1143–94) and Ye Shi (1150–1223) who maintained that scholarship must be of use to the state and to the people; they thus attacked Zhu's doctrine of human nature and principle as promoting the useless and 'empty' talk. Secondly, Zhu's theory was opposed by the idealistic school led by Lu Jiuyuan and later by Wang Shouren who were dissatisfied with Zhu's devotion to isolated details of principle and his advocacy of exegetical studies. The Idealistic School insisted that the Confucian way to sagehood must be easy and simple, and thus labelled Zhu's doctrine of moral cultivation as being aimless, drifting and difficult.

THE IDEALISTIC SCHOOL: LU JIUYUAN AND
WANG SHOUREN

The doctrines of the Idealistic School (*xin xue*, the Learning of the Heart/ Mind) supplemented as well as opposed those of the Rationalistic School (*li xue*, the Learning of Principle). The latter takes Principle as the Supreme Ultimate which contains and underlies all things and beings, while the former holds that the heart/mind is the Supreme Ultimate and contains the whole universe and all principles as well as all virtues. The Idealistic view is best expressed by Lu Jiuyuan when he says that 'The universe is my mind, and my mind is the universe' (Chan, 1963a: 579). In opposition to the Rationalist proposition that (human) nature is principle (*xing ji li*), the Idealistic School argues for a different thesis that the heart/mind is principle (*xin ji li*) and that the heart/mind is 'what Heaven has endowed in us. All men have this mind, and all minds are endowed with this principle' (*ibid.*: 579). It criticises the Rationalistic School for its failure to recognise the wholeness of principle and failure to locate principle in the very heart/mind. Because there is no principle outside the heart/mind and because the heart/mind has already had within it all the sources and resources of principle and virtue, the heart/mind is itself complete and holistic. In addition, it is also active and practical, containing the innate ability to know what is good, to learn how to be good and to do what is virtuous. It is in this sense that the Idealistic School argues for the unity between knowledge and action.

The fundamentals of the Idealistic School may be traced to the *Book of Mengzi* and the *Doctrine of the Mean*. Within Neo-Confucianism the chief architect of the school was Lu Jiuyuan (1139–93). Lu's deliberations on the heart/mind were developed and consummated by the greatest exponent of this school, Wang Shouren (1472–1528) of the Ming Dynasty; and hence this school is also known as the School of Lu–Wang.

Lu Jiuyuan, better known by his honorary title, Xiangshan, was the chief rival of Zhu Xi's interpretation of Neo-Confucianism, and he particularly opposed Zhu's proposition that the investigation of things and the exegetical study of the classics were the path to sagehood. In order to moderate their differences, a mutual friend, Lü Zuqian (1137–81) arranged a meeting at the Goose Lake Temple in 1175. This meeting did not accomplish the task, as the open debate revealed a huge gap between their basic understanding and concepts. Zhu sees principle as the One that manifests itself in the myriad things and as Natural Law that exists both in and outside the heart/mind. Lu sees this as dissipating the unity of principle. Lu considers principle to be nothing other than the heart/mind from which all things and affairs in the universe originate. This different understanding of principle led to their different methodologies. Zhu takes the 'exhaustive study of principle' (*qiong li*) as the path to enlightenment in spiritual cultivation and the increase of knowledge as the way to progress in moral improvement. Lu disagrees with this by stressing that as there is no principle outside the heart/mind, learning is nothing more than 'enlightening the heart/mind' (*ming xin*), which requires knowledge of the fundamentals, with the classics as simply 'footnotes' for one's own heart/mind (Chan, 1963a: 580). Unlike Zhu, Lu does not believe that Confucian Learning consists in exegetical studies of the classics, but in what Mengzi calls 'preserving the heart/mind' (*cun xin*) and 'going after the lost heart/mind' (*qiu fangxin*). Lu termed this the easy, direct and simple way of learning, in direct contrast to Zhu whose teaching he took to be difficult, complicated and ineffective.

For Zhu, material force is the source of existence and as such is responsible for the differences between individuals. He further identifies principle with human nature, and material force with human desires, by which he concludes that in order to manifest the principle of Heaven in human nature, one needs to improve one's 'physical qualities' (*qizhi*). Lu sees this as a dualistic doctrine, as he believes that there is no Way (*dao*) outside things and that principle and material force cannot be separated. For Zhu, the heart/mind is the function of human nature, which appears in two forms, the human and the moral. The human heart/mind owes its origin to material force and is prone to mistakes, while the moral heart/mind comes from the principle of Heaven and takes the Way as its standard. Lu argues against this distinction and states that the heart/mind and [human] nature are unified in an individual or in the entire universe, and 'the mind and principle can never been separated into two' (*ibid.*: 574). Moral virtues are inherent in the human heart/mind and endowed by Heaven, which means that humaneness and righteousness form the original heart/mind of humans. The original heart/mind is indissoluble, shared both by sages and by common people, which was so in the past and will be so for centuries to come. Heaven and humans are originally one and there is no reason to attribute goodness to Heaven and badness to humans nor is it necessary to hold the physical nature responsible for human destiny. It is, nevertheless, important to improve the quality of material force in one's character but the easy and simple way to enlightenment is not through study or investigation but through 'building up the nobler part of one's nature' (*Mengzi*, 6A: 15). This requires a careful exploration of one's heart/mind so that the heart/mind can be rid of all selfishness, partiality and 'material desires', as Lu believes that

> Those who are beclouded by material desires so as to pervert principles
> and violate righteousness, do so because they do not think . . . If they
> can truly examine themselves and things, their sense of right and wrong
> and their choice between right and wrong will have the qualities of quiet
> alertness, clear-cut intelligence, and firm conviction.
>
> (Chan, 1963a: 580)

Zhu's 'following the path of inquiry and study' (*dao wenxue*) and Lu's 'honouring the moral nature' (*zun dexing*) are the two sides of one process expressed in *The Doctrine of the Mean* (chapter 27), and should be complementary to each other. Zhu seemed to recognise the defects of this separation and attempted to combine the two methods (*Sishu Zhangju Jizhu*, 1983: 35–6), whereas Lu insisted that 'honouring the moral nature' must come first, as it was only by so doing that study and inquiry could commence. Their differences mark the final separation between the two leading schools of Neo-Confucianism in the Song and Ming Dynasties.

From the end of the Song Dynasty until the advent of Wang Shouren, the orthodox status of the Cheng–Zhu School was not seriously challenged. The majority of leading Confucian scholars in the Yuan Dynasty, Yao Shu (1203–80), Xu Heng (1209–81), Zhao Fu (1215?–1306) and Jin Lüxiang (1232–1303), to name but a few, and those in the first half of the Ming Dynasty, such as Song Lian (1310–81), Cao Duan (1376–1434) and Xue Xuan (1389–1464), were all the followers and exponents of Zhu Xi. The influence of the Cheng–Zhu School was so overwhelming that it was said that some scholars dared to challenge the views of Confucius and Mengzi, but none dared to challenge the interpretations by Cheng Yi and Zhu Xi. An effort was also made throughout the Confucian schools to explain away the differences between Zhu Xi and Lu Xiangshan, and to harmonise the two schools. Xu Heng (1209–81), Wu Cheng (1249–1333) and Zheng Yu (1298–1358) of the Yuan Dynasty openly propagated 'harmonization of Zhu's teaching and Lu's doctrine (*hehui Zhu-Lu*)'. Wu Cheng believed that Zhu and Lu were originally comparable in their teaching; and that it was their inferior disciples who attacked the other side (*Songyuan Xuean*, 1992, vol. 6: 583). When commenting on the Yuan Confucian schools, Qian Mu noticed that 'He [Wu Cheng] had already completely harmonised Chu and Lu, therefore, during his lifetime, his followers did not dare to pit one school against the other by necessarily rejecting Lu in order to put forth Chu' (Chan & de Bary, 1982: 288). One of his students, Yu Ji (1272–1384), proposed that Zhu and Lu differed in their early writings but were alike in the later works. For example, he picked out the passages in Zhu's writings to demonstrate that Zhu had realised the deficiency of investigating things and agreed with Lu in reflection on one's self (*fanshen er qiu*). Zheng Yu (1298?–1357) insisted that although different in their methods and approaches with respect to learning, Zhu and Lu were the same in the tenets and purpose of their teaching. There were both positive and negative aspects in their doctrines, and thus Zheng proposed that each school should learn the good from the other to amend one's own deficiencies.

The dominance of Zhu Xi and the intellectual tendency of the Yuan and the Ming Dynasty to conflate the difference between Zhu and Lu provided in turn the background for the burgeoning of yet another prominent Confucian scholar, Wang Shouren, better known by his literary name, Yangming. Like most of his contemporaries, Wang was educated in the Cheng–Zhu tradition and was taught to accumulate his knowledge through the investigation of things. But Wang failed to gain enlightenment by this method and this prompted him to turn to the teaching of Lu Xianshan. He systematised and finalised the learning of the heart/mind, and thereby put the Lu–Wang School on the map of the Confucian tradition. This school challenged the teachings of the Cheng–Zhu School, and became of parallel importance in the development of Neo-Confucianism. Wang believes that all humans possess an original heart/mind which has the unifying quality of humaneness, and that the innate heart/mind possesses an intuitive knowledge which manifests innate wisdom and vitalises actual operations. In this sense, Wang believes that everyone has sagehood within and reflection on the innate heart/mind is the only way to enlightenment.

Like Lu Jiuyuan, Wang criticises Zhu Xi's doctrines that principle must be sought in things and affairs, that to acquire wisdom one must extend one's knowledge through investigating things to their utmost and that such an investigation of one thing today and another tomorrow will eventually lead to one's enlightenment. Wang uses his own experience and observations to challenge these views. Firstly, he maintains that the things of the world are so numerous and a person's life-span so limited, that none of us can possibly investigate them all. Secondly, to investigate things one by one is to divide 'principle' (truth) into unrelated pieces, a method which cannot possibly abide by the nature of principle. Thirdly, he objects to Cheng–Zhu's sequential ordering in which the investigation of things is meant to be followed by the extension of knowledge, then by making one's intention sincere, and by rectifying the heart–mind . . . Wang observes that this sequence isolates learning from morality, knowledge from action, the external from the internal, and the beginning from the end, and thus reduces learning to a purely quantitative accumulation of experiences which alone is unable to bring about the qualitative breakthrough to sagehood. Fourthly, Wang believes that by beginning with the external investigation of things, the Cheng–Zhu School sees only the leaves and branches of the tree and ignores the trunk and the root. 'Chu Hsi reversed the proper order of learning, so that the beginner has no place to start' (Chan, 1963b: 12–14; 95–7). This renders the way of the Cheng–Zhu School unproductive and a hindrance to the progress of learning.

Neo-Confucian Learning is a path to sagehood. Since everybody can learn, then it follows that everybody can become a sage. According to Wang, not all doctrines help a person to learn to be a sage. He sees the complicated methods proposed by the Cheng–Zhu School as limiting the possibility of becoming a sage to a very small circle of people, since it is impossible for ordinary people to investigate all things and to study the classics exhaustively, even supposing they were inclined to do so. To counter this, Wang insists that the purpose of learning is to acquire wisdom within, not to accumulate knowledge of external things. He admits that although all people are the same in their nature, they have different natural endowments, and thus the efforts required to attain to wisdom also differ. But Wang further stresses that all people have the capacity to transcend their individual circumstances and develop their original nature to the utmost. Thus, 'the learning of the sages' becomes essentially self-transcendence, and takes the human heart/mind as the starting point and basis. The heart/mind is not completely free of all imperfections such as selfishness, but it does possess the power of self-control and self-correction and is able to lead itself to perfection. In this sense Wang emphasises the unity between knowledge and action: 'Knowledge is the direction for action and action the effort of knowledge', or 'knowledge is the beginning of action and action the completion of knowledge' (Chan, 1963b: 11). Through unifying knowledge and action, Wang gives priority to practice rather than book-reading, to how to realise the principle in life rather than how to memorise the words and sentences of the classics.

The dynamic and idealistic Neo-Confucianism of Wang Yangming exerted a huge influence on later intellectual and political development in China and to some extent, in Japan. Mainly due to the simplicity and directness of its spiritual cultivation elaborated by Wang, the Idealistic School enjoyed a large number of followers. As a rival to the prevailing orthodoxy of the Rationalistic School, and as an opponent of Cheng–Zhu's rigid way of learning, the Idealistic School frequently became the weapon and inspiration for those who rebelled against authority or authorised ideology. After Wang Yangming, the Lu–Wang School developed in different directions; firstly at the hands of Wang's disciples such as Wang Ji (1498–1583), Qian Dehong (1496–1574), Wang Gen (1483–1540), and then by those adherents of the schools generally called 'The Later Learning of Wang Yangming (*wangmen houxue*)'. It was also the cradle of independent thinkers such as He Xinyin (1517–79), Li Zhi (1527–1602), Huang Zongxi (1610–95) and Wang Fuzhi (1619–92), who explored and demonstrated the independent and innovative spirit of Confucianism. Li Zhi, for example, challenged the old tradition and pointed out 'What people consider right and wrong can never serve as a standard for me. Never from the start have I taken as right and wrong for myself what the world thinks right and wrong' (de Bary, 1970: 199).

In the following centuries, Confucian Learning in China was largely characterised by debates between those who were for Wang Yangming and those who were against him. Within the idealistic tradition some propagated an extreme form of the learning of the heart/mind, while others attempted to moderate it. Concerning the relationship between Lu–Wang's idealism and Cheng–Zhu's rationalism, some adopted an inclusive attitude towards each other, while others appeared to be more exclusive. On the negative side, there are some undesirable elements in the teachings of the Idealistic School, which partly explain its misfortune in the hands of orthodox Confucian scholars. For example, its understanding of transcendence bore the hallmark of Chan Buddhism and its emphasis on the intuitiveness of the heart/mind led to something 'socially unconformative and intellectually undisciplined', so much so that later critics blamed it for the downfall of the dynastic system in China (Chan, 1963a: 658). On the positive side, the Idealistic School contributed to reform within Confucian Learning. Its followers challenged the then orthodox learning, rejected the external restrictions placed on individuals, and projected an idealistic vision of a world populated by sages. These imply a number of important ideas including intellectual freedom, moral equality and political progress, being of great instrumental value for encouraging independent thinking and developing the spiritual dimension of Confucian scholarship, which would soon bear fruits in the development of reform movements in both China and Japan.

KOREA: THE SECOND HOME FOR CONFUCIANISM

In spreading to other countries, Confucianism was transformed and was then presented in many different and yet related ways. Of these presentations, two resulted from the efforts made by Korean and Japanese masters in the inculturalisation of Confucian doctrines and practices, where the Chinese tradition was transformed into a culture socially and spiritually indigenous. Apart from China, Korea was perhaps the first country in which Confucianism exerted a sweeping influence. This influence was not only present in the past but is also still visible today, as affirmed by a contemporary Korean scholar that

> Korean Confucianism clearly contributed to the formation of a sense
> of national selfhood and sovereignty and became an important force
> in the unfolding of Korean history. It has provided a universal cultural
> consciousness that has given rise to a value system directly related to
> a highly developed view of ethics and politics and has helped stimulate
> a unique national consciousness directly related to the existence and
> future prosperity of the Korean people.   (Yun, 1996: 113)

Outside China, Korean Confucianism also has the longest and richest history. It is recorded in the *Samkuk Saki* (*Chronicles of the Three Kingdoms*) that a national academy (*taehak*) where the sons of the nobility studied the Confucian classics was established in 372 CE – the second year of the reign of King Sosurim of the Koguryo Dynasty (37 BCE–668 CE). During the same period, a national academy and a doctorate system of studying the Confucian classics were also set up in the Kingdom of Paekche (20 BCE–660 CE) and Paekche functioned as a bridge between China and Japan via which Confucian Learning was 'transported' to the 'land where the sun rises'. Before he acceded to the throne, King Muyol of the Kingdom of Silla (365–935) went to Tang China in the year 648 to inspect the Chinese national university. When he became the King he sent a large number of Silla students to the Tang capital to study Confucian doctrines (Bak, 1983b: 256). A quasi-religious and military system, *hwa-rang do* (the Way of the Flower Youth) was established, based on Confucian and Buddhist teachings – members practised the Confucian way of learning and self-cultivation, and were instrumental to the unification of the Korean Peninsula in 669 (Chung, 1995: 1). Confucianism took firm root and became the centre of learning. The following inscription discovered in 1934 demonstrates how two Korean students in 732 'swore before heaven to conduct themselves with perfect loyalty for a space of three years from that date, and further, they swore to master the Books of Poetry, and Rites, and the Tso Chuan in the like period of three years' (Yang & Henderson: 1958–9: 83). The penetration of Confucianism into Korean culture enabled a great Confucian scholar of the Silla period, Choi Chi-won (858–951), to say that Korean native religion was a composite of Confucianism, Buddhism and Daoism (Bae, 1982: 37). Taking its lead from Tang China, the Koryo Dynasty (918–1392) established the *Kwako* (Civil Service Examination System), and the *Kukjakam* (in Chinese *guozi jian*, the National University). During the reign of King Munjong (1047–82) private Confucian schools (*sowon*, in Chinese *shuyuan*) flourished, and one of their founders, Choi Chung (974–1068), was named 'the Confucius of the East' for his contribution to Korean education and learning.

Even though Confucian scholars had been active in government, education and academic learning since the beginning of the Koryo Dynasty, Confucianism was not yet the dominant force in Korean culture. Buddhism rather than Confucianism was considered to be the state religion. Buddhist monks were allowed to take civil service examinations and could thus engage in the making of state policy. The deep involvement of Buddhism in secular business led to widespread corruption and social discontent. Towards the end of the Koryo era, Confucian scholars made it their priority to revive Confucianism and to reject and criticise Buddhism. Among these scholars, An Hyang (1243–1306), Chung Mong-ju (1320–92), Yi Saek (1328–95) and Kil Chae (1353–1418) contributed greatly to a systematic introduction of the Cheng–Zhu School to Korea. They argued powerfully for Neo-Confucian cosmology, morality, religion and philosophy, and their scholarship presented a viable alternative to Buddhist theories and practices. The replacement of the Koryo Dynasty by the Yi Dynasty (1392–1910) marked the end of Buddhist dominance in Korean politics and saw the beginning of Neo-Confucianism as the foundation of Korean culture and society.

Neo-Confucianism in China turned Confucian Learning from the pedantic exegetical study of the classics (*jing xue*) prominent in the Han and Tang Dynasties to the study of principle and philosophy (*yili xue*). Korean Confucian scholarship also focused on *sôngnihak*, the study of [human] nature and principle, or *tohak* (the learning of the Way). The Neo-Confucian concepts of *li* (principle), *qi* (material force), *xin* (heart/mind) and *taiji* (Great Ultimate) with their practical applications in meditative discipline and self-cultivation gained the heart of Korean scholars and became the centre of academic study and debates. One of the first great Confucian scholars of the sixteenth century, So Kyong-dok (1489–1546), elaborated a monistic theory based on the conception of *qi* (material force), which can be said to be a Korean version of Zhang Zai's theory of material force and primordial harmony (*taihe*) and of Zhou Dunyi's cosmological deliberations. So Kyong-dok argued that the universe was composed of nothing but material force and that material force alone was the source of all things. For him, principle could not reside outside material force and principle was the commanding power of material force. Therefore, principle never precedes material force because it must function in material force. So's monism represented the first Korean attempt to systematise the imported ideas of Neo-Confucianism and to place Confucian ethical teachings on a firm base of metaphysics and cosmology.

Korean Neo-Confucian Learning reached a peak in the hands of great scholars Yi Hwang (better known by his pen name, T'oegye, 1501–70) and Yi I (Yulgok, 1536–84), 'two of the most famous names in Korean history', and 'national symbols, figures that inspire pride and confidence' (Kalton, 1994: xv). Having accepted Cheng–Zhu's interpretations of Confucian teachings, these scholars found some disparities and problems in Zhu Xi's theories, especially with regard to the relation between principle and material force. Thus, different understandings led to intensive debates, which in turn led to further modifications, compromises and syntheses. One of the debates focused on the metaphysical and psychological complexity of human nature and emotions, in the form of the relationship between the Four Beginnings ('the four sprouts of virtues' or 'the four innate good dispositions', *Mengzi*, 2A: 6) and the Seven Emotions (joy, anger, grief, fear, love, hate and desire, *Liji Jijie*, 1989: 606). This so-called 'Four–Seven Debate', unique to Korean Neo-Confucianism, was first engaged in by T'oegye and one of his disciples, Ki Taesung (Kobong, 1527–72), which attempted to define the proper relation between the 'original nature' and the 'physical nature'. The debate was carried on then by Yulgok and Song Hon (Ugye, 1535–98), who re-examined the interdependence of the 'heart/mind of the Way' and the 'heart/mind of humans'. In different forms the Four–Seven Debate remained at the centre of Korean academic scholarship and characterises Korean Neo-Confucianism throughout its history.

T'oegye, the greatest Neo-Confucian scholar in Korea, is the most creative scholar on *Jujahak* (The Studies of Zhu Xi). He is known as 'Zhu Xi of the East' for his contribution to Korean Confucian scholarship. His reinterpretations of Neo-Confucian doctrines 'had permanently fixed the nature and character of Korean Confucianism'; 'His personal traits and scholarly manners became synonymous with the characteristics and methodology of Korean Confucianism'; and if it had not been for him, 'Korean Confucianism would not have been as it were' (Hwang, 1979: 518). T'oegye is also respected and revered in Japan, and it is said that T'oegye's thought 'virtually launched Confucian studies in that country. Kang Hang (1567–1618), a scholar of T'oegye thought taken to Japan as a prisoner of war, was a mentor to Fujiwara Seika (1561–1619) who founded modern Japanese Confucianism' (Lee, 1996: 118). T'oegye compiled *Chu Hsi Su Julyo* (the *Essentials of Zhu Xi's Works*) and *Sunghak Sipto* (*Ten Diagrams of Neo-Confucianism*) to propagate the doctrines of the Cheng–Zhu School. Central to T'oegye's philosophical deliberation is how principle and material force are related and differentiated and how this relationship is applied to society and individual life.

As far as human nature is concerned, T'oegye is clearly in line with Zhang Zai and Zhu Xi, and upholds the view that there are two forms of human nature, the Nature of Heaven and Earth (*tiandi zhi xing*), the original nature (*benran zhi xing*), which is the manifestation of principle, and the nature of physical force (*qizhi zhi xing*), the derived nature, which is the manifestation of material force. T'oegye applies the two aspects of human nature to his understanding of the relationship between [human] nature and emotion. He believes that the original and Heaven-bestowed nature manifests itself as the Four Beginnings (humaneness, righteousness, propriety and wisdom) and that being purely good, the original nature contains no evil elements. He also believes that the sensual nature reveals material force as seven human emotions and that being indeterminate, the physical nature makes no distinction between good and evil. He uses this theory to explain that although there is essentially equality between all people, one can differentiate between people by examining their attitudes and behaviour, and hence there are some good people while others are bad.

Zhu Xi put forward two propositions concerning principle and material force (1) that principle and material force were two different things and (2) that they could not be separated. Between these two seemingly contradictory propositions, T'oegye was inclined more to the first. He insisted that principle and material force must be differentiated and that human nature must be related to principle, and human emotions to material force. He made it clear that 'The issuance of the Four Beginnings is purely a matter of principle and therefore involves nothing but good; the issuance of the Seven Emotions includes material force and therefore involves both good and evil' (Kalton, 1994: 1). This dualistic theory aroused strong reactions, especially from one of T'oegye's disciples, Kobong, who argued against the dualism of principle and material force. In standing up to his master, Kobong showed an independent and creative spirit. Kobong believed that the Four Beginnings and the Seven Emotions could not be regarded as two distinct entities and could not be independent of each other, because the Four Beginnings were merely the best part of the world of the Seven Emotions. The debate between the master and the pupil lasted nearly eight years, during which both sides slightly modified their initial views and in the end reached an agreement which indicated that the Four Beginnings and the Seven Emotions could be differentiated but only in the sense that they were 'essential but different aspects of the self-cultivation process' (*ibid.*: 107–8).

Soon after the deaths of T'oegye and Kobong, their views on the Four–Seven issue again became the subject of a scholarly debate between Ugye and his good friend Yulgok. Both Ugye and Yulgok initially disagreed with T'oegye's dualistic treatment of principle and material force. Then after close study of a passage in Zhu Xi's writing, Ugye changed his position – the passage was concerned with the differentiation between the heart/mind of the Way that arises from principle and righteousness, and the human mind that arises from material force and self-interest (*Sishu Zhangju Jizhu*, 1983: 14). This change led to an open debate between him and Yulgok. Yulgok demonstrated his brilliance as a Neo-Confucian scholar at the early age of twenty-three, and his paper for the Civil Service Examination, *Chondochaek* ('Treatise on the Way of Heaven') established him as an original and independent thinker. Yulgok maintained his monistic position and was not swayed by the newly found views of Master Zhu. He explained the differentiation between the heart/mind of the Way and the human heart/mind as merely differences between terms:

> The mind is single; using [diverse] terms for it such as 'the Tao mind [the mind of the Way]' and 'the human mind' is because of the distinction between our normative nature and our psychophysical constitution. The feelings are single; speaking of them in some cases as 'the Four (Beginnings)' and in others as 'the Seven Feelings' is because of the difference between speaking with exclusive reference to principle and speaking of it as combined with material force. Thus the human mind and the Tao mind cannot be combined, but rather are related in the same fashion as end and beginning. The Four Beginnings are not able to include the Seven Feelings, but the Seven Feelings include the Four Beginnings.   (Kalton, 1994: 113)

Yulgok's monistic view of principle and material force was a rational continuation of Kobong's argument against dualism, and clearly targeted T'oegye. Yulgok insisted that there was no separation of principle and material force, and argued that principle and material force were two in substance but one in function. For Yulgok, principle is the power that enables things to move and to cease to move, while material force moves or ceases to move because of principle. It is important to see that principle issues nothing of its own accord and neither can it emit itself, and that material force is the vehicle by which principle is manifest. There are differences between principle and material force because principle is unlimited and omnipresent while material force is limited and one-sided. Principle penetrates everything and being unobstructed can assume any shape, while material force appears to be either partial or fair, pure or turbid, docile or resistant. That is what Yulgok implies when he says that 'principle communicates and material force is limited' (Bak, 1980a: 68).

The debate divided the whole of Korean Confucian scholarship roughly into two camps, the School of Principle (Yongnam School), and the School of Material Force (Kiho School). On the one hand, this debate consumed the energy of Korean Confucianism and confined its scholarship to purely academic games; on the other, it led Korean scholars to explore many dimensions of Neo-Confucianism, consequently enriching and extending Confucian Learning. Although devoted to scholarly debates, T'oegye and Yulgok did not enclose themselves in 'ivory towers'. They were active in applying Confucian doctrines to everyday life. T'oegye, for example, developed Confucian meditation or quiet sitting to a high degree, as the way to gain true knowledge. He described in a poem how this could be done:

> Burning incense is not to imitate the Chan Buddhists.
> Sitting with a pure heart without any worldly attachments, the
>   thought is concentrated.
> Sending off all the mental activities of the heart/mind, it is
>   completely purified.
> Following this state let the heart/mind stay as clear as deep water.
> (Kim, 1995: 24, with minor changes)

Like T'oegye, Yulgok also took self-cultivation to be the foundation of a peaceful and harmonious society. In his *Kakkyo Mobum* (*Manuals for School*), he prescribed concrete tenets, for example, setting the intention to be a sage; disciplining one's body by right behaviour; reading and reflecting on the classics, and sitting quietly to preserve one's heart/mind (*ibid.*, 30–1).

Traditionally, Korea prided itself on being a more (orthodox) Confucian nation than the homeland of Confucianism, China. Only the Rationalistic School (the Cheng–Zhu School) was taken as the correct transmitter of Confucian Learning, and the Idealistic School (the Learning of the Heart/Mind) was labelled heretical and strictly prohibited shortly after its introduction to Korea. The intensively cultivated orthodox sense of Confucianism gave rise to some of the unique features of Korean scholarship. Neo-Confucianism in China matured by absorbing elements from Buddhism and Daoism, and therefore its relation with other religious traditions was inclusive, not only in terms of doctrines but also in areas of practical living. Neo-Confucianism in Japan was from the very beginning allied with Chan (Zen) Buddhism, and the communication and interaction between Confucianism and Buddhism formed an important dimension in the development of Japanese Confucianism. In Korea, however, Confucian attitudes towards Buddhism were much more exclusive and harsh. The strictly orthodox understanding of the Cheng–Zhu teachings was responsible for debates and arguments typical of Korean Neo-Confucian scholarship, which on the one hand clarified the meanings of Confucian terms, but on the other hand turned the energetic search for truth into trivial quarrels.

The desires for an extreme orthodoxy inevitably suffocated Confucian Learning and allowed it to degenerate into purely scholastic study irrelevant to daily life or into something which was pursued merely for the sake of the Civil Service Examinations. Such study had little or no value for improving people's lives. Dissatisfied with their situation and stimulated by new developments in Confucian Learning pursued in China during the Qing Dynasty (1664–1911), a number of independent Confucian scholars opened up a new trend called *Silhak* (the Practical Learning), in the seventeenth and eighteenth centuries. The Korean Practical Learning can be traced to Chung Mong-ju: 'The Way (Tao) of Confucianism lies in the ordinary affairs of daily life. Even in sexual relations and in eating and drinking there is a meaningful principle. The *Tao* of Yao and Shun is nothing other than this principle' (quoted in Hwang, 1979: 470). However, as a systematic theory and practice, the Practical Learning was advocated in the seventeenth century. Yu Hyang-won (1622–72) and Yi Ik (1682–1764), for example, discarded abstract and 'empty learning', condemned absolute monarchism, denounced the ill effects of the Civil Service Examinations and turned their attention to social reform and public welfare. The scholars of the Practical Learning enthusiastically studied anything that was seen as good for improving governmental institutions and improving living conditions. They attempted to reform land ownership, taxation, and the civil service examinations. They attacked the scholastic debates in Confucian Learning as trivial and irrelevant to the needs of the people, and insisted that the major cause of the country's problems was the separation of morality from industry, and that of Confucian Learning from the people's needs.

For these scholars, 'to honour morality alone and ignore industry is equal to being a widower and to stress industry and neglect morality is equivalent to a widow' (Bak, 1980b: 273). They argued for the unity of the two and believed that the state, the people and Confucian Learning would benefit greatly from this unification. It was Chong Yak-yong (better known as Dasan, 1762–1836), the greatest Confucian scholar after T'oegye and Yulgok, who combined the practical spirit and Confucian Learning, and reoriented Confucian scholarship towards social and political realities. Dasan identified the deficiencies in Zhu Xi's interpretations and called for a return to original Confucian classics. He especially emphasised the importance of the *Analects of Confucius*, because he believed that this book did not contain abstract debates about principle and human nature that were typical of Song Learning, neither was it concentrated on a responsive relationship between Heaven and humans that is characteristic of Han Confucianism. He not only dismissed the Confucian scholarship in the Han and Song Dynasties, but also discarded Mengzi. Instead of searching for the truth in these interpretations, he would rather go directly to the teachings of Confucius himself. The intention of such an interpretation was, by way of Confucius, to bring new life to Confucianism and make it relevant to everyday life because, Dasan argued, Confucianism was by nature a practical doctrine concerned with how to cultivate filial piety and humaneness in one's self, how to apply one's virtues to others, and consequently how to induce a humane government. According to this understanding, Confucian Learning must be a kind of learning which centred on human relationships rather than on the relationship between principle and material force and Confucian scholarship must be an effective and efficient tool of state-craft to remove chaos and achieve social order. Unfortunately, Dasan's thought did not appeal to the then Confucian leadership, nor was it tolerated by the authorities. He was exiled for nearly nineteen years and endured a life of great hardship.

Practical Learning did not make a breakthrough and a new academic trend known as *Tonghak* (the Eastern Learning) developed. *Tonghak* bears a clear hallmark of Confucianism. It propagates 'Oriental Thought' in direct opposition to 'Western Learning', especially that of the Christian teachings of God, salvation and original sin. The initiator of the Eastern Learning movement was Choi Je-wu (1824–64), who was first to use the term *Tonghak* in his work *Tongkyong Daejon* (the *Comprehensive*

Book of Eastern Learning) where he articulated the oriental doctrine of the Way of Heaven. Following the Confucian belief that 'The Way is not far from humans. When one pursues the Way and yet remains away from humans, one's course cannot be considered the Way' (Chan, 1963a: 100), Choi argues that the Way of Heaven is not outside but rather within humans and that the heart/mind of Heaven and the heart/mind of humans are identical. To grasp the Way of Heaven one needs to improve one's own innate nature rather than seeking salvation from an external source. The second leader of the Eastern Learning Movement, Choi Si-hyong (1829–98), developed these ideas further and proposed that if one wanted to 'grasp' the truth and to serve Heaven one must first know oneself. He argued that since 'everyone is Heaven', then to mistreat others was to mistreat Heaven, and to treat others properly was to serve Heaven. He also argues for a universalistic equality that as everything in the universe is a copy of Heaven, then Heaven, humans and things are essentially the same. In the hands of the third *Tonghak* leader, Sohn Byong-hi (1861–1919), the movement developed into a religion, *Chondo-kyo* (The Religion of Heaven's Way). *Chondo-kyo* rejects salvation and eternal life after death, while aiming to realise a paradise on earth by way of peace, moral virtue and propriety. It endeavours to enhance and purify Korean national spirit by reforming the corrupt feudal system and overcoming old customs. *Chondo-kyo* actively engaged in the enlightenment movement, and organised various kinds of demonstrations and uprisings.

Despite the reforming effort made by many Korean Confucians, the insular nature of orthodox Confucian Learning became a major obstacle for Korea which was a nation making an attempt at modernisation at the end of the Yi Dynasty. 'The degree of the stagnancy of Korean Confucianism was evidenced by the simple historical fact that the two philosophical themes of Chong Mong-Chu [Chung Mong-ju] of the late fourteenth century were faithfully preserved as the fundamental issues of Kwak Man-Woo (1846–1919) of the twentieth century' (Hwang, 1979: 469). As a result, Korean Confucianism was the price that had to be paid for the transition from a country 'stifled intellectually by orthodox Confucianism, stagnant economically, and politically bound to the decaying Chinese empire' (Deuchler, 1977: 1) to a more open and thus more vulnerable land. The demise of the Yi Dynasty heralded the collapse of Confucianism: Confucianism was no longer a major player in education and social life. Korean Confucianism was under fierce attack from liberal-minded intellectuals who saw it as a conservative and backward institution. With the advent of a 'new age', Korean Confucianism, like its counterpart in China, had to redefine its own position with regard to its social and moral functions.

JAPANESE CONFUCIANISM: TRANSFIGURATION AND APPLICATION

There are a number of similarities between Korean and Japanese Confucianism. Like Korea, Japan had adopted the Buddhist tradition before the arrival of Neo-Confucianism and only after a long and painful reflection on their Buddhist experience did the Japanese intellectuals come to embrace Neo-Confucian Learning. The realisation of a natural affinity between Confucian cosmology and the native Shintô tradition facilitated this change of attitude. Like Korean scholars, the majority of Japanese Confucians worked within the Rationalistic School of Neo-Confucianism, and transmitted and transformed the Cheng–Zhu tradition to the needs of Japanese society. There are also many differences between Japanese and Korean Confucianism. Unlike the case of Korea where leading Confucian scholars such as Yi Hwang and Yi I indulged in metaphysical and philosophical debates, Japanese Confucians had much less enthusiasm for cosmologicalism, traditionalism and philosophical universalism. Their primary interest was in how to apply Confucian values, ideas and precepts to social and political life. Therefore, the history of Confucianism in Japan is marked by a series of transformations and syncretism which deliberately ignored some aspects of Neo-Confucianism while highlighting and developing others. The combination of Confucian ethics and the Shintô religion enabled Confucianism to become finally part of Japanese indigenous culture and to permeate the national consciousness. Confucian ethics became a cultural tool for national morale and provided practical rules for social behaviour. Japanese Confucians did not succeed in establishing, or perhaps never really tried to establish, a civil examination system as did their counterparts in China and Korea. Consequently the link between Japanese Confucian scholars and governmental bureaucrats was loose, and Japanese *literati* were seldom given supreme power over the state and were never allowed to hold a self-contained position independent of the government. Confucian Learning and practices were used to shape and reshape the conscience of the *bushidô* (the way of warriors) but Japanese Confucians themselves were always considered the 'servants' of the *bakufu* (the government) and the emperors. The Japanese pragmatic attitude toward Confucian Learning greatly affects the way in which the Confucian tradition develops and explains the unique image and functions that Confucianism has had in modern Japan. For most of the twentieth century the majority of the Chinese and Koreans see Confucianism as politically conservative and culturally backward, while in Japan, Confucianism is largely considered to have played an important part in the Meiji Reformation and aided the acceleration of Japanese industrialisation and modernisation.

Two early Japanese chronicles, *Nihon Shoki*, the *Chronicles of Japan* and *Kojiki*, the *Records of Ancient Matters* record that the *Analects of Confucius* and *Qianzi Wen*, the *Book of Ten Thousand Characters* were brought to Japan by a Korean scholar, Wani (Wang In), in the second month of the sixteenth year of Emperor Ôjin. This corresponds to 285 CE. It is now believed that this event occurred actually at the beginning of the fifth century, probably in 405 CE. According to the Chinese records, *Hou Hanshu* (the *Book of the Later Han Dynasty*), *Wei Lue* (the *History of the Kingdom of Wei*) and *Song Shu* (the *History of the Liu Song Dynasty*), diplomatic and business intercourse between Japan and China existed in the Later Han Dynasty and were further promoted via Korea during the Wei–Jin and the Southern–Northern Dynasties (Tsunoda, 1951: 1–16). In the memorial that Japanese envoys presented to the Chinese emperor and in the three bronze/iron inscriptions excavated in Japan and dated at the beginning of the fifth century, the Confucian influence on Japanese politics, morality and social life is clear (Wang, 1990: 5). From the historical facts it is possible to conjecture that Confucian ideas or possibly texts were introduced into Japan via Japanese envoys and Chinese immigrants, and that the introduction was not a single event but a long and slow process. From the historical record that at the beginning of the sixth century Korean academicians (*boshi*) of the Kingdom of Paekche were received at the Japanese court, we can further speculate that Korea functioned as the bridge between China and Japan, and that Koreans as intermediaries brought into Japan not only Chinese and Korean culture but also Confucian classical learning.

Along with Confucianism came Mahayana Buddhism. Ironically, Buddhism rather than Confucianism was quickly absorbed into Japanese society and widely spread among ordinary people. Confucian Learning and scholarship gradually gained prestige among the elite, influencing politics and education. The first Japanese constitution, *Junanô Kenpô* (the Constitution of Seventeen Articles), decreed by Prince Shôtoku (573–621) in 604 CE, was obviously composed under the influence of the Confucian moral–idealist vision of politics, and was written in the light of the Confucian historical–political design. Its primary objective was to define the relations between the sovereign and the state, between the emperor and the subjects (Moore, 1967b: 4–9). The concept of the 'Mandate of Heaven' was introduced to justify the rule of the Emperor. Emperor Tenchi (r. 662–71) established a system of education composed of national and provincial universities (*daigaku*), local academies and private schools, in which the textbooks were mainly taken from the Confucian classics. This dominance of Confucian Learning in the education system did not last long, and was soon minimised when the Japanese writing system superseded Chinese and writers in the Japanese language became popular, and especially when the system of civil service examinations collapsed. The early centuries of the second millennium saw a rise in Buddhist popularity eclipsing that of Confucian scholarship. Confucian Learning came to be seen as an aspect of Buddhism. It is said that until the end of the thirteenth century Confucian influence on Japanese culture was slight, and that Japanese Confucian scholars of this period simply copied and followed the Chinese and Korean interpretations, and failed to incorporate the innovations that occurred in these countries. Confucian Learning in Japan did not vary much from the exegetical studies that had prevailed in Han–Tang China.

The rise of Neo-Confucianism in China and its spread to Korea did little to change the character of Confucian Learning in Japan during the medieval period (1192–1573). The developments of Zen (in Chinese *Chan*) Buddhism, however, brought Neo-Confucian philosophy to the attention of Buddhist scholars. A resemblance between Zen Buddhism and Neo-Confucian Learning, especially the teaching of Zhu Xi, was recognised and well received in Zen monasteries. It was a Zen monk, Keian (1427–1508), who first translated Zhu Xi's *Collective Comment-aries on the Great Learning* into Japanese. This affinity explains another character of Japanese Confucianism: while in China and Korea, Neo-Confucianism responded to the challenges of Buddhism and Daoism by incorporating some of their metaphysical views while criticising their religio-moral system; in Japan, however, Neo-Confucianism was seen from the very beginning as part of Buddhism, and to a great extent has been in harmony with Buddhism and Shintô.

Since Neo-Confucianism was believed to be an aid to understanding the Buddhist Way, both the royal house and Buddhist monasteries promoted its learning. Emperor Godaigo (r. 1318–39), for example, 'summoned scholars to lecture on Confucian topics' and several thousand students, though many of them Zen monks, 'studied a Neo-Confucian curriculum' in *Ashikaga gakko* (the Ashikaga Academy) (Nosco, 1984: 7). Whatever motives might be behind this, the spread of Zhu Xi's teaching paved the way for a new era of Japanese Confucianism in the Tokugawa age (1603–1867), during which Chinese and Korean Confucian Learning were thoroughly studied and transformed. For most part of this period Neo-Confucianism, especially the teaching of the Cheng–Zhu School, was recognised as the foundation of Japanese politics, culture and education, and as the underlying ideas for social and intellectual life.

Under the influence of Korean Zhu Xi Studies and inspired by an intensive search for truth in Confucian classics, Fujiwara Seika (1561–1619) deserted Zen Buddhism and turned to Confucianism. He consequently became the first of the Tokugawa Confucian masters, and proved that Confucian Learning could effectively support the Japanese establishment and provide a moral basis for the *bakufu* system. Seika taught Tokugawa Ieyasu (1542–1616), the founder of the *bakufu* system, Confucian historical and political programmes. In return, Tokugawa Ieyasu became the patron of Confucian Learning and adopted Confucian political programmes as the way of ruling Japan (Tsunoda *et al.*, 1958: 336–7). Seika was the first eminent Japanese Neo-Confucian scholar to annotate the Four Books and the Five Classics in the light of the Rationalistic Neo-Confucian teachings. He believed that all truth lay in human relationships and thereby criticised Buddhism for its attitude of renouncing the world. Being dissatisfied with Han–Tang exegetical studies of the Confucian classics, he turned to the learning of the Song, which he took to be more in keeping with the 'learning of the sages' and a true transmission of Confucianism. Seika favoured the teaching of Zhu Xi but he did not reject other Neo-Confucian masters for he inclined towards an eclecticism rather than extreme exclusiveness. He identified the common principles shared by Neo-Confucian philosophers, and combined them into a single system. He believed that 'the emphasis on quietness' of Zhou Dunyi, 'holding fast to seriousness' emphasised by Cheng Yi, 'investigating principle exhaustively' propagated by Zhu Xi, 'the simple and easy way' of Lu Jiuyuan, 'quiet sitting' proposed by Chen Xianzhang (1428–1500) and 'the innately good knowledge' of Wang Shouren, 'are all from the same source but appear to be different in words' (Wang, 1990: 81). Seika opened up a new aspect of Neo-Confucian discourse and took Confucianism into a new era. His interpretation exerted a great influence on Japanese scholarship, and his followers became leading figures in Confucian Learning who further strengthened the link between Confucianism and the Tokugawa Shogunate.

Following Seika, Hayashi Razan (1583–1657) played a decisive role in promoting Confucianism to be the dominant ideology in Tokugawa Japan: 'It was through efforts of Razan and his descendants that Neo-Confucianism became the official philosophy and code of the Shogunate, in both external and internal affairs' (Tsunoda *et al.*, 1958: 347). Like his master, Seika, Razan turned away from Zen Buddhism and embraced Zhu Xi's learning, attacking Buddhist doctrines and practices as destroying human relationships and Buddhist monasteries as a waste of manpower and material resources. Unlike his master who compromised between Zhu Xi and Wang Shouren by emphasising the sameness in fundamental principles between them, however, Razan held strictly to the Learning of Zhu Xi and insisted that only Zhu Xi represented the orthodox transmission of Confucian teachings. Razan also developed the practical dimension of Confucian Learning by exploring the 'usefulness' of Neo-Confucian teachings for the *bakufu* and giving pre-eminence to the virtue of 'loyalty' rather than 'filial piety'. He believed that the state held undisputed priority over the family and thus successfully turned Confucianism into a useful tool in the unification of Japan and also for justifying and maintaining the system of *bakufu*. Razan undertook the task of harmonising Confucianism and Japanese indigenous culture and pointed out that 'The spiritual tradition of Japan is the Way of Kingliness, which is exactly the same as the Way of Confucianism. Therefore, there is no difference between them' (Wang, 1990: 86–7).

After Hayashi Razan, *Shushigaku* (the Studies of Zhu Xi's Learning) developed in a number of directions. Yamazaki Ansai (1618–82) took Zhu Xi as the first master after Confucius. To express his reverence to Master Zhu, Ansai always wore dark red clothes and used dark red handkerchiefs ('Zhu' in Chinese means 'dark red'). Ansai believed that all Neo-Confucian commentators in China and Japan including Fujiwara

Seika and Hayashi Razan had distorted Zhu Xi's teaching, and therefore took upon himself the task of faithfully transmitting the inner and practical dimensions of Zhu's teaching. He argued that to transmit Zhu's teachings was not simply a case of transplanting them from China to Japan, but more importantly, a case of re-experiencing Zhu's teaching on humaneness and self-cultivation in one's own life and in a Japanese context. With regard to the relationship between Confucianism and Shintô, Ansai took the same line as his predecessors and attempted to fashion a new Shintô theology 'using a Neo-Confucian structure', thereby making these two traditions allies as well as opening a possibility of 'Neo-Confucianism's penetration into the "ground bass" of Tokugawa thought' (Nosco, 1984: 11). Whereas Razan insisted on the sameness of Shintô and Confucianism, Ansai agreed that there was an affinity between Confucianism and Shintô, but he nevertheless stressed the nationalistic aspects of Confucianism and presented Shintô as the Way unique to Japan. To his own question about what the Japanese students of Confucius and Mengzi should do if China sent an army headed by Confucius and Mengzi to attack Japan, Ansai replied that he would take up weapons 'to fight and capture them alive in the service of my country. That is what Confucius and Mencius teach us to do' (Tsunoda *et al.*, 1958: 369–70).

Ansai uncovered and explored a new dimension of Japanese Confucian Learning. For Razan, Confucian Learning served the *bakufu* externally and guided the direction of the *bakufu* by its moral codes and ritual-laws, while Ansai believed that Confucian Learning was part of one's life and had to be cultivated through inner meditation and fulfilled in social justice. The differences between Razan and Seika not only produced two major schools within Japanese Neo-Confucianism, but also engendered two different political attitudes. The followers of Razan would support the *status quo*, while those of Ansai would be most likely to engage in emotionally patriotic movements, and would support the 'restoring the Emperor's authority' against the *bakufu's* monopoly of power, participate in *sonno-joi* (revering the emperor to expel the barbarian), and engage in the Meiji Restoration.

Kaibara Ekken (1630–1714) developed the spiritual quality and the practical application of Neo-Confucianism in Tokugawa Japan. Comparing Ekken with leading Chinese and Korean Confucian masters, Tucker outlines Ekken's contribution to Japanese Confucianism as follows:

As Hsü Heng sought to demonstrate the relevance of Neo-Confucian teachings for the Mongols under Khubilai in thirteenth century China, and as Yi T'oegye adapted the Neo-Confucianism of Chu Hsi for the Koreans in the sixteenth century, Ekken was similarly involved in the transformation of the Way of the sages across cultural and national boundaries. Recognizing the universal elements of Neo-Confucianism, and aware of their particular application for Tokugawa society, Ekken embraced the Way with remarkable dedication. In the teachings of the Sung Neo-Confucian Chu Hsi (1130–1200), he saw a system of personal cultivation, intellectual investigation, political organization, and cosmological orientation that provided a broad context for thought and a functional basis for action which he perceived as essential for his time.   (Tucker, 1989: 3)

Ekken transformed Neo-Confucianism from a rigid moral code of restrictions to a system that was more suited to the 'common sense' of society and politics, thereby completing the process of Japanising Confucian ethics. He was a firm believer in Zhu Xi's teachings, yet under the influence of the general mood in Ming China and Yi Korea, Ekken attempted to revise rationalistic philosophy in the light of his own insights and construct a vitalistic and vibrant doctrine internally rooted in a personal spiritual experience and externally based on a thorough observation of nature. This inevitably led him to challenge part of the orthodox teachings. In his *Taigi-roku* ('Grave Doubts'), Ekken seriously criticised some of Zhu's formulations and sincerely attempted to remodel them into something meaningful and useful to the ordinary Japanese. 'More than anyone else he brought Confucian ethics into the homes of ordinary Japanese in language they could understand' (Tsunoda *et al.*, 1958: 374). He could not tolerate the dualism of principle (*li*) and material force (*qi*), and of heavenly principle and human desires. He articulated the dynamic relationship between the cosmological and human orders and proposed a monistic understanding of material force. In this spirit of realism Ekken emphasised the practical value of Confucian doctrines in everyday life, and believed that the true Way of Confucianism was found in the practical application of its teachings rather than in the old and out-dated codes. Despite his criticism of some aspects of Zhu Xi's interpretations, Ekken was nonetheless emotionally attached to his 'intellectual mentor' and held fast to the teaching of Master Zhu. In this sense Ekken can be said to have reformed Zhu Xi's learning from within as 'Doubt for Ekken was a means of genuine scholarly inquiry, not a sign of a break with the Confucian tradition' (Tucker, 1989: 65, 75).

The prevalence of *Shushigaku* eclipsed the *Yômeigaku* (the Study of Wang Yangming's Learning) in Japan. The Idealistic School in Japan did not enjoy the privileges it had enjoyed in China during the later half of the Ming Dynasty, but neither did it come to be extinguished, as it was in Korea. The *Shushigaku* quickly gained recognition from the *bakufu* and became its official learning and eventually the State Orthodox Ideology (1790), while the scholars who studied and propagated the doctrine of the heart/mind remained in the shadows, and were frequently considered 'heterodox' and even persecuted by the authorities. Nevertheless, a certain degree of tolerance was extended to *Yômeigaku*, so that it was able to develop its teachings and distinctive schools. Scholars like Nakae Tôju (1608–48) and Kumazawa Banzan (1619–91) pioneered the *Yômeigaku* and emphasised the substance and function of the heart/mind. Confronted with the official doctrines, these scholars demonstrated an independent spirit in developing the Japanese idealistic form of Neo-Confucianism.

Neo-Confucianism had been adapted to Japanese needs and this meant that the practical dimensions of Confucianism were emphasised at the expense of its more philosophical deliberations. To enable Confucian doctrines to serve Japanese society efficiently and effectively, Ansai and Ekken deliberately ignored the highly philosophical doctrines of Zhu Xi, and gave their attention to the practical and realistic aspects of his teachings. Yet being bound to Zhu's rationalistic principles, Ansai and Ekken could not make the final breakthrough. In parting with Zhu Xi's dogmas and taking the subjective heart/mind of Wang Yangming as the foundation of Confucianism, Tôju took Japanese Confucianism forward into a new arena, one in which inner experience and personal happiness took precedence over external investigation and universal principles. Tôju called the innate moral senses 'the inner light' or the 'Divine Light of Heaven', and believed that it was only this light, not anything else, that guided one's life. What Tôju did not succeed in was the unification of the notions of subjective experiences and social reforms so that personal happiness could have been guaranteed by institutional structure. This task was accomplished by one of his disciples, Kumazawa Banzan (1619–91). Banzan turned to Mengzi's theory of humane government (*ren zheng*) for inspiration, where he found the resources for how to project one's virtues to the world. He completed the theoretical process of combining the inner and the external, personal experience and social convention, and the individual's happiness and public welfare, and established the tenets that 'Benevolent rule cannot be extended throughout the land without first developing our material wealth . . . If the lord of a province had wealth according to the Great Principle, the entire province would be happy, and if the shogun had such wealth, the whole country would be happy' (Tsunoda *et al.*, 1958: 388–9).

Banzan appeared to follow the same path as Razan in his politicisation of Confucianism. However, while Razan transformed *Shushigaku* into a tool to maintain the *bakufu* regime, Banzan made *Yômeigaku* a servant of political administration in order to reform the social infrastructure.

The early *Yômeigaku* gained new momentum in the hands of prominent eighteenth–nineteenth-century scholars, such as Satô Issai (1772–1859) and Oshio Chusai (1798–1837). These scholars 'emphasised both the importance of understanding based on personal experience, and the study of the mind and human nature' (Okada, 1984: 216). They and their predecessors are characterised by a number of distinct features. Firstly, like the exponents of later Idealistic Learning in China, few of the Japanese scholars of *Yômeigaku* held exclusively to the learning of the heart/mind. They combined Wang Yangming's teaching of innate good knowledge with Zhu Xi's teaching of the investigation of things, which necessitated compromise in these two traditions. For example, Banzan insisted that both were needed and Hayashi Ryosai (1807–49) declared, 'In my humble opinion the special character of Ch'eng-Chu and Lu-Wang is that they all go back to the same thing, they are all teachings of sages' (Okada, 1984: 223). Secondly, although they insisted that the heart/mind was the only reality and the ultimate source of all things, they put greater emphasis on filial piety. When he was twenty-seven years old, Tôju had to make a choice between his service to his feudal lord and the care of his aged mother. He chose to care for his mother and thereby placed filial piety above his social responsibilities. Later he made filial piety the supreme virtue and the main constituent in his interpretation of Confucian Learning, stating clearly that 'Filial piety is the summit of virtue and the essence of the Way in the three realms of heaven, earth, and man. What brings life to heaven, life to earth, life to man, and life to all things is filial piety. Therefore those who pursue learning need study only this' (Tsunoda *et al.*, 1958: 384). Thirdly, the independent spirit and the search for the unity of knowledge and action promoted in *Yômeigaku* cultivated the character of social innovation and practical application in the Japanese scholars. The early masters of *Yômeigaku* devoted themselves to improving practical utility, frequently in defiance of the authority of learning. The later scholars directly challenged what they considered the irrational and immoral institutions of Japan, which was exemplified in the actions of Chusai who led a rebellion in 1837 in order to relieve the starving people, and by Yoshida Shôin (1830–59) and his disciples, many of whom enthusiastically prepared for and were actively involved in the Meiji Restoration.

Alongside these two mainstream Neo-Confucian schools, a third school developed throughout the Tokugawa period and was known as *Kogaku*, the School of the Ancient Studies. *Kogaku* scholars discarded the teachings of Zhu Xi and Wang Yangming and believed that these schools had been formed under a Daoist and Buddhist influence. They went back to the Duke of Zhou, Confucius and Mengzi to discover the real teaching of the sages. They argued that, although the scriptures of the sages 'are self-evident to all the world', they had been led to confusion by later commentators and annotators (Tsunoda *et al.*, 1958: 401). Therefore, the only way to grasp the truth of the sages was to discard the confounding writings and go back to the Sages themselves. Yamaga Sokô (1622–85) described how he went on this course:

> In the 1660s, I learned that my misunderstandings were due to reading works by scholars from the Han, T'ang, Sung and Ming dynasties. I went directly to the works of the Duke of Chou and Confucius, and taking them as my model, I was able to straighten my own line of thought. From then on, I stopped using the writings of later ages, and by diligently studying works of the sage day and night, I finally clarified and understood the message of the sages.   (Nosco, 1984: 14)

Sokô searched the teachings of the sages to find the truth that would provide answers to practical questions, not intellectual diversions. He took the most important one to be how to guide the life of a *samurai* (warrior, or more vividly, 'military scholar'). Sokô applied Confucian ethics to the warrior's creed (*bukyo*) and for the first time he gave a systematic exposition of what later came to be known as the Way of the Warrior (*bushidô*):

The business of the *samurai* consists in reflecting on his own station in life, in discharging loyal service to his master if he has one, in deepening his fidelity in associations with friends, and, with due consideration of his own position, in devoting himself to duty above all . . . It would not do for the samurai to know the martial and civil virtues without manifesting them. Since this is the case, outwardly he stands in physical readiness for any call to service and inwardly he strives to fulfil the Way of the lord and subject, friend and friend, father and son, older and younger brother, and husband and wife.

(Tsunoda *et al.*, 1958: 399)

Kogaku was further developed and deepened in the hands of Itô Jinsai (1627–1705) and Ogyû Sorai (1666–1728). Jinsai deplored the current negligence of the original teachings of Confucius and Mengzi, and insisted that the *Analects* was 'the foremost book of all, rising above the Six Classics', that it alone 'can serve as the standard and guide for the teaching of the Way in all time,' and that 'the *Book of Mencius* is the key that opens the gate of Confucianism at all times', 'is for all of us of later times a magnet', and is like 'a lantern in the dark' (*ibid.*: 419–20). Sorai went even further. By identifying Confucius' words with the Six Classics, he called for a return to the teaching of the early sage kings:

The Way of Confucius is the Way of the early kings . . . failing to achieve a position of authority, he devoted himself to editing the Six Classics so that they might be handed down to posterity. Thus the Six Classics embodied the way of the early kings, and they are quite wrong who say today that the way of Confucius is not the same as the way of the early kings.

(Tsunoda *et al.*, 1958: 425)

The scholars of *Kogaku* took different approaches in their opposition to the Neo-Confucian tenets of distinguishing heavenly principle from human desires, and saw the separation between being righteous and seeking benefits, as man-made contradictions. They followed the Way of the Mean to justify human desires, to sanction properly seeking benefits, and to prioritise politics over morality.

Seika and Razan liberated Confucianism from Zen monasteries as well as from the classrooms of exegetical scholars, thus starting the long process of making Confucianism a living tradition that served the needs of Japanese society. Tôju and Sorai broke through the external restriction imposed by the objective principles of Zhu Xi, and by way of *Yômeigaku* they took Confucianism to be a useful and effective tool for inner experience and social reform. On the one hand, this facilitated the penetration of Confucian moral and political doctrines into Japanese psychology and social life. On the other hand, it also secularised Confucianism and dried up the intellectual fountain of Neo-Confucian Learning. Confucianism was thus deprived of moral idealism and metaphysical deliberation, and became merely the 'art of government'. Therefore, it was unavoidable that after Sorai, Japanese Confucian Learning went into decline, despite the active involvement of many scholars in political life. Most of the schools and movements, such as Setsu Aika (eclecticism) and Kosho (exegetical studies of the classics), lacked a critical and original spirit. The rapid introduction of western learning made Confucian scholarship more or less an 'empty learning' and a 'useless discipline'. The scholars of enlightenment such as Fukuzawa Yûkichi (1834–1901) and Nishi Amane (1829–97) targeted Confucianism as the chief cause of a backward society. Japan was advancing to become a capitalist and militarist state, in which science and technology constantly had the upper hand over Confucian Learning. Yet Confucianism still had a practical value for Japan and Japanese modernisation did not completely expel Confucian ethics. Unlike its counterparts in China and Korea, Japanese Confucianism did not, or was not intended to, hold back Japan from becoming a member of the modern world. Without losing most part of its own culture heritage, Confucianism was successfully transformed into a motivating power and moral assistance for modernisation and industrialisation. The Meiji Restoration (1868) formally established Shintô as the state orthodoxy, and at the same time it allowed room for other traditions to function. Moderation and tolerance brought together all sorts of different traditions and forces. The earlier eclectic maxims such as *Shinju-gôchi* ('Shinto and Confucianism can be combined to one'), *Bumbu-funi* ('Literary and military [training] are not incompatible') and *Chuko-ippon* ('Loyalty to sovereign and loyalty to parents are one in essence') (Tsunoda *et al.*, 1958: 592) continued in a new environment. Thus Confucianism was patronised by the government, partly due to its intimate relationship with Shintô and partly due to its moral power counterbalancing the influence of western culture. It was taken as a symbol of eastern morality in the lasting slogan *Toyo no dotoku, Seiyo no gakugei* ('eastern ethics and western science'), proposed by Sakuma Shôzan (1811–64, Tsunoda *et al.*, 1958: 607). As opposed to China and

Korea, Japan gave Confucianism a chance to be part of the modernisation process: while its learning was criticised and its institutions such as schools and academies dismantled, Confucianism did not cease to be functional. A multidimensional transformation of Confucianism was shortly forthcoming as the New Constitution was established. Traditionally minded scholars such as Motoda Eifu (1818–91) and Nishimura Shigeki (1828–1902) transformed Confucian teachings to suit a rapidly changing Japan, and made it easier for Confucian ethics to be incorporated into the education curriculum. The Imperial Prescript on Education (*Kyôiku chokugo*) issued by the Emperor in 1890 'reflected a powerful reaction to the Westernization tendencies of the early Meiji Period', and was a full-scale reinforcement of Confucian moral education (*ibid.*: 647). Business-minded pioneers of capitalism such as Shibusawa Eiichi (1840–1931) promoted the unity between morality and economics, transforming Confucian teachings into a motivating power for capitalism. In his famous thesis *The Analects and Abacus*, for example, Eiichi proclaimed that there was no contradiction between Confucian morality and market economy. At the same time militarists also strengthened the Confucian moral elements of *bushidô* to cultivate loyalty and militant virtues of the nation, and to justify their military action in East Asia. Through these two channels, elements of Japanese Confucianism were transmitted to the modern era, one in which Confucianism was further altered to suit the social, political and economic needs of a rapidly changing Japan and Japanese society.

The end of the Second World War also terminated the deliberate use of Confucianism by the government. This disruption did not last long, however. After the Japanese economy took off in the 1960s, Confucianism appears again in the nation's agenda, which may be seen from the proposal by former prime minister Yasuhiro Nakasone to reincorporate Confucian ethics into the school curriculum, echoing similar actions taken by Singapore (Küng & Ching, 1989: 85).

Questions for discussion

1. What are the differences and similarities between Mengzi and Xunzi?
2. How did Confucianism win a victory over other schools to become the state religion during the Former Han Dynasty?
3. Is Mysterious Learning (*Xuan xue*) merely a development of Daoism? What is the Confucian dimension of Mysterious Learning?

4. What is the Rationalistic School of Neo-Confucianism? What is the Idealistic School? How should we understand their opposition?
5. Why is it said that Korea is the second homeland of Confucianism?
6. In what way did Japanese Confucianism help to accelerate the modernisation of Japan while Chinese and Korean Confucianism was believed to obstruct the process?

Plate 1 The statue of Confucius at the main hall of the Temple of Confucius, Qufu, the home town of Confucius.

Plate 2 The Apricot Platform where Confucius is said to have taught, in the Temple of Confucius, Qufu, Confucius' home town.

Plate 3 The Sacred Path leading to the tomb of Confucius, the number of trees at one side symbolising his seventy-two disciples and at the other his life of seventy-three years.

Plate 4 The tablet of Confucius in front of his tomb.

Plate 5 The tablet and tomb of Zisi (483?–402? BCE), the grandson of Confucius.

Plate 6 People meditating in front of the hut at the side of the tomb of Confucius where Zigong (502?–? BCE), a disciple of Confucius, is said to have stayed for six years mourning the death of his master.

Plate 7 The tablet and statue of a Former Worthy (*xian xian*), Master Yue Zheng (?–?) who is traditionally regarded as a transmitter of the Confucian doctrine of filial piety, in the Temple of Confucius at Qufu.

Plate 8 The Temple of the Second Sage (Mengzi, 372?–289? BCE), at Zou, Mengzi's home town.

Plate 9 Korean scholars paying homage to Confucius in the ceremonies of sacrifice to Confucius at Songgyun'gwan, the National Academy of Confucius (from: Spencer J. Palmer's *Confucian Rituals in Korea*, Berkeley: Asian Humanities Press and Seoul: Po Chi Chai Ltd, 1984, plate 66).

Plate 10 Two semicircular pools in front of a hall in the Songyang Confucian Academy, near the famous Chan Buddhist monastery, *Shaolin Si*, Henan Province.

Plate 11 The spiritual tablet and statue of Zhu Xi (1130–1200) in White Cloud Temple, a Daoist Temple, Beijing. The inscription on the tablet reads 'The Spiritual Site of Master Zhu Xi'. His hand gesture is certainly a kind of variation of Buddhist ones.

Plate 12 The stage of the Global Celebration of Confucius' 2549th birthday held by the Confucian Academy Hong Kong, 17 October 1998.

3

The Way of Confucianism

According to Confucian understanding, the world is sustained by, and structured around, three ultimates (*sanji*), which are also termed the three powers of the universe (*sancai*): *tian* (heaven), *di* (earth) and *ren* (humans). These three powers work together in an organic cosmos so that 'Heaven, Earth and humans are the origin of all things. Heaven generates them, Earth nourishes them and humans perfect them' (*Chunqiu Fanlu Yizheng*, 1992: 168). The Confucian discussion of Heaven lays down a solid foundation for its metaphysical view of the world, its understanding of Earth links the present to the past, and its approach to humankind seeks the full realisation of human potentiality. The three dimensions of the universe share the same nature, and their relationship is characterised by harmony rather than opposition or confrontation. The *Book of Changes* presents them as three modes of the same Way: the Way of Heaven is called the yin and yang, the Way of the Earth is called the yielding and the firm, and the Way of Humans is called humaneness and righteousness (Chan, 1963a: 268; *Zhouyi Dazhuan Jinzhu*, 1979: 609). Heaven and Earth are sometimes combined to refer to the metaphysical and material world, in which humans live and act, and by which humans organise their life and guide their behaviour.

The Way (*dao*) is fundamental to the Confucian view of the world, concerning the question of the ultimate meaning of human existence (Roetz, 1993: 101–3). Confucian masters focus on how to apply the principle governing Heaven and Earth to human life and society and on how to find the Way to maintain or restore the harmony of the world. In this process, the original meaning of *dao* as a road or a path is enriched to mean the universal Way applicable and existent in every corner of the universe. The universal Way is understood to originate from Heaven and Earth and therefore to be the source of the meaning and value of human life. It is believed to have been manifest in the wisdom of the ancient sage–kings (*xianwang zhi dao*, in *Lunyu*, 1: 12), in the doctrine of Confucius (*fuzi zhi dao*, in *Lunyu*, 4: 15), and in the way of life of good people (*shanren zhi dao*, in *Lunyu*, 12: 20). Understood as such, the Way is the foundation of a harmonious universe, a peaceful society and a good life, and without it the transformation of the universe would break down, human society would fall into chaos, and the state would weaken and collapse. Although Confucians recognise that whether or not the Way prevails in the human world is not entirely a matter for human beings but is more or less predetermined ('It is the Destiny (*ming*) if the Way prevails. It is equally Destiny if the Way falls into disuse', *Lunyu*, 14: 36), they nevertheless believe that within the framework of human destiny, individuals are endowed with responsibilities to practise the Way in their own life. Therefore, the Way is not distinct from human beings and cannot be separated from human life, since it exists in daily life, in ordinary behaviour and in mundane matters. It is up to humans to enlarge or belittle it, to manifest or obscure it.

Central to the Confucian Way is the principle of *tianren heyi*: the harmonious oneness of Heaven and humanity, 'a convenient formula for capturing what is generally perceived as the fundamental characteristic of Chinese religiousness' (Hall & Ames, 1987: 241). Although as early as the Spring and Autumn period rational philosophers and politicians had realised that 'The Way of Heaven is distant, while that of man is near' (Fung, 1952: 32), the Confucian masters seldom separated them or discussed them in their opposition. A rationalistic approach to Heaven as the spiritual Ultimate initiated a humanistic understanding of the Way of Heaven and the Way of Humans. Through a unity between metaphysical/naturalistic Heaven and social/moral humanity the Confucian understanding of the organic universe is extended to human realms, and the perfection of human virtues has acquired a spiritual nature. Various modern scholars have noted the importance of the unity for the Confucian tradition and its profound implications for human spirituality. Tu Wei-ming, for example, elaborates the meaning of the unity in this way:

> The relationship between Heaven and man is not an antinomic biunity
> but an indivisibly single oneness. In this sense, the sage as the most
> authentic manifestation of humanity does not coexist with Heaven;
> he forms a coincidence with Heaven . . . Despite the possibility of a
> conceptual separation between Heaven and man, inwardly, in their
> deepest reality, they form an unbreakable organismic continuum.
>
> (Tu, 1976: 84)

Heaven, humans and harmony are three constituent elements of the
Confucian Way. Consequently, the Way of Heaven, the Way of Humans
and the Way of Harmony become the three most essential aspects of the
Confucian doctrine. In one sense, these three dimensions are only the one
Way, not separable from each other. What is meant by the Way of Heaven
is reflected in the Way of Humans and culminates in the Way of Harmony,
and what is pursued as the Way of Humans has its source in the Way
of Heaven and functions in the Way of Harmony. Keeping in mind the
singleness of the three dimensions and the functional overlaps between
them, for theoretical convenience we will divide our discussion of the
Confucian Way into three parts, each dealing with one of these three
dimensions.

The Way of Heaven

Heaven is the source of Confucian spirituality and is identified as its
transcendental power. It is believed that Confucian doctrines are
primarily the result of observing and following the laws of Heaven and
Earth. The commentators of the *Book of Changes* believed that the
ancient sages looked up to observe the pattern of Heaven, and looked
down to examine the order of Earth, so that they gained the knowledge
about the causes of various affairs and understood the circle of life and
death (Chan, 1963a: 265).

Important as Heaven is for Confucianism, there seldom seems to be
a consensus concerning what Heaven is. The character for Heaven (*tian*)
is traditionally defined as the 'Supreme Ultimate (*zhigao wushang*)'
(*Shuowen Jiezi Zhu*, 1981: 1). Modern scholars vary in their renderings
of this Chinese character. Herrlee G. Creel interpreted *tian* (天) as 'one'
(一) above man (大); or (天) as Large or Great Man, hence 'the rulers
of the past, collectively conceived as living in heaven'. Shima Kunio considered the character in the oracle bones (□) identifiable with *di* (帝)
as Sky-god (Lord on High). Robert Eno hypothesises that *tian* was the

destination of the ashes of cremated sacrificial victims, a meaning of sky 'linked to the image of death by fire', and was recreated by early Confucians as ultimate transcendence (Eno, 1990: 181–9). With so many difficulties in deciphering the character and so many disagreements in rendering its meaning, it is impossible to give a clear-cut definition of what is meant by this character in Chinese philosophical and religious traditions. Therefore, 'Heaven' as we use it throughout the book is only a convenient but inaccurate translation of the Chinese character *tian*.

Heaven in Chinese religions as well as in the Confucian tradition has multidimensional implications and these implications are related to one another. A Neo-Confucian master, Cheng Yi of the Song Dynasty, attempted to unify all the dimensions of Heaven:

> Spoken of as one, Heaven is the Way. Spoken of in its different aspects, it is called heaven with respect to its physical body, the Lord (Ti) with respect to its being master, negative and positive spiritual forces with respect to its operation, spirit (*shen*) with respect to its wonderful functioning, and Ch'ien with respect to its nature and feelings.
>
> (Chan, 1963a: 570)

Among many of its meanings, three are most frequently referred to in a Confucian context. In its metaphysical and physical connotation, Heaven, often in conjunction with, and/or in opposition to, the Earth, refers to the universe, the cosmos, the material world, or simply, Nature. Applied in the spiritual realm, it signifies an anthropomorphic Lord or a Supreme Being who presides in Heaven, and rules over or governs directly the spiritual and material worlds. In a moral context, it is understood to be the source of ethical principles and the supreme sanction of human behaviour, and some scholars suggest that its principle can be identified with Natural Law in modern European philosophy (Eno, 1990: 4). Most importantly, the Confucian Heaven functions as the Ultimate or Ultimate Reality, to which human beings are answerable with respect to fulfilling their destiny. The Way of Heaven predetermines the Way of Humans and underlies the Way of Harmony. The diverse spiritual, ethical and natural meanings of Heaven establish the Way of Heaven as the foundation of Confucian views of the world, the universe, and human society.

HEAVEN AND THE CONFUCIAN ULTIMATE

A much-quoted paragraph concerning the character of Confucianism as a religion comes from Joseph Needham when he put it categorically that

'Confucianism was a religion, too, if you define that as something which involves the sense of the holy, for a quality of the numinous is very present in Confucian temples (the *wen miao*); but not if you think of religion only as the theology of a transcendent creator-deity' (Needham, 1969: 63). While in general we agree with Needham regarding the religious nature of Confucianism and the differences in the conception of the transcendental between Confucianism and theistic religions, it does not follow that there is no theological belief in the transcendental Ultimate or Being within the Confucian tradition. There is no doubt that Heaven is the focal point where all Confucian beliefs converge and that Confucians take Heaven as their ultimate spiritual authority. As the transcendental Being, Heaven is believed to have the power to determine the course of the natural and the human world, although the majority of the later Confucians look askance at an absolute creator or anthropomorphic Lord (*di*), preferring the ultimate enforcement of Natural Law. In the mind of Confucians, Heaven is the transcendental power that guarantees harmony between the metaphysical and the physical, between the spiritual and the secular, and between human nature and human destiny.

In the Confucian classics and in imperial religious practices, Heaven is referred to as a divine being who controls and determines the human world. The references to Heaven in the *Book of Poetry*, the *Book of History*, the *Book of Rites*, *Zuo Zhuan* or *Zuo's Commentary on the Spring and Autumn Annals*, and *Guo Yu* or the *Conversations of the States*, 'seem generally to designate the ruling or presiding anthropomorphic ... Imperial Heaven Supreme Emperor' (Fung, 1952: 31). The actual process of how Heaven became the 'Ruler' will probably always be a matter of dispute. However it is probably reasonable for us to assume that Heaven as a natural deity (Sky God) of the Zhou tribe was transformed into the supreme ruler of the Zhou Dynasty, partly in its association with the anthropomorphic character, *Di*, or *Shangdi*, the Supreme Lord of the Shang Dynasty, which is now believed to have derived its corporate or generic dimension from an early conception of the 'fathers' of a lineage. *Di* or *Shangdi* was continually revered as the Supreme Lord during the first years of the Zhou Dynasty, until it was realised that belief in the Lord would be 'a dangerous antagonist and potential rallying point for the Shang opposition' (Franz, 1986: 27). Political needs accelerated the process of promoting Heaven to the highest rank in the spiritual world and merging Heaven and the Lord in a manner most acceptable to the people. Hence a new title for the spiritual Supreme Ruler, *huangtian shangdi*, the August/Imperial Heaven the Lord on High, became the focus of religious and political practices. Heaven was depicted as an all-powerful, supreme, purposive administrator or ruler of the universe, ruling over and judging all the human and natural affairs throughout time and space. Many Confucian writings strengthened and reconfirmed the supremacy of Heaven. The speech supposed to have been made by the founding father of the Shang Dynasty, Tang, condemned the last ruler of the Xia Dynasty, and claimed that 'Heaven has given me the mandate to destroy him'; and one of his ministers announced that 'Heaven gives birth to the people' (see also Legge, 1992, vol. 3: 173–4, 178). Heaven is said not only to possess the divine executioner, but '[f]or each of Heaven's affairs there is its proper official' (Fung, 1952: 30). The favour or ire of Heaven became the foundation for the extremely important conception of the Mandate of Heaven (*tianming*), which legitimises or disqualifies the taking over of one dynasty by another or the execution of the royal power to crush rebellions. Heaven would make known its approval or otherwise of human affairs by manifesting blessings or condemnations in the form of, for instance, good harvests or natural disasters. This was developed into a sophisticated doctrine during the Han Dynasty that failure to fulfil human duties would annoy Heaven, and Heaven would first warn and then reprimand him by sending down the visitations (*zai*) and prodigies (*yi*) 'to warn the human sovereign of his behaviour, to command him to repent on his wrongdoing and to cultivate his virtue' (*Baihutong Shuzheng*, 1994: 267).

The destiny of a dynasty depended upon the continuing blessings from Heaven, as elaborated by the Confucian sage, the Duke of Zhou, who is credited with the completion of this system that was simultaneously moral, political and religious:

> Heaven, without pity, sent down ruin on the Yin Dynasty
> (1384–1112 BC). Yin having lost the Mandate of Heaven, we,
> the Chou, have received it. But I dare not say with certainty that our
> heritage will forever truly remain on the side of fortune. If Heaven
> renders sincere help, I do not dare say with certainty that the final
> end will result in misfortune. (Chan, 1963a: 6)

Confucians firmly believe that it is essential for any new Dynasty to have received the Mandate from Heaven, and that the preservation of the Mandate is a necessary condition for a dynasty to continue its rule. Any political change could be justified only if it was recognised as what had been 'decreed' by Heaven, and the replacement of one dynasty by another was only possible if it had been blessed by Heaven. Many of Confucius' references to Heaven point to the supreme being who controls the world and determines the destiny of human affairs, because 'Heaven is the greatest in the world' (*Lunyu*, 8: 19). The *Book of Rites* confirms that sacrifice to Heaven is essential for peace and harmony of the state. The spirit will return to Heaven upon death. Dong Zhongshu drew us a picture of Heaven as human ancestor and creator, and in this sense, Fung Yu-lan's comments that for Dong 'Heaven, while possessing cognition and consciousness, is definitely not an anthropomorphic deity' (Fung, 1953: 19), probably overlook the spiritual dimension of Heaven in Dong's discussion of the Way of Heaven. It is clear that Dong considered Heaven 'the most spiritual' and 'the Lord of all gods' (*Chunqiu Fanlu Yizheng*, 1992: 354, 402); he believed that Heaven was the great-grandfather of all humans: 'Humans cannot produce themselves, because the creator of humans is Heaven. That humans are humans derives from Heaven. Heaven, indeed, is the great-grandfather of humans (*zeng zufu*)' (*Chunqiu Fanlu Yizheng*, 1992: 318). As the great ancestor of humans, Heaven is believed to have constructed human life and endowed humans with their nature. As the 'creator' of humans, Heaven is believed to regulate the way of humans and 'commands humans to practise humaneness and righteousness, to be ashamed of what is shameful, and not to be concerned, like the birds and beasts, solely with existence and profit' (*ibid.*: 61).

Heaven is not only the creator of life, the supreme governor of the universe, but also a just administrator of human affairs. Heaven is revered not for the deliverance rewarded to those who have prayed for it. Rather, Heaven is revered and respected with awe in the sense that Heaven is regarded as the final sanction of human behaviour and social changes. For a fixed period, human efforts may succeed or fail, a particular action may or may not be justified, and the character of an individual may or may not be recognised. However, with faith in Heaven in which the final sanction is upheld, the failure of a particular person at a particular time does not frustrate a Confucian to the extent that he abandons his goals. Wrongdoing and violation of moral principles which for the time being cannot be corrected and punished are believed to be eventually corrected and punished by Heaven which is closely 'watching' and passionately concerned with the world below. It is therefore regarded as the most serious crime to offend Heaven or to violate the Way of Heaven. Confucius made it clear that 'He who offends against Heaven has none to whom he can pray' (*Lunyu*, 3: 13). He subsequently believed it to be a devastating fate for an individual to be abandoned by Heaven. This point is illustrated in the following anecdote. Confucius once paid a visit to the notorious court lady Nanzi, and one of his disciples was not pleased. Although Confucius felt that there was nothing inappropriate in his behaviour, he realised that this might be open to serious misinterpretation. In order to clear his name, Confucius invoked Heaven to make a solemn declaration that 'If I have done anything wrong, may Heaven forsake me! May Heaven forsake me!' (*Lunyu*, 6: 28). In this way, Confucius again emphasised the supremacy of Heaven as the religious sanction for human integrity, and showed confidence in the justice of Heaven.

Confucianism directed traditional spiritual belief in Heaven into rational and moral directions. Heaven is not treated merely as a passive sanction or guardian, but more positively as the initiator of virtues. It is believed that the Way of Heaven generates the moral power in human beings. When faced with the danger of being killed, Confucius put his faith in Heaven and gained freedom from fear: 'Heaven has begot the virtue that is in me. What have I to fear from such a man as Huan Dui?' (*Lunyu*, 7: 22). A strong sense of mission that issues from Heaven gives Confucius confidence in the transmission of ancient wisdom and culture. When asked why people did not understand what he had been teaching, Confucius emphasised the fulfilling of one's own mission that was endowed by Heaven: 'I do not complain against Heaven nor do I lay the blame on other people. I study things on the lower level but my understanding penetrates the higher. It is Heaven who knows me' (*Lunyu*, 14: 37). This paragraph contains a number of very important Confucian tenets. Firstly, Confucian confidence in the course of human life and its optimism about the future are grounded firmly in faith in Heaven. The Confucian view of the world and human affairs is inspired by belief in Heaven's justice that governs the world and beyond, and by the Confucian belief in personal fate that the courses of life or death, wealth or poverty, success or failure, depend upon Heaven. For them, whether or not their efforts are recognised or praised by others is of little concern. What matters is whether or not they have done their best to fulfil their duties. Secondly, the Way of Heaven can be known through studying human affairs (things on the lower level), and the study of human life is thus the path to understanding the Way of Heaven (principles on the higher level). Thirdly, Heaven is the final judge of individuals and of their values and merits. With faith in the Ultimate, individuals would not be blown off course by their successes and failures in the world.

As the supreme being with the power to sanction moral behaviour, Heaven naturally becomes the centre of gravity in Confucian theories and practices with regard to religion, politics, ethics, history, literature and the way of life. Confucians are determined to fulfil their mission in the world for they believe that '[t]hose who are obedient to Heaven are preserved; those who are against Heaven are annihilated' (*Mengzi*, 4A: 7). Thus they devote their life to learning, education and the transmission of ancient culture because of their belief in the Mandate of Heaven which can be known through learning, divination and observation (*Lunyu*, 7: 22; 14: 36; 12: 5; 2: 4).

HEAVEN AND MORAL PRINCIPLES

The conception of Heaven as the Supreme Being is closely related to the understanding of Heaven as a set of moral principles (*yili zhi tian*). As a matter of fact, these two aspects are the two closely related sides of Confucian doctrine: Heaven is supreme because it is the embodiment and source of moral virtues, and Heaven can generate and bring out illustrious virtues (in humans) because it is the ultimate principle of transcendence. The close relationship between its moral and its transcendental implications distinguishes Heaven as the Confucian Ultimate from the God of theistic traditions. The Way of Heaven lies primarily in the moral path which people lead in their life. Heaven endows humans with the Mandate, by which the world can be ruled justly. Just rule can be exercised only if the people are satisfied in a moral way. Endowing or withdrawing the Mandate is a matter of moral judgement. Thus, in Confucian politics, the Mandate of Heaven is understood to be the same as the will of the people, by which the legitimacy of a government is given and confirmed. Heaven's generating power is understood as 'conferring' on the people their [moral] nature, so that they can follow and develop the Way from their own nature in a variety of ways. As Heaven embodied in human nature is identified with the Way, cultivation of the Way becomes the source of Confucian doctrine and instruction (*jiao*). It is believed that instruction and education of this kind will lead to goodness, truth and perfection in general, and to personal integrity and sincerity, family loyalty and responsibility, communal reciprocity and sound commonsense in particular. Having only a short span of life and for most part living in a chaotic environment, individuals are not always able to be confident in their destiny. It is the Way of Heaven that gives Confucians an assurance of attaining the Ultimate. In a sense, the attainment of the Ultimate in a Confucian context means to attain to secure the infinite and sacred ideal in a life that is finite, historical, secular and cultural.

Confucians believe that Heaven and its relation to the earth set up a model for, and lay down the principles of, human moral codes. For example, just as Heaven is above and the earth below, so too the sovereign is placed over his ministers and subjects, parents over their children, and a husband over his wife. It is believed that of all creatures born from the refined essence of Heaven and Earth, the human race is the noblest because we alone are able to practise heavenly principles in our life and behave according to proper relationships either at home or abroad. Among humans, only those who have cultivated their nature revere the Mandate of Heaven, while those who lack virtue do not respect it.

The Way of Heaven signifies morality, and to follow the Way of Heaven is to lead a virtuous life. Mengzi believes that there are two kinds of honours, the honours bestowed by Heaven (e.g. humaneness, righteousness, sincerity, etc.), and the honours bestowed by humans (e.g. positions and ranks in the government). The former should be sought after first and the latter will follow as a matter of course (*Mengzi*, 6A: 16), and in this manner, the Way of Heaven would prevail in the world. Contrary to this, however, the people pursued the mundane honours first, and therefore lost the honour of Heaven. Neo-Confucians developed the moral conception of Heaven and applied the Way of Heaven to daily life. Heaven is sometimes identified with the (moral) principle (*li*), hence the Principle of Heaven (*tianli*) becomes another name for the Way of Heaven. On other occasions, Heaven is identified with the (innate) heart/mind, hence the Way of Heaven is nowhere but in the heart/mind. The principle of Heaven cannot be understood unless the heart/mind has been extended; and an individual cannot become one body with Heaven unless he has explored his own nature (Chan, 1963b: 13). In different ways, Heaven, the Way of Heaven, principle, nature and the heart/mind are regarded as being essentially the same, as Cheng Yi put it: 'What is received by man and things from Heaven are called destiny. What is inherent in things is called principle. What is endowed in man is called nature. And as the master of the body it is called the mind. In reality they are all one' (Chan, 1963a: 567). This is what Heaven is and this is how the Way of Heaven runs its course.

HEAVEN AS NATURE OR NATURAL LAW

Heaven as the anthropomorphic divine ruler and as the embodiment and generator of supreme virtues is the key to understanding the Confucian way of Heaven. However, there is also a naturalistic dimension with respect to the Confucian Ultimate in which Heaven is primarily taken as Nature, and the Way of Heaven as something similar to Natural Law. The concept of Nature and Natural Law is an important constituent element of the Confucian doctrine of Heaven, and is one of the underlying ideas of Confucian rationalism. As we will see in the third section of this chapter, the concept of Heaven as Nature leads to the harmony between human beings and their environment.

Although Confucius spoke of Heaven as that which determined the course of human life and which produced the illustrious virtues in him himself, he also seems to have indicated that the Way of Heaven is manifest in natural courses which should be followed. When asked why he did not speak out, Confucius pointed out that transmission of the ancient culture did not need speech, as silent Heaven ran its course by its law rather than by its words: 'What does Heaven ever say? Yet there are the four seasons going round and there are the hundred things coming into being' (*Lunyu*, 17: 19). In *Kongzi Jiayu* or the *School Sayings of Confucius*, compiled in the Later Han Dynasty, Confucius is recorded as having made the following statements about the Way of Heaven:

> As the sun and the moon from East to West succeed each other without cease, such is the Way of Heaven. To be able to last without hindrance, that is the Way of Heaven. That without interference all things are accomplished, that is the Way of Heaven. That, once they are completed, they are clarified by it, that is the Way of Heaven.
>
> (Kramers, 1950: 215)

The majority of Confucians focus their attention on the Way of Humans but do not exclude the Way of Nature. The early Daoist philosophers take people as an extension of Nature and call them to return to

149

their origins, that is, to be one with nature and to follow the way of nature. Because these Daoists were preoccupied with the Way of Nature and had little to say about the distinction of the human way, Xunzi criticised them by pointing out that Zhuangzi 'was blinded by Nature and was insensible to men' (*Xunzi*, 21: 4; Knoblock, 1994: 102). Xunzi nevertheless developed the conception of Heaven as Nature within the Confucian tradition: 'The constellations follow their revolutions; the sun and moon alternately shine; the four seasons present themselves in succession; the Yin and Yang enlarge and transform; and the wind and rain spread out everywhere' (Knoblock, 1994: 15). This opened up a Confucian trend in which a naturalistic understanding of the world and of human beings was developed and extended.

Naturalistic Confucians take Heaven as the ultimate source of human life, i.e., Heaven is the force behind all the diversity and variety resulting from constant and regular changes. Therefore, Natural Law in a Confucian context is the principle of constant changes, by which all things are given life and all events run their course. This is what is meant by the Way of Heaven in the commentaries of the *Book of Changes*. The greatest virtue of Heaven and Earth is said to be in its constant production, because change (*yi*) is a process of production and reproduction (*shengsheng*). Thus the Way is the interaction between the *yin* and the *yang*: 'The successive movement of yin and yang constitutes the Way', and this statement is understood in the later Confucian development as meaning that 'The nature [of humans] and the Way of Heaven are but Change' (Chan, 1963a: 268, 266, 506). The Way of Heaven is in the change of the two cosmic forces and the change is the primary power motivating all changes and developments. Identifying Heaven as the fundamental principle for human existence and activity, Dong Zhongshu made good use of the yin–yang doctrine to explain human nature and destiny, pointing out that humans have within them nature and feelings because the *yin* and the *yang* exist in Heaven (*Chunqiu Fanlu Yizheng*, 1992: 299). Wang Chong developed this understanding to an extremely naturalistic view and made it clear that 'the Way of Heaven is that of spontaneity', that is, the yang and yin arise and decline in the four seasons and things themselves reach maturity. This is the meaning of his phrase: 'The Way of Heaven is one of non-activity' (Fung, 1953: 152–3). The understanding that the Way of Heaven is the Way of spontaneity was accepted and further developed in the Mysterious Learning of the Wei–Jin Dynasties and in Neo-Confucianism of the Song–Ming Dynasties. One of the Neo-Confucian masters, Cheng Hao, once remarked: 'What is spontaneous in Heaven is called the Way (*Tao*) of Heaven. Heaven's allotment of this to all creatures is called the Decree (*ming*, Mandate) of Heaven' (*ibid.*: 514).

As the origin of the universe, Heaven is identified with *taiji*, the Supreme Ultimate, the fountainhead from which all things come into being. The Great Commentary (*dazhuan*) of the *Book of Changes* first speculates on the Supreme Ultimate in the system of changes. The Supreme Ultimate generates the Two Modes, the yin and yang. The Two Modes generate the Four Forms (the major and minor yin and yang, which become the four seasons). The Four Forms generate the Eight Trigrams which represent heaven, earth, mountain, lake, fire, water, thunder and wind (Wilhelm, 1967: 318). The mutual interaction between the Way of Heaven and the Way of Earth (*gangrou xiangmo*) and between the Eight Trigrams (*bagua xiangdang*) generates all beings and things (Zhang, 1982: 27). The outline of the cosmic evolution in the *Book of Changes* was enriched in Neo-Confucianism, and Zhou Dunyi formulated an inclusive doctrine of the Way of Heaven based on the conception of the Supreme Ultimate. The origin of the universe (*wuji*, the Ultimate of Non-Existence) manifests itself as the origin of the existence (*taiji*, the Supreme Ultimate). The activity and tranquillity of the Supreme Ultimate generate the yang and the yin, two forms of the cosmic power from which the Five Elements arise. In the integration of the Supreme Ultimate, yin–yang and the Five Elements, the Way of Heaven and the Way of Earth, feminine and masculine forces come into being, and the inter-action between these two forces engenders the myriad things. The myriad things produce and reproduce, resulting in unending transformation (Chan, 1963a: 463).

Heaven as Nature is closely related to the conception of *qi*, the vital material force. In early Confucian writings, the concept is not clearly defined, as demonstrated in the *Mengzi* where the night force (*yeqi*) and the moral force (*haoran zhi qi*) are discussed. Only in the works of the Later Han scholars, He Xiu (129–182), Zheng Xuan and Liu Shao (182?–245?) was the concept of *qi* used unambiguously to refer to the profound and fundamental material force of the universe. He Xiu said that 'The origin (*yuan*) is material force (*qi*)', Zheng Xuan interpreted the Supreme Ultimate as the material force that was in total harmony and not yet diversified, and Liu Shao understood that the universe came from the original One (*yuan yi*) that is material force (Zhang, 1982: 41). The Confucian doctrine of material force was completed in the hands of Zhang Zai. Zhang identified Heaven with the Great Vacuity (*tai xu*) that is the original state of material force, the Way of Heaven with the Great Harmony (*tai he*) and the Mandate of Heaven with the ceaseless operation in material force (*qi*). He stated that

> The Great Vacuity (hsü) has no physical form. It is the original substance of material force . . . As the Great Vacuity, material force is extensive and vague. Yet it ascends and descends and moves in all ways without ever ceasing . . . If material force integrates, its visibility becomes effective and physical form appears. If material force does not integrate, its visibility is not effective and there is no physical form . . . From the Great Vacuity, there is Heaven. From the transformation of material force, there is the Way. In the unity of the Great Vacuity and material force, there is the nature of (man and things). And in the unity of the nature and consciousness, there is the mind.
>
> (Chan, 1963a: 501, 503, 504)

Zhang also explored the way of material force. Material force changes according to the law of nature: 'In the process of production, some (things) come first and some afterward. This is Heaven's sequence. In the inter-relationship and assumption of shape (by those things), some are small and some large, some lofty and some lowly. This is Heaven's orderliness' (Fung, 1953: 482). Therefore, the cosmic evolution is the process of integration and disintegration of material force, and this is done in accordance with Heaven's sequence (*tian xu*) and orderliness (*tian zhi*). The heavenly order and sequence of material force is the Way of Heaven. As far as human nature is concerned, heavenly principle and material force point to two different directions, and human moral characters can be explained by the difference of their material constitution. According to this interpretation, material force has its gender, the *yin* and the *yang*. The *yin* and *yang* powers flow in their ways, so there are the four seasons; they move in different directions, so there are the Five Elements (*wu xing*). In a similar manner Wang Fuzhi maintains that the heart/mind, nature, Heaven and principle are all based on material force, and without material force 'none of them would exist'. Heaven is nothing other than the total-ity of the yin–yang and the Five Elements, and the Way of Heaven is the order of material force: 'Split apart, we call them the *yin* and *yang* and

Five Elements, inasmuch as they consist of two (major) divisions and five (lesser) parts. But in the totality we call them all Heaven' (*ibid.*: 641–2). Dai Zhen (1723–77) believes that *yin-yang* and the Five Elements possess each other, and their mutual transformation is the Way of Heaven: 'The *yin* and *yang* and Five Elements constitute the true substance of the *Tao* [Way]' (*ibid.*: 653).

The Way of Heaven is that which natural courses follow and by which all things are done. Therefore, it is equivalent to the Confucian conception of principle, and Heaven and principle are used together to indicate the Way of Heaven (*tian li*). The commentaries in the *Book of Changes* identified Principle with Heaven, and the study of Principle with the attainment of the Mandate of Heaven: 'By the exhaustive study of Principle (*li*) and complete development of the nature, one attains to (Heavenly) Decree' (*ibid.*: 650). In the *Book of Rites*, the passage that 'Heaven gives birth to the people' is reinterpreted as meaning that 'All things originate from Heaven, humans originate from their ancestors' and the major sacrifices are 'to express gratitude toward the originators and recall the beginnings' (Legge, 1968, vol. 27: 430–1). Either as Nature or Natural Law, Heaven and the Way of Heaven underlie human life and are therefore closely related to the Way of Humankind.

The Way of Humans

Confucianism is sometimes described as a kind of secular humanism on the grounds that it does not pay sufficient attention to the spiritual dimension. It is indeed the case that Confucianism is first concerned with life rather than death and with humans rather than with spirits. However, it does not follow that the Confucian understanding of the self is totally preoccupied with secularity and temporality. For many Confucians, the self is endowed with a transcendental 'spirit', which if fully developed would enable one to be a co-ordinator of the world, a guardian of natural and social processes, and a partner in the creative transformation of Heaven and Earth. The close relationship between the metaphysical or transcendental Way and secular human life is demonstrated in the first paragraph of *the Doctrine of the Mean*: 'What Heaven imparts to humans is called human nature. To follow our nature is called the Way. Cultivating the Way is called education. The Way cannot be separated from us for a moment. What can be separated from us is not the Way' (Chan, 1963a: 98).

The Way of Humans is essentially the way of moral life, and that is why it is said that in human terms the Way is called humaneness and righteousness. For most Confucian scholars, Heaven is the source of a meaningful life and has provided human beings with the virtuous roots or beginnings of humaneness, righteousness, propriety and wisdom. However, this does not mean that all individuals are predetermined to follow a good course. Whether or not the roots can grow into the great tree of humanity and whether or not the beginnings can be fully developed, depend essentially upon whether or not, and how, humans preserve their heart/mind and cultivate their character. The Way of Heaven cannot be fulfilled unless it has been understood as the human way and consciously carried out by individuals in everyday life. Admitting that Heaven, Earth and humanity are the three Ultimates of the universe, Confucians believe that humans must fulfil their duties to qualify for this role: 'For Heaven there is the Way of Heaven, for Earth there is the Way of Earth, and for man there is the way of man. Unless man fully practices the Way of man, he will not be qualified to coexist with Heaven and Earth' (Lu Jiuyuan, in Chan, 1963a: 575). In exploring how the Way of Heaven and the Way of Humans are related and how the former can be manifest in the latter, Confucians are not interested in the opposition between this world and the next, or between salvation and damnation. Rather, they focus on closing the distance between the human and the non-human, or more precisely, between those who have been instructed in proper behaviour and those who have not, and therefore Confucians establish education and self-cultivation as the centre of the Human Way. The necessity for self-cultivation follows from the fact that the potentiality within individuals that enables them to be finally differentiated from birds and beasts is yet to be developed and cultivated as actual qualities of their character. To cultivate this potential is firstly to preserve it. To preserve it, that is, to fully develop original moral senses, is to become fully human, while to abandon or neglect it is to have a deficient character which is not far from that of an animal.

It is a Confucian belief that Heaven endows human beings with the sense of, and concern with, the transmission of culture, by which we search for the ultimate meaning of life. The Way of Heaven must be cultivated in personal experience and social interchange. The will of Heaven to preserve **this culture** (*si wen*) (*Lunyu*, 9: 5) animates the moral tradition and gives it a cosmological significance on the one hand, and 'imposes' a mission on human beings to carry out what is hidden in this culture on the other hand.

MORALITY AS TRANSCENDENCE

Confucianism is not a purely secular tradition. It has a profound sense of religiosity and spirituality. As a religious humanism, Confucianism identifies the moral or virtuous with the religious or transcendental. To discuss the Way of human beings, therefore, we must start with a moral concept, *de* (德). Although translatable as 'virtue', *de* originally signifies a political and spiritual quality or ability, which was the 'power' or 'charisma' by which a king could rule the state without resorting to force or violence. In this sense, *de* as virtue is defined as 'to obtain' (*de*, 得), and a virtuous man is one who is able to 'obtain' the endorsement of Heaven and the ancestors, to get the capable ministers to support him and the people to work for the state. Initially, offering sacrifices to Heaven and the ancestors was believed to be of the greatest significance for earning the legitimacy and 'power' to rule. Gradually, out of this practice evolved the understanding that the ability and power must also be cultivated by individuals, and thus *de* became 'a moral-making property of a person' that is able to give the person 'psychic power or influence over others, and sometimes even over one's nonhuman surroundings' (Nivison, 1996: 17). To illustrate the process of how the meaning of *de* was extended from 'power' to 'moral virtue', Norden and Nivison point out that

> Humans typically feel gratitude for gifts. However, in some societies, this feeling becomes magnified, so that my gratitude to you comes to seem like a force you exert over me. *De* was originally this 'force', which the Chinese kings acquired through their willingness to make 'sacrifices' to the spirits of their ancestors and for their subjects. However, there is an important difference between a gift given sincerely, and one given with the intention of gaining control over another. Consequently, *de* became connected with humility, generosity, and (in general) the 'virtues'.   (Nivison, 1996: 5–6)

Based on the understanding of the nature and source of the political power, Confucians believe that a good ruler is the one who cultivates his character sincerely, performs rituals reverentially, and accumulates good deeds earnestly. A king who failed to fulfil his duties, for instance deliberately ignoring or violating the rules of ritual, or abusing the political or military powers, would be regarded as one who had lost his virtue which in turn caused him to lose the power and ability to govern. In this way, virtue and rituals (*li*) are closely related and mutually supporting. Further, since the endorsement of Heaven, the ancestors and the spirits are seen in the harmony, peace and order of the state, community and family, rituals are not only oriented to the other world but also morally directed and guided. Religious rituals are thus transformed into rules of behaviour and a sense of propriety in their widest application. These are needed not only at the time of making sacrifices but also in daily life, and are considered necessary not only for one's status as a king or an official but also for anyone's destiny as a particular being. In this way the rules of propriety become what Jaspers calls the 'imperatives of conduct' (1962: 55). The external observance of the rules is further internalised as a moral quality, and practice outwardly exercised becomes an inwardly spiritual journey. This is how the moral and the ethical in the Confucian tradition have gained the significance of the religious and the transcendental.

Virtue is not only a quality, but also an ability to transform oneself and a power to transform others. As the wind sways the grass, a person of virtue is believed to be able to lead the masses in the direction of the morally good. To be a person of virtue is thus no longer the privilege of a ruler or a superior minister. It has become a necessary condition for a personal transition from a crude and uncivilised being to a cultivated and civilised person, or from a being of sensation to a person of virtue. This is considered a person's own responsibility, because whether or not one would be such a person depends on oneself, not on others. Self-cultivation is thus understood as the fundamental path to the spiritual transformation of one's character. By the interaction between the macrocosm and the microcosm, the transformation of one's own character is believed to fulfil the transformation of the cosmos and society.

In self-cultivation it is one's own will that leads. The difficulty in becoming cultivated and then attaining to the ideal comes firstly from our natural weaknesses, for example, from preferring sexual enjoyment to moral transformation, as Confucius observed (*Lunyu*, 9: 18), or being less inspired to pursue learning than to seek the satisfaction of physical desires, as Mengzi warned. Such a difficulty may also result from our social vulnerability in a bad environment. To guard against corruption, Confucianism in the main highly values the preservation of our own nature and the pursuit of righteousness in social interaction. In this respect the heart/mind plays an active part in Confucian self-transformation. It is believed that when the moral and spiritual propensity inherent in human nature is frustrated by the complex of external causes, the heart/mind will be corrupted. While it is important to remove these causes (this is why Confucianism takes it as its first responsibility to participate in political life and to reform social structure), most Confucians insist that the social causes of human corruption cannot be completely removed unless most individuals have cultivated their own nature and made their own character correct and righteous. For them, it is more urgent to start working on one's own nature by engaging in self-cultivation than to blame others or external circumstances for one's failure. The Confucian discourses on the self probe at a deeper level into each individual's moral psychology. They hold individuals to be responsible for their own future and encourage them to search in their own heart/mind for the resource of becoming good, believing that 'Seek and you will get it; let go and you will lose it. Thus seeking is of use to getting and what is sought is within yourself' (*Mengzi*, 7A: 3).

The Confucian discussions of human nature and heart/mind are directly related to their concern about human destiny. This concern is not about the life in the other world, but about the life fulfilled in this world, not about the possibility of salvation from without but about the process of self-transformation or self-transcendence through moral cultivation and social engagement. The question 'how to become good' in the Confucian tradition becomes as resourceful and profound as the question 'how to be saved' in many other religious traditions. In this sense, the search for the morally perfect is also the search for a 'transcendental breakthrough', breaking through one's moral limitations as an ordinary human being. In the process of searching for the breakthrough, the mainstream in the Confucian tradition exhibits its religious idealism in the following three dimensions.

Firstly, it believes that we have the sources and resources of becoming good within ourselves. Many Confucians believe that Heaven endows us with a heart of the Way (*daoxin*), which is subtle but entangled with our physical needs. The heart of the Way provides the foundation for us to be good, and the power and will to search for our own destinies. Within each individual there is also a 'human heart (*renxin*)', which desires and seeks the satisfaction of physical needs. This human heart provides individuals with the materials to be worked on.

Secondly, it holds that human beings have the ability to know how to become good. The Way of Heaven manifests itself in nature, society and individuals. Therefore, there are two methods for us to find out how we can be in line with the Way of Heaven. One is to observe the principles by which everything exists and every being lives. For example, through observing the growing and withering of plants and trees, we can understand the regularity and punctuality of the heavenly principle and understand the importance of abiding by ritual/propriety in human community. The other way is to contemplate on our own heart/mind. Since all the people have in their hearts/minds the resources to become good, reflection and meditation on the internal world will enable us to fully understand our internal potential and to make maximum use of it.

Thirdly, for the majority of Confucian scholars, observation and meditation alone cannot fulfil one's destiny, unless one has fully mastered the classics and lived by the rules of propriety in daily life, so that in every intention and in every action there is nothing other than that which is in full agreement with the Way of Heaven. Such an achievement as this enables a person to 'follow whatever his heart desires, but never go beyond the boundaries [of the Way]' (*Lunyu*, 2: 4), to 'order and adjust the great relations of mankind, establish the great foundations of humanity and know the transforming and nourishing operations of Heaven and Earth' (Chan, 1963a: 112), 'to know and serve Heaven' (*Mengzi*, 7A; 1), and to 'regard that which fills the universe as his own body, and consider that which directs the universe as his own nature' (Zhang Zai, see Chan, 1963a: 497). This is what is meant by 'the transcendental' in the Confucian tradition.

In the Confucian conception of transcendence there is no call for an escape from the world, nor to seek an extraordinary style of life. In the perspective of the possibility of being transformed and cultivated in everyday life, Confucianism establishes its optimism and confidence in human destiny on a solid ground, and by bringing individuals' growth in line with cosmic evolution, Confucians locate their concept of immortality (*buxiu*). The Confucian view of immortality was greatly influenced by a conversation which took place in the year 546 BCE and which defined 'immortality' as the lasting effect of virtue, words and works: 'The best course is to establish virtue, the next best is to establish achievement, and still the next best is to establish words. When these are not abandoned with time, it may be called immortality' (*ibid.*: 13). Based on this understanding, Confucians identify 'immortality' with sagehood. In the Confucian view, the world is not divided between good and evil, heaven and hell, but between the civilised and the barbarian, the learned and the ignorant, the cultivated and the uncultivated. Life as a whole is a process of development from the latter to the former, the goal of which is to become a sage.

The Chinese character for sage, sheng (聖), presents a pictographic understanding that a person of achievement would 'listen' more than speak. The sage 'listens' to the calling from Heaven, 'listens' to the demands of the people, and 'listens' to the 'rhythm' of the natural world, so that he can reproduce the Heavenly principles in terms of human codes, and guide human activities by his wisdom. A sage is believed to have manifested the greatest virtue which corresponds to Heaven and to have been given the blessing of Heaven. For example, Shun, the sage–king of legend, is praised for his great filial piety and virtue, which earned him not only his position (the Son of Heaven, the King), but also wealth and a long life:

> The admirable, amiable prince displayed conspicuously his excellent virtue. He put his people and his officers in concord. And he received his emolument from Heaven. It protected him, assisted him, and appointed him king. And Heaven's blessing came again and again.
>
> (Chan, 1963a: 102)

A sage is morally perfect and intellectually brilliant, and in carrying out the Way of Heaven in the human world he 'extensively confers benefit on the people and sends relief to all' (*Lunyu*, 6: 30). The sage has made the tradition living and everlasting:

> Chung-ni (Confucius) transmitted the ancient traditions of Yao and Shun, and he modeled after and made brilliant the system of King Wen and King Wu. He conformed with the natural order governing the revolution of the seasons in heaven above, and followed the principles governing land and water below.   (Chan, 1963a: 111–12)

He has brought the greatest benefits to the world, established an immortal influence and bequeathed an admirable model to all people of all generations. This is borne out by a widely held saying that 'Had Heaven not sent Confucius into this world, the history of ten thousand years would have been in eternal darkness' (*tian busheng Zhongni, wangu ru changye*). A sage as such becomes one of the three powers sustaining the whole universe and assisting the transformation of the universe. Being able to fully develop his own nature, the sage can likewise develop the nature of all beings and all things; being able to develop the nature of all things and beings, he can assist the transforming and nourishing powers of Heaven and Earth; and being able to assist the transforming and nourishing powers of Heaven and Earth, he can thus 'form a trinity with Heaven and Earth' (Chan, 1963a: 108). In this achievement the sage is identified completely with Heaven and Earth, and being in the unity and oneness with Heaven and Earth the sage demonstrates in his own life their eternal and transcendental nature.

GOOD AND EVIL

Based on the understanding of the Way of Heaven and its relation to the Way of Humans, Confucians come to deal with the problem of good and evil. Fundamental to their belief is that the Way of Heaven is right and violation of the Way is wrong, and that what issues from the Way is good and what obstructs the prevalence of the Way is bad. Most Confucians take the view that evil (*e* 惡) is not a metaphysical concept, because 'what is called evil is not original evil' (Chan, 1963a: 529). That is to say, the Confucian conception of evil does not denote a metaphysical or ontological reality. It is simply a moral concept, designating a kind of moral situation in which the moral and physical activities of a human being are conducted in a wrong way.

Good and evil are considered to be a pair of terms for the moral character of an individual. As all individuals are believed to be able to become good, a natural question that follows is whether they can be good because they already have all the potentialities within or they can become good because they are guided by the rules of propriety and by the instructions of the sage. The Confucian debate about these two options was inaugurated by Xunzi in his argument against Mengzi, and these two options lead to two different theories concerning human nature.

Believing that good is fundamental and evil is the deviation from good, Mengzi insists that human beings are born with goodness, in goodness and for goodness, and that this is as clear as the natural tendency of water to flow downwards and the natural tendency of a tree to grow upwards. As Mengzi presumes that humans are originally good, then where does evil come from? Mengzi answered this question by giving three reasons why a good nature could give way to evil. Firstly, the nature (*xing*) with which we are born has only provided the beginning or potentiality for us to do good, but not all individuals will develop from the beginning or can fully realise their potentiality. In other words, the evil that exists in individuals' character is due to the non-development or non-completion of their innate nature. Secondly, the innate goodness is fragile, and being subject to erosion by external influences, needs to be preserved and cultivated. In his famous metaphor of the Bull Mountain, Mengzi explained how this could happen: the trees on the mountain were once beautiful. But being too near to the capital of a great state, they were hewn down ... even so, nourished by the rain and dew and with the force of growth operating day and night, the stumps sent forth fresh sprouts. But soon cattle and sheep came to browse on them, and in the end the mountain became completely bare. Seeing it thus, people would now imagine that it had never been wooded. According to Mengzi, however, the nature of the mountain was beautifully wooded, and bareness was only the consequence of having being lopped and browsed on. Following the same logic, he argued that the nature of all human beings contained innate goodness, and that some of them became bad or evil because they had been deprived of their 'natural growth' (*Mengzi*, 6A: 8). Thirdly, Mengzi argued that we are ourselves responsible for most of our failure to become fully good. Subject to the same influence, some people become good and even become sages, while others are degenerate. The key lies in whether they retain their good heart/mind or let it go. Very little distinguishes a human person from an animal. If one loses that, one will behave like a beast. As Confucius once remarked: 'Hold on to it and it will remain; let go of it and it will disappear' (quoted in *Mengzi*, 6A: 8). Therefore, to regain one's good heart, one must look after it. Mengzi deplored that having lost chickens and dogs, people would go after them; but having lost their good heart, they were not at all concerned. In this sense, he believed that the Confucian way was nothing but seeking the lost heart (*Mengzi*, 6A: 11). He concludes that evil is none other than underdevelopment, deprivation, degradation and non-completion of our original good nature. Whatever erosion or corruption one may suffer, one's original goodness cannot be totally eradicated. Learning and education would be sufficient to help one seek the lost heart, and by natural growth and conscious cultivation its original goodness could be restored.

Xunzi challenged Mengzi by maintaining that goodness did not exist innately in human nature: 'The nature of man is evil; his goodness is the result of his activity' (Chan, 1963a: 128). The difference in their doctrines of human nature comes from their different understandings of the nature of Heaven. Following the thesis that Heaven is the source of virtue and moral sanction of behaviour, Mengzi reasons that humans are innately oriented towards the good. However, based on the naturalistic doctrine that Heaven is no more than Nature or Natural Law, Xunzi argues that human beings are born with natural instincts which, if not guided and controlled, will cause bad behaviour and jeopardise social justice and communal interests. For example, human beings love profits by nature and when they continue this tendency, bitter conflicts and inordinate greed increases, whereas propriety and righteousness disappears. Human beings are naturally envious and hateful, and when they follow this tendency, injuries and destruction increase, whereas loyalty and faithfulness disappear: 'The strong would injure the weak and rob them, the many would do violence to the few and shout them down. The whole world would be in violence and disorder and all would perish in an instant' (*ibid.*: 131–2). Thus, Xunzi believes that we are born with bad tendencies rather than an inclination to morality. For Xunzi our so-called 'inborn nature' is something that is not acquired by learning and practice, while moral qualities are what we have to pursue and practise. Propriety and righteousness are not innate in us. Rather, they are created by sages to restrict human nature: humans naturally desire to eat when hungry, while propriety requires them to serve their elders first; humans naturally desire rest when exhausted, while righteousness requires them to relieve others first: 'If one follows his natural feeling, he will have no deference or compliance. Deference and compliance are opposed to his natural feeling. From this point of view, it is clear that man's nature is evil and that his goodness is the result of his activity' (Chan, 1963a: 129–30).

Xunzi takes the Confucian teaching as a necessary measure to correct what is wrong in individuals and society. For him, goodness is what is correct, what is in accordance with natural principle, and what leads to peace and order; while evil is what is wrong through partiality, what wickedly contravenes natural principles, what is perverse, what is rebellious and what will cause disorder. If the former already existed in human nature, there would be no need for sages, nor would there be any need for propriety and righteousness. The sages of antiquity saw the wickedness of humans, and 'established the authority of rulers to govern the people, set forth clearly propriety and righteousness to transform them, instituted laws and governmental measures to rule them, and made punishment severe to restrict them' (Chan, 1963a: 131). In this sense, virtues are not innate, but are the result of the activities of the sages. As a potter shapes the clay to create the vessel, or as an artisan carves a vessel out of a piece of wood, ancient sages created propriety and righteousness by accumulating their thoughts and ideas, and established goodness by mastering what had been gained in learning and practice. Although everybody is born with natural desires, any intelligent person can see that it is in his own interests to be virtuous, and any person who lives in society must be under the influence of social conventions. Through conscious activities and social conventions, the innate nature is transformed and an acquired nature is formed. Xunzi argues that what is born with natural life and what is acquired in social life are two sides of the one process: inborn nature is the raw material and original constitution to be worked on, while conscious activity is the form and principle of order, development and completion. If there were no inborn nature, there would be nothing for conscious action to improve; without conscious action, inborn nature cannot refine itself. Only when inborn nature and conscious action are joined, can the concept of the sage be 'perfected, and the merit of uniting the world brought to fulfillment' (Knoblock, 1994: 66).

The two doctrines of human nature propagated by Mengzi and Xunzi were subsequently combined or adapted by later Confucians. Prominent scholars such as Dong Zhongshu, Wang Chong, Yang Xiong, Han Yu and Li Ao produced a variety of theories about human nature. For example, some upheld that human nature contains both good and bad elements, while others maintained that human nature is good in some people and bad in others, and others again insisted that human nature is good while the emotions are bad. Whatever positions they held, their primary task was to reduce evil and to increase goodness. They believed that this could be done through internal cultivation at the personal level and through external instruction at the social level. At the social level, Confucianism emphasises the importance of education. Dong Zhongshu, for instance, argues that Heaven has provided human beings with good material but humans are unable to become wholly good. Thus Heaven establishes kingship to make us good by way of education (*jiao*). 'Following the will of Heaven, the king takes it as his duty to give completeness to the nature of the people' (*Chunqiu Fanlu Yizheng*, 1992: 302). This is the foundation for a complex of Confucian social programmes aimed at transforming society. At the personal level, Dong emphasised the role played by the heart/mind (*xin*) in developing goodness and preventing evil in human nature. For him, although humans are endowed with goodness by Heaven, the material factors (human feelings) prevent us from becoming wholly good. It is important to check the feelings, which is the job of the heart/mind:

> That which confines the multitude of evil things within and prevents them from appearing externally, is the heart/mind. Therefore, the heart/mind is known as the confiner . . . Heaven has its restraints over the *yin* and the *yang*, and the individual has his confiner of feelings and desires, in this way he is at one with the Way of Heaven.
>
> (*Chunqiu Fanlu Yizheng*, 1992: 293, 296;
> see also Fung, 1953: 35)

Neo-Confucianism established Mengzi as the orthodox transmitter of the Confucian way and his understanding of the goodness of human nature as the authentic Confucian doctrine. Based on the belief that human nature is originally good and that evil is a deviation from the good, Neo-Confucians consider good and evil to be related concepts. The relation between good and evil is compared to that of the *yang* and the *yin*, the binary forces of the universe, not in the sense that good is the *yang* and evil is the *yin*, but in that 'Among all things, there is none that does not have its opposite. Thus for the *yin* there is the *yang*, and for goodness there is evil. When the *yang* waxes, the *yin* wanes, and when goodness increases, evil diminishes' (Cheng Hao, quoted in Fung, 1953: 518). In this sense they believe that 'The goodness and evil of the world are both equally Heavenly principles. To say that something is evil does not mean that it is inherently so. It is so merely because it either goes too far or does not go far enough' (*ibid.*). As good and evil are related to the Mean, it is natural for these scholars to hold that evil is nothing more than a departure from the Middle Way. Some Neo-Confucians made use of the clearness and opacity of water to illustrate how good and evil are related and why evil would come into being. Water is originally clear. As streams flow to the sea, some become dirty. Some become extremely muddied while others only slightly so (Zhang Zai, in Chan, 1963a: 528). Cheng Yi interpreted this to mean that evil is not the essence but a manifestation of the heart/mind: 'The mind is originally good. As it is aroused and expresses itself in thoughts and ideas, there is good and evil' (Chan, 1963a: 567). Wang Yangming also argued that there is no distinction between good and evil in the original substance of the mind and such distinction only appears when the will becomes active. Therefore, 'The highest good is the original substance of the mind. When one deviates from this original substance, there is evil. It is not that there is a good and there is also an evil to oppose it. Therefore good and evil are one thing' (*ibid.*: 684). Although emphasising the unity of good and evil, these Neo-Confucians did not mean that good and evil are both desirable. For them, it is important to know what good and evil are, and it is more important 'to do good and to remove evil'.

SACRED KINGSHIP AND HUMANE GOVERNMENT

It needs not only personal cultivation but also proper supervision by a good government to do good and remove evil. Therefore, the Way of Humans inevitably enters the political arena. In the *School Sayings of Confucius*, Confucius is supposed to have made the following remarks about the Way of Humans:

> In the way of man, government is greatest. Now government means: to be correct. In the ancient way of government love of others was greatest. [Among the ways] to regulate love of others, the rites were greatest. [Among the means] by which to regulate the rites, reverence was greatest. [Among the things in which] reverence reached its utmost, the great marriage [rite] was greatest.   (Kramers, 1950: 212)

A logical conclusion follows that 'love and reverence should be the roots of government' (*ibid.*: 213). If this is what Confucians believe concerning the Way of Humans, then we can see that the Way is fundamentally an ethical system and is sustained by moral virtues. In concrete terms, the Confucian Way of Humans is composed of three aspects: government, love of others and rituals. Among these three, government is given priority because it is both the result of the other two and the necessary condition for them to be carried out.

Confucian discourse on government is based on its understanding of the Mandate of Heaven. 'The Way of Heaven is to bless the good and to punish the bad' (Legge, 1992, vol. 3: 186), and how to govern becomes a kind of competition in terms of moral virtues. Those who have demonstrated good virtues would be trusted with the ruling right, while those who have violated the principle of Heaven would consequently lose the right. Heaven does not 'favour' any particular man or tribe. Heaven endows those with the right to rule, only if they have illustrated and continue to illustrate the illustrious virtue. A modern Confucian scholar, Tang Junyi, rephrases this belief in this way: 'The Mandate of Heaven following men's cultivation of virtue, men must be mindful of Heavenly *ming* [mandate] and continue to cultivate their virtue even after they have received *ming*; the more fully men cultivate their virtue, the more fully will Heaven confer its mandate on them' (Tang, 1961: 202).

All the great ancient kings are said to have been virtuous men. Confucius sang eulogies to Yao, Shun, Yu and King Wen, for their great virtues (*Lunyu*, 8: 19–21). Believing that 'he who possesses great virtue will surely receive the appointment [Mandate] of Heaven' (Chan, ed. 1963: 102), the Confucian classics elaborate the belief that the Mandate of Heaven is a reward for the virtues of the former kings. The reason why the Zhou Dynasty could be established is said to be due to the splendid virtues of King Wen:

> King Wen . . . was able to illustrate his virtue and be careful in the use of punishments. He did not dare to show any contempt to the widowers and widows. He employed the employable and revered the reverend; he was terrible to those who needed to be awed . . . The fame of him ascended up to the High God [*shangdi*], and God approved. Heaven gave a great charge to King Wen, to exterminate the great dynasty of Yin, and receive its great appointment, so that the various States belonging to it and their peoples were brought to an orderly condition.
>
> (Legge, 1992, vol. 3: 383–5)

The *Book of Poetry* praises the glorious Mandate of Heaven and the beautiful virtue of King Wen as if they were one thing: 'The Mandate of Heaven, How beautiful and unceasing! Oh, how glorious was the purity of King Wen's virtue!' (Chan, 1963a: 6). Confucius glorified King Wu for his efforts in manifesting his father's virtues when King Wu declared that 'I may have close relatives, but better for me to have benevolent men. If the people transgress, let it be on my head alone' (*Lunyu*, 20: 1). Mengzi emphasised that Heaven alone, and nothing else, could bestow the right to rule the empire: 'Heaven does not speak but reveals itself by its acts and deeds', and the changes of rulers 'could not be brought by humans, but by Heaven alone' (*Mengzi*, 5A: 5). The virtue of the previous kings is described, however, as something like a sum of credit that can easily be used up. The Mandate of Heaven is not constant. It changes according to the virtue of the king and the cultivation of virtue by the king. The Confucian classics repeatedly warn the presiding king that the Mandate of Heaven is not easily preserved, and can only be kept by the continual reverence towards Heaven and by conscientiously increasing rather than decreasing the virtue demonstrated in the life of the former kings. Thus, central to the continuity of the Mandate of Heaven is whether or not a king maintains his reverence and continues to manifest the brilliant virtues of his forefathers. To preserve the Mandate of Heaven, the king is required to conduct rituals and ceremonies correctly, to do administrative work appropriately, and to pray and offer sacrifices to Heaven and the ancestors sincerely. He is also expected to reduce rather than increase the hardship of the people, to be benevolent rather than cruel to the people, and to take care of those who are suffering. Failure to do this will cause the people to complain to Heaven, and Heaven will in turn withdraw the Mandate. In a number of passages in the *Book of History* the last Shang ruler is accused of offending Heaven and committing immoral sins, which is believed to be the reason why he would lost the empire: 'The King of Shang does not reverence Heaven above, and inflicts calamities on the people below' (Legge, 1992, vol. 3: 284).

Heaven is believed to act according to certain ethical principles, which are in turn enforced upon living rulers who, as intermediaries between the supreme ruler above and humans below, are to model their behaviour on those of Heaven in the activities of a rational, moral, harmonious and unified government. The supreme position of the king on earth and the extensive range of his responsibilities give rise to the concept of sacred kingship. Morally sacred kingship in the Confucian tradition is closely related to Confucian religio-politics or ethico-spirituality. In the classics, a king often addresses himself as 'One Man' (*yi ren*), and is addressed as 'the Son of Heaven' (*tianzi*). These terms explain not only his unique authority for ruling the world but also his exclusive responsibility in carrying out the Mandate of Heaven. Heaven and the human world are connected by the king who speaks to Heaven above and governs for the people below. The Han Confucian, Dong Zhongshu, was caught up with this communion and explained that the character for king, *wang* (王), composite of three horizontal lines and one vertical line running through them at the centre, is in fact a representation of how three realms are related in the kingship; three horizontal lines representing respectively

Heaven (above), Earth (below) and humans (in the middle), with the vertical line referring to the king who connects them. In this sense, Dong confirmed that 'The king models himself on Heaven' and therefore 'The Way is the Way of the King, and the King is the beginning of human [life]' (*Chunqiu Fanlu Yizheng*, 1992: 329, 101). Heaven entrusts the king with the task of ruling the human world, and the king therefore 'holds a position of life or death (over other men), and shares with Heaven its transforming power' (Fung, 1953: 47). On the other hand, Confucians emphasise that a king is merely the executive manager of the Way of Heaven on the earth. The ruler must model himself on Heaven and love the people, because Heaven does not establish the people for kingship but establishes kingship for the people: 'Heaven, to protect the people below, made for them rulers and made for them instructors' because 'Heaven compassionates the people. What the people desire, Heaven will be found to give effect to' (Legge, 1992, vol. 3: 286, 288).

Social disruption is largely due to the moral inadequacy of the ruler. Confucians believe that 'Heaven sees as the people see and Heaven hears as the people hear' (*Mengzi*, 5A: 5), and they measure the virtue of a ruler by his conformity to the needs of the people. The ruler who brought suffering to the people is deemed a tyrant, and the ruler who did not take advice from Confucians is considered unworthy. A tyrant would be subject to rebellion against him, and an unworthy ruler must be reprimanded. With the belief in the Mandate of Heaven and the determination to carry out the Way of Heaven, many a Confucian master took it as his greatest duty to persuade princes or kings to behave according to ritual/propriety, to protest persistently against any wrongdoing until it is rectified. This is frequently done at the risk of the Confucian's career or even life. What these Confucians attempted to safeguard is the principle of rule by moral virtue. Rule by virtue is a governing mechanism that maximises the effect of a moral example. Punishment is deemed as an inferior way of government, and maintaining social order by killing those who do not follow the Way is considered a failure of the ruler himself. When asked whether it was permitted to execute people for violating the Way, Confucius absolutely denied its legitimacy and pointed out that there was no justification and need for slaying, because 'If you desire the good, the people will be good' (*Lunyu*, 12: 19). It is believed that 'When the ruler treats the aged as the aged should be treated, then the people will model themselves on him and become filial. When the ruler treats the elders as they should be treated, then the people will be stirred to brotherly love. When the ruler treats the young and the helpless with compassion, then the common people will not follow the opposite course' (*Daxue*, 10, see Chan, 1963a: 92). The only legitimate government is the one based on its consonance with the virtue of Heaven. Consequently, the only righteous ruler is the one who dedicates himself to the well-being of the people, provides them with enough food, establishes justice, enlightens the populace by means of education and rituals, and institutes a meritocracy by which virtuous and diligent scholars are appointed as officials. In this way, a relationship of care and trust between the ruler and the people is established and the Way of Humans is made manifest.

Kingship is important for carrying out the Way of Heaven. But the rationalism and humanism of Confucianism enables Confucian doctrines to extend the responsibility for the Way of Heaven from the ruling class to all individuals, or at least to all educated men. An individual is held responsible not only for his own destiny, but also potentially for the destiny of human beings as a whole and for the destiny of the world. In this way, Confucian doctrines become the guidelines for the life of the people, not merely the statecraft for the ruling class. Because everybody is held responsible for the Way of Humans, the value of a person is seen in his/her manifestation of Confucian virtues. Understood as the moral guidance of life and the principles of human activities, the Way of Humans is essential for peace and harmony in the world, because it is believed that violating this guidance and these principles would seriously disrupt the harmony between Heaven and human society, resulting in disorder and chaos.

The Way of Harmony

In the Confucian doctrines of the Way, there is no clear line that can be drawn between Heaven and humanity, thus the Way of Heaven and the Way of Humans are always related in one form or another. The terms used for the realm of Heaven such as *qi* (material force), *yin–yang*, *tai-ji* (the Supreme Ultimate), *yuan* (the origin) and so forth are all applicable to human beings, while those referring to the human realm such as *xin* (the heart/mind), *xing* ([human] nature), *qing* (emotions or feelings) can also be used to designate Heaven. Other terms like *de* (virtue), *li* (principle), *dao* (way) penetrate the two realms of Heaven and humanity. This demonstrates that the relationship between Heaven and humanity is the foundation of the Confucian world-view, and that the relationship is primarily one of harmony rather than of confrontation or conflict.

Confucian discourses on Heaven and humanity pave the way for its conception of harmony, by which the Way of Heaven and the way of humans are fulfilled in each other and the realisation of each of these ways supports the other. In this sense, harmony is the culmination of the Confucian way and marks the point where the Way of Heaven and the Way of Humans converge. Confucianism took shape in a turbulent time, both as a reaction against disorder, and as a remedy for correcting chaos. Central to Confucian solutions of disorder and conflict is the question of how to rebuild the Grand Unity (*datong*), which is believed to have existed in the ancient Golden Age under the rule of the sage–kings and to have been reclaimed and restored in the time of each generation of the Confucian followers. This mission-like vision was revealed by Confucius in his propagation of a peaceful and harmonious life guaranteed by virtue (*de*) and guided by ritual/propriety (*li*) in opposition to a cruel and unjust reality. This vision was also repeatedly claimed and reclaimed by Mengzi who devoted his life to opposing despotism and tyranny in favour of a humane ruling by a benevolent king. It is illustrated in the *Book of Rites*, especially in its chapters of the *Great Learning*, the *Doctrine of the Mean* and the *Evolution of Ritual/Propriety* (*Li Yun*), which deliberate on how to realise equilibrium and harmony (*zhi zhonghe*) in the world and proclaim a utopian society as a social, moral, political and religious ideal. The Confucians of the Han Dynasty believed that the unity between Heaven and humanity was not only the natural law but also human destiny, while the Neo-Confucians of the Song–Ming Dynasties championed for a harmonious world in which all human beings were brothers and all things companions.

HARMONY: THE CONCEPT AND THE THEME

Harmony (*he*) is not an invention of Confucius. The Chinese character (和) for harmony appears only in bronze inscriptions where it is written as 𣚊, composed of a plant and a mouth. But this character is frequently used to represent an older and more complicated character (龢), composed of *yue* (龠) that denotes its meaning and *he* (禾) that points to its pronunciation. By analysing this character we can see that the Confucian understanding of harmony is primarily related to music. In oracle-bone inscriptions the character *yue* is a pictograph of a musical instrument, probably a short flute or panpipe of two or three holes (𢍰, 龠). It is in this sense that the character *he* (龢) is defined as 'harmonising multi-tones' (*he zhongsheng*) in *Shuowen Jiezi Zhu* (1981: 85). It was commonly recognised among the ancients that music and harmony were closely related, as seen in a statement of the *Book of Zhuangzi* that 'The *Book of Music* speaks of harmony' (Watson, 1964: 363). In the section on music in the *Book of Rites*, tones are said to rise from the human heart, while music is related to the principles of human conduct (*Liji Jijie*, 1989: 928). In this sense music is believed to reflect harmony as well as create harmony through touching the human heart and adjusting our conduct. As in ancient times, music was primarily part of religious and social ceremonies, ritual and music functioned together to establish harmony: 'Music unites, while rituals differentiate. Through union the people come to be friendly toward one another, and through differentiation the people come to learn respect for one another' (Lin, 1992: 565). Further, ritual and music are of metaphysical significance, because 'Music expresses the harmony of the universe, while rituals express the order of the universe. Through harmony all things are influenced and through order all things have a proper place' (Lin, 1992: 571). Confucius believed that music was essential for a good character and that music could not only harmonise human sentiments but also bring order from social chaos. For him as well as for many other Confucians, there are two kinds of music: harmonious and peaceful music and seductive or violent music. The former is believed to be good for improving human character and is conducive to bringing peace to the state, while the latter encourages bad behaviour and fosters immoral sentiments.

From music, harmony is extended to mean an orderly combination of different elements, by which a new unity comes into being. Harmony is compared to a kind of tasty soup in the *Zou's Commentary on the Spring and Autumn Annals*, where 'harmonising' refers to mixing up different ingredients and flavours according to certain measures (Fung, 1952: 36). Confucians consciously differentiate harmony from identity (*tong*), and believe that identification of one thing with another is simply to replicate what one already has, while to be in harmony with others is to produce something new. In this sense it is claimed that to be harmonious is to produce (*sheng*), to transform (*hua*) and to enlarge (*da*).

Manifest in human character, harmony is an inner state in which all feelings and emotions are properly expressed following the Mean: 'When these feelings are aroused and each and all attain due measure and degree, it is called harmony' (Chan, 1963a: 98). Everyone has emotions, but not all of us can express them properly or in due time. To make our emotions harmonious, we must cultivate our character. It is believed that cultivating harmony within, we will become virtuous; while doing the contrary, we will spoil our character. In this sense, harmony is identified with moral virtues, and is deemed as the most important of all virtues. Confucius and his disciples elaborated the meaning and functions of harmony, and believed that among all those things that can be achieved through ritual, harmony is most valuable (*Lunyu*, 1: 12). Dong Zhongshu made it clear that 'Centrality is that by which Heaven and Earth start and end, harmony is that by which Heaven and Earth produce [the myriad things]. Therefore, of all the virtues the highest is harmony' (*Chunqiu Fanlu Yizheng*, 1992: 444).

For Confucians, virtue is of political importance by nature. As the 'highest virtue', harmony is said to be necessary for the peaceful life of individuals, the family and the state. Order and peace must be cultivated internally and externally. The *Book of History* holds the people who have lost harmony in their heart responsible for the disorder in the world: 'It is from yourselves that the want of harmony arises:–strive to be harmonious. In your families there is a want of concord:–strive to be harmonious'; and it is recorded that when King Cheng of the Zhou Dynasty declared his last charge, he commanded his subjects 'to continue the observance of the lessons, and to take the rule of the empire of Chow, complying with the great laws and securing the harmony of the empire' (Legge, 1992, vol. 3: 505, 558).

As Confucians consider politics to be a branch of education, harmony becomes an important content as well as the primary aim of moral training. It is recorded that in the Zhou Dynasty the king 'regulated the emotions of the people with six kinds of music, and educated them with harmony' (*Zhouli Zhushu*, 1980: 708). To realise harmony within and without, individuals are required to play an active, creative role in recasting and reshaping their life, to improve their understanding of the world and to manifest their own nature. Harmony as the highest ideal is thus closely related to nature, politics, ethics and daily life. In this sense it is sometimes addressed as the 'Central Harmony (*zhonghe*)'. By 'central harmony' Confucians mean that harmony is central to all existence and all activities and is rooted in the innate centrality and equilibrium.

The doctrine of harmony propagated by the early Confucian masters was later developed in Neo-Confucianism. Neo-Confucians take harmony not only as a central concept, but also as the spirit animating Confucian doctrines and as the vitality empowering Confucian practices. They believe that harmony is the underlying principle of all relationships, and that harmony is the reason why all virtues can be fully realised.

> When moral principles and human destiny are united in harmony, they
> will be preserved and abide in principle. When humanity [humaneness]
> and wisdom are united in harmony, they will be preserved and abide
> in the sage. When activity and tranquillity are united in harmony, they
> will be preserved and abide in spirit. When yin and yang are united
> in harmony they will be preserved and abide in the Way. And when
> the nature of man and the Way of Heaven are united in harmony,
> they will be preserved and abide in sincerity.
>
> (Zhang Zai, in Chan, 1963a: 507)

As the central theme, harmony penetrates all levels and dimensions of Confucian discourses. However, it is addressed primarily in the context of the relationship between Heaven and human beings. This relationship is discussed and explored from many different points of view. In terms of metaphysics, a harmonious relation between Heaven and humans refers to harmony between spirit and material, between form and matter, between mind and body, and between the one (the universal) and the many (the particular). In a religious sense, it indicates a continual process between this life and the life hereafter, between the divine and the secular, and between heavenly principles and human behaviour. In the area of naturalism, it points to the unity between humans and Nature, between beings (the living) and things (the existent), and between the social and the natural. From the perspective of politics, it effects the unity between the ruled and the ruling, between the government and the mandate to govern, and inspires the people to correct disorder and chaos in order to attain to peace and harmony.

The various Confucian schools differ in their understanding of what Heaven is, and consequently they hold different opinions about the harmony between humans and Heaven. Of these opinions, two constitute the mainstream of the Confucian doctrines of harmony; one locating harmony in the oneness of humans and Heaven, the other finding harmony in human conformity to Natural Law.

ONENESS OF HEAVEN AND HUMANS

For many Confucians the harmony between Heaven and humans denotes a moral correspondence between humans and their Ultimate. Mengzi considered the extension of one's heart and cultivation of one's nature to be the way to know Heaven and to serve Heaven. Influenced by the School of Yin–Yang and the Five Elements, which 'contemplated profoundly the increase and decrease of the yin and yang and wrote . . . on their permutations' (*Shiji*, 1998: 2344), Han Confucians, in the main, understood harmony as a metaphysical oneness, a kind of political/moral mechanism in which so-called 'moral co-operation' is forged between Heaven as the supreme ruler above and the human ruler below. They placed the responsibility for social and natural harmony on the shoulders of the ruler. Harmony is the Mandate of Heaven, but to enjoy harmony, the ruler must first cultivate his own virtue.

Dong Zhongshu established it as the fundamental principle for Confucianism that 'humans and Heaven are of one species' (*Chunqiu Fanlu Yizheng*, 1992: 341). The oneness of Heaven and humans was used to reveal various manifestations of the macrocosmic–microcosmic unity. Firstly, humans and Heaven are believed to be of the same nature and can communicate to each other (*tianren xiangtong*):

> Heaven possesses the *yin* and *yang*, so do humans. When the *yin* force arises in Heaven and Earth, the *yin* force in humans arises in response. In turn, when the *yin* force in humans arises, so does that in Heaven and Earth. When the *yang* force in humans arises, the *yang* force in Heaven and Earth arises too. Their courses are one.
>
> (*Chunqiu Fanlu Yizheng*, 1992: 360)

Secondly, humans are believed to correlate with the numerical categories of Heaven (*renfu tianshu*). According to this theory, humans are produced on the pattern of Heaven, and the human body, mind and morality are shaped exactly in accordance with the principles of Heaven. For example, the human head is round, correlating to Heaven that is believed to be round; the human foot is rectangular, correlating to the square Earth; the human body is believed to be composed of 366 pieces of bone, correlating to the number of days in a year; the four limbs correlate to the four seasons; the five inner organs correspond to the Five Elements; and the eyes correspond to the sun and moon. Human emotions are also believed to correspond to the changes of Heaven, sadness and pleasure corresponding to the yin and the yang (*Chunqiu Fanlu Yizheng*,

1992: 354–7). Thirdly, human affairs would arouse Heaven to respond, and Heaven does so by rewarding the good and punishing the bad (*tianren gangying*). Therefore, 'the root of natural disasters is in the faults of the nation' (*ibid.*: 259). To restore the original harmony between Heaven and humans, Heaven 'commands' humans to behave morally and 'guides' them in their life. The responsive correspondence between heavenly principles and human affairs reveals the vital importance of humans following the universal principles. However, the response between Heaven and humans is not only one-way traffic, in which Heaven gives orders while humans follow passively. Confucians believe that humans can play an important role in maintaining harmony, not only between the universe and ourselves, but also between the fundamental powers of the universe, the *yin* and the *yang*. As early as the Han Dynasty, it was stressed that governmental politics had a responsibility for the harmony of the world, and that 'the duties of the "Three Highest Ministers" included, in addition to their normal administrative work, that of "harmonizing the *yin* and *yang*"' (Fung, 1953: 10). For example, it is recorded that a prime minister of the Former Han Dynasty, Chen Ping (?–179 BCE) once described to his emperor the duties of a prime minister in the following terms: 'It is the duty of the prime minister to be an aid to the Son of Heaven above, to adjust the forces of the *yin* and *yang*, and to see that all proceeds in accordance with the four seasons. At the same time he must strive to nourish the best in all creatures' (Watson, 1961, vol. 2: 166).

The causal responses between Heaven and humans have a wide range of implications, and it is by these that Confucian politics, ethics, education, literature and so forth are constructed and performed.

HUMANS AND NATURE

As Heaven has a dimension of Nature or Natural Law, harmony between Heaven and humans is understood to be a co-operative relationship between humans and their natural environment, in which natural laws should be followed and the natural environment protected. From this, a kind of Confucian eco-ethics develops, aiming at establishing a state of harmony between humans and Nature.

Confucian eco-ethics is based on the perceived agreement between the Way of Heaven and the way of the humans. The laws operating in the world at large are also effected in every human being. The commentaries on the *Book of Changes* proclaimed that:

> Heaven is high, the earth is low, and thus *ch'ien* (Heaven) and *k'un*
> (Earth) are fixed. As high and low are thus made clear, the honorable
> and the humble have their places accordingly. As activity and tranquility
> have their constancy, the strong and the weak are thus differentiated.
> Ways come together according to their kind, and things are divided
> according to their classes. Hence good fortune and evil emerge.
>
> (Chan, 1963a: 265)

This paragraph illustrates the Confucian understanding of the operations of the cosmos, to which humans ideally adjust themselves. To be in
tune with cosmic principles leads to peace, order and happiness, and to
act against them will result in chaos, disorder and misfortune. Human
conformity to Natural Law does not necessarily mean their oneness, and
harmony can be derived from the separation of human affairs from natural
courses. The first Confucian who deliberated on this theme was Xunzi,
who insisted that Heaven as Nature stood outside the human realm.
Against those who believed superstitiously that praying to Heaven would
result in blessing and disobeying Heaven in disasters, Xunzi argued that
the natural course of Heaven could not be changed by human affairs, and
natural laws ran their own course whether humans had behaved morally
or not. Against those who insisted that Heaven was an interfering ruler
and all human fortunes or misfortunes were rewards or punishments from
Heaven, Xunzi maintained that Heaven was none other than Nature and
the harmony between Nature and humans could not possibly be in their
mutual interference. If the people follow the law of Nature and therefore
enjoy peace and happiness, Nature cannot make them unhappy. On the
other hand, if the people neglect their duties and do nothing good with
their life so that they become poor and miserable, Nature cannot reverse
their misfortune.

Since Nature does not have 'emotions' and 'will', it cannot intentionally create harmony for human beings. To secure harmony between ourselves and nature, we should make use of natural laws for our own ends.
We are the architects of our own fate. For this reason, Xunzi argued
passionately that

> Instead of regarding Heaven as great and admiring it,
> Why not foster it as a thing and regulate it?
> Instead of obeying Heaven and singing praise to it,
> Why not control the Mandate of Heaven and use it?
>
> (Chan, 1963a: 122)

Here the Mandate of Heaven is understood as Natural Law, and controlling and making use of natural laws implies understanding them, following them and taking advantage of the knowledge of them. Xunzi suggested two ways to do this. One is to act in accordance with the course of Nature. For example, 'plowing in spring, weeding in summer, harvesting in autumn and storing up in winter' are in accordance with the natural order and thus people will have plenty of grain for food. The other is to protect the natural environment by following the order and law of nature. For example, the season of spring is the time when all things grow, so that all kinds of activities against growth must be forbidden in this season, or in Xunzi's words, 'axes and halberds are not permitted in the mountain forest' and 'nets and poisons are not permitted in the marshes' (Knoblock, 1990: 105).

The understanding that Heaven is Nature, and that harmony comes from abiding by natural laws was accepted and developed by a number of naturalistic or rationalistic Confucians, of whom the most prominent are Wang Chong (27–107), Liu Yuxi (722–843) and Wang Fuzhi (1619–92). These scholars emphasised that Heaven did not create harmony but only provided the conditions for humans to be in harmony, and that a harmonious relationship between humans and their environment is conducive to their well-being. Against those who believe that Heaven produces things purposely to feed and clothe humans, Wang Chong argued that 'Heaven moves without the desire to produce things and yet things are produced of themselves', and that to maintain a harmonious relationship between people and nature, we should behave in the manner of Heaven, acting only when necessary; otherwise letting things run their courses (Chan, 1963a: 298). For Liu Yuxi, Heaven and humanity are different, in terms both of their nature and of their functions, and harmony is the result of the parallel realisation of the natural and the human way. 'Humans cannot do what Heaven can do; neither can Heaven do all what humans are able to do . . . The Way of Heaven is to produce and give forth, which is applied to manifest the strong from the weak; while the way of humans is to establish laws and moral codes, which is used for distinguishing the right and the wrong' (Zhang, 1982: 179). Wang Fuzhi believed that the principle of Heaven was of constant growth and transformation, and we must understand this principle and expand the human way to 'create' our own destiny (*zaoming*) rather than waiting for Heaven to do so (Chan, 1963a: 700). These ideas are, of course, not what we mean today by eco-ethics, and these scholars can hardly be counted as environmentalists. However, they do represent another dimension of Confucian harmony, supplementary to the politicalised and moralised view of the relationship between humans and Heaven.

SOCIAL CONFLICTS AND THEIR SOLUTIONS

The Confucian discourses on harmony are not only a theoretical attempt to search for the secrecy of metaphysical mysteries. They have the strongly practical function of compromising opposition and solving conflict, so that order rather than disorder should prevail. Enthusiastically committed to harmony, Confucians attach a great significance to the resolution of conflict and opposition. Harmony is not considered a static identity, in which everything holds to its *status quo* and nothing is to be changed. Rather, harmony is regarded as a result of constant changes and reconciliation of conflict. It is the Confucian view that opposition arising from the fundamental forces of the cosmos will necessarily lead to harmony, which is classically summarised by Zhang Zai as such: 'As there are forms (*xiang*), there are their opposites (*dui*). These opposites necessarily stand in opposition to what they do. Opposition leads to conflict, which will necessarily be reconciled and resolved' (Chan, 1963a: 506).

Opposition creates tension, and the accumulation of tension will burst into conflict. Conflict will then be reconciled and harmony obtained. In this sense the concept of harmony itself contains conflict and its resolution, and the Confucian Way of Harmony indicates not only the need for adjustment and refinement, but also the need for overcoming tension. Metzger observes that the tension between the good and the bad or between ideal and reality 'was central to Neo-Confucianism, a point misunderstood by Max Weber and often overlooked by scholars focused on the theme of "harmony"' (Metzger, 1977: 108). Admitting the necessity and unavoidability of tension and opposition, however, does not mean that Confucians are content with them. The Confucian Way of Harmony works on the solution and resolution of conflict and search for the effective methods to reconcile and resolve various kinds of conflict.

Within the human realm, the Confucian resolution of conflict concentrates on three kinds of relationship. Firstly, it searches for peace and harmony between the self and others by working on human nature, calling for cultivating one's virtues conscientiously. Secondly, it seeks to harmonise family relationships through cultivating the sense of mutual responsibilities between family members. Thirdly, it looks for a way to diminish the possibility of violent conflict by establishing a humane government in which virtues overwhelm selfish contention. By these three methods Confucianism attempts to build up a mechanism that sustains and maintains a comprehensive social structure in which no conflict goes unnoticed and no opposition is allowed to exceed certain limits. On the one hand, these methods were useful in the past and some of them may still be of value for today. On the other hand, they were designed within certain historical conditions and created new problems while solving old ones. Therefore, a careful examination of these three aspects of Confucian resolution is needed for an overall view of the Confucian Way of Harmony.

According to Confucianism, conflict first arises from the relation between oneself and others, and harmony is the result of an appropriate accommodation of one's own needs to the requirements of others. Confucianism holds that a human is by nature a social being, who knows innately, or can be taught to know, how to relate to others and how to treat others properly. To be a human, therefore, is not merely to look after one's own interests and satisfy one's own desires. The Confucian solution of the conflict between oneself and others is that one must start with the personal cultivation of one's own character, and then be in harmony with others by extending one's virtue to others. It believes that lack of self-cultivation leads to the dominance of self-centredness in personal relations and to the misunderstanding and mistrust of others, which, if not dealt with properly, will result in conflict. The difference between a morally superior and a morally deficient person is that the former has understood what is righteous in one's own self and then extends it to others, while the latter has misinterpreted human relations in order to satisfy one's own interests. Conflict has its causes in one's own heart, and a harmonious relationship with others is only a reflection of one's inner peace. 'Those who are not virtuous cannot abide long either in a condition of poverty and hardship, or in a condition of enjoyment', while those of virtue will still experience enjoyment and be full of happiness even when living a life in a mean and narrow lane with only 'a single bamboo dish of rice and a single gourd of water' for a meal. It is believed that when our heart is at peace and our character is harmonious we will naturally have peaceful relations with others, because it is not riches nor powers but virtuous manners that 'constitute the excellence of

neighbourhood' (*Lunyu*, 4: 1, 4: 2, 6: 11). On the contrary, an uncultivated character causes one not only to be discontented and complaining,
but also to have an eye only on profit and benefit for oneself. Mengzi
took this selfish contending for profit to be the source of conflict and
killing. He believed that if everybody chose what was most profitable
as the only guideline for behaviour, then there would be no virtue and
morality in the world, while murder, killing and violence would replace
ethical norms and the human world would become a kingdom of
beasts in which everyone was engaged in the war against everyone else
(*Mengzi*, 1A: 1).

Virtues or the lack of them can be revealed through self-examination.
Zengzi, a disciple of Confucius famous for his conscientiousness, remarked that he would examine himself many times a day to see whether
or not he had done his best in what he undertook on another person's
behalf, whether or not he had been faithful in dealing with his friends, and
whether or not he had mastered and practised what he had been taught
(*Lunyu*, 1: 4). Such an examination is necessary because it can help us to
find out what is wrong in our own character and what is needed in dealing with others. Any failure to have a harmonious relation with others is
said to have its root in our own character, and to find out the cause one
should reflect on our own self. Confucius took archery as an illustration:
'In archery we have something resembling the Way of the superior man.
When the archer misses the center of the target, he turns around and
seeks for the cause of failure within himself' (Chan, 1963a: 102). The
same attitude is also held by Mengzi when he proposed that we should
look into our own self whenever we are not in harmony with others:

> If one loves others and no responsive attachment is shown to him, one
> should turn inward and examine whether or not one has had sufficient
> benevolence; if one is trying to rule the state but unsuccessfully, one
> should turn inward and examine whether or not one has gained enough
> wisdom; if one treats others according to the rules of propriety but is
> not responded to with appropriate proprieties, one should turn inward
> and examine whether or not one has shown proper respects to others.
>
> (*Mengzi*, 4A: 4)

Ill-treatment by others should not be taken as a reason for one to
return evil with evil. When we are misunderstood or ill-treated, we should
not blame Heaven nor accuse others, but have firm faith in Heaven, as
instructed by Mengzi that

One who loves others is constantly loved by them; one who respects others is constantly respected by them. If one is treated in a perverse and unreasonable manner, a person of virtues will still turn round upon himself: 'I must have been wanting in benevolence; I must have been wanting in propriety . . . I must have been failing to do my utmost [in dealing with them].'

(Mengzi, 4B: 28)

The Confucian solution of personal conflicts are first tested and applied in the family, which, according to Confucianism, is the cornerstone of order and peace in the world. As the family is the basic unit of human community, harmonious family relationships are believed to be crucial for a harmonious society and a peaceful state: 'If only everyone loved his parents and treated his elders with deference, the whole world would be at peace' (*Mengzi*, 4A: 11). For those who are of the ruling class, their virtues in family affairs are even more significant, because it is believed that when these people feel profound affection for their parents, the common people will naturally be humane (*Lunyu*, 8: 2). It was in this sense that Confucius put family harmony above all other considerations, and family responsibilities above all other social duties. In some extreme cases, Confucius was even prepared to consolidate family relations at the price of social regulations, because in his view social justice was nothing other than an extension of family affection and could not be realised unless affectionate family relationships were sustained. His disciples highlighted the importance of family harmony for the stability of the whole society, and made use of family virtues to correct disorder (*Lunyu*, 1: 2).

Family relationships in the Confucian classics are threefold, that is, between parents and children, between a husband and his wife, and between elder and younger brothers. Of these three relations the first and the foremost is that between parents and children, in which the primary responsibility for family harmony is laid on the children. The tension between different generations is reduced through the respect, reverence and service that the younger pays or provides to the elder. It is believed that the cause of any conflict between parents and children is in the latter's inappropriate attitude and behaviour, and whenever a conflict arises, it is the children's responsibility to seek reconciliation by apology and self-criticism. For a long period in history, this solution contributed to a stable family structure at the price of children, and its prejudice against children was open to extreme applications. In the later period of imperial China it was indeed carried to such an absurd extreme that the meaning and value of a son's life could be found only in his absolute obedience to his father: even if a father ordered his son to die, the son would not be deemed filial if he was unwilling to die (*fu jiao zi wang, zi buwang buxiao*).

To some extent, Confucianism was responsible for such an extremely politicised practice of filial piety. It was not without reason that Confucianism was attacked at the beginning of the twentieth century as a 'ritual religion' (*lijiao*) and was accused of 'murdering people' by means of ritual/propriety (*yili sharen*). However, as Julia Ching argues that the ritualism that maintains hierarchically rigid family and social relationships was based on the Confucian vision of social life, but historically speaking, it 'was less the product of Confucianism, and more the combined product of Confucian philosophy developed under the influence of Legalism and its theory of power, and Yin–Yang philosophy with its arbitrary correlation of cosmic forces and human relations' (Ching, 1997: 267), it would not do justice to the Confucian Way of Harmony if we conclude that the Confucian masters did not leave behind them a balanced view of the parent–child relationship. As a matter of fact, Confucius opposed that filial piety was simply to obey one's father. In the *Book of Filial Piety*, he was supposed to remark that

> [T]he father who had a son that would remonstrate with him would not sink into the gulf of unrighteous deeds. Therefore when a case of unrighteous conduct is concerned, a son must by no means keep from remonstrating with his father, nor a minister from remonstrating with his ruler. Hence, since remonstrance is required in the case of unrighteous conduct, how can (simple) obedience to the orders of a father be accounted filial piety? (Legge, 1968, vol. 3: 484)

Many other early Confucian thinkers insist that both a father and his son are equally responsible for a harmonious family. While the son must show filial piety towards his parents, the father is required to be kind and affectionate to their children (*fuci zixiao*). In the parent–child relationship, children's education, especially their moral training and cultivation of character, is the first duty of their parents. If a son was not educated well, it was his father who should be blamed (*zi bu jiao, fu zhi guo*). Further, Confucians believe that a harmonious family needs a contribution from both parents and children, and that their contributions must not be conditional upon each other. Parents' love or children's respect must be given for its own sake, and the fault of a parent should not be used as an excuse for his or her children not to fulfil their own duties, nor should a disobedient child justify the parents giving up their parental responsibilities.

As a traditional doctrine that came into being in a patriarchal society, Confucianism held a low opinion of women. In the family, the primary virtues of a young woman were considered to be her filial piety towards parents and parents-in-law, assistance to her husband and education of her children (*xiangfu jiaozi*). Mengzi once described the common practice of that time in the following terms:

> When a girl marries, her mother gives her advice, and accompanies her to the door with these cautionary words, 'When you go to your new home, you must be respectful and circumspect. Do not disobey your husband.' This is the way of a wife or concubine to consider obedience and docility the norm. (*Mengzi*, 3B: 2)

Under the guidance of such a code, a wife was confined to housework and family services, and was considered less worthy of respect than her husband. It was against this social background that Confucius once put a woman and a morally deficient person on an equal footing: 'In one's household, it is the women and morally inferior men (*xiao ren*) that are difficult to deal with. If you let them get too close, they become insolent. If you keep them at a distance, they complain' (*Lunyu*, 17: 25). The discrimination against women was further developed in the name of Confucianism. It became an established norm in traditional Confucian societies that a virtuous woman was the one who had no political ambition and even had no exceptional abilities *(nuzi wucai jiu shi de)*, and who would always follow her husband, no matter who and where he was *(jia ji sui ji, jia gou sui gou,* which literally means that if married to a rooster a woman should follow the rooster, and if married to a dog she should follow the dog).

Confucianism should not be held solely responsible for such discrimination against women in East Asia; for this was characteristic of almost all the traditional patriarchal societies, and it was only in a later stage when Confucianism became rigidly dogmatic that all measures against women were associated with Confucian doctrines. In a Confucian society mother/grandmother enjoyed respect and admiration. The achievements of many great men were said to come, directly or indirectly, from the virtues of their mothers. Thus behind Confucius stood his mother who supported and educated him to become the greatest sage. The story that the mother of Mengzi moved her home three times for the sake of a better educational environment for her child was known to every family and every schoolchild. Confucianism favoured the labour division between male and female in the household: a husband was in charge of external responsibilities while a wife was responsible for internal matters, and considered this to be the principle of the universe: 'The correct place of the woman is within; the correct place of the man is without. That man and woman have their proper places is the greatest concept in nature' (Wilhelm, 1967: 570). This division gave senior female members in a family a clear range of responsibilities so that they could exercise their wisdom and manifest their feminine virtues. In a sense these understandings and measures contributed to a stable family structure in a traditional society, although they are far from the modern concept of equality between men and women.

Confucians maintain that politics is an extension of family and personal ethics, and political conflicts must be dealt with according to the same principles used in a family context. Confucianism developed its solution of political conflicts by laying down rules for handling internal and external problems. In a Confucian context, a state (*guo*) is nothing other than an enlarged form of family (*jia*) and the relations between the ruler and the subjects, and those between those who govern and those who are governed are equivalent to the relations between parents and children. However, unlike in the family where children are held primarily responsible for dissolving conflict, in the state the chief responsibility for reducing tension and solving conflict is laid on those who rule and govern. It is a Confucian conviction that with a cruel and immoral ruler no state would be at peace, and only humane and virtuous rulers could bring the end to conflict and make the state prosperous and harmonious. For the faithful followers of Confucianism, to take part in politics is to be engaged primarily in moral cultivation and moral education, sincerely carrying out the moral principles in government. Only those who have love and affection in their heart are considered to have the right to rule. With this moral orientation, Confucianism opposes the policies of ruling simply by legal or military punishments. Confucius criticised the imposition of the death penalty on people without properly educating them, and Mengzi condemned a ruler as a tyrant if he killed a single innocent person. For faithful

Confucians, a good politician must be the one who morally loves and takes care of all the people and the one who is concerned before anyone else in the world but enjoys only after everyone else has enjoyed.

Economic considerations often play an important part in political conflict. Poverty leads to discontent and discontent leads to contention and conflict. Confucianism has been regarded as a tradition which gives priority to the moral side. However, there are also teachings within the tradition which are aimed at harmony between morality and materiality. When seeing the flourishing of population in a state, Confucius remarked that the next step was to enrich them, which should then be followed by 'educating them' (*Lunyu*, 13: 9). Here Confucius gave priority to developing economic well-being rather than to moral training by listing 'moral education' as the last. While proposing that one should die for righteousness, or should be virtuous rather than rich if these two were in opposition, Mengzi affirmed that the people must have a decent material life before being taught with virtue and propriety (*Mengzi*, 1A: 7).

On the one hand Confucians believe that it is a priority to dissolve conflict by enriching people and making it possible for them to have a decent life. On the other hand, they emphasise that moral virtues like humaneness, righteousness and faithfulness, rather than merely wealth and riches, are the meaning and goal of life. To rid the state of conflict, one 'worries not about poverty but about uneven distribution, not about underpopulation but about disharmony' (*Lunyu*, 16: 1). In other words, one of the Confucian ways of solving conflict caused by economic concern is to distribute wealth evenly among people, and to decrease the gap between the rich and the poor. Distribution could not be even and fair unless the ruler and the ruling class were moral, decent and virtuous, unless they could 'reduce their own expenditure and love the people' (*jieyong airen*) and unless they put the interests of the people above their own interests.

However, the two-sided understanding of life was developed in two directions in later Confucianism. Some Confucians pushed it to the extreme that morality was all that one should strive for, and thereby called for 'preserving the Heavenly Principle and extinguishing human desires (*cun tianli, mie renyu*)' as a way to personal integrity and social harmony. Other utilitarian-minded Confucian scholars emphasised that material sufficiency is the only foundation on which morality can be built up: 'When social results are achieved, there is virtue; when success is attained, there is principle' (Tillman, 1982: 133). Some of them even reduced the meaning of ethical codes to the satisfaction of material needs: 'All the ethical codes of human relationship and the principles of affairs are about wearing clothes and having meals' (*Fenshu Xufenshu*, 1975: 4). Neither of these two sides reflects the balanced view held by Confucius who indicated that however much human beings desired wealth and high ranks, they must acquire these things in a righteous way (*Lunyu*, 4: 5). In his view, material well-being and moral virtue can be harmoniously related, the former being the basis while the latter its guidance. Wealth and riches do not necessarily contradict the Way as long as they are acquired in accordance with moral principles.

As in all predemocratic societies, the Confucian solution for political conflicts faces the problem that it lacks the practical measures to supervise and monitor the ruling classes. Keen Confucian watchers have noticed this problem: 'From the point of view of Western political thought, the most glaring absence in this highly idealistic picture is that of any legislation through which the benevolence of the ruler and the obedience of the people could be guaranteed and enforced' (*The Times Literature Supplement*, 19 July, 1998).

For a Confucian, this is a problem of morality rather than of legislation. To solve this problem, Confucianism provided three measures to bind the ruler to moral principles, although whether or not these measures could be fully implemented in imperial politics was always an open question. The first is its doctrine of the Mandate of Heaven. Without the support of the spiritual and metaphysical Ultimate, no government could be legitimised. It was in the light of the supreme sanction of Heaven that Mengzi put forward the doctrine of 'sovereignty in people'. When weighing the three most important elements for the stability and prosperity of a country, Mengzi said that 'The people are of supreme importance; the altars to the gods of earth and grain come next; last comes the ruler' (*Mengzi*, 7B: 14). Having identified the Mandate of Heaven with the will of the people, wise Confucian politicians used the water-boat to illustrate the relationship between the people and the ruler. The people are like water and the ruler is like a boat. As a boat may float in water or be capsized by water, a *good* ruler enjoys peace and harmony supported by the people, while a *bad* ruler brings in chaos and disaster that will eventually lead to his being overthrown. The second measure to call the ruler to his responsibilities is the ancestral tradition. Confucianism is a tradition based on the reverence of ancestors and the preservation of ancient culture. No matter how lofty an emperor was in the world, he was a descendant of the ancestors, whose blessing, protection and approval were believed to be essential for his identity and legitimacy. Loyalty to the ancestors thus became not only a way to link him to his powerful ancestors but also a means by which the ruler engaged in self-examination and repentance of his faults in exchange for the ancestors' continual support. The third measure is the doctrine of removing the Mandate (*geming*) from an unworthy ruler. Under an immoral rule people would complain to Heaven, and Heaven would then 'withdraw' its Mandate and give it to those of brilliant virtues. A king or an emperor who did not possess virtues, who treated his subjects cruelly, and who exploited the people to an unbearable degree was deemed to have lost his legitimacy to rule and to govern. The Confucian doctrine of 'revolution' is essentially ethico-religious, based on the harmony between humanity and Heaven, and revolution is believed to be a dynamic process of great transformation, which recreates harmonious relationships and renews the human mission to carry out the Mandate of Heaven on earth by removing the primary source of chaos and disorder from society.

War between states is the most violent conflict and is believed to be the main cause of miseries and the chief destroyer of social harmony. The Confucian condemnation of war comes from its deep concern for people's life, because in war 'The people are robbed of their time so that they cannot plow and weed their fields, in order to support their parents. Thus their parents suffer from cold and hunger, while brothers, wives, and children are separated and scattered abroad' (*Mengzi*, 1A: 5). To stop war, Confucian masters explored ways to reduce conflicts of interest between states, and sought to bring peace and harmony to the world by means of moral influence and the power of virtue. Confucians were not pacifists in a strict sense. Brutal reality forced them to seek effective ways to end war, and the conception of 'just war' was upheld. A just war is the one waged by righteous people, for good causes and for 'punishing the tyranny and consoling the people' (*diaomin fazui*). However, Confucianism is generally more in favour of influence through virtue than violence. Confucian masters preferred to bring peace and harmony to the world by virtue rather than to secure peace by war. Confucius demonstrated this preference in his differentiation of Shun who was believed to have won the empire by his virtue and King Wu (the actual founder of the Zhou Dynasty) who overcame the Shang Dynasty by war. The music of the former was said to be both perfectly beautiful and perfectly good, while that of the latter was said to be only perfectly beautiful but not perfectly good (*Lunyu*, 3: 25). For Confucius, the most efficient way to defend one's country against aggression was not to strengthen its arms but to strengthen its own people's trust. As far as the security and peace of a state were concerned, trust from the people was of the first priority, while food and arms were only the second and the third (*Lunyu*, 12: 7).

As an old tradition, the Confucian Way of Harmony and its solutions of conflict are contingent on historical conditions, and they have been critically examined but not yet replaced by new ones. Confucians emphasised that harmony could not be achieved unless there is constant change and adaptation, as stated by Dong Zhongshu, 'When change (*genghua*) is obviously needed [in the state] but is not subsequently made, the state cannot be governed well even in the hands of great sages' (*Hanshu*, 1997: 2505). However, in reality the emphasis on harmony was frequently used to strengthen hierarchically fixed and rigid human relationships and to maintain the *status quo*. Another problem in the Confucian Way of Harmony is the tension between its highly inspiring theory and its less practical measures of implementation and this kind of tension frequently caused more conflicts than the Confucian solution could solve. As an inspiring ideal, Confucian harmony encourages its followers to strive devoutly for peace and harmony, for which they were even prepared to give up their riches, ranks and lives. However, it relies on self-cultivation to enhance personal virtues to resolve all kinds of conflicts, this renders the Confucian Way of Harmony quite weak in creating peace and harmony out of conflict and disorder, nor sufficient enough to reduce the tension within society and eliminate social causes of conflict.

The Confucian Way of Harmony has its modern values. Extreme Maoist Communists in Mainland China followed the Lenin–Stalinist doctrine of 'class struggle' and opposed the traditional Confucian appreciation of harmony. These people believed that contradiction rather than harmony was the essence of the world and was the power pushing a society forward. Therefore, a philosophy of struggle (*fendou*), struggling against Heaven, against Earth (Nature) and against humans, was inaugurated as the guiding ideology and was believed to bring endless fulfillment to those engaged in the struggles. This resulted in disastrous conflict between the people and the natural environment and between the people themselves, which culminated in the ten years' Cultural Revolution (1966–76). Reflecting on history and the ideologies of the twentieth century, many contemporary Confucian or non-Confucian intellectuals of Mainland China endeavour to rediscover and explore the theme of harmony in the Confucian tradition, focusing on its significance for Chinese life and its guidance in dealing with conflict. They argue that harmony must be reinstalled as the centre of Chinese culture and re-established as the ideological foundation of the twenty-first century for guiding all the nations in dealing with conflict between people, between human beings and nature, and between nations (Zhang, 1996, vols. 1–2).

Questions for discussion

1. How should we understand the importance of 'Heaven' for the Confucian view of the world, society and human destiny?
2. What is the Confucian Way of Humans? How is the human way related to the Way of Heaven?
3. What is meant by 'harmony' in the Confucian tradition? Why is it said that harmony is the central theme running through Confucian doctrine?
4. Can Confucianism provide a useful resource for a modern eco-ethics?
5. How can we evaluate the Confucian attitudes towards family relationships?

4

Ritual and religious practice

The Confucian understanding of ritual and the Confucian practice of spiritual cultivation reveal the distinctiveness of Confucian religiosity. The co-existence of Confucianism with other religious traditions has enabled Confucians to engage in dynamic dialogue with many different doctrines. This enriches Confucian religio-ethics on the one hand and cultivates a syncretic culture on the other hand. To examine the spiritual dimension of the Confucian tradition, therefore, we shall look into three areas of Confucian practice. Firstly, we shall explore how Confucianism was involved in grand religious sacrifice and its contribution to the formation and transformation of the state religion. Collective and official ritual is but one aspect of Confucian religiosity, and individual Confucians also actively engage themselves in a range of spiritual practices, in which a sense of eternity and transcendence is sought through the pursuit of secular learning and personal discipline. In the second section of this chapter, therefore, we shall come to examine how individual Confucians endeavour to bridge the temporal and the eternal through learning and spiritual cultivation. Confucianism has existed and functioned in the context of a multireligious society and its intercourse with other religious traditions, such as Daoism, Buddhism and more recently Christianity, not only has an impact on its own doctrines and practices but also exerts a great deal of influence over these traditions. The interaction between Confucianism and these three religious traditions will thus be the focus of the third section.

Confucianism: a tradition of ritual

Confucianism is known as a tradition of ritual/propriety (*lijiao*), and as such was deeply entwined with the state religion in traditional China and Korea. Although Confucianism is not wholly identical with the state religion and the religious practices of the state cannot be said to be exclusively Confucian, there is nevertheless a significant overlap between the key elements of Confucian doctrine and the religious ceremonies of the imperial government. Confucianism transformed the religious practices prevailing in the Shang and Zhou times and helped establish a systematic doctrine that was used as the guidelines for official and private religious practices. Confucian scholars/officials had great influence in the understanding and performance of ceremonies, and contributed to the formation of a political-ethical-religious society essentially based on moral and religious rites. In these ways Confucianism became the foundation of the imperial system of administration and provided the authority for the interpretation and organisation of religious beliefs and practices. Confucianism benefited greatly from associating itself with the state, and consequently Confucian elements became embedded in the whole imperial system, dominating the way of thinking, acting and living for a long period. In a sense we may say that without a proper understanding of religious and non-religious rituals, it would not be possible for us to understand the fundamentals of Confucianism and its function in traditional society. Yet it is also true that without an appreciation of Confucian spirituality it would be difficult to grasp how imperial governments in China and Korea justified and exercised their authority in the social and religious life of the masses.

RITUAL AND SACRIFICE

'Ritual' in Chinese is *li*, translated variously as ritual, rites, ceremonies, moral codes or the rules of propriety. *Li* (禮) is a character portraying a sacred (示) ritual vessel (豊) and its original meaning is 'to arrange ritual vessels'; hence 'serving gods and praying for good fortune' (*Shuowen Jiezi Zhu*, 1981: 2). The understanding of the character was later extended and developed, and consequently the character becomes a complex term denoting the basic principles of the universe which underlie all the laws, codes and rules of the natural and human world. *The Book of Rites* describes *li* in the following terms:

> While the rules of ceremony [*li*] have their origin in heaven, the
> movement of them reaches to earth. The distribution of them extends
> to all the business (of life). They change with the seasons; they agree in
> reference to the (variation of) lot and condition. In regard to man, they
> serve to nurture (his nature). They are practised by means of offerings,
> acts of strength, words, and postures of courtesy, in eating and drinking,
> in the observances of capping, marriage, mourning, sacrificing, archery,
> chariot-driving, audiences, and friendly missions.
>
> (Legge, 1968: vol. 27: 388)

Confucians believe that in the human realm *li* has religious, social and
psychological dimensions, and that its meaning extends from ritual to
propriety, from civil laws to codified customs, and from moral rules for
behaviour to ethical senses for thinking, feeling and acting. The religious
dimension of *li* indicates the means by which humans communicate with
spiritual powers. It is believed that the orderly performance of dance and
music combined with offerings and sacrifice pleases the ancestors and
the spirits to whom it is dedicated; in this way the descendants are able
to express their gratitude and commitment. During this process, faults
are repented, confidence gained, and happiness and success secured.
In its social dimension, *li* 'is the principle by which the ancient kings
embodied the laws of heaven and regulated the expressions of human
nature. Therefore, he who has attained *li* [ritual] lives, and he who has
lost it, dies' (Lin, 1992: 493). The web of ritual gives everyone a special
position in family, community and society, which in turn enables one to
assess what one should or should not do in a particular circumstance
and to formulate one's words and actions accordingly. It is believed that
if everybody acts in accordance with *li*, then the world would be peaceful
and orderly, ruled without ruling, governed without governing, and
ordered without ordering. The psychological dimension of *li* is somewhat similar to the harmony embodied in music, poetry and dance, and
makes following rules an enjoyable personal experience and not the dull
performance of duties. This experience is believed to be necessary for
cultivating one's character and to enable all feelings and emotions to be
harmonised and expressed in proper measure.

The early Confucians are mostly recorders, preservers, modifiers and
editors of ancient literature, of which a large quantity is on various kinds
of *li*. Confucian masters and students took these records as textbooks
for education, and gradually developed a systematic understanding

concerning the nature, function and value of various rituals. When Confucianism was promoted as the state ideology in the Han Dynasty, its ideas about ritual were integrated into the state religion and played an important role in the development of the imperial theo-political system. Confucian records and interpretations of ancient ritual underpinned imperial practices concerning the communication between the human and the spiritual, and provided much needed help to the the government in its efforts to consolidate the empire.

The most important aspect of ritual is sacrifice. There are three Chinese characters for 'sacrifice': *ji* (祭), a hand (⺬) holding a piece of meat (⺼) offering it to the spirits or on a sacred altar (示); *si* (祀, 祀), a combination of a sacred altar (示) and a human embryo (㔾); and *xiang* (享, 會 a pictograph of an ancestral temple). Each of these characters has a special meaning linked to a special purpose: *si* is to offer sacrifices to heavenly spirits, *ji* to earthly spirits and *xiang* to the spirits of the ancestors (*Zhouli Zhushu*, 1980: 757–8). In general, however, all activities in relation to sacrifice can be called *jisi* or *si*. According to the *Rites of the Zhou*, a collection of rituals edited during the late Warring States period or the early Han time, there are three grades of sacrifice, the grand sacrifice (*dasi*) with offerings of jade, silk and animals, the medium sacrifice (*zhongsi*) with offerings of animals and metal; and the small sacrifice (*xiaosi*) offering only animal victims. In later imperial China, the grand sacrifice was made to Heaven and the Lord on High in the Temple of Heaven, to Earth in the Temple of Earth, to *sheji* at the Altar of the Spirits of Land and Grains, to the royal ancestors in the Temple of Ancestors, and to Confucius in the Temple of Confucius. The medium sacrifice was offered to the sun and moon, to the gods of agriculture and sericulture and to the former emperors, while the small sacrifice was offered in ordinary temples (Shryock, 1966: 160).

Confucianism was closely related to these practices. Ritual and sacrifice are recorded, described and interpreted in the Confucian classics. Faithful Confucians always treat ritual with care, sincerity and reverence, and they observe and follow the rules in accordance with the sacred texts, and consider sacrifice to be the 'utmost expression' of reverence and humanity, in which each offering was endowed with a symbolic meaning. According to the provisions in the *Book of Rites*, the animal victims, the fish and the flesh, were

the richest tributes for the palate from all within the four seas and the
nine provinces. The fruits and grains presented in the high dishes of
wood and bamboo were the product of the harmonious influences
of the four seasons. The tribute of metal showed the harmonious
submission (of the princes). The rolls of silk showed the honour they
rendered to virtue.   (Legge, 1968, vol. 27: 413)

The strict performance of ritual is believed to be necessary to ensure
harmony, happiness and prosperity for the state, the land and the
people. The majority of Confucians considered the proper execution of
ritual with the proper number of animal, silk and vegetable offerings to
be of great importance for effective communication between the human
and the spiritual realms. When discussing the meaning and significance
of ritual, the *Book of Rites* makes it clear that 'Of all the methods for
the good ordering of men, there is none more urgent than the use of
ceremonies [rituals]. Ceremonies are of Five kinds [the auspicious, the
mourning, hospitality, the military and the festive], and there is none of
them more important than sacrifices' (Legge, 1968, vol. 28: 236).

Being a rational doctrine, Confucianism interprets ritual and sacrifice in
a humanistic way. It believes that sacrifice is not imposed on individuals
and the state from the outside; rather it issues from the hearts of the
people. Only those of virtue can fulfil this condition and fully display the
meaning and purpose of ritual and sacrifice. Confucianism appreciates
that sacrifice may bring about good fortune, such as material gain, physical longevity and spiritual protection, but it constantly emphasises that
personal gain is not the primary purpose. The important thing is to have
a sincere attitude, a reverential heart and a virtuous motive, and to offer
'sacrifices without seeking for anything to be gained' (Legge, 1968, vol.
28: 237). Those who are engaged in ritual should experience a spiritual
and moral reunion with the spirits: ' "Sacrifice as if present" is taken to
mean "sacrifice to the gods as if the gods were present" ' (*Lunyu*, 3: 12).
This requires more than merely ceremonial performance. Confucians
stress the importance of ceremonies in refining human piety and emphasise
the moral effect of ritual on the people. Ritual is not merely about playing music and offering jade and silk (*Lunyu*, 17: 11). It is meant to achieve
moral perfection. When a person of virtue performs a sacrifice, he 'brings
into exercise all sincerity and good faith, with all right-heartedness and
reverence; he offers the (proper) things, accompanies them with the
(proper) rites; employs the soothing of music; does everything suitably

to the season' (Legge, 1968, vol. 28: 237). Therefore, reverence runs through the whole process of sacrifice which begins with a reverential heart and extends to the greatest reverence toward the spirits (*Liji Jijie*, 1989: 1298; Legge, 1968, vol. 28: 330).

Confucians maintain that ritual is a vehicle by which virtue and the meaning of life are manifest. Rather than casual observance, it is important to live a good life and to fulfil one's mission with reverence. When seriously ill and reminded of the need to pray to the spirits, Confucius first asked whether there was such a thing as prayer and then said that 'I have been offering my prayers for a long time' (*Lunyu*, 7: 34). For him, praying is not a moment of expiation; it is the direction of one's whole life. In this sense Confucius was confident that the life he had lived was in accordance with the Way of Heaven and that his pursuit of goodness and his untiring teaching of others were the most reverent form of prayer, far more effective than any particular praying words even at the time of his approaching death.

As a morally oriented tradition, Confucianism transformed ancient rituals and made them closely related to moral achievement. The majority of Confucians understand spirits and sacrifice to spirits in humanistic terms, and believe that the needs of the spirits are in fact the needs of the people. They argue against those who believe that a good performance of ritual can be achieved by well-prepared victims like fat sheep and beautiful silk, and urge people to understand that 'the *state of* the people is what the Spirits regard. The sage kings therefore first secured the welfare of the people, and then put forth their strength in *serving* the Spirits' (*Chunqiu Zuozhuan Zhu*, 1990: 111; Legge, 1992, vol. 5: 48). They propose that only those who have gained moral perfection, or have made a great contribution to the spiritual and material well-being of the people, are entitled to sacrifice. According to this understanding, great rituals should be observed only to honour those who have done great service to the people and to the state. It is indeed described in the section on the way of sacrifice of the *Book of Rites* that

> According to the institutes of the sage kings about sacrifices, sacrifice should be offered to him who had given (good) laws to the people; to him who had laboured to the death in the discharge of his duties; to him who had strengthened the state by his laborious toil, to him who had boldly and successfully met great calamities, and to him who had warded off great evil.   (Legge, 1968, vol. 28: 207–8)

Further, Confucians insist that ceremonies be performed not only for an effective communication between the human and the spiritual, but also for the ethical transformation of the living people. They believe that the proper and sincere performance of ritual has a corresponding effect on the perfection of the character of the people, assuming that through engaging and observing ritual, performers would be purified, observers educated and the people taught about what is good and what is not good so that they would naturally follow the good and reject the bad.

SACRIFICE TO HEAVEN

Traditional government based on Confucianism was by nature a theo-political entity, and functioned with the religious belief that political power was endowed by Heaven and that Heaven sanctioned political decisions. In this respect all state affairs were religious and all religious practices had a political significance.

In the Chinese context 'state religion' is a vague term and covers a vast area including religious sanction for policy-making, official sacrifices, court ceremonies, royal marriage, funeral and mourning rites. Among the numerous sacrifices offered in the name of the state, three are directly related to Confucianism: sacrifice to Heaven, to royal ancestors and to Confucius, and these three grand rituals formed the pillars of the state religion. Sacrifice to Heaven and to the royal ancestors originated in the Shang–Zhou period long before Confucianism became a distinctive school, but Confucians incorporated them into their own system and made them part of their own tradition. Confucians invested greatly in these ceremonies, and paid great attention to perform them according to the rites recorded in the Confucian classics.

In the previous chapter we have examined the way the Confucian Heaven underlies its doctrine of the universe and humanity, and how it provides the gravitational centre for religious, political, moral and daily life. In the earlier part of Chinese history 'Heaven' was used frequently in a spiritual sense and it was indeed that 'many of the religious influences in Chinese political life stemmed from the basic concept of Heaven and its subordinate system of deities as a supernatural force that pre-determined the course of all events in the universe' (Yang, 1961: 127). Subsequently, sacrifice to Heaven became the first and foremost important ritual of the state. Sacrifice to Heaven was used for many purposes depending upon historical, social and cultural circumstances. It might be used to request relief from drought, insect infestation, enemy invasion, or to obtain a peaceful reign, a good harvest or a successful campaign, or to justify and strengthen the sovereign power. In many ways it was the prevailing circumstances that determined the focus of sacrifice to Heaven with the ultimate aim of harmonising the relationship between the human and the spiritual realms.

Generally speaking, there are two kinds of sacrifice, one performed in the Temple of Heaven and the other at the Eastern Peak, Mount Tai. Confucians maintained that both had been performed in the past by legendary sage–kings, and it is recorded in the *Book of History* that when the eastern capital was build at Luo, the Duke of Zhou had an altar established in the southern suburb, where he offered two bulls as victims to Heaven (Legge, 1992, vol. 3: 423). In other classics, sacrifice to Heaven is said to be made by the 'Son of Heaven', and the number of animals used in the sacrifice varied. The *Book of Rites* states that the Son of Heaven 'sacrificed to Heaven with a single victim' (Legge, 1968, vol. 27: 398), and that '[a]t the (Great) border sacrifice, he [the Son of Heaven] welcomed the arrival of the longest day. It was a great act of thanksgiving to Heaven and the sun was the chief object considered in it' (*ibid.*: 427). Due to the influence of yin–yang and the Five Elements theory, the Lord of Heaven (*tianzhu*) was later represented as the Five Lords, residing respectively at the centre and in the four quarters. During the Han Dynasty there was a temporary separation of Heaven (*tian*) from the Lord on High (*shangdi*): sacrifice to Heaven was carried out in the southern suburb while that to the Lord on High in the *Ming Tang*, the Bright Hall or Luminous Hall – a cosmic temple with a conical top conforming to Heaven and a square base in accord with the Earth (Soothill, 1951: 90). Gradually, these two kinds of sacrifice were combined into one ceremony and the southern suburb sacrifice became the only occasion on which the earthly ruler communicated with Heaven and expressed his gratitude to Heaven by offering sacrifices. Since then until the beginning of the twentieth century, all dynasties observed the sacrifice, regulated the ritual and considered it to be the most august religious activity. The ritual is composed of nine steps, and the performance includes music, dance, reading prayer documents and offering sacrifices. The single qualified worshipper for this great sacrifice was the emperor, the Son of Heaven, and in making the sacrifice to Heaven he 'served' Heaven (*shitian*, in *Chunqiu Fanlu Yizheng*, 1992: 405). Throughout the year the emperor ruled the whole country and sat on his throne facing south, but on the occasion of the sacrifice to Heaven he had to face north to acknowledge his humble and subordinate position, and to prostrate himself in front of the spiritual tablet of *Huangtian Shangdi* (August Heaven the Lord on High).

Sacrifice to Heaven was also made at Mount Tai and this ritual is known as *feng* (封). *Feng* was said to have been a practice adopted by all the ancient sage–kings and in the *Book of History* the Sage–King, Shun, is said to have presented a burnt-offering to Heaven on the Mount (Legge, 1992, vol. 3: 35). When the First Emperor of the Qin Dynasty toured the country, he wished to follow ancient kings to perform the *feng* at the foot of Mount Tai. But the Emperor and his retinue were ignorant of the ritual, so he 'summoned seventy Confucian masters and scholars' to advise him of the 'procedures for carrying out the Feng and Shan [for Earth] sacrifices' (*Shiji*, 1997: 1366; Watson, 1961, vol. 2: 23). Emperor Wu of the Han Dynasty was an assiduous performer of the ritual, and it is recorded that he performed the grand ceremony at the foot of the Mount five times during his reign.

Whatever form it took, sacrifice to Heaven was at the centre of state religion and politics, and was highly regarded by Confucian scholars. There is no doubt that worship of Heaven was always an official matter and an exclusive privilege of the emperor, and that sacrifice to Heaven was used to strengthen the power of a political regime. Dong Zhongshu asserted that 'the greatness of the Way originates from Heaven. As Heaven remains unchanging, so does the Way' (*Hanshu*, 1997: 2518–19). This was frequently taken as an excuse for resisting the call for changes. However, it does not follow that Heaven and sacrifice to Heaven had nothing to do with ordinary Confucians and the common people. Rational Confucianism transformed the supernatural concept of Heaven into an understanding of the unity between humans and Heaven based on moral principles, but this does not reduce the Confucian reverence to Heaven much. In the Confucian system *jingtian* (敬天 treating Heaven with reverence) and *wei tianming* (畏天命 standing in awe of the Mandate of Heaven) underlie all human behaviour and social programmes. Obedience to the emperor was considered to be a religious act by the people, who accepted that the power of the royal house was endowed by Heaven, and that the emperor was the representative of Heaven on earth. It was also believed that Heaven controlled not only the fate of the dynasty but also the destiny of each individual within the empire. Confucianism was no doubt instrumental in spreading these ideas, which intertwined the fate of the state and the destiny of the nation with the Mandate of Heaven.

The worship of Heaven was not merely a tool for restraining the people. It could also be a positive leverage for the state. The power and authority of Heaven were reconfirmed on each occasion of the sacrifice and the ruler was reminded of his duty to Heaven and thereby to the people at each step of the ceremony. Confucian scholars saw this as the religio-political value of the ritual. Only in the light of their mission to carry out the Mandate of Heaven on the earth can we understand why so many Confucians in history would risk their lives to reprimand a dissolute emperor for his failure to fulfil his duties to the state. Many of the so-called Former Scholars (*xianru*), whose tablets were admitted to the Temples of Confucius, had demonstrated their loyalty to the mission. They were believed to have served Heaven by inculcating the ruler with Confucian principles and integrity. Of these Former Scholars, famous examples were Han Yu (768–823) who twice rebuked the emperor and was twice banished, and Ouyang Xiu (1007–72), who fearlessly rebuked the emperor, the Empress Dowager and the powerful prime minister (Watters, 1879: 112, 121). On the other hand, the Confucian belief that 'Heaven sees as the people see and Heaven listens as the people listen' provided a powerful weapon for Confucians and the common people alike to fight against a corrupt superior. Sacrifice to Heaven aroused the sense of dignity in the people. Believing that the Way of Heaven was just, the common people would take Heaven as their justification for expressing dissatisfaction and anger against a 'rotten regime' and for launching revolutionary movements to overthrow it.

SACRIFICE TO ANCESTORS AND FILIAL PIETY

Ancestral worship is thought by many scholars to be the root of all religions. The family occupies a central position in Confucian culture, in which reverence and glorification of one's ancestors is seen not only as one's greatest duty but also one's greatest honour. Originally referring to the temple of the ancestors, the Chinese character *Zu* (祖, ancestors) is composed of two radicals: 示 (spiritual sacred altar) and 且 (male genitals, or meat for sacrifice), which shows a combination of sacredness and sacrifice. Archaeological discoveries and historical records demonstrate that the Shang culture was based on sacrifice to ancestors, and that the replacement of matriarchy with patriarchy had been completed by the early years of the Zhou Dynasty:

> References to females are also evident in oracle bone inscriptions of the Shang period (c. 1200 BC). Mentions of a deceased mother (*bi*) are more numerous than those of a father or male ruler, and it has been suggested that the predominance of female names points to a matriarchal society. This situation appears to have changed during the Zhou period, by the end of which no special sacrifices seem to have been directed at female ancestors. (Rawson, 1996: 271)

In this culture death was not seen as a total end to family connection, but an event that would continue to have an effect on the destiny of the family. Through sacrifice, the past and the present were believed to be reunited, and the dead and the living to support each other. The oracular and bronze inscriptions bear testimony to an intimate and daily communication between the reigning king and his royal ancestors. Sacrificial bronze vessels, human and animal remains, chariots and numerous other artefacts found in excavated tombs point to some belief that the dead had needs similar to those of the living. The motive for sacrifice is twofold, one a concern for the dead, the other for the living. Sacrifice on behalf of the deceased was to provide sustenance, and the materials offered through sacrifice would allow the ancestors to live in the manner to which they had been accustomed in life. For the living, sacrifice to the ancestors brought about blessings and help, which would enable the descendants to overcome disasters and cope with difficulties. They believed that failure to perform sacrifice would dissociate them from their ancestors and result in the anger of the unsatisfied ancestors who would then lay a curse upon their family.

The early practice in relation to ancestral worship also demonstrated a close relationship between sacrifice to the ancestors and the conception and value of the Ultimate. It was believed that the great ancestors of the royal house were in Heaven sitting besides the Lord on High, and that the most efficient way to communicate with Heaven was via sacrifice to the great ancestors. It was the Shang and Zhou custom that royal ancestral spirits were worshipped as correlates of Heaven or the Lord on High. The Duke of Zhou was believed to have offered sacrifices to Heaven via his ancestor (*hou ji* 后稷, the Lord of Grains) and to the Lord on High via his father, King Wen (Watson, 1961, vol. 2: 16–17).

Sacrifice to ancestors was not only a religious matter but also the foundation of government, culture and society. The royal ancestral temple used to be the most important place in the state and was considered the political symbol of sovereignty. The temple was the location for more than just the sacrifice to the ancestors; it was the place where divination was carried out, where a new king was enthroned and imperial marriage was announced. It was also the storehouse for things of value and military weapons. It was in this temple where kings held their audiences with officials and feudal lords, where orders concerning both civil and military matters were issued, where the ruler and ministers heard news of victory in battle, and where they dispensed rewards to meritorious officials (Bilsky, 1975: 66). These actions bear testimony to a deep belief that politics could not proceed without religious support and that religion would not be complete without political programmes.

From these early customs developed a general practice in relation to ancestral sacrifice. Early Confucians believed that the life of human beings came from the combination of two parts, the *hun* 魂, the spirit from Heaven, and the *po* 魄, the soul from the earth. When a person was born, these two parts combined and life began, and when a person died they departed, with the *hun* ascending to Heaven and the *po* descending to the earth. In ancestral sacrifice individual ancestors were symbolised by spiritual tablets that were installed on an altar, located either in a special room or in a temple. When sacrifice was made before the tablets, the descendant would recall the deceased: the spirit from Heaven by music and the soul from the earth with wine. It was believed that when the music and fragrance of the offerings ascended to the palace of heaven and the smell of wine descended to the Yellow Spring of earth, the spirit and soul of the ancestors would return to their 'home' and reside in the tablets. Confucius was believed to have highly valued this sacrifice, and the *Book of Rites* records his words to the effect that 'It is the union of *kwei* [*gui* 鬼, soul] and *shan* [*shen* 神, spirit] that forms the highest exhibition of doctrine' (Legge, 1968, vol. 28: 220).

Sacrifice to ancestors was considered to be an occasion that required emotional care and reverence. 'The rites of mourning are the extreme expression of grief and sorrow' (Legge, 1968: vol. 27: 167), but sacrifice to ancestors was not confined to offering food and materials. It was a way that descendants submitted themselves to the ancestors and demonstrated their reverence to the past. In this way sacrifice to the ancestors is believed to lead to the perfection of moral virtues, as stated by Zengzi that 'the virtue of the common people will reach its fullness when the dead are looked after carefully and sacrifice is extended to the ancestors of the past' (*Lunyu*, 1: 9).

Not only did the Confucians of all generations make reverent sacrifice to their ancestors at home but they also paid great attention to the continuity of the ancient ritual and the establishment of it as a national institution. For them, sacrifice to ancestors was important because it gave the descendants a religious dependency and spiritual reliance, and made possible the continuity of the chain linking the ancestors and descendants. The belief that 'All things originate from Heaven, and humans originate from ancestors' (*Liji Jijie*, 1989: 694; Legge, 1968, vol. 27: 430) is central to Confucian doctrine, and Confucianism endows ancestral worship with the meaning of not forgetting one's origin. Ancestral worship requires filial piety. Filial piety (*xiao*) characterises the Confucian attitude towards the past and the Confucian efforts to associate descendants with the ancestors and parents. In earlier texts *xiao* meant piety towards the spirits of ancestors or deceased parents. For example, in the *Book of Poetry* it states that a filial descendant would provide unceasing service to his ancestors, and for such filial piety the ancestors would confer blessings on him (Legge, 1992, vol. 4: 477). In the *Book of Rites* Confucius is quoted as to say that: 'The repairing of the ancestral temple and the reverential performance of the sacrifices were intended to teach the people to follow their dead with their filial piety' (Legge, 1968, vol. 28: 291). In the *Analects* filial piety is still frequently used in this sense, but it becomes mainly applied to living parents. Confucians insist that ancestors exist not only in the past but also in the present and they emphasise that an individual owes everything to the remote ancestors as well as to the immediate 'ancestors', as one's body is nothing other than that which has been 'bequeathed to one by one's parents' (Fung, 1952: 358). Therefore, one's duty to parents is the same as, or perhaps even more important than, the duty to ancestors. The shift of focus from the dead to the living was the result of the development of Confucian rationalism and humanism. When filial piety is paid to the 'living ancestors', ancestral worship becomes more than a tradition or custom; and when ancestral worship is considered an extension of family life, filial piety is more than a secular attitude; it has become part of religious ritual and a constituent element of spirituality. Later Confucians promoted filial piety to the summit of all virtues, stressing that the spiritual value of filial piety comes from Heaven and that Heaven instills filial piety and respect for elders when it produces all things in the world (*Chunqiu Fanlu Yizheng*, 1992: 168). In the *Book of Filial Piety* it is deemed the first principle of Heaven and Earth, 'surrounded by the mystical halo' (Waley, 1938: 39). This short book thus became one of the most important texts for effectively enforcing filial piety on the people and for propagating the fundamental Confucian virtue. It contributed to the final establishment of filial piety as the cornerstone of the Confucian state.

Filial piety is regarded as lifelong service to one's parents. When asked about how to be filial, Confucius said that a filial son must provide his parents with sufficient food and clothes, must do this with a pleasant attitude, and must act according to the rules of propriety. Zengzi described three grades of filial piety (*Liji Jijie*, 1989: 1225). At the highest level, one would honour and glorify one's parents by one's achievement in moral cultivation and by one's service to the people and the state. At the second level, one would not bring disgrace to one's parents through one's own failure; as warned in the *Book of History* that if the sovereign did not do his job properly he would disgrace his ancestors (Legge, 1992, vol. 3: 201). At the lowest level, one would serve one's parents with reverence and ensure that they had a decent life.

The Confucian practice of sacrifice to ancestors and filial piety to parents demonstrates another characteristic of the Confucian understanding of human destiny. 'In Buddhism, the ego disappears into the cosmos, in Confucianism [it] disappears into the family' (Tu, *et al.*, 1992: 6, 12). The family provides an individual not only with the source of life, by which he is related to the past, but also with a sense of continuity, by which he is extended to the future. From this we can see that the Confucian understanding of continuity and eternity is different from that of other religious traditions. In Christianity, it is atonement and incarnation that give a person a sense of continuity and allows him to enter eternity after his bodily life has ceased. In Buddhism, the ego is seen as an illusion and the cosmos as flowing forever. The individual is caught in a constant cycle of reincarnation until he can forget his small self and become part of the great cosmic self. In Daoism, the physical body is believed to be capable of living forever, and to acquire immortality one should cultivate *Dao* by leading one's life according to natural law.

In Confucianism eternity exists in self-cultivation as well as in the collective and practical life of the family. Confucians believe that a sense of eternity can be obtained through the continuity of the family in which each generation is treated as a necessary link in the family chain and every life is considered a contribution to the huge enterprise that was initiated by the ancestors and continued by their descendants. Confucians taught that through the performance of their duties in the family, the young would obtain a sense of moral responsibility, the elderly gain respect, the dead live in the hearts of their descendants and the newborn be given a mission. In these ways an individual would last as long as his family lasted, and would acquire a sense of eternity in the midst of temporal life.

THE CULT OF CONFUCIUS

Modest as Confucius was, his disciples praised him as the highest ideal – although the praises recorded in the *Analects* might perhaps have been added at a much later date. Confucius said that he did not dare to claim to be a sage or a man of virtue (*ren ren*) (*Lunyu*, 7: 34), yet his disciples believed that it was Heaven that set him on the path to being a sage (*Lunyu*, 9: 6). Confucius saw himself as an ordinary man who only distinguished himself through his eager seeking of the truth: 'In a hamlet of ten households, there are bound to be those who are my equals in being loyal and faithful, but few of them would love learning as eagerly as I do' (*Lunyu*, 5: 28). However, his disciples compared his character to that of the sun and moon, far beyond the reach of others: 'Other men of excellence are like hills which one can easily climb over. Zhongni [Confucius] is like the sun and moon which one has no way of climbing over' (*Lunyu*, 19: 24). Confucius portrayed himself as a transmitter of ancient culture, a man eager to learn and tireless to teach, but for his disciples, the Way of their Master was profound and sublime beyond description: 'The more I look up at it, the higher it appears. The more I bore into it the harder it becomes. I see it before me. Suddenly it is behind me' (*Lunyu*, 9: 11). When Confucius was criticised for not being as good as one of his disciples (Zi Gong), this disciple took a house with an enclosing wall to illustrate the difference between himself and his master: The wall of his own house was only several feet high, so everybody passing by could see the beautiful things in the house. It was quite different in the case of his master, where the wall was tens of feet high. Unless one gained admittance through the gate, one could not possibly see how beautiful it was (*Lunyu*, 19: 23). In his life Confucius did not succeed in persuading rulers to implement his doctrine, but this did not affect the views of his disciples who continued to believe that his achievements were so great that they could not possibly be matched:

> It would be as hard to equal our master as to climb up on a ladder to the sky. Had our master ever been put in control of a state or of a noble family, it would have been as it is described in the words, 'He raised them and they stood, he led them and they went. He steadied them and they came. He stirred them and they moved harmoniously. His life was glorious and his death bewailed.' How can such a man ever be equalled?
>
> (*Lunyu*, 19: 25)

This admiration for Confucius was further developed by later Confucians, who believed that Confucius had reached the highest level in the world: 'Since humanity came into this world, there has never been one greater than Confucius' (*Mengzi*, 2A: 2). Having confirmed that Confucius did compose (*zuo*) the *Spring and Autumn Annals*, Mengzi claimed that what Confucius did was nothing other than 'the business of the Son of Heaven' (*Mengzi*, 3B: 9). In the *Doctrine of the Mean* the contrast between the modesty of Confucius and his achievement is interpreted as part of the Way: 'The Way of the superior man [*junzi*] functions everywhere and yet is hidden', and Confucius' work in human society is said to be of transcendental significance, and as a sage he is believed to have been part of the transforming and nourishing process of Heaven and Earth (Chan, 1963a: 100, 108). The Confucians of the Han Dynasty worshipped Confucius as the 'Uncrowned King' (*su wang*), and they believed that the capture of a *lin* (unicorn) in 481 BCE recorded at the end of *the Spring and Autumn Annals* was a sign from Heaven that the 'Mandate of Heaven' had passed to Confucius and in a moral sense he was the founder of a new dynasty (Fung, 1953: 71).

Praises and eulogies of this kind were soon used in the ritual of sacrifice to Confucius, and Confucian followers facilitated the elevation of the sacrifice from an ordinary ceremony to the major cult of the state. The history of sacrifice to Confucius shows how he gained importance in political, cultural and educational areas. Confucius was undoubtedly mourned by his disciples and students for three years and in one case for six (*Mengzi*, 3A: 4), but the traditional belief that a temple was erected by the Duke of Lu as early as 478 BCE cannot be authenticated (Shryock 1966: 94). It was recorded that the founder of the Former Han Dynasty paid a visit to the tomb of Confucius in 195 BCE and he offered a *tailao* sacrifice composed of an ox, a sheep and a pig, but many people believed that this was more of a political gesture than a sincere act of worship. The full state sacrifice to Confucius did not begin perhaps until Confucianism became the state orthodoxy. It was during the Han period that the scale and importance of the sacrifice grew rapidly. In 8 BCE, the descendants of Confucius were given a hereditary fief to enable them to conduct sacrifices to Confucius and to their forefathers of the Shang Dynasty. In the year 1 CE, the Confucian Temple in his home town was repaired at the expense of the state and Confucius was given the title of 'Duke'. An imperial decree was issued in 57 CE to link the sacrifice to Confucius with that to the Duke of Zhou. Emperor Ming (r. 57–75) gave an order in 59 CE that sacrifics to Confucius be made in all educational institutes therefore establishing Confucius as the patron of education. In 492 Confucius was given the title of 'the Venerable Ni, the Accomplished Sage', and in 609 his temple at the capital was separated from that of the Duke of Zhou. The founder of the Tang Dynasty decreed in 630 that all districts and counties establish temples in honour of Confucius, and in 647 the tablets of the seventy-two disciples of Confucius were placed in the Temple of Confucius in the capital – prior to this the only disciple who had received sacrifice with the Master in the state temple was Yan Hui. In 657 Confucius was titled 'the perfect Sage, the ancient Teacher' (*zhi sheng xian shi* 至聖先師), and this title has remained to the twentieth century.

In each city of traditional China and Korea there were one or more temples dedicated to Confucius, where his followers, students, scholars and governmental officials offered sacrifices during festivals. In the first decade of the seventeenth century Ricci observed that

> In every city and school where the literati congregate, according to an ancient law, there is a very sumptuous temple of Confucius, in which there stands his statue with his name and title; and every new moon and full moon, and four times in the year, the literati offer to him a certain kind of sacrifice with incense and dead animals which they offer up, although they acknowledge no divinity in him and ask nothing of him. And so it cannot be called a true sacrifice. (Rule, 1986: 27)

Watters noticed in the nineteenth century: 'According to the laws of China there must be a Wen-miao (文廟) or Temple of Confucius attached to every Prefecture, Sub-Prefecture, District, and in every market-town throughout the empire. Consequently not only has each town its temple but all prefectural cities contains two and some three' (Watters, 1879: v).

Confucian temples have had various names: *xiansheng miao*, the Temple of the Former Sage, *wenmiao*, the Temple of Culture or Literature, and *kongzi miao*, the Temple of Confucius. Temples of Confucius are normally connected with the Confucian academies, which led to them acquiring titles such as *xuegong*, the Palace of Education, and *bangong*, which refers to the semicircular pools (see figure 10) found before the temples imitating the college design of the Zhou Dynasty (Shryock, 1966: 144). In the temple, sacrifices were made to Confucius, his ancestors, family members, disciples and prominent scholars. Besides the Four Associates (*sipei*) – Yan Hui, Zengzi, Zisi and Mengzi, each having his own temple (see figure 8), there are the Twelve Philosophers (*shier zhe*), Former Worthies (*xian xian*) and Former Scholars (*xian ru*), the numbers of the lists varied throughout history. Korean Confucians retained the original number of the Ten Philosophers and made various other changes to the scholars worshipped in their temples. The most recent one dramatically reduced the number of figures worshipped from 208 to 39, namely, Confucius, the Four Associates, the Ten Philosophers, the Six Neo-Confucian Masters and the Eighteen Korean Sages (Palmer, 1984: 62). Regardless of the changes, Korean Confucians treat the ritual and sacrifice with deep reverence and thereby pay homage to their Former Teacher (see figure 9).

The worship of Confucius was always an important part of the imperial system in China. In 1906 an imperial decree announced that sacrifice to Confucius should be placed on an equal footing with those to Heaven and Earth. After the overthrow of the Qing Dynasty (1644–1911), the first generation of republicans carried on this tradition. The representatives of the parliament convened in 1914 to discuss the rites paid to Confucius and they unanimously agreed that the rites 'should be the *Ta ssu*, and the ceremony, clothes, and vessels should be similar to those of the sacrifice to Heaven' (Shryock, 1966: 206, 216). As late as 1918 it was still observed that Confucius 'is worshipped in a similar spirit as the Buddhists worship the Gautama Buddha, the Enlightened One, the Christians worshipped Jesus Christ, as the Messiah of Israel and the Saviour of all mankind, and the adherents of Islam look reverently up to their prophet Mohammed' (Carus, 1918: 155).

Is sacrifice to Confucius a kind of theistic cult or simply an act of moral reverence? It is perhaps a combination of both with each aspect having a greater or lesser significance at different times in the long history of the tradition. Shryock believed that 'The cult of Confucius was a hero worship deliberately adopted by the state at the insistence of a social group, the scholars, who acknowledged the leadership of the sage. This hero worship occupied a place in the state religion between the cults of nature deities and the worship of ancestors, from both of which it borrowed' (Shryock, 1966: 105).

On the one hand Confucius was treated as a deity and was believed to have been sent by Heaven to save the world from destruction. Due to the influence of Buddhism and Daoism, Confucius was considered a god with spiritual powers. This lasted from the Tang Dynasty to 1530 when, under the guidance of rational Confucianism, major reforms were instigated to eliminate the images and the titles of nobility previously given to Confucius and his followers. On the other hand, Confucius was regarded as a great man and a great teacher, and Confucians always placed emphasis on the moral and educational values of the rites. The prayer used in the sacrifice illustrates the moral excellence of Confucius and expresses the admiration of his followers:

> O Great teacher, thy virtue surpasses that of a thousand sages,
> And thy way excels that of a hundred kings.
> Rivaling the sun and moon,
> Thy light shines forever . . .
> The reverent and constant observance of thy moral teaching is the
> expression of our gratitude to thee. Mayest thou enjoy this sacrifice.
> (Shryock, 1966: 169–70)

As with all other major Confucian rituals, sacrifice to Confucius and Confucian sages is intended to augment human moral development and to transform the character of the people. Daily or seasonal offerings of food and drink placed before statues, portraits or tablets are taken as a reminder of the great virtue of the sages, and the Confucian sages are seen as great examples for education and moral cultivation. Even after the official sacrifice to Confucius was abolished, Confucius continues to be the symbol of education and social ethics, and his birthday (the 27th day of the 8th month in the Chinese calendar) continues to be celebrated in his temples and in Confucian academies (see figure 12). The worship of Confucius is also continued in Korea, whereas Palmer notices that 'The oldest Confucian ceremonies surviving today are the semi-annual sacrifices to Confucius and other Chinese and Korean sages carried out in the premises of Songgyun'gwan, the historic National Confucian Academy in Seoul', and that underlying the ritual is the idea that 'by ritual commemoration of Confucius, participants emulate practices of filial piety, virtue, loyalty, honor, social harmony, and faith; and the principles of moral management of personal, familial, and state affairs are reaffirmed' (Palmer, 1984: 1, 40).

Learning and spiritual cultivation

Confucianism invests greatly in official rituals and sees ceremonies and rites as necessary in attaining personal virtues and moral perfection. Yet the spirituality of Confucianism is far more than the engagement in collective rituals. The majority of Confucians understand transcendence in terms of self-transformation and maintain that self-transformation cannot be fulfilled unless the traditional values are manifest in one's own life. Weber did not read this out of the Confucian tradition, and therefore wrongly concluded that 'the Confucian way of life was rational but determined, unlike Puritanism, from without rather than from within' (Weber, 1968: 247). Tu Wei-ming examines Confucian spirituality in the integration of four dimensions of humanity: self, community, nature and Heaven, in which the self is the centre and the power house of ultimate transformation (Tu, 1993: 142). To understand Confucian spirituality, therefore, we need not only look at Confucian understanding of Heaven and its relation to humans, but also examine how Confucians have transformed the seemingly external 'Mandate' into a moral sense of mission and transformed the interaction between the spiritual Ultimate and an individual into a process of personal experience and growth. This transmission is the key for secular learning to be imbued with sacred meaning and for self-cultivation to be closely associated with spiritual purity and sincerity.

LEARNING AS A SPIRITUAL PATH

'How to be good' or in other words 'how to be human' is a perennial theme in Confucian intellectual and spiritual discourse. Of the many ways explored by Confucian masters, learning is considered to be the most important path towards perfection. Confucius began his lifelong endeavour by setting his mind on learning (*Lunyu*, 2: 4). He took learning to be the way to balance one's own character and actions. He attached great importance to the virtues of humaneness, righteousness, wisdom and courage, but believed that all these virtues must be firmly based in learning and study:

> To love humaneness (*ren*) without loving learning is liable to
> foolishness. To love intelligence (*zhi*) without loving learning is liable to
> deviation from the right path. To love faithfulness (*xin*) without loving
> learning is liable to harmful behaviour. To love straightforwardness
> (*zhi*) without loving learning is liable to intolerance. To love courage
> (*yong*) without loving learning is liable to insubordination. To love
> unbending strength (*gang*) without loving learning is liable to
> indisciplining.   (*Lunyu*, 17: 8)

To learn extensively while having a firm and sincere will, and to inquire with earnestness while reflecting what one has learnt, are believed to be essential for a good character. Confucius used his own experience to illustrate that it would be a waste of time to concentrate on thinking and meditation if one failed to study: 'I have spent the whole day without food and the whole night without sleep in order to meditate. It was of no use. It is better to learn' (*Lunyu*, 15: 31). He also took so much enjoyment in learning that he frequently forgot to eat (*Lunyu*, 7: 19).

Most Confucians have little or no interest in 'salvation', if by salvation we mean deliverance by a supernatural power, because it is indeed that 'The Confucian desired "salvation" only from the barbaric lack of education' (Weber, 1968: 228). Through learning, humans can develop moral strength and move forwards to moral virtue. Therefore, in the hands of the Confucian masters, learning becomes a primary tool to facilitate the process of transformation from what is realised to what should be realised, from the animal-like to the fully human, from the uncivilised to the civilised, and from the uncultivated to the cultivated. In this process it is neither prayer nor repentance, but learning that plays a central role. In this way Confucianism demonstrates that 'to learn' is synonymous with 'to live', 'to improve', 'to be mature' or even 'to be eternal'.

By its very nature Confucian Learning is not simply a reading of books but a special kind of practice or moral training. This moral training covers all aspects of social life and students are required to 'be filial at home, reverent abroad, to be sincere and faithful, to love the people and cultivate the friendship with the good. When having time and opportunity after performing these, they should devote to the study of literature' (*Lunyu*, 1: 6). To guide these practices, Confucians designed a number of training programmes based on the recognised texts. At the time of Confucius the most important works were those on ritual/propriety, music, poetry and history. Confucius taught that it was not enough only to be wise, courageous and versatile, but that in order to be a 'complete man', one must be refined by ritual/propriety and music (*Lunyu*, 14: 12). Confucius extended the traditional understanding of ritual to be of a wide application and made it the core of the way of life. When asked about how to become a person of virtue, Confucius answered with four 'nots': not looking, not listening, not speaking, and not acting, unless it was in accordance with ritual/propriety (*Lunyu*, 12: 1). Confucius emphasised the importance of music, partly because Confucian Learning was built upon an ancient tradition of education in which 'The process of education was built around training in music and dance: the idealized education institutions of such texts are presided over by music masters, and the curricula consist largely of graduated courses in ceremonial dance' (Eno, 1990: 196). Along with music and ritual/propriety, poetry was also a very important aspect for moral training: without studying the *Book of Poetry*, it is impossible for any individual to speak properly, while without studying the *Book of Rites*, one cannot establish one's character (*Lunyu*, 16: 13). Confucianism was recognised as a distinguished school through its great emphasis on these subjects, and the early Confucians were well known for their tireless chanting of ancient texts, singing of ancient songs and playing music, even in the face of death. It is recorded in the *Records of the Historian* that Liu Bang (r. 206–195), having defeated his chief rival and being about to become the first emperor of the Han Dynasty, 'marched north and surrounded the state of Lu with his troops, but the Confucian scholars of Lu went on as always, reciting and discussing their books, practicing rites and music, and never allowing the sound of strings and voices to die out' (*Shiji*, 1998: 3117; Watson, 1961, vol. 2: 397). This demonstrated that the Confucians practised ritual, played music and read poems not merely for enjoyment but because they found the value and the meaning of life in these pursuits. In other words, Confucians internalised the external learning so that learning itself became a process by which the temporality of the learner could be transformed into a sense of eternity, and their short lifespan could gain lasting meaning.

Thus, to learn is to experience and to study is to do. Confucius never placed much emphasis on the recitation of the classics. Rather, he asked for a personal understanding of the sayings and a personal experience of the wisdom embodied in the texts. This method was adopted as the guideline for the Confucian academies (*shuyuan*) that flourished during the Song and later dynasties, where moral and spiritual improvement is central within the curriculum. In his 'Articles of Instruction of Bailu Dong Academy', Zhu Xi instilled the following principles for Confucian Learning:

1. The Five Teachings: between father and son there should be love; between prince and subject there should be just dealing; between husband and wife there should be distinctions; between the old and young there should be precedence; between friends there should be good faith.
2. The Order of Learning: study extensively; inquire accurately; think carefully; sift clearly; practise earnestly.
3. The Essentials of Self-Cultivation: in speaking be loyal and true; in acting be serious and careful; control anger and check desires; correct errors and move to the good.
4. The Essentials of Managing Affairs: stand square on what is right, do not scheme for what is profitable; clarify the Way, do not calculate the honours.
5. The Essentials of Getting along with Others: Do not do to others what you would not like yourself; if a man pursue a course, and his way is impeded, let him see the remedy in himself (Meskill, 1982: 50–1).

Zhang Huang (1527–1608), once the headmaster of the same academy, laid down the following 'Steps in Learning':

1. The foundation of learning is an established will.
2. The principle of learning is to promote humaneness (*ren*) through gathering with friends.
3. The pathway to learning is the investigation of things and the extension of knowledge.

4. The regulator of learning is caution and fear.
5. The true ground of learning is filial piety, respect for elders, earnestness and faithfulness.
6. The certification of learning is the controlling of anger, checking of desires, and moving to the good.
7. The last measure of learning is the complete development of one's nature until destiny is fulfilled.
8. The proof of good faith in learning is in searching out the ways of old and mining the classics (*ibid.*: 145–6).

These examples show the emphasis that Confucians place upon learning as a method for improving one's own character and not for the sake of fame or praise from others. Thus we see that learning is a process of transformation pursued by one's self for one's self. Learning begins with one's self but should not end with one's own satisfaction. Students are required to extend their knowledge and virtue to others and to the world, and by this extension to help bring about peace and harmony in society. Confucius insists that self-cultivation is the means by which peace and harmony can be manifest in the world, and that undertaking learning for the sake of self-realisation (*weiji*) one accomplishes all things, while undertaking learning 'for the sake of others' (*weiren*) one ends only with the loss of one's self (*Lunyu*, 14: 24).

The chief aim of Confucian Learning is to understand Heaven and to apply this understanding to social, family and personal life, and it is therefore a process of generating virtue within and learning to be a person of virtue. Among the many virtues taught by Confucius, the most important one is *ren* (仁) that is regarded as the thread running through all other virtues. *Ren* has been translated variously as humaneness, humanity, love, goodness, benevolence, man-to-man-ness, human-heartedness, kindness etc., and these translations themselves reveal its rich content and wide extension. *Ren* deals primarily with how people relate to each other, as shown by the combination of the two parts of the character, 'two' (二) and 'humans' (人). In this sense 'humaneness' is a better rendering. Humaneness is the core of Confucius' teaching, and he introduced two further concepts to help people understand the practice of *ren* in their daily lives. These two concepts are *shu* (恕), 'reciprocity' and *zhong* (忠), 'loyalty', which are pathways leading towards the realisation of *ren*. *Shu* is expressed by the injunction 'what you do not like yourself do not do to others' (*Lunyu*, 15: 24). The underlying commitment of *shu* is not only to refrain from doing harm to others by abiding by rules, but also to integrate one's self and others by following the Way. Compared with *shu*, *zhong* is more positive: 'One who wishes to establish oneself must first establish others; one who wishes to be prominent oneself must first help others to be prominent' (*Lunyu*, 6: 30). *Zhong* denotes a positive intention to act. In order to integrate oneself with others, it is not enough merely not to impose upon them the things one does not like oneself. It is more important to help others to achieve what one wants, and only in this positive way can one be said to be 'loyal' to others.

Humaneness is considered to be 'a person-making process' (Hall & Ames, 1987: 84), a necessary quality of human beings and a dynamic force for creating and renovating one's self and others. 'The completion of the self means humanity [humaneness]' (Chan, 1963a: 108). The Confucian discourse on humaneness is always related to what humans can become and humaneness is considered the essential qualification of a person of virtue, *junzi* (君子). *Junzi* has been translated as 'a person of virtue', 'a superior man', 'a princely man', 'an ideal man' or 'a gentleman'. Etymologically this phrase means a 'son of the ruler', referring to the descendants of the ruling house and members of the upper classes and indicating their aristocratic birth and noble descent. Although this ancient meaning was still adopted in some passages of the *Analects*, Confucius expanded the term to signify the totality of superior human qualities and the embodiment of humaneness. For him, a man cannot be a *junzi* if he does not manifest humaneness. 'A *junzi* who parts company with humaneness does not fulfil that name. Never for a moment does a *junzi* quit humaneness' (*Lunyu*, 4: 5). At a lower level, a *junzi* is someone whose actions are free from violence, whose bearing is completely sincere and whose speech lacks vulgarity (*Lunyu*, 8: 4). On a higher level a *junzi* is someone who can be entrusted with the destiny of the whole state, one who willingly bears such a heavy burden as serving the state and the people, and who perseveres in fulfilling humaneness in the world (*Lunyu*, 8: 6 & 7). The Way (*Dao*) is the only thing that a *junzi* seeks, even if his doing so brings him into poverty (*Lunyu*, 15: 31). A *junzi* is a man of wisdom who has no perplexities, a man of humaneness who has no anxiety, and a man of courage who has no fear (*Lunyu*, 14: 30). A *junzi* acts before speaking and then speaks according to his actions

(*Lunyu*, 2: 13), and would therefore be ashamed if his words exceeded his deeds (*Lunyu*, 14: 29). A *junzi* has the power and ability to transform the uncivilised way of life, as illustrated in the following conversation between Confucius and his disciples: the Master (Confucius) wanted to settle among the Nine Barbarian Tribes of the East. Someone said: 'They are rude. How can you put up with them?' Confucius said, 'If a *junzi* lives there, what rudeness would there be?' (*Lunyu*, 9: 13).

A *junzi* is someone who has made great achievement in cultivating his virtues and is thereby distinguished from those who are uncultivated. The contrast between a *junzi* and a *xiaoren* (a small man) is the contrast between a person of virtue and a mean or vulgar person. This contrast is manifest in all areas of life. In terms of a psychological character, the former is broad-minded while the latter is partisan (*Lunyu*, 2: 14). In terms of behaviour, the former always aims at what is righteous while the latter understands only what is profitable (*Lunyu*, 4: 16). Internally the former is calm and at ease while the latter is full of distress and ill at ease (*Lunyu*, 7: 36). In personal relations, the former only makes demands upon oneself, while the latter makes demands upon others (*Lunyu*, 15: 20). On the surface, the qualities of a *junzi* are common and secular. However, together the integrated qualities constitute an ideal personality that Confucians strive hard to achieve. In this sense, to become a *junzi* is not only the content of Confucian Learning but also the process by which one attains to self-realisation. The aspiration to become a *junzi* provides the power and the motive for Confucians to engage in learning and to put that learning into practice. Thus the scholars learn how to cultivate and control their disposition and to harmonise their emotions, which is then manifest in their actions with regard to all worldly affairs. To think and act as a *junzi* is to be a truly cultivated and disciplined human being. Subjectively, these activities are designed to enable one to manifest one's innate nature, and objectively they lead one to manifest maturity in social and community life. Mengzi compared the original state of human nature to seeds and remarked that 'Of all seeds the best are the five kinds of grain, yet if they are not ripe, they are not equal to the weeds. So the value of humaneness depends entirely on its being brought to maturity' (*Mengzi*, 6A: 19). In the growth of the virtuous 'seeds' the five constant virtues of humaneness, righteousness, propriety, wisdom and faithfulness are confirmed and affirmed, and thereby the natural (human senses) become the ideal (moral virtues).

That is what Confucian Learning intends to achieve and is where the meaning and value of Confucian Learning are to be found.

SPIRITUAL CULTIVATION

Confucian Learning has a strong spiritual dimension, for the ultimate goal of the learning is to be a sage, an ideal whose intelligence and virtue have been manifest to the utmost. All the programmes in Confucian Learning and practice are designed to help the learner to attain to sagehood, a goal which is believed to be attainable through spiritual cultivation in one's secular life. One of the fundamental beliefs in the Confucian tradition is that everybody is capable of becoming a sage (*Mengzi*, 6B: 2; *Xunzi*, 23: 5). However prior to Neo-Confucianism the only people who were called sages were the sage–kings of antiquity and Confucius. Instead, most Neo-Confucians see sagehood as a realistic outcome of moral transformation and the ultimate aim of spiritual cultivation, the final journey in one's moral progress: 'The sage aspires to become Heaven, the worthy (*xianren*) aspires to become a sage and the gentleman (*junzi*) aspires to become a worthy' (in *Jinsi Lu*, Chan, 1967: 29). To be a sage is all one should do in the life and is all Confucian Learning is about. Neo-Confucians reconfirm that it is within everyone's ability to be a sage and they also deliberate on the complex meaning of sagehood. For most of them, sagehood can be roughly said to be a state of consciousness by which one is aware of the oneness with the universe. This is known as 'one body with Heaven and Earth', of which the realisation is taken as the sign of 'enlightenment', an achievement in self-cultivation that results from the clear awareness of one's own nature. There are differences between Neo-Confucian scholars with regard to the method one should use to achieve this so-called enlightenment, and consequently, these differences lead to the emergence of two distinct schools. One school teaches that the final breakthrough could only come after the gradual accumulation of learning through the external investigation of things, while the other looks to a sudden and immediate realisation of the oneness of Heaven and humans through an internal search in one's own heart/mind. The latter school especially propagates the universality of sagehood. As everyone has the heart/mind that is the same as the heart/mind of the sages, sagehood is universal, open to all the people, the educated or the uneducated, the superior or the inferior, in equal measure (de Bary, 1970: 171).

Confucianism considers spiritual cultivation to be a personal experience that needs 'carefulness when alone' (*shendu*) and 'sincerity' (*cheng*). *Cheng* 'means not only sincerity in the narrow sense, but also honesty, absence of fault, seriousness, being true to one's true self, being true to the nature of being, actuality, realness' (Chan, 1963a: 465, fn. 28). Believing Heaven and humans to be the same in essence, the *Book of Mengzi* and the *Doctrine of the Mean* see sincerity as central to the unity of Heaven and humanity because sincerity is the Way of Heaven while to think how to be sincere is the way of humans. Thus sincerity is taken as the foundation of the five human relations (ruler–subject, father–son, elder–younger brother, husband–wife and friend–friend) and the guarantee of achievement in moral cultivation: without sincerity, one cannot please one's parents and cannot understand what is good (*Mengzi*, 4A: 12). One who possesses complete sincerity can transform oneself as well as others, and one who cannot transform oneself and others has not yet been full of sincerity. Neo-Confucians inherited this tradition and considered sincerity to be the root of spiritual growth. They believed that in sincerity, being and non-being, tranquillity and activity, the internal and the external were harmonised and unified. Zhou Dunyi, for instance, deliberated that 'Sincerity is infinitely pure and hence evident. The spirit is responsive and hence works wonders. And incipient activation is subtle and hence abstruse. The sage is the one who is in the state of sincerity, spirit, and subtle incipient activation', and thereby identified sincerity with the Confucian ideal: 'Sagehood is nothing but sincerity' (Chan, 1963a: 467, 466). Zhang Zai further elaborated why sincerity was said to be the way of Heaven: sincerity 'is the way according to which heaven can last for long and is unceasing', and therefore 'without sincerity, there will be nothing'. For him, true sincerity is more than a sense of being sincere; it is an enlightenment which comes only when one's nature has been developed and things investigated to their utmost, because spiritual breakthrough cannot be attained without true sincerity (*ibid.*: 507–8).

With sincerity, one may become new every day and become 'liberated' in every disposition and action. This organic process is not only the character of humanity but also the principle of the universe, the natural and moral law of Heaven. The *Book of Changes* takes 'daily renewal' (*rixin*) as the 'glorious virtue' (*shengde*) and identifies 'production and reproduction' (*sheng sheng*) as the principle and essence of eternal change. The idea of daily renewal seems mystical, but it is described in the

Doctrine of the Mean as a very natural process that enables one to bring all emotions and feelings and action into harmony. In equilibrium or in action one can experience the original quietude of the heart/mind and keep the motivated heart/mind adjusted so that 'reflecting on sincerity' and 'being sincere' are seen to be as profound as 'ultimate respectfulness' and 'oneness of the self with the cosmos'.

To be sincere one must engage in spiritual cultivation, which has both an internal and an external dimension. Internally one cultivates one's nature in the form of 'nourishing the vital force' (*yangqi*) and externally one practises virtues and accumulates righteous deeds (*jiyi*). Influenced by Chan Buddhist and Daoist meditation, the Neo-Confucians developed their own understanding of spiritual contemplation and concentration conducive to calming the heart/mind as a path to sincerity and enlightenment. Some of them therefore became fond of a special method called quiet sitting or sitting quietly in meditation (*jingzuo*) and believed that it was an effective way to examine one's learning and achievements, and was the path leading to enlightenment. They traced the ideas and practices of quiet sitting to Confucius and Mengzi, as Confucius talked about tranquillity and quietude (*Lunyu*, 6: 23), and Mengzi practised nourishing the heart and cultivated the vital force of the night (*Mengzi*, 6A: 8).

For Neo-Confucians there is no universally applicable formula for spiritual cultivation, and the way to sagehood has to be found in one's own experience. Various Neo-Confucian masters place different emphasis on how one should proceed with spiritual cultivation, and there is a wide divergence of opinion between scholars as to what constitutes the stages of this process. Zhou Dunyi, for instance, insisted that the most important element is 'quietude or tranquillity', which leads him to emphasise the spiritual practice of 'holding fast to tranquillity' (*zhujing*). When asked if it were possible to become a sage, Zhou answered positively and described the essential way for so doing as follows:

> The essential way is to [concentrate on] one thing. By [concentrating on] one thing is meant having no desire. Having no desire, one is vacuous (*hsü*, being absolutely pure and peaceful) while tranquil, and straightforward while in action. Being vacuous while tranquil, one becomes intelligent and hence penetrating. Being straightforward while active, one becomes impartial and hence all-embracing. Being intelligent, penetrating, impartial, and all-embracing, one is almost a sage.
>
> (Chan, 1963a: 473)

Having seen danger in this approach, Cheng Hao replaced tranquillity (*jing*, 靜) with 'reverence/seriousness' (*jing*, 敬), thereby inserting a positive attitude into spiritual cultivation. Cheng Yi felt that 'reverence/ seriousness' was still not enough, as this represented only an inward effort. He believed that regardless of the form it took, spiritual cultivation must be related to the external world. While believing that inward meditation is concerned with moral life and with one's external behaviour, Chen Yi argued that it would difficult for us to deal with the affairs of the world, if we were simply to 'sit there quietly' (*Songyuan Xuean*, 1992, vol. 3: 774). To adjust the one-sidedness of Zhou Dunyi and of Cheng Hao, Cheng Yi added the idea of 'extending knowledge' (*zhizhi*) to 'reverence/ seriousness', and thereby greatly reduced the significance of tranquillity for spiritual cultivation. In order to extend one's knowledge one must investigate things to gain knowledge of principle (*li*), and to gain knowledge of principle is to fulfil one's own destiny. Cheng Yi insisted that the exhaustive study of principle is the only way in which one could efficiently and effectively practise spiritual cultivation. For him, 'The investigation of principle to the utmost, the full development of the nature, and the fulfillment of destiny are only one thing. As principle is investigated to the utmost, one's nature is fully developed, and as one's nature is fully developed, destiny is fulfilled' (Chan, 1963a: 563).

Following his spiritual master, Zhu Xi also emphasised the significance of the investigation of things. However, as a great synthesiser of Neo-Confucian teaching, Zhu paid more attention to the compromise between the two dimensions of spiritual cultivation, namely, 'holding fast to reverence/seriousness' and 'extending one's knowledge'. For him, these two things 'are really the essentials for the student to advance in establishing himself in life' (Chan, 1963a: 606). In Zhu's mind, 'holding fast to reverence/seriousness' is to preserve and nourish one's nature, and investigating principle is to extend and enrich it. These two things are not mutually exclusive; they are mutually contained: 'the effort of investigating principle to the utmost is already found within that of preserving and nourishing, and the effort of the preserving and nourishing is already found within that of the investigation of principle to the utmost'. They are also mutually dependent: 'If one is not able to preserve the mind, he will be unable to investigate principle to the utmost. If he is unable to investigate principle to the utmost, he will be unable to exert his mind to the utmost' (*ibid*.: 605, 606). Following Cheng Yi, Zhu interpreted 'holding fast to reverence/seriousness' as nothing more than 'being orderly and dignified' and 'being grave and austere', and 'extension of knowledge' as no less than finding out 'where principle is' in learning and in dealing with things (affairs). For Zhu, 'reverence/seriousness' does not mean to 'sit still like a blockhead, with the ear hearing nothing, the eye seeing nothing, and the mind thinking of nothing'. Zhu regarded this way of quiet sitting as 'dead seriousness'. On the one hand, holding fast to reverence/seriousness is 'to be apprehensive and careful and dare not give free rein to oneself', so that 'both body and mind will be collected and concentrated' (*ibid.*: 607). On the other hand, 'reverence/seriousness' must be supported with 'righteousness' to distinguish between right and wrong, and reverence/seriousness and righteousness are the two sides of the same coin: 'wherever there is seriousness, there is righteousness, and wherever there is righteousness, there is seriousness'. Zhu called this 'living seriousness' (*ibid.*: 608). Based on the unity of righteousness and reverence, Zhu emphasised the balance between tranquillity and activity in mutual support: 'Tranquillity nourishes the root of activity and activity is to put tranquillity into action.' He insisted on the oneness of the internal and the external: 'Things and the principle [inherent] in my mind are fundamentally one.' He also believed that knowledge and action always require each other, the one leading to the other: 'As one knows more clearly, he acts more earnestly, and as he acts more earnestly, he knows more clearly' (*ibid.*: 607–9). According to this understanding, spiritual meditation is like a circular journey of tranquillity and activity, or of preserving [the mind] and investigating [the principle], or of knowledge and action.

Idealistic Confucians discuss spiritual cultivation in different terms. According to them, the heart/mind is not simply the seat of consciousness, it is a metaphysical reality and a psychological substance that necessitates and activates moral activity. Self-cultivation is not the outward investigation of things but is primarily an inward process of looking into one's own heart/mind and reflecting on one's own innate sources of sagehood. Idealists considered this form of self-cultivation to be the 'easy and simple' way to the realisation of 'one body with Heaven and Earth' (*yu tiandi wei yiti*). This is contrasted with the so-called 'difficult and complicated' way proposed by some Rationalists who taught that each thing must be thoroughly investigated before one was able to know the holistic truth of the universe. The Idealistic School described the rationalistic way of investigation as painstaking and fragmentary as well as dissipating and irrelevant. As the proponents of the idea that 'the principle fills the universe' and 'the universe is my mind', idealists believed that it was right to search for sagehood within and there was no need to seek it in things and affairs outside. Self-examination and inward exploration are enough for one to gain true knowledge and to be a sage. Therefore Lu Xiangshan emphasised 'knowing the fundamentals' and 'building up the nobler part of one's nature' in direct contrast to those who taught that 'book-reading' was sufficient for the attainment of sagehood. Lu believed that concentrating on reading books misled students and that the Confucian classics were only useful to illustrate what had been gained from self-examination: 'If in our study we know the fundamentals, then all the Six Classics are my footnotes' (Chan, 1963a: 580). Chen Xianzhang (1428–1500), an important intermediary thinker between Lu Xiangshan and Wang Yangming, challenged the rationalistic conception of truth: 'Is there any idea not in one's own mind? Why is it necessary to copy the ancients?' (de Bary, 1970: 74). For Wang Yangming, spiritual cultivation is purely an internal exploration of one's own heart/mind, or in his own words, an extension of the innate good knowledge (*liangzhi*) and the employment of one's innate good ability (*liangneng*). As learning is to extend one's innate knowledge, then learning is not merely book-reading, but essentially a process of moral activity, in which knowledge is unified with action, because knowledge is the direction and beginning of action, while action is the effort and completion of knowledge. With the unity of knowledge and action, Wang takes it for granted that an immoral intention is equal to an immoral action. To learn is not only to refrain from acting wrongly; it is more important to have no evil thoughts and intentions. Wang believed that this was the basic purpose and meaning of his teaching about the unity between knowledge and action (Chan, 1963b: 201). Since 'knowledge' and 'action' are two words for the same effort, quiet sitting is considered to be a technique useful for students to obtain genuine knowledge and a necessary step at certain stages of self-cultivation. Wang believed that quiet sitting could help students directly see the true Way and that it would help them refrain from being occupied with intellectual explanations and trivial debates. However, if indulged in, it would develop 'the defect of fondness of tranquillity and disgust of activity' and would degenerate 'into lifelessness like dry wood'. Wang said this was why he later taught only the doctrine of the extension of innate good knowledge and why, in his later years, he took a dislike of quiet sitting. 'If one's innate knowledge is clear, it will be all right either to try to obtain truth through personal realization in a quiet place or to discover it through training and polishing in the actual affairs of life' (Chan, 1963a: 684). To be a sage, one must have 'sageliness within' and 'kingliness without', that is, one must manifest one's virtue not only by cultivating one's self, but also by allowing self-cultivation to overflow into the fulfillment of responsibilities toward the family, the state and the world (Chan, 1963b: 191, 216–17). Wang believed that in this way the innate humaneness would be fully realised, and one would consciously become one body with all things and beings in the universe.

Although there is no consensus with regard to what is spiritual cultivation and how to cultivate one's self spiritually among Neo-Confucians, most Neo-Confucian masters consider spiritual cultivation a practical way to enlightenment, and find 'quiet sitting' effective in putting their view of life into practice and in overcoming the obstacles in their spiritual journey. Luo Congyan (1072–1135), for example, developed this understanding and 'taught his students to observe in quiet sitting the states of happiness, anger, sorrow and joy before they are aroused' (*Songyuan Xuean*, 1992, vol. 4: 567). Quiet sitting was also frequently used as an alternative way in the personal search for 'truth'. According to Chen Xianzhang's own records, he had followed the ideas of a number of important teachers, yet failed to make any progress. This led him to casting aside the complexities and to searching 'for a simple one of my own, entirely through "quiet sitting"' (Fung, 1953: 594). Chen practised quiet sitting earnestly, as he once 'wrote to one of his pupils: "Everyday, after eating my dinner, I sit with closed eyes till the end of the day'; he also told his students that 'For learning, you must engage in quiet-sitting, from which will come forth a "beginning"' (de Bary 1970: 79).

Fond of quiet sitting, Neo-Confucians took great pains to differentiate their practice of spiritual cultivation from Buddhist or Daoist meditation. They argued that quiet sitting was oriented to this world and aimed at perfecting one's self, whereas Buddhist and Daoist meditation focused on forgetting the world and abandoning one's self. Meditation in other religious traditions proscribed strict procedures which must be followed in minute detail and it would normally invoke supernatural powers. Neo-Confucian scholars take quiet sitting to be only a way to help understand one's gain in self-cultivation and they do not see it as a means to isolate oneself from human affairs. They believe that it is only within this world and among worldly affairs that one can progress in the path of spiritual cultivation. Zhan Ruoshui (1466–1560) gave an excellent illustration to this understanding by pointing out that one can realise 'the principle of Heaven wherever one might be and whatever one might be doing' (Meskill, 1982: 68). Gu Xiancheng (1550–1612) confirmed that quiet sitting was a method to probe into the depth and profoundness of human nature, and believed that this could be achieved either when one was alone or occupied, whether one was with other people or was suddenly overtaken with affection, anger, grief or pleasure (*Mingru Xuean*, 1992, vol. 8: 742). Another Ming scholar, Gao Panlong (1562–1626), emphasised the naturalness and ordinariness of spiritual cultivation and said, 'In considering the method of quiet sitting, there is no need for any particular procedure. Just act in an ordinary fashion and let quietude come forth from silence' (*Mingru Xuean*, 1992, vol. 8: 766). Gao further confirmed that quiet sitting is the method by which the beginner cultivated his character and the new student entered the door of spiritual cultivation (*ibid.*, 767). Gao used his own experience to illustrate this spiritual journey. When he experienced spiritual anguish and intellectual stagnation, Gao would undertake quiet sitting to engage in spiritual cultivation and thereby gained a sense of oneness with all. In his own words, 'I was merged with the Great Transformation until there was no differentiation. And yet even further there was no partition between Heaven and man, exterior and interior' (Taylor, 1983: 25–7). This is the kind of experience and enlightenment that most Neo-Confucians constantly search for in their spiritual cultivation.

Confucianism and other religious traditions

Confucianism is not confined to China, nor is it an insular or isolated tradition. Throughout its history Confucianism has been in constant exchange with other cultural and religious traditions, which include Daoism, Buddhism, Shamanism, Shintô, Islam, Christianity, Marxism, Western Rationalism and Humanism. Confucianism has drawn from many sources and in so doing it has gained strength and an ability to change and adapt to new circumstances and conditions. The inquiry into Confucian spirituality, therefore, inevitably involves multidimensional research into the interaction and exchange between Confucianism and these traditions. Among the religious traditions with which Confucianism has come into contact, Daoism, Buddhism and Christianity are of special interest for us. It is the interaction between Confucianism and these three traditions that has exerted the greatest influence on what we know as the Confucian tradition.

THE UNITY OF THREE DOCTRINES

Confucianism, Daoism and Buddhism are traditionally known as 'the three doctrines or three religions' (*sanjiao*). In dealing with the other two, Confucianism was at times dogmatic and at times flexible. Like many other so-called orthodox traditions in the world, Confucianism used to regard itself as the only truth in the world and the only correct way to peace and harmony. In order to establish or preserve their dominant position, Confucian masters campaigned against Daoism and Buddhism. At times this dogmatic approach gave rise to the political persecution of Buddhism or Daoism and was partly responsible for the conflict between the three traditions. Yet within the Confucian tradition there is indeed a flexible attitude towards different theories and practices. Confucius once rebuked some of his disciples who could only follow what had been taught and insisted that 'A person of virtue (*junzi*) in the world does not set his mind either for or against anything; he follows whatever is right' (*Lunyu*, 4: 10). In a similar vein, Mengzi criticises those people who either hold on to the middle without the proper measure or hold to one extreme, because he believes that both will damage the Way (*Mengzi*, 7A: 26). The Confucian attitude towards other religions is thus characterised by the co-existence of dogmatism and flexibility, and of exclusivity and inclusivity. While dogmatism and exclusivity frequently create new, and intensify old, conflicts, flexible and inclusive attitudes help to reduce tension, modify conflict and cultivate a common sense of the unity between the three traditions.

In the traditional social and religious life in China, there seems to be a recognised division of labour between the three doctrines. Confucianism was expected to provide the moral principles for social and political life, while Daoism and Buddhism were to sanction Confucian morality and deal with psychological and spiritual issues. This labour division played a key role in maintaining the balance between them and contributed to the co-existence and mutual acceptance that existed in all the three doctrines. Various statements are used to express the unity and harmony of these three traditions, such as 'the one body of the three doctrines' (*sanjiao yiti*), 'the three parallel doctrines' (*sanjiao binxing*) or 'the three converged doctrines' (*sanjiao heliu*). The three religious traditions are likened to the three legs of a bronze sacrificial vessel, an ancient and sacred ritual tripod, with each leg being indispensable to the stability of the vessel. This three-in-one structure reflected the political intent to balance different doctrines, as W. E. Soothill observed that 'Each of the three religions has been the recipient of Imperial recognition and favour, and the three may be considered as three aspects of the established religion of the country' (Soothill, 1929: 11). The three-in-one unity was universally accepted as the ideal and was embraced by most members of all the three traditions. As a matter of fact, Buddhists and Daoists were the most enthusiastic supporters of the three-in-one deal. Johnston begins his book *Confucianism and Modern China* with the triunity of Buddhism, Confucianism and Daoism. According to his description, within the grounds of one of the most famous Buddhist monasteries in China, *Shaolin* Monastery in Henan Province, this triunity is vividly presented in an inscribed picture that is believed to be more than seven hundred years old. This picture shows us the figures of the 'founders' of the three traditions standing side by side, Sakyamuni of Buddhism, Laozi of Daoism and Confucius, the 'most holy sage' (Johnston, 1934: 1–2).

The origin of the three-in-one doctrine can be traced to the introduction of Buddhism when Buddhist sutras were understood and interpreted in the terms of Daoist and Confucian classics. The Dark or Mysterious Learning of the Wei–Jin Dynasties merged Daoism and Confucianism, which had an implication that different doctrines were the same in essence, thereby theoretically facilitating the acceptance of the three-in-one doctrine by the government and by Confucian scholars, Daoist hermits and Buddhist monks alike. It was the fashion among the intellectuals during the Southern and Northern Dynasties (386–581) to reconcile the otherworldly creed of Buddhism with this-worldly social virtues of Confucianism. In one of the essays entitled *Yu Dao Lun* or 'Treatise Illustrating the Way' Sun Chuo (c. 300–80) argued that the two traditions were the same in essence and their difference to be mainly one of expediency; with Buddhism representing the inner teaching and Confucianism the outer, and that 'the Duke of Chou and Confucius are identical with the Buddha; the Buddha is identical with the Duke of Chou and Confucius' (Ch'en, 1964: 68). Efforts were also made to accommodate Buddhism to Daoism and the Buddha was defined as 'the one who does nothing and yet there is nothing that he does not do' (*ibid.*). A prominent Daoist master, Tao Hongjing (456–536) proposed that a hundred doctrines represented a hundred ways, but that none of these ways was beyond the boundaries of the three religions (*wanfa fencou, wuyue sanjiao zhijing*). Unity does not necessarily exclude competition, and in the competition between Daoism, Buddhism and Confucianism, many stories were invented to show the supremacy of one over the other. One story relates how Laozi, the supposed founder of Daoism, travelled to the West and arrived in India where he taught Sakyamuni the Buddha his doctrine on the Way. Another story counters this by saying that the Buddha sent three of his disciples to the East, the Scholar Bodhisattva (*rutong pusa*) became known as Confucius, the Bright and Pure Bodhisattva (*guangjing pusa*) as Yan Hui, and Mahakasyapa as Laozi. Imaginary and absurd as these stories are, they were instrumental in leading the people to believe that the three doctrines came from one source and led to the same end. It became a popular view that the three traditions were the same in essence, and their differences, if any, were not fundamental. It was believed that the differences were caused by time and space, just as a bird, flying over different countries, might be called by different names while still being the same bird. Severely critical of Buddhism in his thesis entitled *Yi Xia Lun* (*Treatise on the Barbarians and Chinese*), Gu Huan (390?–483?) nevertheless argued that opposites implied unity and that these opposites were combined and unified by the sages. For him, Confucius, Laozi and Sakyamuni were one, and the apparent differences between them were caused by customs, rules and ceremonies. The presentations of the three doctrines might differ but their essence was the same: 'A boat sailed over the water, while a carriage traveled on land, yet both were vehicles for moving from one place to another' (Shryock, 1966: 118).

The political unity of the Sui and Tang Dynasties promoted the ideological unity of the three traditions, and a recognised 'common sense' of the three doctrines gathered fruition as the three systems matured. The belief that all the teachings of the three religions were the same in essence, but differed only in their forms, became popular and penetrating. In his *Zhuzi Jiali* (the *Zhuxi's Family Rituals*) Zhu Xi quotes a passage written by a Tang poet and writer, Li Zhou (735–89), that well illustrated this popular belief: 'If Sakyamuni had been born in China, he would have founded a teaching like that of [the Duke of] Chou and Confucius. If [the Duke of] Chou and Confucius had been born in the west, they would have founded a teaching like that of Sakyamuni.' This is interpreted as 'Li Chou [Li Zhou] intended to suggest that Confucianism and Buddhism are equivalent as teachings, but that each is suited to, and by implication should be restricted to, the region in which it originated' (McMullen, 1995: 59).

The merger of the three doctrines was instrumental in the development of a new type of Confucianism in the Song and Ming Dynasties. Neo-Confucianism is well known for its stance against Daoism and Buddhism, yet the essence of Neo-Confucianism is a syncretic product of Chan Buddhism, Daoist philosophy and traditional Confucianism. Almost all Neo-Confucian masters spent a longer or shorter period in the study of Daoist and Buddhist doctrines, and their presentation of Confucian philosophy was a result of their transformation and incorporation of some aspects of these non-Confucian theories and practices. Alongside the Neo-Confucian ascendancy, Daoists made a great effort in renovating their own doctrine in the light of the three-in-one theory. Wang Chongyang (1112–70), the founder of a new Daoist sect, Perfect Truth (*Quanzhen*) Daoism, propagated that the three doctrines were in fact one family and required his disciples to study the Buddhist *Heart Sutra*, the Daoist *Dao De Jing*, and the Confucian *Book of Filial Piety*. Wang taught the unity, equality and harmony of the three religions, and named the five societies he established as organisations of the three-in-one (*sanyi*). He made it clear that his sect did not exclusively venerate its Daoist root, but revered all the three founders of Daoism, Buddhism and Confucianism equally, as 'all the three religions do not deviate from the True Way, and they are like the three branches from a single tree' (Qing, 1993, vol. 3: 54). Many Buddhist masters also dedicated themselves to the three-in-one doctrine, but it was Chan Buddhists who pushed forward the argument that the three doctrines of Confucianism, Buddhism and Daoism came from the same root. They insisted that one could not understand Confucianism if one did not study Buddhism and that only true Confucians were able to grasp the true meaning of Buddhism, because the three doctrines originated from the same source, namely, the self-mind. They propagated that learning must include three disciplines, the Confucian classics that helped one to live in the world, the Daoist scriptures that helped one to forget the world and the practice of *dhyana* that helped one to leave the world behind. In this way the five Confucian virtues became identical with the five Buddhist commandments, the Confucian expression of 'conquering oneself and returning to humaneness' (*Lunyu*, 12: 1) was equated with the Buddhist 'meditation' and 'sudden enlightenment', and Confucius and Laozi were taken as the incarnations of the Buddha.

The three-in-one doctrine is not only a purely theoretical speculation. For many centuries it was the foundation of social and political life in China. The attempts to harmonise Confucianism, Buddhism and Daoism were made by scholars and ordinary people alike. Those who embraced Buddhism would also support Confucianism and Daoism, and vice versa. Under the influence of the syncretic doctrine, schools and religious sects were established based on the unity of the three religions which emphasised that the teachings of Confucius, Laozi and the Buddha were essentially the same and that there was no conflict between them at all. A Confucian scholar, Lin Zhaoen (1517–98), having widely read the writings of the three traditions, created a new religion that unified the three, and this led to him being named the 'Master of the Three-in-One Religion' (*sanjiao xiansheng*). In 1584, a temple of the Three-in-One Religion (*sanjiao si*) was established, in which four statues were worshipped: Confucius, the Founder of the Sage Religion (*shengjiao*), Laozi, the founder of Mysterious Religion (*xuanjiao*), the Buddha, the Founder of Chan [Buddhist] Religion (*chanjiao*), and Lin himself, the Founder of the Three-in-One Religion (*sanyi jiao*). On the one hand, Lin critically examined the three doctrines and pointed out the illness of each tradition; on the other hand, his three-in-one religion was founded on Confucian doctrines, and he subjected Buddhism and Daoism to Confucianism and to the teachings of Confucius (Qing, 1993, vol. 3: 513–15). This three-in-one religion had a great impact on Chinese religious life during the later part of the Ming Dynasty. In the Qing Dynasty the three-in-one religion was branded as 'heresy' and was persecuted; yet its influence remained and the teachings of this religion penetrated the religious fabric of the state. In many temples or monasteries, whether Confucian, Daoist or Buddhist, there were often tablets or statues of Confucius, Laozi and the Buddha and they were worshipped together. Antonio de Caballero (1602–69), a Catholic missionary in China in the seventeenth century, reported that

The statues of these three personages [Confucius, Buddha Sakyamuni and Laozi], the authors of these three sects, are usually placed on the same altar, which is dedicated to them with the following inscription at the door of the temple, 'san kiao tank [*sanjiao tang*],' the Temple of the Three-in-One religion.   (Gernet, 1985: 65)

The three-in-one religion is by no means a religion of the past: 'according to a book published 1988, there are seven temples in Taiwan where incense is offered to Confucius, Lao-tzu, the Buddha, as well as the religion's founder' (Ching, 1993: 217–18). More importantly, the three-in-one understanding has penetrated the Chinese religious doctrines and practices and modern scholars of Chinese religions often find it difficult to clearly define most popular beliefs and cults without resorting to the combination of the three doctrines.

CONFUCIANISM AND DAOISM

Confucianism and Daoism are indigenous doctrines in China that emerged in roughly the same period, and both gained their ascendancy during the Han Dynasty. They evolved from the same source of the Shang–Zhou culture; yet each had its own focus. Confucianism is more ethico-politically oriented, while Daoism put more emphasis on the mysterious and spiritual dimension. Since they were established as distinctive schools during the Spring and Autumn period and the Warring States period, they have both complemented and opposed each other. They both base their doctrines on the unity of Heaven and humanity, but Daoism teaches that the only way to the unity is to follow natural law, while Confucians believe that it is by self-cultivation and the instruction of sages that humans come into harmony with Heaven.

Of the many stories that surround the 'founders' of the two traditions, the most famous is the one that talks of Confucius as a younger contemporary of Laozi and describes how Confucius learned about rituals from Laozi. Nevertheless, it is recorded in the *Records of the Historian* that Confucius remarked that Laozi was a man of wisdom and mystery beyond description (*Shiji*, 1998: 2140). The Daoist philosophers of the Warring States period, epitomised by Zhuangzi, attacked the Confucian emphasis on humaneness and righteousness and taught that these ideas were the source and cause of social chaos, while Xunzi criticised Zhuangzi for his blindly following the natural way and thus being ignorant of human affairs. There were disputes and confrontation between the two doctrines, but the historically held confrontation between Daoism and Confucianism seems to have taken place at a much later date than previously assumed. A recent excavation of bamboo strips from a grave dated to around 300 BCE reveals that the Daoist attack on Confucian ideals (sageliness and wisdom) does not exist in the original text of the *Dao de Jing* (*Guodian Chumu Zhujian* 1998: 111). Even after the difference between Confucianism and Daoism developed into open debates, debates did not exclude them from 'borrowing' from each other. The ideas attributable to different schools of Confucianism and Daoism were in fact found in various kinds of contemporary collections such as *Guanzi*, *Lüshi Chunqiu*, *Jingfa* and a later eclectic work *Huainanzi*. This mixture of ideas in literature prepared the way for the merger of the two doctrines in the Han Dynasty. Through their adaptation of the ideas of Daoism, the Yin–Yang and the Five Elements, and Legalism, Han Confucians created a new version of Confucianism that was acceptable to the imperial government as the guideline for political, social and personal life. Confucianism thus became the state orthodoxy, while Daoism a subordinate philosophy. The dominance of Confucianism in social life was not seriously challenged until the emergence of the Dark or Mysterious Learning in the Wei–Jin Dynasties, when scholars subjected Confucianism to Daoist interpretation. Daoist religion took shape during the Later Han Dynasty and matured during the Southern–Northern Dynasties. The key figures in this further development were Ge Hong (284–364), Kou Qianzhi (365–448), Lu Xiujing (406–77) and Tao Hongjing (456–536), who successfully transformed the earlier mass movements and philosophical theories into an organisation with a systematic doctrine. Central to their efforts in the process of transformation was their incorporation of Confucian ethics, especially loyalty and filial piety, into religious Daoist doctrines. For example, Ge Hong composed his book *Baopuzi* or *The Master who has Embraced Simplicity* in two parts; the inner chapters deal with alchemy, immortal elixirs, methods to prolong life and drive away evil, while the outer chapters deal with social and family affairs based on Confucian ethics. Ge maintained that the Daoist cultivation of immortality must be based on the virtues of loyalty, filial piety, humaneness and faithfulness. He wrote that 'Those who desire longevity must strive to accumulate goodness, win merits, be kind and affectionate to others, and practise the Golden Mean' (Ware, 1966: 116). He argued that without these virtues one could not become an immortal, however hard one worked on it.

The Daoist–Confucian alliance was frequently forged in order to combat Buddhism. In the Tang Dynasty Daoism was promoted to the religion of the royal family, and its founder, Laozi (with the same surname as the Emperor, Li), was worshipped as the ancestor of the royal house. But even this move did not change the roughly balanced structure of Confucianism, Daoism and Buddhism. Daoists deliberated on 'mystery' (*xuan*), 'quietness' (*jing*) and 'cultivation of the heart/mind' (*xiuxin*) and these kinds of elaboration paved the way for the Neo-Confucian philosophy of the Song Dynasty. The two-way traffic between Confucianism and Daoism accelerated with the rise and dominance of Neo-Confucianism. Under the influence of the three-in-one eclecticism and admitting the dominant position of Neo-Confucianism, the Daoists elaborated on the unity and mutual benefit between the two traditions, and the language, arguments and logic employed in Daoist works were very much in the same manner as those of the Neo-Confucian masters. The two major sects of Daoism, the Heavenly Master in the south and the Perfect Truth in the north, were both devoted to the unity between Confucianism and Daoism. Wang Daoyuan (?–?) at the beginning of the Ming Dynasty, for example, played an important role in the integration of Neo-Confucian doctrine and Daoist practice. He made use of the Neo-Confucian theory of substance (*ti*) and function (*yong*) to explain the Daoist understanding regarding the 'cultivation of [human] nature (*xing*) and destiny (*ming*)'. Many Neo-Confucian masters had emphasised the unity and interaction of substance and function. Shao Yong believed that 'In the interaction of substance and function, the principles of man and things are complete', while Cheng Yi taught that 'Substance and function come from the same source, and there is no gap between the manifest and the hidden' (Chan, 1963a: 485, 570). Wang followed them and proposed that human nature and destiny were related in the same way as substance and function, and that the Way existed only in their integration. But how could such an integration be achieved? Wang believed that he found an answer by following the Neo-Confucian method of extinguishing desires and restraining the heart/mind. In cultivating the heart/mind, Wang adopted the Neo-Confucian doctrine of dual human nature: the Nature of Heaven and Earth or the original nature, and the Nature of material force or physical nature. All beings have their original nature that is good and what makes them bad is contamination by physical nature. Therefore, Wang called for cleansing human nature of contamination in order to return to the original nature. Wang also incorporated Neo-Confucian social ethics into Daoist doctrines and argued that the Five Constant Virtues (humaneness, righteousness, ritual/ propriety, wisdom and faithfulness) were the fundamental way of the world, and that loyalty (*zhong*) and filial piety (*xiao*) were the path to Daoist truth (Qing, 1993, vol. 3: 500–2).

Neo-Confucians of the Ming Dynasty were in general indebted to Daoism. Wang Yangming, for example, was for a long time under the influence of Chan Buddhism and Daoism. In his own words during his life of fifty-seven years, he spent about thirty years studying Daoist and Buddhist writings and in spiritual cultivation. His biographies written by his disciples record many of his visits to Daoist masters. One of them records that on the first night of his marriage, he went alone to a Daoist master to discuss the way of nourishing life, and he 'sat face to face [with the Daoist] and forgot to return' (*Wang Yangming Quanji*, 1992: 1222). After Wang fully transferred his allegiance to Confucianism he still continued to use Daoist theories to illustrate Confucian concepts. For example, he used the three Daoist terms *shen* the spirit, *qi* the vital force and *jing* the essence to explain his doctrine regarding innate good knowledge (*liangzhi*): '[I]nnate knowledge is one. In terms of its wonderful functioning, it is spirit; in terms of its universal operation, it is force; and in terms of its condensation and concentration, it is sperm [essence]' (Chan, 1963b: 133). He believed that his doctrine of the innate good knowledge held the key to understanding the Daoist formulas to prolong life. Many of his disciples were also interested in pursuing Daoist spiritual cultivation. Wang Ji (1498–1583), for example, followed the Daoist ideas with regard to 'inner alchemy' in order to explain how to extend 'innate good knowledge':

> A human is a human because of his spirit (*shen*) and vital force (*qi*). Spirit is the lord of the force, and the force is the flow of the spirit. Spirit is [human] nature and the vital force is [human] destiny. The innate good knowledge is the secret of spirit and vital force, and is the spiritual pivot of nature and destiny. When the knowledge is extended, then spirit and the vital force are united. Thus our nature and destiny are completed.   (*Mingru Xuean*, 1992, vol. 7: 289)

As the state orthodoxy, Confucianism demanded homage from Daoists, and Daoists were ready to acknowledge this dominance. It has become a tradition that in many Daoist monasteries or temples, worship is given not only to Daoist deities/immortals but also to Confucian masters. This can be seen in the White Cloud Temple in Beijing where Confucius, the Four Associates and Zhu Xi are revered – their statues are established in *Wenchang Gong*, the Palace of the God of Literature (see figure 11).

MUTUAL TRANSFORMATION BETWEEN CONFUCIANISM AND BUDDHISM

The relationship between Confucianism and Buddhism is more complicated. It is not only concerned with the interaction between two different traditions but also with the mutual transformation between an indigenous and a foreign culture. In the first stage of its introduction into China, Buddhism was interpreted and understood mainly through Daoism and Confucianism. The Buddha was seen as a figure similar to a Daoist deity or a Confucian sage, and was offered sacrifices alongside the Yellow Emperor and Laozi. When more accurate translations of the Buddhist texts were available, people became aware of the differences and contradictions between Buddhist doctrines and the teachings of Confucius and Laozi. The integration between Confucian and Daoist thought in the development of the Mysterious Learning led to the incorporation of Confucian ethics into religious Daoism. It became imperative that Confucianism and Buddhism attain a similar accord. The flexibility of Buddhist practices helped to alleviate some of the tension between this foreign importation and indigenous Chinese traditions. Confucian responses to the philosophical and spiritual challenges of Buddhism resulted in a further development of Confucian Learning.

According to a third-century author, Mouzi (c. 200), the early arguments against Buddhism were such that Buddhism was a barbarian doctrine which propagated reincarnation, violated filial piety, and was inferior to the teaching of Confucian sages (Keenan, 1994). The debates reflected the differences between Confucian teachings based on the family and the Buddhist doctrine centred on reincarnation. For a Buddhist, the sufferings of this life are evidence of one's previous life, and it is one's action in this life that indicates what will happen in the next life. This was contrary to the Confucian belief that an individual's life is only one link in the chain from ancestors to future descendants (Nivison & Wright, 1959: 71–2). In order to have a widespread appeal, Buddhism had to accommodate its teaching to Confucian ethics of the family. Thus a special Buddhist doctrine of filial piety was created and extended, which according to Ch'en, was done in the following three ways:

> First, by pointing out the numerous sutras in the Buddhist canon which stress filial piety; second, by forging a body of apocryphal literature which emphasizes piety as its central theme; and third, by contending that the Buddhist concept of filial piety was superior to that of the Confucians in that it aimed at universal salvation (this would include all previous ancestors in different forms), while the Confucian piety was limited to just one family. (Ch'en, 1973: 18)

To enhance their appeal, Buddhists argued for a deeper understanding of filial piety and they deemed that a person who became a monk/nun could accumulate merits for his/her ancestors and parents. They also argued that this was in agreement with the Confucian requirements of filial piety for not only doing service to one's parents but also glorifying them and manifesting the virtues of the ancestors. Arguments of this kind run through the whole history of Buddhism in China, and are supported by numerous writings, literature, poems and dramas about how a monk or nun saved his/her parents by his/her faith in the Buddha. The Buddhist *literati* also published a large number of treatises which argued for the consistency of Buddhist and Confucian ideas of filial piety. Qisong (1007–72), for example, wrote a treatise entitled *On Filial Piety* that is regarded as the most systematic and comprehensive discussion of the Buddhist theory of filial piety. Following the pattern of the Confucian classic on filial piety, Qisong maintains that filial piety is the fundamental principle of heaven and earth, is the first of all the commandments, and is the way to gain eternal happiness. In his opinion, 'Filial piety is honoured by all religions, but it is in Buddhism that filial piety is given the highest position' (Lai, 1995: 91), and 'The Confucians humanise piety but the Buddhists spiritualise it. Supreme and great is Buddhist piety' (Ch'en, 1973: 49). In this way, the Confucian virtue of filial piety became the primary purpose of Buddhist practices.

The debates between Confucians and Buddhists covered many areas. But the most important of them was concerned with the political and social effects of Buddhist practices. Confucians found it intolerable that Buddhist monks and monasteries drained the brain and treasures of the state, and believed that these created disorder and unrest. The Confucians opposed the Buddhist claim to be independent of the sovereign and of the state, because they believed that this seriously damaged the cohesion of the state and undermined the unifying power of the emperor. Some Confucian scholars argued that before the arrival of Buddhism, the Chinese people had enjoyed a peaceful and harmonious life, and that after its arrival, the state was in constant chaos. From this argument it is easy to come to the obvious conclusion that the miseries of life were caused by Buddhism because Buddhist doctrine and practice damaged or destroyed all human relationships. These Confucians attacked Buddhist monks and nuns as parasites, because monks and nuns did not cultivate the land nor did they weave cloth, and because by their refusal to marry they wasted their procreative functions, a practice that was contrary to nature and that deprived the country of much-needed manpower. Through the Confucian efforts to restrain the extreme practices of Buddhism and by the Buddhist efforts to accommodate Confucian politics, 'the gradual acculturation of Buddhism to the Chinese scene' took place, and 'the Buddhist monk became a Chinese subject, the monastic community a Chinese religious organization subject to the jurisdiction of the imperial bureaucracy. Buddhism had become Sinicized politically' (Ch'en, 1973: 124). This was achieved at the loss of Buddhist independence and led to the vulnerability of Buddhism as a part of social structure. Among the many persecutions Buddhism suffered in China, the persecution in 845 CE was the most thorough and sweeping, when more than 4,600 Buddhist monasteries were destroyed, and more than 260,500 monks and nuns were forced to return to secular life (Ch'en, 1964: 232).

Indebted to Buddhism as it was, Neo-Confucianism marked the return by the Chinese thinkers to their own cultural heritage and presented an alternative to the Buddhist way of life and doctrines. The Buddhist concepts of emptiness, impermanence and the Buddha-nature gave way to the Confucian concepts of principle, material force, the heart/mind, human nature and sagehood. The Buddhist doctrine of *sunyata* – that the phenomenal world is empty of essence – was replaced by a metaphysical philosophy of material force and principle. The Buddhist view of death and life was substituted by Confucian humanism which believes that in life one should serve unresistingly, and when death comes one will be at peace.

Due to the overwhelming position of Neo-Confucianism, the Buddhists of the Song–Ming Dynasties became even more eager to accommodate themselves to the Confucian doctrine. Zhi Yuan (976–1022) of Tian Tai Buddhist School explained the Buddhist Middle Way as the Confucian Mean (*zhongyong*), and called himself the 'Master of the Mean'. He pointed out that all his writings were based on Confucian principles, because without the teaching of Confucius, the state would be in disorder, the family would be in chaos, which would cause all the people including Buddhists to have no food for meals and no houses for shelter. Confucianism calls for cultivation of one's character and Buddhism concentrates on the heart. Their functions are like the inside and outside [of the clothes], interdependent on each other (Lai, 1995: 149–51). A Chan Buddhist master, Xingxiu (1166–1246), advised one of his disciples, the minister of the Jin dynasty (1115–1234), to govern the state by Confucianism and to control the mind of the people by Buddhism. After the Yuan Dynasty, Buddhists in general attached themselves to the Confucian system. Zhu Hong (1535–1615), for example, was originally a Confucian scholar but later converted to Pure Land Buddhism. He believed that there was nothing contradictory between Confucianism and Buddhism and that in fact they complemented each other, since Buddhism could 'do the job' that could not be done by Confucianism, while Confucianism could make manifest the Buddhist Dharma. Among the twenty laymen listed as his followers, two attained such prominence in official life that they were included in the biographical section of the *History of the Ming Dynasty (Mingshi)* and nine of them obtained *jinshi* degrees which were the highest in the civil service examination system (Ch'en, 1964: 439). Yuan Xian (1578–1657) considered that the Buddha was the sage of the other world while Confucius was the sage of this world. He likened the inherent nature of humans as stressed by Mengzi to the *zhenru* or Genuine Thusness of Buddhism (*ibid.*: 439).

Confucianism also benefited greatly from its contact with Buddhism. Without Buddhism, Confucianism would not have developed into the tradition that we know today. Many Neo-Confucian masters were fond of Buddhist doctrines. Zhou Dunyi, for example, was so deeply influenced by Buddhist compassion and universalism that he did not even cut the grass in front of his window, although he claimed that he did not do this from the Buddhist view that killing was evil, rather he was motivated by his observation of how creatures grew and flourished (Bruce,

1923: 29). Zhou compared a Buddhist sutra (*Saddharmapundarika Sutra*, the *Lotus Sutra*) with one of the hexagrams in the *Book of Changes* (*gen*, signifying 'keeping still', or ceasing to take pleasure in worldly goods), and used the Buddhist symbol of the lotus to illustrate his ideal personality, 'growing out of the shiny mud and yet being not defiled, and living in the pure and rippling water without appearing to be too fascinating and seductive' (Chang, 1958: 139–40). In general, Neo-Confucianism was formulated against the background of Buddhism, as Ch'en affirmed that 'While the Neo-Confucianists used terms found in the Confucian classics, they interpreted those terms in the light of the dominant Buddhist atmosphere, and the Neo-Confucian system would be incomprehensible to one not familiar with the prevailing Buddhist ideas of the age' (Ch'en, 1964: 471).

As far as religious practice is concerned, four of the Confucian practices were reshaped under the Buddhist influence. Firstly, the list of the Confucian worthies and scholars in Confucian temples indicates the influence of the Mahayana Buddhist worship of bodhisattvas, arahants and other saints. Following the model of Buddhist temples, statues of Confucius and a large number of Confucian worthies and scholars were established in Confucian temples, which was a move away from the ancient rites recorded in the classics where only a limited number of the important personages were represented by spiritual tablets. Secondly, Confucius and Confucian worthies were worshipped in a manner similar to the Buddhist bodhisattvas. Although Confucian ritual still followed the ancient rites for making sacrifice, their content and form were subtly changed and adjusted under the influence of Buddhist worship. Thirdly, Confucian pilgrimage and sacred places reflect a Buddhist understanding of the holy. Pilgrimage to these places became a feature of Confucian Learning. Fourthly, the Neo-Confucian understanding and practice of meditation, its spiritual cultivation and its conception of sagehood were clearly indebted to Chan Buddhist practice and doctrine.

CONFUCIANISM AND CHRISTIANITY

The first contact between Confucianism and Christianity most likely occurred during the Tang Dynasty, when the Nestorians came to China via Persia. The evidence for this is an inscribed stone stele, which was established in 781 and excavated in 1623. According to the inscription written by a Nestorian priest, Adam (*Jingjing*), a Syrian Nestorian called

Aloben arrived with a number of other priests in the Tang capital of Changan in the year 635, where he was welcomed by the Prime Minister and then received by the emperor. Three years later, they set up a monastery in the capital, known as *Daqin Si* or the 'Temple of Persia'. Nestorian Christianity was called *Jing Jiao*, an Illustrious Religion, but many people saw it as a sect of Buddhism. In Chinese, the priests were called *seng* (monks), the churches *si* (temples), God *fo* (the Buddha), and prophets, apostles, angels and saints were all known as *fawang* (Kings of the Dharma). The Christian symbol was known as the 'cross of victory', but it was frequently pictured in a (Buddhist) lotus flower. Not only was Nestorian Christianity closely associated with Buddhism, it was also attached to Confucianism. There is evidence that shows that Nestorianism was deliberately adapted to Confucian ethics. For example, in the translated messianic books of the Bible, the ten commandments were rephrased in such a way that the first four were summarised as 'humans must honour and fear the Heavenly Father', while the other six concentrated on filial piety. The Nestorians combined the service to the sovereign, the service to parents and the service to God into a three-in-one requirement for the believers. To accommodate themselves to Confucian political requirements, they followed Chinese rituals including prostrating themselves in front of the Emperor and establishing the statues of Tang emperors in their places of worship (Dong, 1992: 19–20). It was said that Nestorianism, alongside other established religions such as Daoism, Buddhism and Manichaeism, flourished in the whole country for around two hundred years. Towards the end of the Tang Dynasty, however, the imperial tolerance of 'foreign religions' had worn out, and the cry to curb 'barbarian cults' was encouraged by Confucians. In 845 when Buddhism was persecuted, Nestorianism and all other foreign religions were also swept away. It was recorded that as many as two thousand Nestorian missionaries were banished.

There is some evidence that Catholic Christianity was present in the Mongolian Yuan China, although this contact did not leave significant impact on Confucianism. The next serious attempt for their encounter was not made until the end of the sixteenth century when Jesuit missionaries met Confucian scholars. The most famous of these missionaries was an Italian Matteo Ricci (1522–1610) who devoted his time to the study of the Confucian classics and to the translation of the Confucian Four Books into Latin. Ricci focused his efforts on Confucian *literati* and officials, and deliberately adapted Christian teachings to Chinese customs and culture. He also introduced the Chinese to western science and technology, such as astronomy, mathematics, geography and mechanical devices. In these ways he earned a good reputation at court and amongst the upper classes. Many Confucian scholars/officials admired his knowledge of the Confucian classics and his respect of Confucius and Confucian sages. The most important thing that Ricci did was to make 'such "adjustments" in the Christian religion that his Chinese converts could not differentiate it from Confucianism' (Young, 1983: 26). In his renowned book entitled *Tianzhu Shiyi* or *The True Meaning of the Master of Heaven*, Ricci began with the following words, reminiscent of the Confucian text, the *Great Learning*:

> All doctrines about making the whole world peaceful and governing a
> country rightly are focused on the principle of uniqueness. Therefore,
> worthies and sages have always advised the ministers to be loyal, that
> is not to have a second [lord in their mind]. Among the Five Human
> Relationships the most important is that regarding the king, and the first
> of the Three Bonds in Human Relations is that between the king and the
> minister.   (Ricci, 1985: 57)

Ricci believed that there was a fundamental agreement between Confucianism and Christianity: 'When we examine their books closely, we discover in them very few things which are contrary to the light of reason and many of which are in conformity with it, and their natural philosophers are second to none' (Gernet, 1985: 28). Whether or not this approach is considered to be in accordance with the Christian doctrine, Ricci made his teaching appealing to the Chinese literati, and thus introduced a new element to Confucian Learning. This tailoring of the Bible and the Confucian classics facilitated the conversion of a number of leading Confucian scholars to the Christian faith, of whom Xu Guangqi (1562–1633), Li Zhizao (1569–1630) and Yang Tingyun (1557–1627) were most famous. There was an element of faith in their conversion to Christianity, but the underlying reason was their desire to transform Confucianism by way of Christianity. They sought to turn away the Han–Song versions of Confucian Learning, to rid Confucianism of Buddhist contamination and to reclaim the earlier classical tradition, namely, the beliefs and rituals recorded in the Confucian classics, which they thought would be possible through the ideas presented in the Christian faith. Xu

Guangqi made this point very clear when he argued that the purpose of Ricci's book the *True Meaning of the Lord of Heaven* was 'to do away with Buddha and to complete the law of the literati' (Covell, 1986: 54).

In later Ming China the intellectual trend was towards the belief that all religions, doctrines and traditions were the same in essence. It was in this framework that the association between Confucianism and Christianity was forged. Scholars believed that not only did the three doctrines of China share the same purpose of 'establishing one and the same principle of the universe', but also that they 'were all in perfect agreement with the teachings of the missionaries' (Gernet, 1985: 33). Many a Confucian scholar took the view that the Christian 'teaching is one with that of the Duke of Zhou and Confucius'. Among the ideas shared by Confucian and Christian faiths that they believed to be 'exactly those of our Confucianism', was that 'one must serve and fear Heaven'. These scholars took this understanding as a new stimulus for the people to follow more closely the teachings of Confucius. On one occasion it was even stated that 'In the China since Confucius, it has no longer been possible to imitate Confucius. By coming to China [the doctrine of the] Master of Heaven teaches men to act rightly and thus causes each person to imitate Confucius' (*ibid.*: 35–6). The converted Christians interpreted their new faith in the light of their Confucian understanding. In the preface to the 1628 edition of Ricci's *The True Meaning of the Master of Heaven*, Li Zhizao insists that the book contains an excellent moral teaching which 'in its essentials, requires that people repent their errors and rediscover the meaning of their duties (*yi*), that they repress their desires and retain intact within themselves the meaning of humanity (*ren*)' (*ibid.*: 37).

However, the co-operation and mutual admiration between Christian missionaries and Confucian scholar–officials did not last long. The majority of Confucians soon found out the fundamental differences between the two teachings. Wang Fuzhi, for example, criticised Ricci because Ricci had turned 'his back upon the ancestors in favour of an unclean ghost', and pointed out that although Ricci dressed his theories with speeches full of artifice, they 'are the ideas of those we call Barbarians' (*ibid.*: 69). Another scholar accused the Christians of confusing truth and the false: 'How could our Saints and Sages of Antiquity possibly have abandoned cultivating their virtue in order to concentrate upon cultivating favours from Heaven? But there is even worse to come: what these Barbarians consider to be good and evil are the exact opposite to what our Saints and Sages mean' (*ibid.*, 168). Meanwhile, other Christian sects and the court in Rome had also become impatient and intolerant of the Confucian tradition. Controversies surrounded the understanding and translations of terms such as Heaven (*tian*) and the Lord of Heaven (*tian zhu*), and conflicts between Confucianism and Christianity arose with regard to the nature of ancestral worship, the worship of Confucius and to the question of who had jurisdiction over mission activities in China. In 1704 and again in 1715 the Pope issued orders prohibiting Chinese converts from performing rites to Confucius and to the ancestors. This created a split between the Chinese court and the Roman Church, which led the Qing Emperor, Kang Xi (r. 1660–1720), to reverse his policy in regard to the activities of the Christian missionaries. In 1720 a decree was issued stating that: 'They [the missionaries] preach heresy like Buddhist monks and Daoist priests. From now on it is not necessary for Westerners to engage in religious activities in China, and we forbid it' (Fang, 1959: vol. 5: 140). This marked the end of the great encounter between Confucianism and Christianity.

European and American Protestant missionaries arrived in China in the earlier part of the nineteenth century. In order to facilitate the translation of the Bible they found it necessary to study the Confucian classics, and some of them took Confucianism as a frame of reference to introduce the Christian gospel. Confucius and Mengzi were used to illustrate the Christian tenets, and many tracts made use of the Confucian theories of human nature and destiny to explain that although God created humans as 'good', the human ancestors sinned and fell from grace and therefore everybody was in need of perfection. James Legge (1815–97), a Scottish Presbyterian missionary, engaged upon the huge project of systematically translating the Confucian classics into English. For Legge, 'Confucianism is not antagonistic to Christianity, as Buddhism and Brahmanism are. It is not atheistic like the former, not pantheistic like the latter' (Lee, 1991: 13). Legge's translations were of enormous value in introducing Confucianism into the West, as well as for initiating a dialogue between Confucians and Christians. On the other hand, Christian doctrines added a new element in the chaos and unrest that was spreading through China in the middle of the nineteenth century, and led to a military movement aimed at establishing the heavenly paradise on earth that almost brought down the Qing Dynasty. This movement was known as the Heavenly State of Grand Peace, led by Hong Xiuquan

(1814–64), who established a short-lived Heavenly Dynasty (*tianchao*). Having failed in civil service examinations, Hong Xiuquan was attracted to the Christian faith by some Protestant pamphlets and created a new faith by combining Christian beliefs and Confucian ethics. He called upon the starved and ill-treated people to establish an equal society by the power of the God of Grand Peace (*taiping shangdi*). God was recognised as Father, Jesus the eldest son, Hong as the second son, and Hong's generals as younger sons. In his evangelistic zeal, Hong abolished Confucianism, decreeing that all Confucian books be burnt, and Confucian temples and tablets smashed. He also ordered the Confucian classics to be re-edited to fit the new faith. These measures were not, of course, carried out thoroughly, and Hong's new policies were in fact a revision of Confucian moral codes rather than a total departure from them. For example, he insisted that filial piety to parents was the same as filial piety to the Heavenly God (Father in Heaven). This eclectic merger of Confucianism and Christianity was condemned by Confucians and Christians alike, and the movement was crushed through an alliance of the Qing government, local Confucian generals and the western powers.

The end of the nineteenth century and the beginning of the twentieth century saw a new relationship between Confucianism and Christianity. In general there was some degree of agreement between these two traditions in the eyes of most newly converted Chinese Christians, as Lee observes, '[M]ost scholarly-minded Chinese Christians acknowledge their indebtedness to Confucianism. Seldom do you find a Chinese Christian who repudiates Confucianism wholesale. Not to speak of repudiation, criticism of Confucianism is uncommon among Chinese Christians' (Lee, 1991: 16). Many Chinese converts made use of Confucian philosophy and ethics to reformulate Christian ideas. At the same time, the contact with the Christian West became a powerful driving force for the people rooted in the Confucian tradition to re-examine their own tradition. This double heritage has a serious impact on modern Confucianism in the twentieth century, and all the modern New Confucians have to take the challenges arising from the compatibility and incompatibility between Confucianism and Christianity. While admitting that Confucianism can learn from the Christian tradition, many New Confucians point out the fundamental differences between these two doctrines. In his dialogue with younger Chinese Christians, Mou Zongsan once remarked that

You should not insist that there is only one Christ, while others can be merely Christians. If you rejected that 'all the beings can become Buddhas' and 'everybody can become a sage', then we would not agree with you. Why must [salvation] go through Christ? . . . Jesus is merely a sage, why must we be saved through him? Why is Jesus able directly to be [in God], while we cannot? . . . If you say that Christ is not from humans, but sent by God; if you say that everybody cannot become Christ but merely Christians, then [Christianity] would not be fit for Chinese culture and there of course arises mutual rejection [between Christianity and Chinese culture].

(*Er Hu Monthly*, No. 3, 1997: 3)

Most modern Confucians see the necessity for the dialogue between Confucianism and Christianity, but they strongly resist the overwhelming influence of Christianity and search for the mutual benefit in a two-way flow, as emphasised by Liu Shuxian that 'the dialogue between contemporary New Confucianism and Christianity does not mean to convert one from another, but to expand one's horizon so as to incorporate some of the values, experiences and insights from the other' (Lee, 1991: 68). The value of the dialogue between Confucianism and Christianity cannot be fully appreciated unless we understand this dialogue against the wider background of Confucian survival and renovation in the twentieth century. To evaluate the efforts modern intellectuals made in accommodating the two traditions, we must examine the intellectual trends in modern China and other parts of East Asia and investigate the themes on which Confucian scholars formulate and develop their new understandings. This will be the chief aim of our conclusive chapter.

Questions for discussion

1. How can we understand the Confucian sacrifice to Heaven? Is it a theistic cult?
2. In what sense can we say that ancestral worship is the root of the Confucian tradition?
3. 'In spite of the enormous influence of Confucius, it is doubtful whether he ever received worship from large numbers of people at any time . . . Confucius was a patron, not of the Chinese as a whole, but of a sharply marked class in Chinese society' (Shryock, 1966: 224). Do you agree? If so, why?
4. What is the spiritual meaning of Confucian Learning?

5. How can we tell the differences between Confucian cultivation and Buddhist/Daoist meditation?
6. How was the three-in-one doctrine accepted as the best one to deal with different religious traditions in China?
7. What can be learned from the historical interchange between Confucianism and Christianity?

5

Confucianism and its modern relevance

The modern era of Confucianism began with its responses to the challenges of Western powers. Emotionally being engaged in and holding to tradition, Chinese and Korean Confucians did not initially respond to modernity as quickly and rationally as their counterparts in Japan, and fatally slowed down the process of Chinese and Korean modernisation during the second half of the nineteenth century. Confucianism came into the twentieth century burdened with scholasticism, accompanied by extreme moralism and blamed for intellectual, political and social failures of East Asia in the modern time.

The vulnerable situation of Confucianism in East Asia in general did not change until rapid industrialisation brought about cultural confidence and the need for traditional values in the 1970s. Since then, more and more people, academics and politicians alike, have come to rethink the tradition more positively and to reclaim their lost identity by asserting that cultural idiosyncrasy lies in the very heart of modernity. In examining the cultural elements in economic and political courses, they find that East Asia, though divergent economically and politically, is an area that shares a common cultural background provided by Confucian values. They have also come to realise that Confucianism as the shared culture in the 'Confucian world' CAN be a positive, progressive and valuable factor in promoting economic and cultural development. In the enthusiastic search for the 'cultural root', Confucianism is brought into focus, and becomes relevant to people's lives again.

Are we coming to a new era of Confucianism? Or in other words, has Confucianism been revived into a modern tradition? There are no ready answers to the questions about modern Confucianism. The modern relevance and vitality of Confucianism lie nowhere but in its ability to help people understand and solve their problems, and modern Confucian scholars have to rise to a challenge to answer all the questions that science and democracy have raised, and how to revitalise Confucian values in the context of modern life.

China or the so-called 'Sinic world' was, and continues to be, the main source of modern Confucian Learning, the powerhouse for changes and the pioneer of the Confucian future. Therefore, in this concluding chapter we will base our observation and discussion of the modern relevance of Confucianism on the Chinese efforts in updating and transforming the Confucian tradition, with an awareness that Korean and Japanese Confucians have made and are making similar progress.

Following its ups and downs in the modern era, we will first examine the contributions made by leading Modern New Confucians, and then revisit the key issues in modern Confucian studies, assessing the problems and challenges modern Confucianism has so far faced and taken. Lastly, we will come to re-examine the cultural, moral and spiritual legacies of Confucianism, thereby speculating its values for the future in relation to the following questions: how can Confucianism contribute to a multicultural modern society in which people of different cultures are learning to co-exist with one another while reasonably admitting their differences? How can Confucianism shake off its negative elements while enhancing its positive relevance for the coming twenty-first century?

Confucianism: survival and renovation

Modern Confucianism has engaged in a long process of survival and renovation originated as early as the end of the Ming Dynasty. As an array of social, cultural and spiritual traditions, Confucianism had been undergoing constant changes, which were both the source of its energy and the basis of its vitality. The arrival of western culture in the nineteenth century, however, essentially rejected the self-change or self-adjustment preferred by Confucians. The collapse of Confucian states meant that old Confucianism was already out-dated, and to survive, Confucianism had to change itself more rapidly and fundamentally. Confucian scholars were pressed into a painful soul-searching with profound self-reflectiveness, and had to find answers to the questions of why it had lost its political, religious and cultural influence, and whether it could maintain its moral and spiritual power bases. Facing a life-or-death choice, those who had deep fondness for tradition started to redirect the trends and fashions, and Confucian Learning thus made the transition to the new era of 'Modern New Confucianism'. The modern new Confucians attempt to 'modernise' Confucianism in a new context by creating 'a cultural space and an authentic possibility for the creative transformation of Confucian humanism as a living tradition in modern East Asia' (Tu, 1996b: 19).

STEPPING INTO THE MODERN AGE

Confucian Learning from the end of the Ming Dynasty to the beginning of the Qing Dynasty was for most part a continuation and redirection of the early Neo-Confucian scholarship. A great number of scholars saw defects in both Rationalistic (Cheng–Zhu) and Idealistic (Lu–Wang) Schools, and attempted to synthesise them into a better system. Some of them, like Gu Xiancheng (1550–1612), opted to overcome the 'emptiness' of the Idealistic school by emphasising the scholarly learning of the Cheng–Zhu teaching, while others, like Huang Zongxi (1610–95), took another path by trying to reduce the scholastic tendencies of Cheng–Zhu by promoting the self-cultivation of the Lu–Wang School.

Looking to the ancients was a hallmark of leading scholars of the Qing Dynasty (1664–1911). Dissatisfied with the Confucian scholarship of the Song (宋學), Gu Yanwu (1613–82) and Wei Yuan (1794–1857), for example, were determined to return to the Han Learning (漢學), believing that the Song Learning destroyed the spirit of Confucianism, that the study of principle (*li xue*) was a kind of 'false learning', and that the Han study of classics (*jing xue*) was the true way to the restoration of Confucian values. Wang Fuzhi (1619–92), Yan Yuan (1635–1704) and Dai Zhen (1724–77) went even further: Confucianism had been corrupted as early as, if not earlier than, the Qin–Han period, after which learning was no longer really of Confucian studies, but a 'false Confucianism' (*wei ru*). Yan Yuan believed that the Way of Confucianism was in the classics, and that the commentaries of the classics produced from the Han to the present were the means for transmitting the principles of the sages and worthies, but that they did not themselves constitute these principles. The Confucians of the Song–Ming Dynasties whose tablets were given places in the Temple of Confucius contributed to the commentaries but not to the Confucian way. Their understanding of Confucianism was contaminated by Buddhism and Daoism, and became the source of confusion and distortion. For Yan, the Song–Ming Learning was nothing but an ossified form of the Way, misleading the people and weakening the state, and he therefore concluded that the Neo-Confucian masters were not 'the true followers of Yao, Shun, the Duke of Chou, and Confucius . . .' (Fung, 1953: 633).

The Manchu Qing Dynasty promoted religious and political Confucianism to an unprecedented high position in history and strengthened the orthodox position of the Cheng–Zhu School on the one hand, and ruthlessly suppressed any new interpretation of Confucian Learning on the other. This produced another characteristic of the Qing scholarship: while being unable to do anything to oppose the political regime, Confucian scholars engaged themselves in evidential studies of the ancient classics (*kaozheng xue*) to rebel against the highly speculative scholarship established by the great Song masters. Both Cheng–Zhu and Lu–Wang explored in depth the moral significance of the Confucian classics, but in so doing they did not examine the philological evidence of the sage's words. Believing that only correct understanding of the words and phrases of the classics can lead one to the true Way, preeminent Qing scholars such as Dai Zhen and Zhang Xuecheng (1738–1801) embarked on an odyssey to critically examine all the Confucian texts and commentaries. The desire to provide solid and concrete evidence for every sentence of these writings led to a great number of philological, historical and textual criticisms, all of which contributed dramatically to the extension of authentic knowledge of the texts.

The scholars of evidential studies did not confine their attention to the Confucian classics. They paid great attention to the way Confucian Learning could be used to improve people's lives. Since the Han era, the majority of Confucian scholars had been less enthusiastic towards the material needs of the people than towards the self-cultivation of humaneness and righteousness. Dong Zhongshu proposed that 'one should manifest the righteous but not seek its profit, and should illustrate the Way but not calculate what one can achieve from it' (*zheng qiyi bumou qili, ming qidao buji qigong*, in *Hanshu*, 1998: 2524). The Cheng–Zhu School calls for conscientious reading of the books; while the Lu–Wang School concentrates on the illumination of the heart/mind. To oppose what is believed to be the one-sided attention to purely scholarly work or an inward journey, the great Song Confucian, Chen Liang (1143–94) dedicated his teaching to the utility of society. While this redirection did not produce much political and academic influence in his own time, Chen's teaching had an effect on the Qing scholarship where the practical concerns with 'man in society' were embraced by those who sought after the evidential and critical examination of the Confucian classics. In the mind of these scholars, action is more important than words, and study of literature is intended to serve efficiently the practical life, and self-cultivation is intended to govern the state properly. Confucianism must be a doctrine useful to its time, as argued by Li Yong (1627–1705) that 'Confucian teachings stood for a specific content, involving ideas and actions morally and socially useful to a Confucian society' (Birdwhistell, 1996: 81). Li rejected Zhu Xi's interpretation of *gewu* (格物) of the *Great Learning* as theoretically 'investigating things' and maintained that *gewu* meant 'to practice a thing with one's own hand' in relation to such tasks as the exemplification of the illustrious virtue, loving the people, (making) one's thoughts (sincere), (rectifying) the mind, (cultivating) the self, (regulating) the family, etc. (Fung, 1953: 634). Wang Fuzhi emphasised at the philosophical level the practical means of the Confucian way. He opposed the separation of the Way (*dao*) and instrument (*qi*), believing that 'without instrument there would be no *Tao* (Way)' (*ibid*.: 642). This 'new scholarship' not only led to the rise of Korean and Japanese 'practical learning', but also fundamentally influenced the later development of Confucian scholarship in China.

The Opium War (1940–2) between Britain and China forced the Qing Court to open the gate to the world, and this cruel reality led many Confucian scholars to search for a solution to overcome China's weaknesses and illnesses and to empower the state. 'Learning technologies from the West in order to stop the western advance' (*shiyi zhi changji yi zhiyi*) was proposed by Wei Yuan and followed up by almost all the then leading Confucians. Studying and introducing European culture became a powerful current. Admitting that there were serious problems in the Confucian tradition, most of them still firmly believed that the real solution was in Confucianism. For them, Confucianism was the substance of culture, while western science and technology merely applications, and the latter merited adoption only to make up the shortcomings of Confucian Learning (*zhongti xiyong*).

None the less, the once self-confident Confucian scholars were deeply puzzled by the advances of the western power and the humiliating weakness of China, a perception which caused many of the new-generation scholars to adopt a critical and suspicious attitude toward traditional values. Reform of both imperial politics and Confucian doctrines became urgent for the intellectuals, who called for a departure from the then orthodox Song Learning (*song xue*) in order to acquire from the West the 'new learning' (*xin xue*) of science and philosophy. Liao Ping (1852–1932), Kang Youwei (1858–1927) and others revived the debate between the Old Text School and the New Text School, and propagated reformation in the name of opting for the New Text School of the Han Dynasty. In his widely circulated book, *Kongzi Gaizhi Kao* (*A Study of Confucius as a Reformer of Institutions*, 1898), Kang presented all the masters of philosophical schools emerging during the Spring and Autumn period as the founders of religious traditions. Of these founders, Confucius was the most influential and successful, and was the King of Constitution and Institutions (*zhifa zhi wang*), the New King (*xinwang*), the Uncrowned King (*suwang*), the King of Culture (*wengwang*) and the Sage King (*shengwang*) (*Kang Youwei Quanji*, 1992 vol. 3: 224). Kang reconfirmed that by reforming the earlier tradition of *ru* Confucius actually created Confucian religion (*rujiao*) and opened up a new era in Chinese history. What was created differed from any system of the previous three dynasties (the Xia, the Shang and the Zhou) and also differed from what was later falsified by the Old Text School of the Han Dynasty. Through so-called evidential research (*kao*), Kang told a story of how Confucius transformed the old culture and set up a model for the people to reform their institutions so that the institutions could serve their own times. For a while a cry echoed loudly from south to north to establish Confucianism as the state religion, in order to enable it to be a Chinese equivalent to Christianity in the West. In this reformed version, Confucius was taken to be a divine being with the same status as Jesus and the Buddha, who came to the world to reform the institution by way of editing and transmitting the Classics. Thus Confucianism, as understood by the reform-minded scholars like Kang Youwei and Tan Citong (1865–98), was believed to have been *the* doctrine that was able on its own to lead the Chinese from the 'Age of Disorder' to the 'Age of Great Unity'.

The scholars of the New Text School failed to bring China out of her abyss and the political reform in 1898 lasted only a hundred days. A group of Confucian scholars attempted in other ways to modernise Confucianism. Yan Fu (1853–1921) and a number of others translated and introduced western philosophical writings to China, of which the most influential ones were *Tian Yan Lun* (*Evolution and Ethics* by T. H. Huxley), *Yuan Fu* (*The Wealth of Nations* by Adam Smith) and *Fa Yi* (*L'Esprit des lois* by Montesquieu). Ironically, these and many other translated works soon became new and powerful weapons in the fight against the old tradition, and signalled that Confucianism had arrived at yet another crucial juncture. The confrontation and reconciliation between Confucianism and the western tradition provided the background for Confucianism to be innovated and developed.

THE RISE OF MODERN CONFUCIANISM

The start of the twentieth century brought to Confucianism both hope and pessimism, and Confucianism was deeply involved in the struggle of two political forces, where both conservatives and reformers made use of Confucianism for their own purposes. In the mood of pessimism and even despair throughout the whole of Confucian scholarship and the chaotic situation of the republic, debates over the value and function of Confucianism were fiercely engaged. The reformers of the past, such as Kang Youwei, Yan Fu and Liang Qichao (1873–1929), became new 'conservatives', in the sense that they were against republicanism and launched a movement to restore the dominant position of Confucianism. The new conservative movement called for the study of the Confucian classics (*du jing*) and restoration of Confucianism as the state religion (*guo jiao*). Their views were used as the rallying slogans by those who attempted to revive the imperial system (*fugu pai*), and unfortunately coincided with the assumption of the crown by Yuan Shikai (1859–1916).

Having seen the problems of Confucian Learning, a number of leading intellectuals were sympathetic and took a more constructive attitude towards Confucianism. On the one hand, they criticised Confucianism for its stupefying of the people and the learning (Zhang, 1976: 250), and proposed to replace the idol of Confucius with 'truth' as the supreme guide for the Chinese: 'I love Confucius, but I love truth more' (Liang Qichao, in Chow, 1967: 300). On the other hand, they devoted much of their energy to Confucian studies, including editing and annotating Confucian classics, as in the case of Zhang Binglin who became a renowned master of classical studies in the modern age.

An introduction to Confucianism

A powerful anti-Confucianism movement was carried out after the
republican revolution that succeeded in overthrowing the Manchu Qing
Dynasty in 1911; Confucianism was blamed for all the illnesses of China
and was seen as the obstacle for the Chinese people to move forward.
'Smashing Confucius' Shop' (zalan kongjia dian) became an exciting
slogan of the May Fourth Movement (1919) led by radical liberals such
as Chen Duxiu (1879–1942), Yi Baisha (1886–1921), Li Dazhao (1889–
1927) and Hu Shi (1891–1962). The movement aimed at establishing
a new culture without Confucianism and new China of 'science and
democracy'. Apart from these political reformers, a group of scholars
led by Gu Jiegang (1893–1980) introduced a new fashion of bringing
the Confucian tradition into suspicion, whilst scrutinising the whole
of ancient history, especially the Confucian history and classics with a
critical eye. Their studies of the classics brought the classical learning
of two thousand years to an end. At the same time their negation of
the Confucian tradition induced a strong reaction from other leading
scholars, which soon opened up a new age for Confucianism, intellectually Modern New Confucian Learning (xiandai xin ruxue) being born
both as a rational response to radical anti-traditionalism and as a conscious movement to reclaim the value and spirit of the Confucian way
of life in modern times.

Modern new Confucians claimed that their efforts were contiguous
with the early tradition and aimed at reviving two traditional themes
in the modern age: how to unify the inner virtue (neisheng, sageliness
within) and the external merits (waiwang, kingliness without), and how
to unify the moral order and the natural order. Xiong Shili (1885–1968),
Liang Shuming (1893–1988), Fung Yu-lan (1895–1990), Qian Mu
(1895–1990), Zhang Junmai (Carsun Chang, 1886–1969), and He Lin
(1902–), to name but a few, stood out as the leaders of this new
trend; their activities constituted the first phase of Confucianism in the
twentieth century.

As far as the basic principle used for reinterpreting Confucian
doctrines is concerned, these early prominent Confucian scholars may
be roughly divided into two interrelated groups, Modern New Idealists
and Modern New Rationalists. The former is represented by Liang
Shuming, Xiong Shili and He Lin, who followed and developed the
Lu–Wang's teaching on the heart/mind, and combined it variously with
western philosophies of life or with Buddhist idealism, to create a

'New Learning of the Heart/Mind' (*xin xinxue*). The latter finds its best representation in Zhang Junmai and Fung Yu-lan, who traced their origin to the Cheng–Zhu's Learning of Principle with a combination of western rational philosophies to form a 'New Learning of Principle' (*xin songxue*, or *xin lixue*).

Xiong Shili was indebted to the influence of the Buddhist *Vijnaptimatra* or better known in China as the *Wei-shi* ('Consciousness Only') tradition, which is characterised by the subtlety of its understanding of the mind (consciousness). In fact Xiong himself had been devoted to the teachings of Asanga and Vasubandhu and searched inwardly for the true self and true heart/mind before abandoning Buddhism to become a Confucian advocate. This conversion came as he found that his inner experience was in complete harmony with what was recorded in the Confucian classics. Differing from another new idealist, Liang Shuming, who emphasised the intuitive heart/mind, Xiong stressed more the significance of the rational heart/mind. Following the line of the Lu–Wang School and incorporating Buddhist idealism into his own thinking, Xiong constructed a new system based on the heart/mind as the ultimate reality. For him, the heart/mind is not only a cognitive knowing but also an effectively acting faculty, and the unity of knowledge and action is fundamental to any theoretical deliberation or any practical work. The heart/mind manifests itself in a creative process wherein the division of the external and the internal is completely transcended. As the ultimate reality, the heart/mind is identified with humaneness (*ren*) and with the original substance that humans, Heaven, Earth and all things share. The heart/mind guards and dominates body and experiences. As the substance of humaneness the heart/mind is the source of all transformations and the foundation of all existences. Social reformation cannot be attained unless the heart/mind has been fulfilled and humaneness realised. He maintained that Chinese culture could not be revived unless the Confucian view of life had been readopted and practised. This deep love for Confucianism and complete identification with the Confucian values converted Xiong from a scholar to a faithful believer. In the last few years of his life when Confucianism was banned by extreme Maoism, Xiong did not give up his faith. He hung on the wall, pieces of paper with the names of Confucius, Wang Yangming and Wang Fuzhi, the three most revered spiritual masters for him, because he felt that he would gain strength and courage when looking at these 'spiritual tablets' (Xiong, 1996: 11).

Xiong's book, the *New Exposition of Consciousness-Only* (*Xin Weishi Lun*, 1932) was met with both great enthusiasm from the Confucian circus, and strong criticism from Buddhists, the Westernised intellectuals and Marxists. It stands as one of the most representative works of Confucian Learning in the twentieth century. His disciples and students such as Tang Junyi (1909–78), Mou Zongsan (1909–95) and Xu Fuguan (1903–82) carried on his teaching and opened up the second stage of Modern New Confucianism.

From the 1930s to the 1940s, Fung Yu-lan published a good number of books and articles to propagate a new version of Neo-Confucianism. In a series of writings known as 'the Six Books of Zhenyuan' (*zhenyuan liushu*), Fung follows up and develops the Rationalistic tradition of the Song–Ming Dynasties, reshaping the rationalistic doctrines of the Cheng–Zhu School by way of the western neo-realism to create a new form of rationalistic Confucianism. Unlike other Confucian scholars like Liang Shuming and Xiong Shili who essentially rejected and refuted the impact of western philosophy on Confucian doctrine, Fung insisted that western philosophies could be used as a means to criticise and reconstruct Confucian metaphysics, moral and social philosophies. This approach enabled him not only to follow simply (*zhao zhuo*) but also to develop further (*jie zhuo*) Neo-Confucianism of the Song–Ming Dynasties. The metaphysical doctrine of Fung's system comes from a combination of Rationalistic Confucian principles and western realistic philosophy, using the latter to adapt and explain the former. The centre of this metaphysics is found in the concepts of principle (*li*) and material force (*qi*), the universal and the particular existing in a harmonious and interactive relation. Applying this understanding to daily and social affairs, Fung reasoned that the conflict between China and the West was one between the ancient and the modern, and that their essential difference was that the former was a society based on family while the latter was based on community. The path of adapting the traditional culture to modern China was through industrialisation. Nature and society are where humans live and act, and metaphysical and moral principles must be carried out in daily life. As a human being, one must understand the proper relations between individual and society, and between humanity and the cosmos, a proper understanding of the former leads one to become an ideal person, while a proper grasp of the latter leads one to oneness with Heaven and Earth, in which Confucian sagehood will be manifested.

The systematic expression of Confucianism by Fung has had a great effect on Confucian studies in the twentieth century, the widely circulated *A History of Chinese Philosophy* has made Fung the most influential source of Confucian studies in the West. Fung's understanding of Confucianism in particular and Chinese intellectual history in general, has to a great extent, shaped the conception of many of the western students and readers of Confucianism. However mainly due to political reasons and to the separation of the Mainland from Hong Kong and Taiwan after 1949, Fung's new rationalism was not followed up by prominent Confucians in Taiwan and Hong Kong; consequently its influence on modern Confucian Learning is not as widespread as that of new idealism propagated by Xiong Shili has been.

UNFOLDING OF THE CONFUCIAN PROJECT
The second period of Modern Confucianism was instigated by those who followed Xiong Shili and other early Confucian masters to continue the exploration of Confucian values for modern life. Of them, the prominent and influential figures include Tang Junyi, Mou Zongsan, Xu Fuguan, and Fang Dongmei (Thomé H. Fang, 1899–1977).

After the victory of Communism in 1949, Confucian studies on the Mainland were carried out only in line with Marxism and Communism, and the social and academic status of Confucian Learning was in a constant decline. The main platform of Modern Confucianism moved from the Mainland to Hong Kong, Taiwan, and the USA, and Confucian Learning was carried on there by the students and disciples of the Confucian masters of the first generation. The first effort in reviving Confucianism in the 1950s was a document drawn up by Tang Junyi, Mou Zongsan, Zhang Junmai and Xu Fuguan and published on the first day of 1958, entitled 'A Declaration of Chinese Culture to the Scholars of the World' (*wei zhongguo wenhua jinggao shijie renshi xuanyan*). The Declaration restates the authors' concern about the direction of human development, and the value of Chinese culture, and urges Western and Chinese scholars to understand Chinese culture, claiming that without a proper understanding of Chinese culture, the perception of China will be distorted and the Chinese, a quarter of the world's population, will have no future. They state that the core of Chinese culture is the Confucian Learning of the human heart/mind and nature (*xin xing*), which presents a unique approach to metaphysical problems, and harmonises moral senses, transcendental vision and religious spirit. Admitting the lack of western democracy, science and technology in Chinese culture, the authors maintain that Confucianism is not against democracy, nor is it anti-science, and that the seeds of democracy, science and technology rooted in Chinese culture could have developed into a modern political system and scientific spirit if properly cultivated, while showing a cultural character different from that of the West. They further declare that a critical turning point for humankind is when humans develop a unified and common heart to prepare for the co-existence and interdependence of different cultures and different nations, and that Confucian tradition can make a great contribution to the unity and harmony of the world (*tianxia yi jia*).

These scholars propagated Confucianism not only by declarations but also by their efforts in reorganising Confucian institutions. The Academy (College) of New Asia (*xinya xueyuan*), Hong Kong, pioneered this direction. According to its founder and the first President, Qian Mu (1895–1990), the Academy aims at opening up a new education system that revitalises the spirit of learning and teaching spirit in the Confucian academies of the Song and Ming Dynasties, borrows the tutorial system of European Universities, directs students in the studies of humanities, and facilitates communication between eastern and western cultures. With a clear Confucian orientation, the Academy became the centre of Confucian Learning and the base camp for the revival of Confucianism.

The new Confucians published a great deal of articles and books to propagate Confucian thought and ideals. The most well known include *Wenhua Yishi yu Daode Lixing* (*Cultural Consciousness and Moral Rationality*, Hong Kong, 1958) and *Zhongguo Renwen Jingshen zhi Fazhan* (*The Development of Chinese Humanistic Spirit*, Hong Kong, 1958) by Tang Junyi; *Zhongguo Renxinglun Shi* (*A History of Chinese Theories of Human Nature*, Taipei, 1963) by Xu Fuguan; *Xinti yu Xingti* (*The Substance of the Mind and of the Nature*, Taipei, 1968–9) by Mou Zongsan; and *The Chinese View of Life: The Philosophy of Comprehensive Harmony* (The Union Press, Hong Kong, 1957) by Thomé H. Fang. Central to their writings is an attempt to explore and answer questions such as how to return to the true spirit of Confucian Learning and how to adapt the Confucian tradition to a new era. Like the earlier Confucian scholars such as Liang Shuming and Xiong Shili, Tang Junyi holds on to Idealistic Neo-Confucianism and takes the heart/mind as the substance of the world and the foundation of life. As the heart/mind is the source of values, which if manifested will enable one to be perfect, Tang equates it with Truth, Goodness and Beauty, and says that 'My Heart/mind is my God and my Spirit' (Fang & Li, 1995, vol. 3: 152). Starting from the original heart/mind, Tang further states that human nature is good, and that humans are able to realise what is good in the heart/mind and to establish their moral self. His theory aims at improving the real world and bringing reality to perfection, which is what Tang believes to be the Chinese spirit of religion. Many people consider Confucian culture a secular culture without belief in God and without religious emotions. Tang objects to this as superficial. For him, Confucian moral and social codes are not merely regulations for external behaviour. Rather they are intended for the inner spirit that comes from Heaven and is embodied in morality and politics. The human heart is the heart of Heaven, and thus 'The spiritual core of Chinese culture is fully manifested in the heart of humaneness, transcendentally covering both nature and human life.' Therefore 'developing fully what is taught in humaneness (*ren*)' is all that Chinese culture needs (*ibid.*: 286, 313).

Tang believes that the introduction of western methodology and institutions has eroded the fundamental principles of Confucianism. To revive and regenerate Chinese culture, therefore, we must re-establish its humanistic spirit and reconstruct its moral system. The first step to re-establishing and reconstructing Chinese culture is to know what real problems obstruct it from further developing, and to learn how to over-come these problems by incorporating the useful elements of Western culture. For example, although Confucianism emphasises the equal im-portance of sageliness within and kingliness without (*neisheng waiwang*), Chinese culture did not extensively develop the property of how to extend the inner spirit to the external activities. In this respect, western science, technology and democracy are of use to balance these two dimensions. Accepting and transforming these western elements, while responding to their challenges as well as transcending their limits will enable Chinese culture to be rebuilt in a new system, like the ancient Chinese who created a new system of Buddhism in accepting and trans-forming Indian Buddhism. Therefore, to reform Chinese culture does not necessarily require the abandonment of its traditions. Returning to the tradition (*fan ben*) and developing the new (*kai xin*) are related and mutually promoted. Tang believes that the scholarship of the last three hundred years has nearly destroyed the foundation of Chinese culture.

Therefore, the chance for a revival of Chinese culture lies in the return to learning before the Qing Dynasty, namely, to Neo-Confucianism of the Song–Ming era. As in the case of European culture which created a new era by returning to the ancient Greek culture for a new spirit at the beginning of the modern age, the return of Chinese learning to Neo-Confucianism will signal the dawn of a new epoch. 'The return to the root of the Chinese spirit of humanism will be enough to be the foundation of its innovation, and will enable it to make a contribution to the Western world' (*ibid.*: 308).

Instead of concentrating on the Song–Ming learning, Xu Fuguan extends his study to the whole history of Chinese culture and gives special attention to the thoughts generated in the pre-Qin period and the Han era. He believes that central to Chinese philosophies are the theories of human nature, which are also the principle and motivating power of the spirit of the Chinese nation. Among various doctrines, Confucianism has been the mainstream in intellectual endeavour. Confucianism starts with self-cultivation and extends this to the regulation of others; the former is the way to sagehood within and the latter the way to kingliness without: 'They are the two sides of one thing' (Huang, 1993, vol. 8: 112). Xu attacks radical liberals in the twentieth century for their negative attitudes toward Confucianism and for their call for wholesale westernisation, which in his opinion has not done any good to the Chinese but rather resulted in the worst system in the history of China. When coming to compare Confucianism and Christianity, Xu first points out that there are discrepancies between these two cultures. For example, Confucianism holds on to the goodness of human nature, while Christianity insists on original sin. There is no recognition of an omnipresent, omniscient God in Confucianism, while God lies at the centre of the Christian faith. Chinese culture is fundamentally inclusive and harmonious, while Christianity tends to be exclusive and competitive. However, he also agrees that these two cultures share some common ground. For example, Chinese culture has had a religious and moral spirit, which can be considered the same as the spirit of Christianity; Confucian understanding of humaneness (*ren*) also corresponds to Christian 'love' as far as their attitudes towards the world are concerned (*ibid.*: 610–11).

Following the route of Liang Shuming and Xiong Shili, Mou Zongsan traces his sources to the Idealistic Learning of Lu–Wang and develops it into a modern view of life. Mou maintains that the essential meaning of

Neo-Confucianism is that of awakening moral consciousness. Instead of following the traditional dual division between Cheng–Zhu and Lu–Wang, Mou believes that there exists a third branch of learning led by Hu Hong (Hu Wufeng, 1106–61) and Liu Zongzhou (Liu Jishan, 1578–1645), which constitutes the mainstream of learning directly transmitted from the pioneers of Neo-Confucianism, Zhou Dunyi, Zhang Zai and Cheng Hao. The third stream of Hu–Liu and the second of Lu–Wang are further combined to form the mainstream of Song–Ming Learning, representing a return to the teaching of Confucius and Mengzi, and to the tradition of the *Doctrine of the Mean* and the *Commentaries of the Book of Changes*. In this sense, the traditional orthodoxy of the Cheng–Zhu School is only a collateral branch, whose teaching is based on the *Great Learning* and lets intellectual studies overwhelm the study of sagehood (Fang & Li, 1995, vol. 3: 512–14). The truth of Confucianism is the learning of humanism, something superior to a mere intellectualism. Establishing human dignity and humans as an absolute subject, Confucianism leads us to explore the inner ultimate and extend the innate goodness so that everybody is able to become a sage. Learning to be a person of humaneness is the learning of sagehood within, and learning to be a person of knowledge is the way to kingliness without. The first stage of Confucianism (from Confucius to Dong Zhongshu) and the second (Neo-Confucianism of Song–Ming Dynasties) have fully developed the inner side of learning, while leaving how to extend the inner virtues to the outside world unelaborated. This is why there is a need for the third stage of Confucianism, whose mission is to unfold the Confucian dimension of politics and science (*ibid.*: 520–2).

Differing from many modern Neo-Confucian masters, Fang Dongmei went through a transition from Confucian Learning to the study of western philosophy and then back to Confucianism. This enabled him to look at Confucianism from the point of view of comparative philosophy. His training in western philosophy and his research on Bergson's philosophy of life led him to search for the value and meaning of life, and drew him to the Confucian Learning of human nature and the human heart/mind. However, Fang did not limit his thinking to traditional Confucianism. He examined Confucianism in its relation to the four traditions in the world: the Greek, the Modern European, the Indian and the Chinese, the four which together have formed the wisdom of humankind. There are also four traditions within Chinese culture, Original

Confucianism, Daoism, Mahayana Buddhism and Neo-Confucianism, and these four together constitute the wisdom of Chinese life. Being one of the four traditions, the way of Neo-Confucianism manifests a huge capability of synthesis and creation, which enables it not only to synthesise the other three Chinese traditions, but also to absorb the wisdom of Greece, Europe and India to create a harmonious world of 'transformation and retransformation' (Fang & Li, 1995, vol. 1: 34).

The unfolding of the Confucian project in the modern world is being carried on by the students and disciples of the above-mentioned masters. Cheng Chung-ying, Tu Wei-ming, Liu Shuxian, Yu Yingshi are prominent members of this group, and the study, propagation and transformation of Confucianism made by them and many others in the West, Mainland China, Taiwan, Hong Kong and other countries constitute the third stage of Modern New Confucianism. This, however, is not a unified group. Of them, some are more liberal minded, being critical of the Confucian tradition, while others are more traditionally oriented, taking it as their mission to revive or regenerate Confucian Learning. Some are strict historians or philosophers, treating Confucianism as a purely historical phenomenon or a system of philosophy, while others reject the western methodology and insist that Confucianism is a holistic tradition and culture, thereby emphasising Confucian ethics, politics, religion and spirituality, and opening them to the modern world and to the future. Instead of confining their research to the classical learning, these scholars consciously examine and re-examine the positive and negative effects Confucianism has had or will have on the multicultural 'global village', and conscientiously adapt traditional Confucian values to modern life, striving to establish the healthy interaction between the Chinese tradition and many other great traditions in the world.

Having been educated and having taught in the West, the third generation of modern Confucian scholars continue the Confucian enterprise to bridge the Confucian tradition and the world, and Confucian Learning and western culture, and strive to reconstruct Confucianism in modern and even post-modern contexts. Like their predecessors, they carefully examine the reason and cause of the Confucian failure in the face of western challenges. They attempt to draw lessons from the unsuccessful efforts in revitalising and reformulating Confucian Learning and institutions in the last one hundred or so years. Some of them challenge the views of established western scholars such as Max Weber and Joseph Levenson who have fundamentally rejected the adaptability of Confucianism to modernisation. They make efforts to explore the cultural background of the process of modernisation in East Asia, in which they identify Confucianism as a shared living culture, as a motivating force for modernisation and as the strength that has made the post-Confucian states and areas, such as Japan, Korea, Taiwan, Hong Kong and Singapore, competitive in the international arena. Some of them go even further to argue that not only Confucian values but also its institutions are positive and conducive to a balanced life in a modern society: 'From this perspective, seemingly outmoded Confucian institutional imperatives and preferences have re-emerged as more sophisticated ways of dealing with an increasingly complex pluralistic world than the single-minded attention to instrumental rationality and its attendant features such as efficiency' (Tu, 1991: 34).

How far the third generation can go in promoting modern Confucianism is an open question, and the effects of its efforts in 'modernising' Confucian values are yet to be seen. Although it is still too early to define what characteristics this generation will bear, there is no doubt that they have become a recognisable force both in academic areas and in social and political markets, and their contribution to the wide spread of Confucian Learning in the West has already surpassed their predecessors. Among many of the attempted tasks, one is perhaps to be of the greatest importance for the future of Confucianism: bringing Modern New Confucian thinking back home, i.e., from Hong Kong, Taiwan, Europe and North America to its original place, Mainland China, where having been silenced for almost half a century, Confucianism is in a process of recovery and revival.

The themes of modern Confucian studies

Before extending our coverage of Confucianism in the modern world, we need first to delineate the difference between Modern New Confucianism and modern Confucian studies, and consequently between Confucian scholars and the scholars in Confucian studies. Modern New Confucianism is a continuity of the Confucian tradition, an attempt to adapt the traditional Confucian system to a modern environment, and in addition, is a process of transformation from within the Confucian tradition while being fully aware of other world traditions, primarily Buddhism, Christianity, modern European rationalism and humanism. The modern transformation is undertaken by those who, to a greater or lesser extent, have laid their faith in Confucianism. Those who are engaged in reviving Confucian values, regenerating Confucian Learning and transforming the Confucian tradition are called therefore New Confucians; and the leaders of this intellectual trend are named New Confucian masters (*xin rujia*). Each of the early masters is distinguishable not only by his literary style and philosophical depth but also by his students and even by his geological location, which is more or less reminiscent of the Confucian school system in the past. The aforementioned 'three generations' are in a kind of master–disciple transmission. A great number of them share some common concerns about, and meanwhile try to work out a solution for, the clashes between Confucianism and western culture, in the firm belief that this is the main reason that has caused traditional values to collapse and the self-dignity of the Chinese to be eroded. Most of these scholars have a sense of mission to re-establish Confucianism as a moral spirituality and a system of comprehensive metaphysics to explore the ultimate meaning of life. In searching for such a system, they explore and examine many dimensions of the traditional view of the world and of life. They make a great effort in understanding and solving the modern problems such as the tension between individuals and society, between the internal and the external, between the particular and the universal, and between human needs and the environment. Their intellectual achievements have fundamentally changed Confucian philosophy on the one hand and make Confucian values relevant to modern life on the other hand.

'Modern Confucian Studies' is a discipline including not only the evolution and transformation of Confucianism from within, but also the study of Confucianism from without, examining the Confucian tradition either in a sympathetic and engaged way or by a critical and phenomenological approach. This is a wide, loosely connected area, covering history, philosophy, religion, ethics, politics, sociology, natural sciences, linguistics, and textual criticism. The scholars in Confucian studies include not only a great number of Chinese liberal or even Marxist intellectuals, such as Hu Shi, Lin Yutang, Kuang Yaming and Fang Keli, but also many western scholars and Chinese, Japanese, Korean scholars who work in a variety of locations around the world introducing and teaching on Confucianism. Of them, the best known to western readers are scholars and translators such as James Legge, Max Weber, Arthur Waley, Wing-tsit Chan, Wm. T. de Bary, D. C. Lau, Julia Ching, Rodney Taylor and Roger Ames. Their translations of Confucian texts and research on

Confucianism constitute the other side of the picture of Confucian studies in the modern world. Though the scholars in Confucian studies in general do not consciously identify themselves with Confucian values, their work converges with those of Modern New Confucians insofar as they have made Confucianism better known and more influential. They are confronted with the same questions as those that New Confucians have been attempting to answer, including how to compare Confucian culture with western culture, how to define the living and the dead within the Confucian tradition, and how to draw useful elements from the Confucian tradition. Among numerous themes Confucian studies and New Confucian Learning have engaged, debated and explored, the following three are of primary importance, namely, Confucianism and the fate of China, Confucian culture and western culture, and Confucianism and modernisation.

CONFUCIANISM AND THE FATE OF CHINA

Within the circle of Chinese intellectuals, the twentieth century started with an intensive search for the way to save Chinese culture from disintegration and to save China from humiliation. Two extreme trends evolved from the search, one 'conservative' and the other 'radical'. The former identified the fate of China with the revival of Confucianism, while the latter associated it with the elimination of Confucianism. These two extremes and the debates between them have dominated Confucian studies in and out of China throughout the twentieth century.

The first intellectual movement of anti-Confucianism took place in 1916–20 as part of the New Cultural Movement. Most of the radical liberals who came back from Europe, the United States and Japan joined forces in a wave of attacks on Confucianism as the chief cause of the Chinese failure, and in a movement aiming at cleansing China of the contamination of Confucian ritualism, moralism and mysticism. For example,

> I Pai-sha was the first of this new generation of intellectuals to attack Confucianism. In an article which appeared in *New Youth* early in 1916, he referred to K'ang Yu-wei's ideas on Confucian religion in his attack on the concept of Confucius as an uncrowned king. He criticized not only the institutional forms of Confucianism, but also the writings of Confucius himself, contending that Confucius, in identifying monarchs with Heaven, had given them unlimited authority, thus promoting an autocratic form of society. (Louie, 1980: 5–6)

A left-wing writer and later one of the founding fathers of the Communist Party in China, Chen Duxiu, published a series of articles in the forum of the May Fourth Movement, the *New Youth*, to refute Confucianism by means of republicanism, and to attack Confucianism as feudalistic and aristocratic, aiming the attack especially at those who attempted to restore Confucianism and who revered the Confucian values. In general, the intellectuals as such believed that Confucianism was a path to decay and death, and that only by destroying Confucianism or replacing it with, say, science, could China be saved. This trend was carried on in socialist China where Maoism identified Confucianism with the ideology of the exploitative class. Condemnation and denunciation of Confucius reached their peak during the Cultural Revolution (1966–76), and Confucianism appeared doomed.

To act against the cultural pessimism, early Modern New Confucians went to the other extreme, propagating that China could not be saved and strengthened unless Confucian Learning was propagated and Confucian values revived. Liang Shuming, for example, believed that the future of China, and the future of the whole human race, to a great degree, depended on Confucianism. Zhang Junmai insisted that only Confucianism, the learning of Neo-Confucianism of the Song–Ming Dynasties, held the key to the gate leading to the prosperity of China. The Japanese invasion in the 1930s further strengthened these scholars' faith in the traditional culture, and many of them believed that Confucianism must be revived in order to re-establish Chinese culture; whether or not this could be done would prove to be an issue of life or death. For example, in an article entitled 'The Future Development of Confucian Thought' (*Rujia Sixiang de Xinkaizhang*) published in 1938, He Lin argued that the weakness of China had stemmed from the weakness of modern Chinese learning, and that saving China lay not in allowing it to become a cultural colony but in promoting and carrying forward Confucian culture. The revival of the Chinese nation was thus essentially identified with the revival of Confucianism. He Lin predicted that in the new development of Confucianism the modern and the traditional, the new and the old, and the Chinese and the western, would become a holistic unity, and therefore would be the future of China and the Chinese nation (Pang, vol. 1, 1997: 396).

Such an exchange of thesis and antithesis with regard to the relation between Confucianism and the fate of China in particular, and with regard to Confucianism and the fate of East Asia in general, is a defining characteristic of the intellectual debates in Confucian studies. Generally speaking, between the two voices in the debate, the louder one comes from the anti-Confucian camp, which commands the central position on the Mainland until the 1980s. The earlier anti-Confucian intellectuals were mostly embedded in the Confucian tradition and thus their criticisms were those of a reassessment and re-evaluation, while the later generations in the anti-Confucian camp have, to a great degree, lost touch with this tradition. They issued criticisms of all kinds upon Confucianism. But for them Confucianism was merely a historically remote and personally irrelevant phenomenon, as evidenced in the criticisms made during the Cultural Revolution and more recently in an anti-tradition television documentary series entitled *He Shang*, 'The Elegy of the Yellow River' (1989).

For the western writers on Confucianism, the situation is quite different. With his attempt to explain China's failure, Max Weber turned his attention to a comparison between Confucian ethic and Protestant ethic. He found deficiencies in the former, which he subsequently deemed the essential elements for the development of capitalism. From the general theme that capitalism in non-western nations would be 'impeded only by the presence of rigid traditions' and therefore 'the impediments to the development of capitalism must be sought primarily in the domain of religion' (Weber, 1963: 269), Weber reasoned that

> Confucianism, the dominant system of ultimate values, was consistently traditionalistic, enjoining adaptation to the given world and not the transformation of it . . . which, together with the literati's lack of interest in economic production enterprises, inhibited socio-economic innovation in the direction of Western capitalism.
>
> (Quoted in Yang, 1961: xxxvi)

For a substantial period of time, the Weberian view of Confucianism dominates the western thinking of Confucianism and China, and its supreme position has not been seriously revised or challenged until very recently. The revision of Weberianism has produced two arguments, explaining Confucianism and the fate of China from two different perspectives. The first perspective indicates that Confucianism has permanently withdrawn from the historical stage. Levenson, for example, inferred from the fact that for so many centuries Confucianism and monarchy were tied in companionship, that as the Monarchy was gone and Confucianism had lost its institutional context, the intellectual continuity of the Confucian tradition was inevitably imperilled (Levenson, 1965: 3). The second perspective envisages Confucianism to be not only alive but also so powerful that it poses a threat to the western way of life. Huntington, for example, calls for 'a more profound understanding of the basic religious and philosophical assumptions underlying other civilizations and the ways in which people in these civilizations see their interests' (Huntington, 1993: 49); he asserts that the clashes between the West and the East lie in the conflict between their cultures, Christianity on the one side and Confucianism and Islam on the other.

On the other hand, challenging the Weberian view also enables some scholars to conclude that Confucianism is a tradition containing elements which lead to modernisation. Neither totally denying nor simply confirming the relation between Confucianism and the fate of China, these scholars come to the conclusion that the real influence of Confucianism does indeed have its limits for further change, but it is still visible in motivating China and East Asia to modernity. Therefore, on the one hand, they argue that the co-existence of industrial capitalism and Confucian values in East Asia has contradicted Weber's conclusion, and 'the thesis that the Confucian ethic is incompatible with the spirit of capitalism is untenable' (Tu, 1996b: 10). They call for going 'beyond questions of wealth and power to comprehend the rise of industrial East Asia not only as an economic and political reality but also as a form of life laden with ethics-religious implications' (Tu, 1991: 41), which is believed to have underlain 'the second model of modernity'. On the other hand, scholars in Confucian Studies have also identified, or are identifying various difficulties, for example, the tension between the Confucian ideal and social reality, and they believe that these difficulties have to be overcome before Confucianism can make a real contribution to the future prospects of China and East Asia (de Bary, 1991b).

CONFUCIANISM AND WESTERN CULTURE

Another key issue in Confucian Studies is how to evaluate the relationship between Confucianism and western culture. Generally speaking, those who are sympathetic to Confucianism likewise object to westernisation, attempting to find a path to a new culture by transforming the Confucian tradition, while those who criticise Confucianism tend to identify the new culture with western culture.

It is ironically illuminating that the early Chinese intellectuals called for learning from the West in order to fight against the West. In the face of a powerful western advance, the Confucians of the nineteenth century accepted the reality that western technologies and administration must be adopted in order to strengthen military power and industrialise the nation. Subsequent generations of Chinese elite soon realised that modernisation was not only in the form of industry and military technology but also had an economic, political, social and cultural basis. With a devotion to science and democracy, radicals proselytised that China had to break with the past and replace Confucian values with European culture. Accepting the European dichotomy of tradition and modernity, many intellectuals identified modernisation with westernisation, in the belief that Confucianism was inferior to western culture and could not play a positive role in the process of modernisation. Wu Zhihui (1865–1953), for example, took national learning (*guo xue*, mainly the study of the Confucian classics) as the source of backwardness:

> When national learning was at a height, all politics were rotten. This is because Confucius, Mencius . . . were products of the chaotic world of the Spring and Autumn and the Warring States. They must be thrown into the latrine for thirty years . . . What is national heritage and what bearing has it on our present world? It is nothing more than a relic of the world, worthy of preservation and nothing more.
>
> (Kwok, 1965: 49)

Hu Shi, a radical cultural reformer and liberal writer who believed that the energy of Confucianism had long been used up and a new life of Chinese culture must be given by the introduction of western culture, called for 'wholesale westernisation' as a way to be out of the problems of China (Hu, 1974: 35–52).

In order to preserve the Confucian tradition while learning from the West, traditional-intended intellectuals were imbued with a pattern of thinking which had been phrased variously as 'Chinese learning for the essential principles, while western learning for the practical applications' (China), or as 'Eastern ethics and Western science' (Japan); or as 'Eastern morality and Western technology' (Korea) (Fairbank *et al.*, 1989: 629). This 'formula' was further applied directly to the relation between Confucianism and western culture in the hands of modern New Confucians and becomes the clear-cut slogan: 'The spirit of Confucianism as substance and the Western culture as applications' (*rujia jingshen wei ti, xiyang wenhua wei yong*). Therefore, the central issue for them is how to 'confucianise Western culture (*ruhua xiyang wenhua*)' (Fang & Li, 1995, vol. 1: 16). In such a 'deliberate response to the modern West', modern New Confucianism reaffirms the value of the Confucian tradition. In his book the *Eastern and Western Culture and their Philosophies* (*Dongxifang Wenhua jiqi Zhexue*, 1921) Liang Shuming made it clear that modernisation must not be identified with westernisation; and that it was essentially a process of recreating and reapplying Confucian values (Pang, 1997, vol. 1: 390). In defiance of the Japanese onslaught, He Lin insisted that the future of Chinese culture should not be based on learning from the West. For him, Chinese culture is fundamentally correct; it needs only to be adjusted to modern society. It is his belief that a new culture will be born when the Confucian moral tradition of loyalty, filial piety, humane love, faithfulness, righteousness and harmony is restored, and when self-cultivation, regulation of the family, the rule of the state and the peace of the world are realised (Fang & Li, 1995, vol. 2: 277–90).

In general, Modern New Confucians, though holding fast to Confucianism and its superiority over other cultures, do not blindly reject western culture. They carefully compare the western and the Chinese, identifying the values of western culture and the problems in Confucian culture. For Tang Junyi, the fundamental difference between Chinese and western culture is that Chinese culture is oriented in humanism, while western culture in materialism. This brings about further differences: Chinese culture puts more emphasis on morality and arts, human responsibilities and unity, while western culture stresses science and religion, individuals' freedom and differentiation. Tang believes that it is important for Chinese culture to learn how to develop in multidirections from western culture, while at the same time for western culture to learn from Chinese culture about how to unify and harmonise. To the question why Chinese culture, though of great values, collapsed in the face of western challenges in the last hundred years, Tang answers that western scientific methodology and the democratic political system have forced Chinese culture to abandon its tradition: modern science is rooted in the spirit of doubt and is manifested in rational analysis, which have eroded the spirit of Chinese culture; while democracy has produced the by-products of extreme individualism and self-centrism, which have destroyed its ethics (Pang, 1997, vol. 1: 442–7). For Mou Zongsan, the mainstream of

Chinese scholarship in modern times is to learn from the West. However, the majority of Chinese intellectuals consider only the side of science in western culture, without paying attention to its literature, arts and religion. It is in the latter rather than in the former that lies the key view of western culture. Due to this one-sided introduction, what the Chinese have learned from the West seems to have focused on material well-being, while lacking consideration about western life and ideals. To overcome this imbalance, Mou calls for awakening the cultural consciousness and the spirit of value embedded in Chinese culture, that is, to return to the Confucian idealism. In developing the idealistic learning of the Song–Ming Dynasties, Mou concentrates on how to innovate Confucian moral idealism to meet the demands of modern science, economics and politics. Mou argues that Confucianism can promote modernisation, not by adapting itself to the West but by realising what is already within Chinese culture while incorporating some values of western culture into the way of life in China. In other words, modernisation is regarded as a process of extending 'sageliness within' to 'kingliness without'. While Confucianism provides us with the former, we also need to develop the latter with the help of western culture. However, since sagehood is the substance and kingliness, the application, the ultimate concern for life and value cannot be found in western culture, but only in Confucian moral and spiritual idealism (Fang & Li, 1995, vol. 3: 522–58).

This self-affirmation finds unusual support from a corner of western intelligentsia. Following post-modernism, especially deconstruction philosophy, western post-modernists indulge themselves in a self-negation of western culture, especially western modernity. Following this trend, some western Asia watchers moved to the camp of New Confucians claiming that as the key to the miraculous success of East Asia, Confucianism has proved to be superior to western culture in the pursuit of modernisation (Kahn, 1979: 124).

A definitive comparison between Confucianism and western culture needs much more than these kinds of simple assertions. There is no doubt that Confucianism has had its serious problems and needs to be transformed in the light of western culture. Clear-minded scholars would take a more rational and realistic approach to it. They tend to highlight the modern value of Confucianism in its interaction with western culture, and adopt the key elements of western culture into the Confucian doctrines to make them relevant to the modern world.

CONFUCIANISM AND MODERNISATION

Derived from the debate of Confucian culture and western culture, Confucians and radicals engaged in the debate concerning whether Confucian Learning can or cannot support the process of modernisation, and about whether modernisation is or is not a process of introducing science to industry and democracy to politics. The mainstream of intellectual discourses since the beginning of the twentieth century has been leaning upon science and democracy, two main factors of western modernity, which alone are believed to be able to 'deliver' East Asia to modernisation. Mr Science (*sai xiansheng*) and Mr Democracy (*de xiansheng*) became the symbol of the New Culture and the sole power to promote industrialisation and modernisation, not only for the Japanese and Koreans but also for the Chinese.

To counter the liberals' claim that Confucianism is against modernisation, Modern New Confucians argue with great emotion that Confucianism can be a part of modernity and can support and guide the process of modernisation. For those who are deeply engaged in the revival of Confucianism in modern times, the differentiation between modernisation and westernisation and the justification of the coalition of Confucianism and modernisation were central to their argument against westernisation. This argument was well illustrated in the great debate between (western) science and the (Chinese) philosophy of life in the 1920s. Based on Liang Qichao's theory that western scientism had proved to be more destructive than constructive, and on Liang Shuming's view that only Chinese culture could save humanity from being destroyed, Zhang Junmai gave a speech at Qinghua University, Beijing on 14 April 1923, asserting that human culture was in transition from the emphasis on material to the emphasis on the mind, from external exploration to self-examination, and thus from the western to the eastern. He argued that the philosophy of life was characteristic of intuition, subjectivism, syncretism and freewill, while science bore the converse of these characteristics. This is why science is powerless in the face of the problems of how to live. Science has its values; yet it would be damaging if it was adopted blindly. Zhang believed that if China adopted European scientism, China would have to follow the western countries to accumulate its power on the base of industry and commercialism, and therefore would pursue the temporary material pleasure while ignoring the ideal and sublime meaning of life. Zhang argued that this is not the way to modernisation, but a way to destruction and oblivion (Huang, 1993, vol. 3: 110–68).

In opposition to the New Confucians who hold that there is a unity between Confucianism and modernity, modern critics of Confucianism went to the other extreme arguing that Confucianism contradicted modernisation. For them, 'Confucianism underlay the political system which kept China in a conservative straitjacket, promoting a way of life which made the rigours of hierarchical order the aim and resting-point of a culture which sprung from the certainties of agricultural obsession' (Hugh Baker, in the *Times Literature Supplement*, 30 Jan. 1998). They conclude that Confucianism has no positive role to play in modern life because it is related, as it always was, to political despotism, social inequality and economic conservatism. Based on the observation of Korean Confucianism and on a comparative study of the roles played by Confucianism respectively in Chinese, Korean and Japanese history, Hwang Byung Tai (1935–), a Korean scholar and politician, argues that there are six fundamental contradictions between traditional Confucianism and modernity. Firstly, modernisation requires a consciousness about the separateness of humanity from social environment and the physical world, while Confucianism offers 'a single continuum covering the entire spectrum of society and the whole physical universe' which interfuses individual and society, and society and nature. Secondly, modernisation requires a utilitarian view of society and nature, while Confucianism tends to moralise history and nature, and to naturalise morality and social life. Thirdly, modernisation requires an evolutionary view of culture and nation, while Confucianism 'had two cardinal orientations: cultural eternalism and cultural universalism'. Fourthly, modernisation presupposes egalitarian democratisation, while Confucianism 'was designed for use by the ruling class of superior men in a divided nationhood'. Fifthly, modernisation requires a social system that differentiates social sectors so that each of them is given a unique role to play in life, while Confucianism is based on the morally organic unity of the world. Lastly, modernisation excludes the dominance of a single bloc either in the sense of political power or in the sense of knowledge and skills, while Confucianism 'had resisted any internal impulse toward democratization'. The conclusion from these arguments is that traditional Confucianism does not fit into the modern world, and obstructs the process of modernisation in China and Korea. 'Confucianism has a bias against modernisation . . . It opposes modernising society, state, economy and culture and cannot contribute to the process of modernisation. Only after the modernisation has been realised should we start searching for the potential elements within Confucianism that support modernity' (Hwang, 1979: 644–52).

Many scholars in Confucian Studies argue against this kind of conclusion by singling out the Confucian theories or practices that are in agreement with science and democracy. For them, there is a scientific spirit in the Confucian tradition. The earlier examples are found in the commentaries in *the Book of Changes*, where it is proposed that knowledge comes from 'observing the pattern of the heavens and examining the order of the earth' (Chan, 1963a: 265). Xunzi calls for 'understanding nature' and 'understanding the division between Nature and mankind' (Knoblock, 1994: 15–17). Neo-Confucianism explores the world in metaphysical as well as physical terms, and its view of the world is even said to be 'one extremely congruent with that of the natural sciences' (Needham, 1956: 493). The object of Neo-Confucian investigation is 'principle' (*li*) or 'Way' (*dao*), a conception with implications similar to those of Natural Law in the West, governing the whole universe, i.e. Heaven, Earth and humans. As Confucian philosophy or epistemology 'affirmed the reality of the external world as a manifestation and confirmation of the Way', it may well be said to be scientific, or at least pre-modern scientific (de Bary & Bloom, 1979: 2).

Democracy is the other wing of modernity. Consequently the matter of relating Confucianism and democracy becomes a crucial argument to justify or disqualify the ally of Confucianism and modernisation. The overall opinion within the intellectual mainstream in China since the May Fourth Movement has been that Confucianism runs contrary to democracy and that 'Confucian democracy' is itself a contradiction in terms. In order to discredit these arguments, modern new Confucians argue that Confucianism contains the seeds of democracy and that therefore there is no contradiction at all between them. They point out that there are democratic elements, if not a system itself, in traditional Confucian doctrines. What is proclaimed in the Confucian classics can be roughly termed as a theo-democratic political theory: 'Heaven watches and listens as the people do' (*Shang Shu*, 11: 10a), and the will of Heaven has been understood as the will of the people. The Confucian moral/ spiritual optimism that 'everybody can become a sage' indicates that all people have equal potential (Pang, 1997, vol. 1: 402). Others have explored the positive elements in Confucian tradition which are believed to be in the same spirit of western democracy further, arguing that if these elements had not been distorted and suppressed by an autocratic system, they would have developed into democracy in China. Therefore, what we need now is not to introduce a wholesale western democracy, but to develop and reinterpret Confucian democratic elements and to put them into political practice in the light of a western political system. Revival of the Confucian tradition is also believed to be a solution to the problem of western politics: 'Only by further accepting Confucian thought can democratic politics root firmly and manifest its highest value' (Huang, 1993, vol. 8: 117).

There may be democratic elements in the Confucian system, but the system lacks a political model because it regards the political and social system as one and the same thing. In order to enable Confucianism to be of value in modern politics, it is crucial for it to enhance its democratic elements and to correct its deficiencies in establishing a rational and humanistic political structure. Modern new Confucians confirm on the one hand that 'there is no contradiction between Confucian thought and the spirit of democracy and science', and on the other they intend to expand the traditional elements and transform them into a modern system, serving democratic institution and freedom of academic discourses. In this way they attempt to overcome the aristocratic tendency and the authoritarian character rooted in the tradition and to carry Confucianism into the structure of the modern state by developing its democratic elements and scientific spirit (Cai, 1998: 199–201).

Confucianism and its modern relevance

As an old tradition, many aspects of the Confucian doctrine are related to specific historical periods, and many requirements of the Confucian moral codes are justifiable only under certain conditions. For example, Confucian political designs are attached to the imperial constitution and institution in China (to the monarchy in Korea, and, to a lesser extent, to the *bakufu*, military government in Japan), the Confucian family ethic is based on patriarchy requiring the young to obey the elder, and the female to obey the male, and Confucian social programmes are rooted in, and in return serve, a small-scale peasant economy. In place of a feudal infrastructure and institution, modern politics, family relations, mass-production industry and commercial business render the Confucian tradition for the most part outdated, superfluous or at least unimportant. The changes in the twentieth century have not only diminished the political, economic and social foundation of the Confucian system, but also made the system itself irrelevant in practice and to daily life. What has ceased to function in the Confucian tradition leads many people to accepting Levenson's understanding of Confucianism only as 'a tradition of museum' or 'a historical monument', an ossified culture like Egyptian and Mayan civilisations, 'eliciting (instead of inculcating) a piety towards the past', interesting only to those who are concerned with human history and archaeology (Levenson, 1965: 100). Will Confucianism go into the twenty-first century merely as a remnant of history? Or will it have much to offer and to contribute to a meaningful life in a rapidly changing society? What elements or parts of the Confucian tradition would enable it not to be a dead culture, nor to be a tradition of the past, but continually to be a living organism comprehensively functioning in a multicultural society, emotionally and rationally motivating the people, and naturally making contributions to world peace and prosperity?

THE REVIVAL OF CONFUCIAN VALUES

With the Confucian retreat from political, social and economic stages in East Asia since the end of the nineteenth century, the Confucian influence has been limited to a small area of learning, seemingly viable only among the traditionally minded people and merely as a social and psychological background of their activities. The political and religious role of Confucianism in Mainland China has long been deemed the 'doctrinal furnishing' of feudalism and aristocracy, and its values and ideals have been severely undermined both by radical revolutionaries and by radical liberals. For most academics and lay people, Confucianism represented the shadow of the past, the symbol and the reason for a backward, disadvantaged and powerless China. As a result, three irreversible changes have taken place in relation to Confucianism: Confucian organisations and institutions have disappeared, Confucian scholars have lost their social identity, and Confucian rituals no longer have spiritual values. Confucianism seems to have been reduced to being merely a theory or a doctrine without practical meaning, an old paradigm lacking influence on and relevance to modern life, and Mainland China, the homeland of Confucianism, appears to have become the least Confucian in East Asia.

This is, of course, only one side of the story. The umbilical cord between the Confucian tradition and modern China cannot easily be severed. Elements of Confucian heritage have been transmitted to the present, either hidden in Nationalist and Communist doctrines, principles, ethics, public opinions and the system of a bureaucratic elite, etc., or implicitly underlying the whole structure of Chinese community (family, community, society and the state), in whatever forms it may take, either capitalist or socialist, Nationalist or Communist. The link between the Three Principles of the People (Nationalism, Democracy and the Livelihood of the People) initiated by Sun Zhongshan (1866–1925) and the Confucian vision of the Grand Unity Society (*datong shehui*) is so strong that very few people would deny that there exists a succession from the latter to the former. And Communism inherited a great deal from the Confucian moral code, so much so that David Nivison argued a long time ago that Communist ethics and Confucianism were not very different in practice (Nivison, 1972: 207–30). This hidden heritage makes it possible for a revival of Confucianism after many years in which its development was impeded.

Since the beginning of the 1980s Confucianism has been on the rise again in many states and areas of East Asia, although the reasons and motives behind its popularity are quite different from one state to another. In any case, the revival of Confucianism is not simply a return to tradition, nor is it intended as a wholesale restoration of the old practice and learning. The awakening consciousness of Confucianism is related to the renewal of culture and the transformation of traditions in order to redefine cultural identity and to guide social and economic development. In the search for a new form of Confucianism, traditional Confucianism is consciously divided into two parts, 'Confucianism as the source of moral values' and 'Confucianism as the structure of a traditional society', which correspond, to some extent, to Ninian Smart's separation between 'doctrinal Confucianism' and 'religious Confucianism' (Smart, 1989: 104), or to Modern New Confucians' division between 'the Confucian tradition' or 'idealistic and cultural Confucianism' and 'the Confucian China' or 'dynastic and social Confucianism' (Li, 1994: 340–5). It is agreed among scholars in Confucian Studies that while the social structure of old Confucianism has long been demolished, its doctrinal and idealistic values remain inherent in Chinese psychology and underlie East Asian peoples' attitudes and behaviour: 'Recent anthropological, sociological, and political surveys all point to the pervasive presence of Confucian ethics in belief, attitude, and behaviour across all strata throughout China' (Tu, 1996b: 259); and that 'Confucian culture is still at work in the everyday lives of the Korean people, and it is now being renovated or reproduced' (Kim, 1996: 203).

Despite criticism and caution about the relevance of Confucianism to modernisation, Confucianism is nevertheless gradually regaining some of the space it traditionally held in people's lives and in the mind of intellectuals. As a traditional organisation, Confucianism may not yet have obtained any new identity, and the old systems and social structures may never be appreciated again. But Confucian values are no longer disliked, and some of them have become appealing, albeit with certain political motives. For example, self-cultivation (*xiu shen*) as the basis for governing the state and bringing peace to the world has been accepted as politically correct and therefore has deliberately been adopted as a means of re-establishing moral standards among students, as shown when the Graduates' Society of Beijing University published its manifesto on self-cultivation in 1994, calling for all students to start with cultivating good habits and moral virtues. The combination of Confucian values and modern qualities creates a new title for business leaders, 'Confucian entrepreneurs' (*ru shang*), praising their Confucian virtues demonstrated in industrial and commercial activities, such as humaneness (*ren*), trustfulness (*xin*), sincerity (*cheng*) and altruism (the *People's Daily*, 15 January 1998). Some people enthusiastically talk about 'Marxist Confucianism' or 'Confucian Marxism', while others see an opportunity in the economic experience of East Asia to merge Confucianism and free-market economy to formulate a new doctrine, Capitalist Confucianism or Confucian Capitalism (*rujiao ziben zhuyi*). Along with these new understandings of the nature and functions of Confucianism, efforts have also been made to rejuvenate and rehabilitate Confucian institutions, and interests in the Confucian education system, including its examinations and academies, are on the increase. For example, after the interval of more than half a century, the traditional civil service examination, which bears the hallmark of Confucianism and which was 'adopted by Western nations in the 19th and 20th centuries' (Ching & Oxtoby, 1992: 23), has partly been adopted as a modern means to recruit civil servants in Mainland China. Confucian academies (*shu yuan*) are no longer regarded as 'feudal institutes' but praised as centres of learning and education, as indicated clearly in the celebration of the 1,000th anniversary of Hunan University in 1996, during which a modern university seems to have been deemed a legitimate successor of the famous Neo-Confucian Academy, Yuelu Shuyuan. In some Chinese communities in Hong Kong, Taiwan and South East Asia, a variety of Confucian organisations have been established aiming at restoring the religious functions of Confucianism. For example, the Confucian Academy of Hong Kong (*Kongjiao Xueyuan*) and its three affiliated schools list the following four objectives in their constitution (1) to strive for the Government's recognition of Confucianism as a religion (2) to strive for designating Confucius' birthday as a national holiday (3) to incorporate Confucian doctrines into the curricula of primary, secondary and tertiary education institutions; and (4) to encourage the establishment of Confucius Temples or Confucian Youth Centres in cities and towns far and wide across the country.

These may not be enough for Confucianism to reclaim the glorious image of its past. However, nobody would deny that it has become gradually relevant again to today's social/personal and religious life. There are obvious signs indicating that aspects of the Confucian ethics are still useful and valuable, that the uniqueness of Confucian religiosity is being recognised as an important dimension of human spirituality, and that the Confucian speculation on metaphysical views is considered conducive to the healthy growth of the global village. If in the past it was true that an understanding of the Chinese and East Asian peoples and their societies was impossible without an appreciation of Confucianism, then it has now become true that a picture of China and East Asia which takes no account of Confucianism is partial and superficial. It is against this background that Bak argues that 'Confucianism still continues to exert a die-hard influence and it is concluded that without sufficient knowledge of Korean Confucianism it is difficult to predict what the future of Korean thought might be' (Bak, 1980b: 278).

Confucianism thus revived does not exist as an isolated tradition behind the process of East Asian modernisation. It is essentially a moderation of the disagreement between Confucian traditionalism and moralism on the one side, and western democracy, capitalism and individualism on the other. New Confucianism is not a wholesale revival of the tradition, but as a transformed doctrine provides useful elements for modern society. New Confucian values are really 'post-Confucian' values, as they have been transformed into modern values. The deep concern with human nature and destiny is what new Confucianism accounts for. It is in this sense that Japanese Confucian scholar Okada Takehiko even said that 'We don't really need to have Confucianism as Confucianism in the future. All we need is the respect for human life and human dignity . . . thus one's focus must remain upon the issue of respect for human life and human dignity, not the name of the tradition' (Taylor, 1988: 212).

To the question of what key element makes Confucianism relevant to modern life and modern society, some people single out Confucian clanism (*jiazu zhuyi*) as the sole reason for its modern relevance. It is indeed that Confucian clanism is culturally and psychologically very important for an East Asian society. Family values are indeed important for the stability and continuity of a modern society, and it has been observed that 'In the post-Confucian states, family continues to serve as a vital institution for social cohesiveness, moral education, spiritual growth and, not infrequently, capital formation' (Tu, 1991: 38). However, there are also arguments opposing any identification of the Confucian modern value with traditional clanism. At least three reasons have been put forward with regard to why clanism cannot be the key for the Confucian relevance to the twenty-first century. Firstly, clan structure in East Asia is going through rapid changes, and traditional family relations as defined by Confucian legal and moral codes have fallen short of the requirements of mobility, flexibility, equality, and democracy that characterise a modern society. Confucianism in conjunction with clanism contributes to a social fabric in which personal connections rather than codes of public conduct are of importance, and that is against the fundamental principles of modernity. Secondly, traditional clanism has brought about too many negative by-products. It is argued that the core of traditional family ethics hinders the implementation of market economy and economic reform, because it would generate a modern version of the old customs including the precedence of seniority, favouritism, hierarchy, patriarchal attitudes, and sheer moralism, which slow down, if not stop, the process of modernisation (Krieger & Trauzettel, 1991: 350–7). Thirdly, while family values are the driving force behind the emerging East Asian economies, 'family businesses' are facing serious challenges from international market economies and competition. What Kim has examined in Korea where business is run in kinship networks (Kim, 1996: 220) and what Yamamoto has observed in Japan where the familistic link is seen as part of the 'Spirit of Japanese Capitalism' (Yamamoto, 1992) have been refuted by recent evidence that traditional family businesses are becoming more a problem than an advantage for East Asian economies. East Asia is being forced to give up its economic pattern based on traditional clan structure.

What makes Confucianism a living tradition for the twenty-first century cannot be any fixed pattern of family, social and political life but rather its moral and spiritual values. Among these values, three are especially of significance for the Confucian future: its concern about moral responsibilities, its emphasis on the importance of transmission of values, and its humanistic understanding of life. It is believed that these three values are the most important elements for Confucian relevance to the future, because they will make a significant contribution to an ethic of responsibility, give a new momentum to the establishment of a comprehensive education system, and help people in their search for ultimate meaning in a temporary life.

AN ETHIC OF RESPONSIBILITY

Humans are not merely political and economic animals. They are also moral beings, characterised by freedom of choice and by a sense of responsibility, being responsible for their own behaviour and being concerned not only with the process of an action but also with its motives and results. In a sense, we may say that one of the key issues in all the existent traditions in the world is how to attain a kind of balance between action and responsibility. Due to cultural differences, however, some traditions are more concerned with free choice and individual rights, while others deal more with responsibility. Confucianism is a tradition that places much emphasis upon human responsibility.

Free choice is the foundation of modern society and is the presupposition of a market economy. However, freedom without responsibility would result in both the collapse of the social network and strife among individuals and between individuals and society, and would lead to the sacrifice of the future in order to satisfy the short-term needs. This has become a serious challenge to human wisdom and to human integrity. In this respect, Confucianism can make a contribution to a new moral sense, a new ecological view and a new code for the global village. Confucian ethics insists that the self be the centre of relationships, not in order to claim one's rights but to emphasise one's responsibilities, that daily behaviour be guided by the rules of propriety, not merely for restricting individuals but more for cultivating the sense of holiness and mission in their hearts, and that knowledge is important for developing a good character, not primarily for conquering what is unknown, but for co-operating with others and for contributing to the harmony of the universe. It is in this kind of ethics that Confucianism finds a new expression of its tradition, something which makes it relevant to modern and post-modern ages.

The Confucian effort in establishing an ethic of responsibility coincides with the growth of a global conscience, and has become part of the international co-operative search for a universal ethic to guide communities of the world in the twenty-first century. A series of events aiming at dealing with the moral problems of the world has already been planned and effected. For example, a Conference of World Religions was convened in Chicago in 1993, where 120 participants signed 'The Declaration toward a Global Ethic' drafted by Hans Küng, a Swiss theologian. The Commission on Global Governance led by the former Chancellor of Germany, Willy Brandt, published a report entitled 'Our Global Neighbourhood' in 1995, promoting the conception of a global civic ethic. The World Commission on Culture and Development of the United Nations calls on a global ethic to preserve our creative diversity and to enhance our sense of the global village. Against this background, UNESCO established the Universal Ethics Project in 1997 to discuss the possibility of a declaration on universal ethics, 'A Universal Declaration of Human Responsibilities', again drafted by Hans Küng. The project convened two meetings in 1997, involving politicians, philosophers, religious specialists and representatives of different cultures and traditions, of whom two were from the camp of modern Confucianism, Tu Wei-ming of Harvard, and Liu Shuxian of Hong Kong (Liu, 1998: 98–100). In a sense, whether such a proposal for a universal ethic is successfully put in place is not of primary importance. The great significance of these events is the ethical attention of the world shifting in a fundamental way from a rights-based morality to a responsibility-emphasised ethic. In this process, Confucian ethics will have an instrumental role to play.

A COMPREHENSIVE UNDERSTANDING OF EDUCATION

Education proves to be the most important way to balance stability and change, innovation and continuity, and modernisation and tradition. All religious and non-religious traditions emphasise the value of education, though their understandings of what education is and how to educate differ greatly. Confucian intellectualism is essentially a tradition based on learning and education. Confucius initiated private and 'equal education' in China and his followers made Confucian Learning a social institution. As the state orthodoxy, Confucianism underlay and regulated traditional education in 'pre-modern' East Asia. However, this fact does not necessarily exclude it from making a great contribution to 'modern' and 'post-modern' views of teaching and learning.

As far as the contents and methods of learning and teaching are concerned, education in the twentieth century has been thoroughly 'modernised' or 'westernised'; whether in Asia or in Africa, the curricula of schools are almost the same, and the subjects taught in school are mainly science, technology, business, history and humanities that originated in European culture. For the majority of the twentieth century, 'modern education' is praised as the only 'correct' way of moving forward, while all traditional ways of education are labelled backward and pseudo-scientific, if not anti-scientific. The early twentieth-century Chinese critics drew us a dim and depressing picture of Confucian education in which human nature was distorted and human knowledge was confined to memorising a few outdated classics, while early western scholars on Confucianism saw problems in both the aim and the methods of Confucian education. Max Weber, for example, pointed out that Confucian education aimed at cultivating a well-adjusted man who rationalised his conduct only to the degree requisite for adjustment, that Confucianism is 'a rational ethic which reduced tension with the world to an absolute minimum' or an ethic of 'unconditional affirmation of and adjustment to the world', and that Confucian Learning therefore 'does not constitute a systemic unity but rather a complex of useful and particular traits' (Weber, 1968: 227, 229, 235). For Levenson, the problem is of another kind. 'Confucian education, perhaps supreme in the world for anti-vocational classicism, sought to create a non-professional free man (*pace* Hegel) of high culture, free of impersonal involvement in a merely manipulative system'. This leads the majority of Confucians to a depreciation of specialisation and science, of rationalised and abstractly legalistic economic networks, and of the idea of historical progress (Levenson, 1965: 109).

Weber's view is not to the point, because Confucian education does not stay at the surface of human behaviour. It is important for a Confucian student to learn how to be well adjusted and how to adapt himself to his environment. But this is only one side. Confucian education is designed to penetrate the inner world of a learner, based on the conviction that cultivation of inner virtues is more important than adjustment of external behaviour. Levenson is wrong to conclude that Confucian education necessarily depreciates modern science and economy and is against historical progress. Early Confucian masters are concerned with the economic foundation of education, and in this sense insist upon the priority of enrichment over moral training (*Lunyu*, 13: 9; *Mengzi*, 1A: 7). The Confucian vision of the Grand Unity Society demonstrates a historical optimism for the future of humanity, though the vision is said to be a mere reflection of the ancient golden age. Confucian education is not scientific by definition. However, it does not follow that it completely lacks a scientific spirit. Confucian education is to cultivate the 'scientific spirit' in the educated by teaching them how to explore their inner world, and by encouraging them to learn what they have not yet learnt. The first enables them to be deep, and the second leads them to be open-minded. Searching for depth and being open to new things are central to the spirit by which modern sciences develop, and both are essential for a progression and continuity of human knowledge. Furthermore, the emphasis of modern education is shifting from purely accumulating knowledge to cultivating the ability to handle knowledge, and education is no longer meant for transmission only. Rather, education is intended to transmit in creation and to create in transmission. In this respect, Confucian education also has something to contribute, because it places great emphasis on the balance between the old and the new, between class learning and social performance, and between book knowledge and the capacity to act and think independently.

There is no doubt that Confucian education has its flaws and is unable to cope adequately with modern subjects. Its methods are far from able to equip people with technical tools to deal with modern problems. It would therefore be naïve or even foolish to try to replace modern education with Confucian moral training, and unprofessional to give too much credit to the traditional ways while rejecting modern methodology and training programmes. Nonetheless, it is still legitimate to raise such a question as: 'Are there any useful elements in Confucianism that may be drawn out to serve the goal of a comprehensive understanding of education?' Many scholars in Confucian studies do not simplistically rebuke Confucian education for insufficiency and partiality. Instead, they start to reassess the supposed weak and strong points of modern and premodern education. Some of them are convinced that

Past studies of traditional education have too often been based on the
twin assumptions of Asian backwardness and Western superiority, and
their goal was simply to show how traditional attitudes and methods
had come to be replaced by 'modern' ones. Now, with 'modernization'
itself being considered to benefit from the persistence of traditional
attitudes, the latter are due for some reassessment.

(de Bary & Chaffee, 1989: x)

Emerging from this reassessment, Confucian education catches the
attention of educationalists as well as scholars, who find the Confucian
programmes to establish voluntarism and social reciprocity through
collegial inquiry and discussion extremely illuminating, because they help
maintain a balance between elitism and egalitarianism, between universalism and particularism through state curriculum and private academic
schools. The purpose of Confucian education is not only to transmit and
develop knowledge, but also to deliver and apply values. Confucian Learning is seldom meant to be merely a scholarly exercise. It has a wide practical extension and employs tools to help students put into practice the
doctrinal understanding of individual, family, community and society:
the core of values fostering a spirit of self-discipline, family solidarity,
public morality and social responsibility. Confucian education is fundamentally humanistic. Its chief aim is to educate the learner to be fully
human and to become a qualified member of the community of trust,
and its primary approach is to enhance self-cultivation and develop
students' capabilities of fulfilling their responsibilities for themselves,
for their families and for society at large. These programmes are of
course designed for a premodern society. However, this does not mean
that they cannot be of use for modern education. The comprehensive
understanding of education can be used to offset the negative elements
of modern education such as pragmatism, extreme scientism and commercialism. Thus, in the eyes of many scholars, 'Confucius' educational
philosophy poses a welcome alternative and in many instances a challenge
to so many ossified, dull teaching practices and dangerous educational
ideologies in the past and in our present time' (Sprenger, 1991: 458).
In this sense, Confucian education is far from being useless and anti-
progressive. It can be adapted and transformed not only to become part
of modern life, but also to contribute to a more comprehensive education
system for a 'post-modern' society.

A HUMANISTIC MEANING OF LIFE

From among the three essentials for the state, arms, food and trust, Confucius insisted that trust be the sole foundation on which the state could survive and flourish, because 'Death has always been with us since the beginning of time, but when there is no trust, the people will have nothing to stand on' (*Lunyu*, 12: 7). Here the trust (*xin*) actually has two dimensions, one objective and the other subjective. In the first, it refers to the mutual commitment between the people and the government, without which the ruling will not be justified and the social order cannot be maintained. In the second, it refers to a personal or collective faith, which enables people to leave behind them a lasting influence and to endure in life the sufferings that cannot be normally endured.

Faith is fundamental to any nation or society, and different traditions have different kinds of faith, or put it more appropriately, different expressions of faith. Currently theo-centric faith dominates the religious world, which is upheld by many religious and cultural traditions, such as Christianity, Islam, Hinduism, part of Buddhism, Shintô, Shamanism, Daoism etc. In a different way to express its concern about human destiny, Confucianism represents an essentially anthropo-centric faith, characterised by the belief in human ability to transform the world, and in human educability and perfectibility. Due to the unique expression of Confucian faith, Confucianism is frequently described as a purely pragmatic system promoting human material welfare only, and thus as a secular doctrine in which there is no position for eternity and universality. Is Confucianism able to provide a faith by which its followers find eternal meaning in temporal life? This is the key question about the spiritual values of Confucianism, and failing to explore the spiritual dimension of Confucian doctrine frequently leads people to the perception that Confucianism lacks metaphysical depth: 'Much misunderstanding of the Confucian project by modern interpreters, especially those under the influence of May Fourth (1919) positivism and pragmatism, is due to an insensitivity to or an ignorance of this dimension of Confucian concern' (de Bary & Chaffee, 1989: 139). This is also of importance to the question of how a great number of people in East Asia lead their spiritual life in a multicultural society. It is argued that since faith is essential for a society and since Confucianism does not hold such a faith, then Confucianism is unable to make any contribution to the spiritual life and an alternative has to be found in the sources and resources outside the Confucian tradition (Weber, 1968: 243).

The flaw in the aforementioned reasoning is that it allows only one type of faith, while denying the existence of different kinds of spirituality. The Confucian faith is fundamentally humanistic, which lays the responsibility for a better world and for a secured future, not in the hands of a supremely detached God, but in the hands of ordinarily engaged humans (Yao, 1996a: 15). In this sense, Confucianism opens up a different approach to the meaning of life and the meaning of death. When Zengzi felt a resting peace at his impending death (*Lunyu*, 8: 3–7), he demonstrated the completion of his mission in the world. When Fan Zhongyan (989–1052) said that he was the first to be concerned with the problems of the world and the last to enjoy its pleasure (*xian tianxia zhi you er you, hou tianxia zhi le er le*), he was summarising the Confucian meaning of life in a paradigmatic statement. For a Confucian, the meaning of life can be realised only in learning and practice through self-cultivation and self-transformation, in committing oneself to the welfare of the family, community and society, and in effecting a lasting influence over the world by one's achievement in moral and cultural realms.

Humanistic as the Confucian concern for the ultimate meaning of life is, Confucianism does not lack a transcendental dimension, nor does it want in metaphysical depth. The belief in Heaven and the Heavenly endowed mission underlies Confucian philosophy, politics and religion. Heaven in the Confucian tradition functions in a way similar to that of the 'Transcendent' functions in a theistic tradition, or as the 'thing-in-themselves' in the Kantian system, the supreme sanction for human behaviour and social action, and the unknown source for the phenomenon world. This enables non-theistic Confucians to engage in dialogue with the people of theistic traditions and to adapt the humanistic belief to meet the spiritual demands of a multicultural society. In the interaction between Confucianism and western traditions, Tu Wei-ming, for example, attempts to reshape the Confucian perspective on the meaning of life by tracing the humanistic understanding of life to transcendental sources, and therefore pinpointing the spiritual value of Confucianism for a twenty-first-century society:

> Copernicus decentered the earth, Darwin relativized the godlike image of man, Marx exploded the ideology of social harmony, and Freud complicated our conscious life. They have redefined humanity for the modern age. Yet they have also empowered us, with communal, critical self-awareness, to renew our faith in the ancient Confucian wisdom that

the globe is the center of our universe and the only home for us and that we are the guardians of the good earth, the trustees of the Mandate of Heaven that enjoins us to make our bodies healthy, our hearts sensitive, our minds alert, our souls refined, and our spirits brilliant.

We are here because embedded in our human nature is the secret code for heaven's self-realization. Heaven is certainly omnipresent, may even be omniscient, but is most likely omnipotent. It needs our active participation to realize its own truth. We are Heaven's partners, indeed cocreators. We serve Heaven with common sense, the lack of which nowadays has brought us to the brink of self-destruction. Since we help Heaven to realize itself through our self-discovery and self-understanding in day-to-day living, the ultimate meaning of life is found in our ordinary, human existence.   (Tu, 1993b: 221–2)

This may not be typical of the faith confessed by all modern Confucian scholars; but most of them must have experienced a similar process by which they acquire their faith and perceive the spiritual meaning of their secular lives. Most modern Confucian believers agree that the search for a spiritual meaning in temporary life is crucial for Confucian spirituality, and that this search cannot be completed by isolating itself from other religious and non-religious traditions. In the dialogue and interaction between Confucianism and other doctrines, the diversity of human spirituality is manifested and the modern Confucian confidence in human destiny is re-established.

Questions for discussion

1. Levenson defines Confucianism as 'a tradition of museum', 'eliciting (instead of inculcating) a piety towards the past'. Would you agree?
2. What are the major stages of the innovation and transformation made by Modern New Confucians?
3. Is Confucianism contradictory to modernisation? What is the second model of modernity? Is Confucianism ever related to the rise of East Asian economies?
4. What kind of role will the Confucian family ethic play in people's lives of the twenty-first century?
5. What key elements in traditional Confucianism enable modern Confucianism to continue and to contribute to the understanding of human nature and destiny?

Select bibliography

I. Primary texts and commentaries

Baihutong Shuzheng 白虎通疏證, vols. 1–2, Beijing: Zhonghua Shuju, 1994.

Baopuzi Neipian Jiaozhu 抱朴子內篇校注, Beijing: Zhonghua Shuju, 1985.

Boshu Zhouyi Zhuyi 帛書周易注譯, Zhengzhou: Zhengzhou Guji Chubanshe, 1992.

Chunqiu Fanlu Yizheng 春秋繁露義正, Beijing: Zhonghua Shuju, 1992.

Chunqiu Zuozhuan Zhu 春秋左傳注, vols. 1–4, Beijing: Zhonghua Shuju, 1981.

Dongxi Fang Wenhua Jiqi Zhexue 東西方文化及其哲學, Shanghai: Shangwu Jinshu Guan, 1922.

Er Cheng Ji 二程集, Beijing: Zhonghua Shuju, 1981.

Fenshu Xufenshu 焚書續焚書, Beijing: Zhonghua Shuju, 1975.

Guodian Chumu Zhujian 郭店楚墓竹簡, Beijing: Wenwu Chubanshe, 1998.

Hanzi Qianshi 韓子淺釋, Beijing: Zhonghua Shuju, 1960.

Hanshu 漢書, in 二十四史, vol. 2, Zhonghua Shuju, Beijing, 1997.

Han Changli Wenji Jiaozhu 韓昌黎文集校注, Shanghai Guji Chubanshe, 1987.

HuaiNanzi Yizhu 淮南子譯注, Shenyang: Jilin Wenshi Chubanshe, 1990.

Jinshu 晉書, *in* 二十四史, vol. 4, Beijing: Zhonghua Shuju, 1997.

Kang Youwei Quanji 康有為全集, vols. 1–3, Shanghai Guji Chubanshe, 1992.

Kongzi Jiyu Yizhu 孔子集語譯注, Shenyang: Jilin Wenshi Chubanshe, 1996.

Liezi Jishi 列子集釋, Beijing: Zhonghua Shuju, 1979.

Liji Jijie 禮記集解, vols. 1–3, Beijing: Zhonghua Shuju, 1989.

Lu Jiuyuan Ji 陸九淵集, Beijing: Zhonghua Shuju, 1980.

Lunyu Yizhu 論語譯注, Beijing: Zhonghua Shuju, 1980.

Menzi Zhengyi 孟子正義, Beijing: Zhonghua Shuju, 1987.

Mengzi Yizhu 孟子譯注, Beijing: Zhonghua Shuju, 1960.

Mingru Xuean 明儒學案, in 黃宗羲全集, vols. 7–8, Hangzhou: Zhejiang Guji Chubanshe, 1992.

Mozi Xiangu 墨子閒詁, in *Zhuzi Jicheng* 諸子集成, vol. 4, Beijing: Zhonghua Shuju, 1959.

Rizhilu Jishi 日知錄集釋, Changsha: Yuelu Shushe, 1994.

Shangshu Zhengyi 尚書正義, in *Shisanjing Zhushu* 十三經注疏, pp. 209–58, Beijing: Zhonghua Shuju, 1980.

Shangjun Shu 商君書, in *Zhuzi Jicheng* 諸子集成, vol. 5, Beijing: Zhonghua Shuju, 1959.

Shiji 史記, in 二十四史, vol. 1, Beijing: Zhonghua Shuju, 1997.

Shi Jing 詩經, in *Shisanjing Zhushu* 十三經注疏, pp. 259–630, Beijing: Zhonghua Shuju, 1980.

Shisan Jing Zhushu 十三經注疏 (The Thirteen Classics and their Commentaries), Beijing: Zhonghua Shuju, 1980.

Shishuo Xinyu Jiaojian 世說新語箋, Zhonghua Shuju, 1984.

Shuowen Jiezi Zhu 說文解字注, (漢)許慎撰, (清)段玉裁注, Shanghai Guji Chubanshe, 1981.

Sishu Zhangju Jizhu 四書章句集注, Beijing: Zhonghua Shuju, 1983.

Songshi 宋史, in 二十四史, vols. 14–16, Beijing: Zhonghua Shuju, 1997.

Songyuan Xuean 宋元學案, in 黃宗羲全集, vols. 3–6, Hangzhou: Zhejiang Guji Chubanshe, 1992.

Wang Yangming Quanji 王陽明全集, Shanghai Guji Chubanshe, 1992.

Weishu Jicheng 緯書集成, vols. 1–2, Shanghai Guji Chubanshe, 1994.

Yan Yuan Ji 顏元集, Beijing: Zhonghua Shuju, 1987.

Yili Yizhu 儀禮譯注, Shenyang: Jilin Wenshi Chubanshe, 1996.

Xiaojing Zhushu 孝經注疏, in *Shisanjing Zhushu* 十三經注疏, pp. 2537–62, Beijing: Zhonghua Shuju, 1980.

Xinyu Jiaozhu 新語校注, Beijing: Zhonghua Shuju, 1986.

Xunzi Jijie 荀子集解, in *Zhuzi Jicheng* 諸子集成, vol. 2, Beijing: Zhonghua Shuju, 1959.

Yanshi Jiaxun 顏氏家訓, in *Zhuzi Jicheng* 諸子集成, vol. 8, Beijing: Zhonghua Shuju, 1959.

Zhangzi Quanshu 張子全書, Taipei: Shangwu Jinshuguan, 1979.

Zhouli Zhushu 周禮注疏, in *Shisanjing Zhushu* 十三經注疏, pp. 639–939, Beijing: Zhonghua Shuju, 1980.

Zhouyi Yizhu 周易譯注, Beijing: Zhonghua Shuju, 1991.

Zhouyi Dazhuan Jinzhu 周易大傳今注, Jinan: Qilu Shushe, 1979.

Zhouzi Quanshu 周子全書, Beijing: Zhonghua Shuju.

Zhuangzi Yigu 莊子譯詁, Shanghai Guji Chubanshe, 1991.

Zhuzi Jicheng 諸子集成, vols. 1–8, Beijing: Zhonghua Shuju, 1959.

Zhuzi Yulei 朱子語類, vols. 1–4, Changsha: Yuelu Shushe, 1997.

II. Confucian studies and translations

Alitto, Guys (1979) *The Last Confucian – Liang Shu-Ming and the Chinese Dilemma of Modernity*, University of California Press.

Allee, Mark A. (1994) *Law and Local Society in Late Imperial China*, Stanford University Press.

Ames, Roger T., Dissanayake, W. and Kasulis, T. (eds. 1994) *Self as Person in Asian Theory and Practice*, Albany: State University of New York Press.

An, Byung-ju (1996) 'Sônggyun'gwan: Sanctuary of Korean Confucianism', in *Korean Cultural Heritage*, vol. 2, *Thought and Religion*, Seoul: The Korean Foundation, pp. 132–6.

Angurarohita, Pratoom (1989) *Buddhist Influence on the Neo-Confucian Concept of the Sage*, Philadelphia: Department of Oriental Studies, University of Pennsylvania.

Ariel, Yoav (1989) *K'ung-Ts'ung-Tzu: The K'ung Family Masters' Anthology*, Princeton University Press.

Bae, Jong-ho (1982) 'The "Four-Seven" Controversy in Korean Confucianism', in Chun Shin-yong (ed.), *Korean Thought*, Seoul: International Cultural Foundation, Si-sa-yong-o-sa Publishers.

Bak, Jong-hong (1980a) 'Main Currents of Korean Thoughts', in *Collected Works of Bak Jong-Hong, vol. 1, A History of Korean Thought*, Seoul: Min Um Sa, pp. 61–75.

    (1980b) 'Historical Review of Korean Confucianism', in *Collected Works of Bak Jong-Hong, vol. 1, A History of Korean Thought*, Seoul: Min Um Sa, pp. 255–78.

Berling, Judith A. (1980) *The Syncretic Religion of Lin Chao-En*, New York: Columbia University Press.

Berthrong, John H. (1998) *Transformations of the Confucian Way*, Boulder and Oxford: Westview Press.

Billington, Ray (1990) *East of Existentialism – The Tao of the West*, Unwin Hyman Ltd.

Bilsky, Lester James (1975) *The State Religion of Ancient China*, Taipei: The Chinese Association for Folklore.

Birdwhistell, Anne D. (1989) *Transition to Neo-Confucianism – Shao Yung on Knowledge and Symbols of Reality*, Stanford University Press.

    (1996) *Li Yong (1627–1705) and Epistemological Dimensions of Confucian Philosophy*, Stanford University Press.

Bloom, Irene T. (tr. 1987) *Knowledge Painfully Acquired: The K'un-Chih Chi by Lo Ch'in-shun*, New York: Columbia University Press.

Boot, William Jan (1982) 'The Adoption and Adaptation of Neo-Confucianism in Japan: The Role of Fujiwara Seika and Hayashi Razan', Ph. D. dissertation, University of Leiden.

Select bibliography

Bowker, John (1973) *The Sense of God – Sociological, Anthropological and Psychological Approaches to the Origin of the Sense of God*, Oxford: Clarendon Press.

Brandauer, Frederick P. and Chun-chien Huang (eds. 1994) *Imperial Rulership and Cultural Change in Traditional China*, Seattle and London: University of Washington Press.

Bruce, J. Percy (1922) *The Philosophy of Human Nature by Chu Hsi*, London: Probsthain & Co.

(1923) *Chu Hsi and his Masters*, London: Probsthain & Co.

Cai Renhou 蔡仁厚 (1998) *Kongzi de Shengming Jingjie: Ruxue de Fansi yu Kaizhan*, 孔子的生命境界: 儒學的反思與開展 Taipei: Xuesheng Shuju.

Carus, P. (1918) 'Ceremony Celebrated under the Chinese Republic in Honor of Confucius', in *Open Court, A Quarterly Magazine*, vol. 32, no. 3, pp. 155–72.

Chan, Adrian (1996) 'Confucianism and Development in East Asia', in *Journal of Contemporary Asia*, vol. 26, no. 1, pp. 28–45.

Chan, Hok-lam and Wm. Theodore de Bary (eds. 1982) *Yuan Thought – Chinese Thought and Religion under the Mongols*, New York: Columbia University Press.

Chan, Wing-tsit (1953) *Religious Trends in Modern China*, New York: Columbia University Press.

(1955) 'The Evolution of the Confucian Concept Jen', in *Philosophy East and West*, no. 4, pp. 295–319.

(1957) 'The Neo-Confucian Solution of the Problem of Evil', in *The Bulletin of the Institute of History and Philology*, Academia Sinica, 28, pp. 773–91.

(ed. 1963a) *A Source Book of Chinese Philosophy*, Princeton University Press.

(tr. 1963b) *Instructions for Practical Living and other Neo-Confucian Writings by Wang Yangming*, New York: Columbia University Press.

(tr. 1967) *Reflections on Things at Hand by Chu Hsi and Lu Tsu-Ch'ien*, New York and London: Columbia University Press.

(tr. 1986) *Neo-Confucian Terms Explained by Ch'en Ch'un*, Columbia University Press.

(1987) *Chu Hsi – Life and Thought*, Hong Kong: The Chinese University Press.

(1989) *Chu Hsi: New Studies*. Honolulu: The University of Hawaii Press.

Chang, Carsun (1958) *The Development of Neo-Confucian Thought*, London: Vision Press Ltd.

(1962) *The Development of Neo-Confucian Thought*, vol. 2, London: Vision Press Ltd.

Chang, Hao (1971) *Liang Ch'i-Ch'ao and Intellectual Transition in China, 1890–1907*, Cambridge, MA: Harvard University Press.

Chen Lai 陳萊 (1996) *Gudai Zongjiao yu Lunli – Rujia Sixiang de Genyuan* 古代宗教与倫理 – 儒家思想的根源 (Ancient Religion and Ethics – The Origin of the Confucian Thought), Beijing: Sanlian Shudian.

Chen, Lifu (1972) *The Confucian Way – A New and Systematic Study of the 'Four Books'*, tr. by Shih Shun Liu, Taipei: The Commercial Press.

Ch'en, Kenneth K. (1964) *Buddhism in China: A Historical Survey*, Princeton University Press.

(1973) *The Chinese Transformation of Buddhism*, Princeton University Press.

Cheng, Chung-ying (1991) *New Dimensions of Confucian and Neo-Confucian Philosophy*, Albany: State University of New York Press.

Chih, Andrew (1981) *Chinese Humanism: A Religion beyond Religion*, Taipei: Fu Jen Catholic University Press.

Ching, Julia (1976) *To Acquire Wisdom: The Way of Wang Yang-Ming*, New York: Columbia University Press.

(1977) *Confucianism and Christianity*, Tokyo: Kodansha International.

(1992) 'Some Problems of Modernization in Confucianism', in Peter K. H. Lee (ed.), *Confucian–Christian Encounters in Historical and Contemporary Perspective*, The Edwin Mellen Press.

(1993) *Chinese Religions*, The Macmillan Press.

(1997) *Mysticism and Kingship in China: The Heart of Chinese Wisdom*, Cambridge University Press.

Ching, Julia and Willard G. Oxtoby (eds. 1992) *Discovering China: European Interpretations in the Enlightenment*, Rochester, New York: University of Rochester Press.

Chou, Min-chih (1987) *Hu Shi and Intellectual Choice in Modern China*, Ann Arbor: The University of Michigan Press.

Chow, K. W. (1994) *The Rise of Confucian Ritualism in Late Imperial China*, Stanford University Press.

Chow, Tse-tsung (1960) 'Anti-Confucianism in Early Republic China', in Arthur Wright (ed.), *The Confucian Persuasion*, Stanford University Press, pp. 288–312.

(1967) *The May Fourth Movement*, Stanford University Press.

Chowdbury, Anis and Iyanatul Islam (1993) *The Newly Industrializing Economies of East Asia*, London and New York: Routledge.

Chung, Edward Y. J. (1995) *The Korean Neo-Confucianism of Yi Toegye and Yi Yulgok*, New York: SUNY Press.

Clegg, Steward R., Winstin Higgins and Tony Spybey (1990) 'Post-Confucianism, Social Democracy and Economic Culture', in Steward R. Clegg and S. Gordon Redding (eds.), *Capitalism in Contrasting Cultures*, Berlin and New York: W. de Gruyter.

Covell, John Carter (1982) *Korea's Cultural Roots*, Elizabeth, NJ: Hollym International Corp.

Covell, Ralph R. (1986) *Confucius, The Buddha and Christ – A History of the Gospel in Chinese*, Maryknoll: Orbis Books.

Creel, Herrlee G. (1949) *Confucius: The Man and the Myth*, John Day.

(1953) *Chinese Thought: From Confucius to Mao Tsetung*, University of Chicago Press.

(1960) *Confucius and the Chinese Way*, New York: Harper Torchbooks.

(1970) *The Origins of Statecraft in China*, vol. 1, Chicago and London: The University of Chicago Press.

Crumo, J. I. (1973) *Chan-Kuo Ts'e*, Ann Arbor: Center for Chinese Studies, The University of Michigan.

Cua, A. S. (1983) 'Li and Moral Justification: A Study in the Li Chi', in *Philosophy East and West*, vol. 33, no. 1, pp. 1–16.

Dardess, John W. (1983) *Confucianism and Autocracy – Professional Elites in the Founding of the Ming Dynasty*, Berkeley, Los Angeles and London: University of California Press.

Davis, Walter W. (1992) 'China, the Confucian Ideal, and the European Age of Enlightenment', in Julia Ching and Willard G. Oxtoby (eds.), *Discovering China: European Interpretations in the Enlightenment*, New York: University of Rochester Press.

Dawson, Raymond (ed. 1964) *The Legacy of China*, Oxford University Press.

(1981) *Confucius*, Oxford University Press.

de Bary, Wm. Theodore (ed. 1970) *Self and Society in Ming Thought*, New York and London: Columbia University Press.

(1975) *The Unfolding of Neo-Confucianism*, New York: Columbia University Press.

(1981) *Neo-Confucian Orthodoxy and the Learning of the Mind-and-Heart*, New York: Columbia University Press.

(1983) *The Liberal Tradition in China*, Hong Kong: The Chinese University Press; New York: Columbia University Press.

(1988) *East Asian Civilisation: A Dialogue in Five Stages*, Cambridge, MA: Harvard University Press.

(1989) *The Message of the Mind in Neo-Confucianism*, Columbia University Press.

(1991a) *Learning for One's Self: Essays on the Individual in Neo-Confucian Thought*, New York: Columbia University Press.

(1991b) *The Trouble with Confucianism*, Cambridge, MA: Harvard University Press.

(1995) 'The New Confucianism in Beijing', in *Cross Currents*, winter, pp. 479–92.

de Bary, Wm. Theodore and Irene Bloom (eds. 1979) *Principle and Practicality: Essays in Neo-Confucianism and Practical Learning*, New York: Columbia University Press.

de Bary, Wm. Theodore and John W. Chaffee (eds. 1989) *Neo-Confucian Education: The Formative Stages*, Berkeley, Los Angeles and London: University of California Press.

de Bary, Wm. Theodore, Wing-tsit Chan and Burton Watson (eds. 1960) *Sources of Chinese Tradition*, vols. 1 and 2, New York: Columbia University Press.

de Bary, Wm. Theodore and Jahyun Haboush (1984) *The Rise of Neo-Confucianism in Korea*, New York: Columbia University Press.

de Groot, J. J. M. (1969) *The Religious System of China – Its Ancient Forms, Evolution, History and Present Aspect, Manners, Customs and Social Institutions connected therewith*, vols. 1–6, Reprinted by Ch'eng-wen Publishing Co., Taipei.

Deuchler, Martina (1977) *Confucian Gentlemen and Barbarian Envoys: The Opening of Korea, 1875–1885*, Seattle and London: University of Washington Press.

(1992) *The Confucian Transformation of Korea: A Study of Society and Ideology*, Cambridge, MA: Council on East Asian Studies, Harvard University.

Dimberg, Ronald G. (1974) *The Sage and Society: The Life and Thought of Ho Hsin-yin*, Honolulu: The University Press of Hawaii.

Dong, Conglin, 董叢林 (1992) *Long yu Shangdi – Jidujiao yu Zhongguo Chuantong Wenhua* (龍與上帝 – 基督教與中國傳統文化), Beijing: Sanlian Shudian.

Dreyer, June Teufel (1993) *China's Political System: Modernization and Tradition*, New York: Paragon House.

Dubs, H. H. (tr. 1928) *The Works of Hsüntze*, London: Arthur Probsthain.

(1951) 'The Development of Altruism in Confucianism', in W. R. Inge *et al.* (eds.), *Radhakrishnan, Comparative Studies in Philosophy*, London: Allen and Unwin, pp. 267–75.

Durkheim, Emile (1961) *The Elementary Forms of the Religious Life*, New York: Collier Books.

Duyvendak, J. J. L. (1928) *The Book of Lord Shang – A Classic of the Chinese School of Law*, tr. from the Chinese with introduction and notes, London: Arthur Probsthain.

Eastman, Lloyd E. (1988) *Family, Fields and Ancestors: Constancy and Change in China's Social and Economic History, 1550–1949*, New York and Oxford: Oxford University Press.

Eber, Irene (ed. 1986) *Confucianism: The Dynamics of Tradition*, Macmillan.

Ebrey, Patricia Buckley (1991a) *Confucianism and Family Rituals in Imperial China*, Princeton University Press.

(1991b) *Chu Hsi's Family Rituals – A Twelfth-Century Chinese Manual for the Performance of Cappings, Weddings, Funerals, and Ancestral Rites*, Princeton University Press.

Ebrey, Patricia Buckley and P. N. Gregory (1993) *Religion and Society in Tang and Sung China*, Honolulu: The University Press of Hawaii.

Elman, Benjamin A. (1990) *Classicism, Politics and Kinship: the Ch'ang-Chou School of New Text Confucianism in Late Imperial China*, Berkeley: University of California Press.

Elman, Benjamin A. and Alexander Woodside (eds. 1994) *Education and Society in Late Imperial China, 1600–1900*, Berkeley: University of California Press.

Elvin, Mark (1996) *Another History: Essays on China from a European Perspective*, Sydney: Wild Peony.

Eno, Robert (1990) *The Confucian Creation of Heaven: Philosophy and the Defense of Ritual Mastery*, Albany: State University of New York Press.

Fairbank, John K. (ed. 1957) *Chinese Thought and Institutions*, The University of Chicago Press.

Fairbank, John. K., O. E. Reischauer and A. M. Craig (1989) *East Asia: Tradition and Transformation*, revised edition, Boston: Houghton Mifflin Company.

Fang, Hao 方豪 (1959) *Zhongxi Jiaotong Shi* (中西交通史, *The History of Communication between China and the West*), vols. 1–5, Taipei: Shang Wu.

Fang, Keli and Li, Jinquan 方克立 李錦全 (ed. 1995) *Xiandai Xinrujia Xuean* 現代新儒家學案 (*Anthology and Critical Accounts of Modern New Confucians*), vols. 1–3, Beijing: Zhongguo Shehui Kexue Chubanshe.

Fang, Thomé H. (1973) 'A Philosophical Glimpse of Man and Nature in Chinese Culture', in *Journal of Chinese Philosophy*, vol. 1, pp. 3–26.

(1981) *Chinese Philosophy: Its Spirit and Its Development*, Taipei: Lienjing.

Fehl, Noah Edward (1971) *Li: Rites and Propriety in Literature and Life – A Perspective for a Cultural History of Ancient China*, Hong Kong: The Chinese University of Hong Kong Press.

Ferm, Vergilius Ture Anselm (ed. 1976) *An Encyclopedia of Religion*, Westport, CT: Greenwood Press.

Fingarette, Herbert (1972) *Confucius: The Secular as the Sacred*, New York: Harper Torchbooks.

Forke, Alfred (tr. 1962) *Lun-Heng: Part I Philosophical Essays of Wang Ch'ung; Lun-Heng: Part II Miscellaneous Essays of Wang Ch'ung*, second edition, New York: Paragon Book Gallery.

Franz, M. (1986) *China Through the Ages*, Boulder, CO: Westview Press.

Fung, Yu-Lan 馮友蘭 (1947) *The Spirit of Chinese Philosophy*, tr. by E. R. Hughes, London: Kegan Paul.

(1952) *A History of Chinese Philosophy*, vol. 1, tr. by Derk Bodde, Princeton University Press.

(1953) *A History of Chinese Philosophy*, vol. 2, tr. by Derk Bodde, Princeton University Press.

(1961) *A Short History of Chinese Philosophy*, New York: Macmillan.

(1991) *Selected Philosophical Writings of Fung Yu-Lan*, Beijing, Foreign Languages Press.

(1997) *Zhenyuan Liushu* 貞元六書, Shanghai: Huadong Shida Chubanshe.

Gardner, Daniel K. (1986) *Chu Hsi and the Ta-hseuh – Neo-Confucian Reflection on the Confucian Canon*, Cambridge, MA: Council on East Asian Studies, Harvard University.

(1990) *Learning to Be a Sage – Selections from the Conversations of Master Chu*, University of California Press.

Gernet, Jacques (1985) *China and the Christian Impact: A Conflict of Cultures*, tr. by Lanet Lloyd, Cambridge University Press.

(1996) *A History of Chinese Civilization*, tr. by J. R. Foster and Charles Hartman, second edition, Cambridge University Press.

Giles, Herbert A. (1915) *Confucianism and its Rivals*, London: Williams and Norgate.

(1926) *Chuang Tzu – Mystic, Moralist, and Social Reformer*, Shanghai: Kelly and Walsh.

Gong, Yanxing and Wang Zhengyu 宮衍興 & 王政玉 (1994) *Kongmiao Zhushen Kao* 孔廟諸神考, Jinan: Shandong Youyi Chubanshe.

Graham, A. C. (1958) *Two Chinese Philosophers: Ch'eng Ming-Tao and Ch'eng Yi-Ch'uan*, London: Lund Humphries.

(1991) *Disputers of the Tao: Philosophical Argument in Ancient China*, La Salle, IL: Open Court.

Granet, Marcel (1975) *The Religions of the Chinese People*, Basil Blackwell.

Gregor, A. James (1981) 'Confucianism and the Political Thought of Sun Yat-Sen', in *Philosophy East and West*, vol. 31, no. 1, pp. 55–70.

Grider, Jerome B. (1970) *Hu Shi and the Chinese Renaissance: Liberalism in the Chinese Revolution 1917–1937*, Cambridge, MA: Harvard University Press.

Gu, Jiegang (ed. 1926) *Gushi Bian* (A Critical Study of Ancient History), reprinted in Hong Kong (no publisher), 1962.

Hall, David L. and Roger T. Ames (1987) *Thinking Through Confucius*, Albany: State University of New York Press.

Hartman, Charles (1986) *Han Yü and the T'ang Search for Unity*, Princeton University Press.

Henricks, Robert (tr. 1983) *Philosophy and Argumentation in Third-Century China: The Essays of Hsi K'ang*, translation with introduction and annotation, Princeton University Press.

Hinnels, John (ed. 1991) *A Handbook of Living Religions*, London: Penguin.

Holzman, Donald (1976) *Poetry and Politics: The Life and Works of Juan Chi, A.D. 210–263*, Cambridge University Press.

Hsiao, Kung-Chuan (1975) *A Modern China and a New World – Kang Yu-Wei, Reformer and Utopian, 1858–1927*, University of Washington Press.

Hori, Ichiro (ed. 1972) *Japanese Religion: A Survey*, Tokyo: Kodansha International.

Hu, Shi 胡適 (1953) *Shuo Ru* 說儒 (*Discussion on Ru*), in *Hushi Wencun*, 胡適 文存, Taipei: Yuandong Tushu Gongsi, vol. 4.

(1974) *Chongfen Shijiehua yu Quanpan Xihua* 充分世界化与全盤西化 (On the Full Universalisation and Complete Westernisation), in *Hu Shi yu Zhongxi Wenhua* 胡適与中西文化 (Hu Shi and Chinese and Western Cultures), Hong Kong: Lienyi Shudian, pp. 35–52.

(1997) *Zhongguo Zhexueshi Dagang* 中國哲學史大綱, Shanghai Guji Chubanshe.

Huang, Kejian 黃克劍 (ed. 1993) *Dangdai Xinruxue Badajia Ji* 當代新儒學 八大家 (*Collections of the Writings of Eight Modern New Confucian Masters*), vols. 1–8, Beijing: Qunyan Chubanshe.

Huang, K'uei-yuen and J. K. Shryock, (1929) 'A Collection of Chinese Prayers – Translated with Notes', in *Journal of the American Oriental Society*, 1929, no. 49, pp. 128–55.

Hucker, Charles O. (1985) *A Dictionary of Official Titles in Imperial China*, Stanford University Press.

Hughes, E. R. (1942) *The Great Learning and The Mean-in-Action*, newly translated from the Chinese, with an introductory essay on the history of Chinese Philosophy, London: J. M. Dent and Son Ltd.

Huntington, Samuel P. (1993) 'The Clashes of Civilisations?', in *Foreign Affairs*, Summer, vol. 72, no. 3.

Hwang, Byung Tai (1979) 'Confucianism in Modernisation: Comparative Study of China, Japan and Korea', Ph. D. thesis, University of California Berkeley.

Jaspers, Karl (1962) *The Great Philosophers: The Foundations*, London: Rupert Hart-Davis.

Jochim, Christian (1981) 'Naturalistic Ethics in a Chinese Context: Chang Tsai's Contribution', in *Philosophy East and West*, vol. 30, no. 2, pp. 163–77.

Johnson, Wallace (tr. 1979) *The T'ang Code*, vol. 1, *General Principles*, translated with an introduction, Princeton University Press.

Johnston, Reginald F. (1913) *Buddhist China*, London: John Murray, reprinted by Chinese Materials Center, Inc., San Francisco, 1976.

(1934) *Confucianism and Modern China*, London: Victor Gollancz Ltd.

Kahn, Herman (1979) *World Economic Development: 1979 and Beyond*, Boulder: Westview Press.

Kalton, Michael (1977) 'The Neo-Confucian World View and Value System of Yi Dynasty Korea', Ph. D. thesis, Harvard University.

(1994) *The Four-Seven Debate: An Annotated Translation of the Most Famous Controversy in Korean Neo-Confucian Thought*, Albany: State University of New York Press.

Kang Youwei (1958) *Ta T'ung Shu, The One-World Philosophy of K'ang Yu-Wei*, tr. by Laurence G. Thompson, London: Allen and Unwin.

Kasoff, Ira E. (1984) *The Thought of Chang Tsai (1020–1077)*, Cambridge University Press.

Keenan, John P. (1994) *How Master Mou Removes our Doubts*, Albany: State University of New York Press.

Kendall, Laurel and Griffin Dix (eds. 1987) *Religion and Ritual in Korean Society*, Berkeley: Institute of East Asian Studies, University of California Berkeley.

Kenji, Shimada (1990) *Pioneer of the Chinese Revolution – Zhang Binlin and Confucianism*, tr. by Joshua A. Fogel, Stanford University Press.

Kiang, Shao-Yuen (1922) 'The Philosophy of Tang-Szu-Tung', in *The Open Court*, vol. 36, pp. 449–71.

Kim, Byung Whan (1992) *Seniority Wage System in the Far East: Confucian Influence over Japan and South Korea*, Aldershot and Brookfield: Avebury; Ashgate Publishing Co.

Kim, Ha Tai (1977) 'The Religious Dimension of Neo-Confucianism', in *Philosophy East and West*, vol. 27, no. 3, pp. 337–48.

Kim, Kwang-ok (1996) 'The Reproduction of Confucian Culture in Contemporary Korea: An Anthropological Study', in Tu Wei-ming (ed.), *Confucian Tradition in East Asian Modernity: Moral Education and Economic Culture in Japan and the Four Mini-Dragons*, Cambridge, MA: Harvard University Press.

Kim, Sung-Hae (1995) 'Active Contemplation: A Confucian Contribution to Contemporary Spirituality – A Study on "Quiet Sitting" in Korean Confucianism', in *Ching Feng*, vol. 38, no. 1, March, pp. 21–41.

Knechtges, David R. (1976) *The Han Rhapsody – A Study of the Fu of Yang Hsiung (53 B.C. – A.D. 18)*, Cambridge University Press.

(1982) *Wen Xuan or Selections of Refined Literature*, Princeton University Press.

Knoblock, John (tr. 1988) *Xunzi: A Translation and Study of the Complete Works*, vol. 1, Stanford University Press.

(tr. 1990) *Xunzi: A Translation and Study of the Complete Works*, vol. 2, Stanford University Press.

(tr. 1994) *Xunzi: A Translation and Study of the Complete Works*, vol. 3, Stanford University Press.

Select bibliography

Koh, Byong-ik (1996) 'Confucianism in Contemporary Korea', in Tu Wei-ming (ed.), *Confucian Tradition in East Asian Modernity: Moral Education and Economic Culture in Japan and the Four Mini-Dragons*, Cambridge, MA: Harvard University Press.

Kong, Demao and Ke Lan (1984) *In the Mansion of Confucius' Descendants*, tr. by Rosemary Roberts, Beijing: New World Press.

Kong Fanyin 孔繁銀 (1992) *Yanshengong fu Jianwen* 衍聖公府見聞, Jinan: Qilu Shushe.

Kramers, R. P. (tr. 1950) *K'ung Tzu Chia Yu – The School Sayings of Confucius*, Leiden: E. J. Brill.

Krieger, Silke and Rolf Trauzettel (ed. 1991) *Confucianism and the Modernization of China*, Mainz: v. Hase & Koehler Verlang.

Ku, Hung-ming (1898) *The Discourses and Sayings of Confucius*, a new special translation, illustrated with quotations from Goethe and other writers, Shanghai: Kelly and Walsh Ltd.

Kuang, Yaming 匡亞明 (1990) *Kongzi Pingzhuan* 孔子評傳 (*A Critical Biography of Confucius*), Beijing: Shangwu Chubanshe.

Küng, Hans and Julia Ching (1989) *Christianity and Chinese Religions*, New York: Doubleday.

Kuo, Eddie C. Y. (1987) *Confucianism and the Chinese Family in Singapore: Continuities and Changes*, Singapore: Department of Sociology, National University of Singapore.

Kwok, D. W. Y. (1965) *Scientism in Chinese Thought, 1900–1950*, New Haven: Yale University Press.

Lai Yonghai 賴永海 (1995) *Foxue yu Ruxue* 佛學与儒學, Taipei: Yangzhi Wenhua.

Lang, Olga (1964) *Chinese Family and Society*, New Haven: Yale University Press.

Lau, D. C. (tr. 1970) *Mencius*, with an introduction, Penguin Books.

(tr. 1979) *Confucius: The Analects (Lun yu)*, translated with an introduction, Penguin Books.

Le Blanc, Charles (1985) *Huai-Nan Tzu – Philosophical Synthesis in Early Han Thought*, Hong Kong University Press.

Lee, Ki-dong (1996) 'T'oegye Thought', in *Korean Cultural Heritage*, vol. 2, *Thought and Religion*, Seoul: The Korean Foundation, pp. 114–20.

Lee, Peter K. H. (ed. 1991) *Confucian–Christian Encounter in Historical and Contemporary Perspectives*, The Edwin Mellen Press.

Legge, James (tr. 1968) *Hsiao King: The Classic of Filial Piety*, in *The Sacred Books of the East*, vol. 3, Oxford: The Clarendon Press, 1885, pp. 464–88, reprinted by Motilal Banarsidass, 1968.

(tr. 1968) *The Yi King*, in *The Sacred Books of the East*, vol. 16, Oxford: Clarendon Press, 1885, reprinted by Motilal Banarsidass, 1968.

(tr. 1968) *The Li Ki or the Collection of Treatises on the Rules of Propriety or Ceremonial Usages*, in F. Max Muller (ed.), *The Sacred Books of the East*, Oxford: The Clarendon Press, vols. 27–8, 1885, reprinted by Motilal Banarsidass, 1968.

(tr. 1991) *The She King or the Book of Poetry*, in *The Chinese Classics*, Oxford: Clarendon Press, reprinted in 1991 by SMC Publishing Inc., Taipei, vol. 2.

(tr. 1991) *The Shoo King, or Book of Historical Documents*, in *The Chinese Classics*, Oxford: Clarendon Press, reprinted in 1991 by SMC Publishing Inc., Taipei, vol. 3.

(tr. 1991) *The Ch'un Ts'ew, with the Tso Chuen*, in *The Chinese Classics*, Oxford: Clarendon Press, 1895, reprinted by SMC Publishing Inc., Taipei, 1991, vol. 4.

(tr. 1992) *The Four Books*, in *The Chinese Classics*, vols. 1–2, Oxford: Clarendon Press, reprinted by Culture Book Co., Taipei, 1992.

Levenson, Joseph R. (1958) *Confucian China and Its Modern Fate – Volume One: The Problem of Intellectual Continuity*, London: Routledge and Kegan Paul.

(1964) *Confucian China and Its Modern Fate – Volume Two: The Problem of Monarchical Decay*, London: Routledge and Kegan Paul.

(1965) *Confucian China and Its Modern Fate – Volume Three: The Problem of Historical Significance*, London: Routledge and Kegan Paul.

(1959) *Liang Ch'i-ch'ao and the Mind of Modern China*, Cambridge, MA: Harvard University Press.

Li, Qiqian 李啟謙 (1988) *Kongmen Dizi Yanjiu* 孔門弟子研究, Jinan: Qilu Shushe, 1988.

Li, Yi 李毅 (1994) *Zhongguo Makesi Zhuyi yu Xiandai Xin Ruxue* 中國馬克思主義与現代新儒家 (*Chinese Marxism and Modern New Confucianism*), Shenyang: Liaoning University Press.

Liang, Qichao (1959) *Intellectual Trends in the Ch'ing Period*, tr. by Immanuel C. Y. Hsu, Cambridge, MA: Harvard University Press.

Liao, W. K. (tr. 1960) *The Complete Works of Han Fei Tzu* – A classic of Chinese Political Science, tr. from the Chinese with introduction and notes, vols. 1–2, London: Arthur Probsthain, 1939, 1960.

Lin, Yu-tang (ed. and tr. 1992) *The Wisdom of Confucius*, Random House, 1938, reprinted in Taipei: Zhengzhong Shuju.

Liu, Kwang-Ching (ed. 1990) *Orthodoxy in Late Imperial China*, Berkeley: University of California Press.

Liu, Shu-hsien (1996) 'Some Reflections on Mencius' Views of Mind–Heart and Human Nature', in *Philosophy East and West*, vol. 46, no. 2, pp. 143–64.

(1998) *Qicao Shijie Lunli Xuanyan de Bozhe*, 起草世界倫理宣言的波折 in *The Nineties Monthly*, no. 2, pp. 98–100.

Liu, Shu-hsien and Robert E. Allinson (1988) *Harmony and Strife: Contemporary Perspectives, East & West*, Hong Kong: The Chinese University Press.

Liu, Wu-chi (1955) *A Short History of Confucian Philosophy*, Baltimore: Penguin Books.

Lloyd, G. E. R. (1996) *Adversaries and Authorities: Investigations into Ancient Greek and Chinese Science*, Cambridge University Press.

Loewe, Michael (1994) *Divination, Mythology and Monarchy in Han China*, Cambridge University Press.

   (ed. 1993): *Early Chinese Texts: A Bibliographical Guide*, The Society for the Study of Early China and the Institute of East Asian Studies, University of California, Berkeley.

Louie, Kam (1980) *Critiques of Confucius in Contemporary China*, Hong Kong: The Chinese University Press.

Lu, Shengfa 盧升法 (1994) *Foxue yu Xiandai Xinrujia* 佛學与現代新儒家 (*Buddhism and Modern New Confucians*), Shengyang: Liaoning Daxue Chubanshe.

Lynn, Richard John (tr. 1994) *The Classic of Changes: A New Translation of the I Ching as Interpreted by Wang Bi*, New York: Columbia University Press.

Makeham, John (1997): 'The Earliest Extant Commentary on Lunyu: Lunyu Zhengshi Zhu', *T'oung Pao – International Journal of Chinese Studies*, vol. 83, pp. 260–99.

Makra, Mary Lelia (tr. 1991) *The Hsiao Ching*, New York: St John's University Press.

Maruyama Masao (1974) *Studies in the Intellectual History of Tokugawa Japan*, tr. by Mikiso Hane, Princeton University Press and University of Tokyo Press.

Maspero, Henri (1981) *Taoism and Chinese Religion*, tr. by Frank A. Kierman, Jr, Amherst: The University of Massachusetts Press.

Masson, Michel C. (1985) *Philosophy and Tradition: The Interpretation of China's Philosophic Past, Fung Yu-lan 1939–1949*, Ricci Institute, Taipei, Paris, Hong Kong.

Mather, Richard B. (tr. 1976) *Shih-shuo Hsin-Yu: A New Account of Tales of the World by Liu I-Ch'ing with Commentary by Liu Chun*, with introduction and notes, Minneapolis: University of Minnesota Press.

McCune, Evelyn (1962) *The Arts of Korea: An Illustrated History*, Rutland and Tokyo: Charles E. Tuttles Company.

McMullen, David L. (1995) 'Li Chou, a Forgotten Agnostic of the Late-Eighth Century', in *Asia Major*, 3rd series, vol. viii, part 2, pp. 57–105, Taipei: Institute of History and Philology, Academia Sinica.

Mei, Y. P. (tr. 1929) *The Ethical and Political Works of Motse*, London: Arthur Probsthain.

Meskill, John (1982) *Academies in Ming China – A Historical Essay*, Tucson, Arizona: The University of Arizona Press.

Metzger, Thomas A. (1977) *Escape from Predicament: Neo-Confucianism and China's Evolving Political Culture*, New York: Columbia University Press.

Moore, Charles A. (ed. 1967a) *The Chinese Mind: Essentials of Chinese Philosophy and Culture*, Honolulu: University Press of Hawaii.

(ed. 1967b) *The Japanese Mind: Essential of Japanese Philosophy and Culture*, Honolulu: East–West Centre Press.

Morgan, Evan (1935) *Tao The Great Luminant* – essays from Huai Nan Tzu, Shanghai: Kelly and Walsh Ltd.

Mou, Jun-sun (1966) *On the Indulgence in 'Discourse and Polemics' by Scholars of the Wei–Chin Time and Its Influence in Subsequent Ages*, Hong Kong: The Chinese University Press.

Mou Zongsan 牟宗三 (1970) *Xinti yu Xingti* 心体与性体, vols. 1–3, Taipei: Zhengzhong Shuju.

(1985) *Yuan Shan Lun*, 圓善論, Taipei: Xuesheng Shuju.

Mungello, David E. (1977) *Leibnitz and Confucianism: The Search for Accord*, Honolulu: The University of Hawaii Press.

Munro, Donald J. (1969) *The Concept of Man in Early China*, Stanford University Press.

(1985) *Individualism and Holism: Studies in Confucian and Taoist Values*, Ann Arbor: Center for Chinese Studies, The University of Michigan.

(1988) *Images of Human Nature – A Sung Portrait*, Princeton University Press.

Needham, Joseph (1956) *Science and Civilization in China*, vol. 2: *History of Scientific Thought*, Cambridge University Press.

(1969) *Within the Four Seas – The Dialogue of East and West*, London: George Allen & Unwin Ltd.

(1970) 'China and the West', in *China and the West: Mankind Evolving*, London: Garnstone Press.

Nivison, David S. (1972) 'Communist Ethics and Chinese Tradition' in John Harrison (ed.), *China: Enduring Scholarship Selected from the Far Eastern Quarterly – The Journal of Asian Studies 1941–1971* (Arizona: The University of Arizona Press, 1972), vol. 1, pp. 207–30.

(1996) *The Ways of Confucianism – Investigations in Chinese Philosophy*, Chicago: Open Court.

Nivison, David S. and Arthur F. Wright (1959) *Confucianism in Action*, Stanford University Press.

Nosco, Peter (ed. 1984) *Confucianism and Tokugawa Culture*, Princeton University Press.

Select bibliography

O'Hara, Albert Richard (1945) *The Position of Woman in Early China – According to the Lieh Nu Chuan 'The Biographies of Eminent Chinese Women'*, Washington, DC: The Catholic University of America Press.

Okada, Takehiko (1984) *Neo-Confucian Thinkers in Nineteenth-Century Japan*, in *Confucianism and Tokugawa Culture*, ed. by Peter Nosco, Princeton University Press, pp. 215–50.

Palmer, Spencer J. (1984) *Confucian Rituals in Korea*, Berkeley: Asian Humanities Press and Seoul: Po Chin Chai Ltd.

Pang, Pu 龐仆 (ed. 1997) *Zhongguo Ruxue* 中國儒學, vols. 1–4, Shanghai: Dongfang Chuban Zhongxin.

Paper, Jordan D. (1987) *The Fu-Tzu: A Post-Han Confucian Text*, Leiden: E. J. Brill.

Park, Sun-yong (1996) 'Confucian Influence on Education', in *Korean Cultural Heritage*, vol. 2, *Thought and Religion*, Seoul: The Korean Foundation, pp. 138–45.

Paul, Gregor S. (1990) *Aspects of Confucianism: A Study of the Relationship between Rationality and Humanity*, Frankfurt am Main: Peter Lang.

Pye, Lucian W. (1994) *China: An Introduction*, 4th edition, HarperCollins Publishers.

Qian, Mu 錢穆 (1966) *Zhongguo Jinsanbainian Xueshushi* 中國近三百年學術史 (*A History of Chinese Thought During the Last Three Hundred Years*), vols. 1–2, Taipei: Shangwu Yinshuguan.

(1982) *Traditional Government in Imperial China – A Critical Analysis*, tr. by Chun-tu Hsueh and George O. Totten, Hong Kong: The Chinese University Press.

Qing, Xitai 卿希泰 (ed. 1993) *Zhongguo Daojiao Shi* 中國道教史 (*The History of Chinese Daoism*), vols. 1–4, Chengdu: Sichuan Renmin Chubanshe.

Queen, Sarah A. (1996) *From Chronicle to Canon: The Hermeneutics of the Spring and Autumn, According to Tung Chung-Shu*, Cambridge University Press.

Rawson, Jessica (ed. 1996) *Mysteries of Ancient China – New Discoveries from the Early Dynasties*, London: British Museum Press.

Ricci, Matteo (1985) *The True Meaning of the Lord of Heaven (T'ien-Chu Shih-I)*, Taipei: Ricci Institute for Chinese Studies.

Roetz, Heiner Roetz (1993) *Confucian Ethics of the Axial Age – A Reconstruction under the Aspect of the Breakthrough Toward Postconventional Thinking*, Albany: State University of New York Press.

Rosemont, Henry (ed. 1991) *Chinese Texts and Philosophical Contexts*, Chicago: Open Court.

(1997) 'Feng Youlan: Something Exists', in *Philosophy East and West*, vol. 47, no. 1, pp. 79–81.

Rubin, Vitaly A. (1976) *Individual and State in Ancient China*, New York: Columbia University Press.

Rubinger, Richard (1982) *Private Academies of Tokugawa Japan*, Princeton University Press.

Rule, Paul A. (1986) *K'ung-Tzu or Confucius – The Jesuit Interpretation of Confucianism*, London: Allen and Unwin.

Rutt, Richard (1996) *Zhouyi: the Book of Changes*, Richmond: Curzon Press.

Rozman, G. (ed. 1990) *The East Asian Region: Confucian Heritage and its Modern Adaptation*, Princeton University Press.

Sailey, Jay (1978) *The Master who Embraces Simplicity – A Study of the Philosopher Ko Hung*, A.D. 283–343, San Francisco: Chinese Materials Center.

Sharpe, Eric J. (1994) *Understanding Religion*, London: Duckworth.

Schwarts, Benjamin (1985) *The World of Thought in Ancient China*, Cambridge, MA: Harvard University Press.

Shih, Joseph (1969–70) 'The Notions of God in Ancient Chinese Religion', in *Numen*, vols. 16–17, pp. 99–138.

Shryock, John K. (tr. 1937) *The Study of Human Abilities – The Jen Wu Chih of Liu Shao*, New Haven: American Oriental Society.

 (1966) *The Origin and Development of the State Cult of Confucius: An Introductory Study*, New York: Paragon Book Reprint Corporation.

Shun, Kwong-loi (1997) *Mencius and Early Chinese Though*, Stanford University Press.

Slingerland, Ted (1996) 'The Conception of Ming in Early Confucian Thought', in *Philosophy East and West*, vol. 46, no. 4, pp. 567–81.

Smart, Ninian (1989; 2nd edition 1998) *The World's Religions*, Cambridge University Press.

Smith, Warren W. (1959) *Confucianism in Modern Japan: A Study of Conservatism in Japanese Intellectual History*, Tokyo: Hokuseido Press.

Sommer, Deborah (ed. 1995) *Chinese Religion – An Anthology of Sources*, Oxford University Press.

Soothill, W. E. (1951) *The Hall of Light: A Study of Early Chinese Kingship*, London: Lutterworth Press.

 (1973) *The Three Religions of China*, 3rd edition, London: Curzon Press.

Space, Art (1996) 'Sôwon: Confucian Academies, Confucian Rites', in *Korean Cultural Heritage*, vol. 2, *Thought and Religion*, Seoul: The Korean Foundation, pp. 122–30, 146–53.

Sprenger, Arnold (1991) 'Confucius and Modernization in China: An Educational Perspective', in Silke Krieger and Rolf Trauzettel (eds.), *Confucianism and the Modernization of China*, Mainz: v. Hase & Koehler Verlang, pp. 454–74.

Steele, John (tr. 1917) *The I-li or Book of Etiquette and Ceremonial*, vols. 1–2, London: Arthur Probsthain & Co., reprinted by Ch'eng-wen Publishing Company, Taipei, 1966.

Streng, Frederick J. (1985) *Understanding Religious Life*, Belmont: Wadsworth Publishing Co., third edition.

Tai, Hung-chao (ed. 1989) *Confucianism and Economic Development: An Oriental Alternative?*, Washington, DC: The Washington Institute Press.

Tang, Junyi, 唐君毅 (1955) *Renwen Jingshen zhi Chongjian* 人文精神之重建, vols. 1–2, Hong Kong: Xinya Yanjiusuo.

(1961–2) 'The T'ien-Ming (Heavenly Ordinance) in Pre-Ch'in China', in *Philosophy East and West*, vol. 11, pp. 195–218; vol. 12, pp. 29–49.

(1972) *Zhongguo Wenhua zhi Jingshen Jiazhi* 中國文化之精神价值, Taipei: Zhengzhong Shuju.

Taylor, Rodney L. (1978) *The Cultivation of Sagehood as a Religious Goal in Neo-Confucianism: A Study of Selected Writings of Kao P'an-lung, 1562–1626*, Missoula: Scholars Press.

(1983) 'The Sudden/Gradual Paradigm and Neo-Confucian Mind-Cultivation', in *Philosophy East and West*, vol. 33, no. 1, pp. 17–34.

(1986a) *The Way of Heaven*, Leiden: E. J. Brill.

(1986b) *The Religious Dimensions of Confucianism*, Albany: State University of New York Press.

(1988) *The Confucian Way of Contemplation: Okada Takehiko and the Tradition of Quiet Sitting*, Columbia: University of South Carolina Press.

Teng, Ssu-yu (tr. 1952) *Family Instruction for the Yen Clan*, Leiden: E. J. Brill.

Teng, Ssu-yu and Knight Biggerstaff (1971) *An Annotated Bibliography of Selected Chinese Reference Works*, Cambridge, MA: Harvard University Press.

Thompson, Laurence G. (tr. 1958) *Ta Tung Shu: The One-World Philosophy of K'ang Yu-wei*, London: George Allen and Unwin.

Tillich, Paul (1963) *Christianity and The Encounter of the World Religions*, New York: Columbia University Press.

Tillman, Hoyt Cleveland (1982) *Utilitarian Confucianism – Ch'en Liang's Challenge to Chu Hsi*, Cambridge, MA: Council on East Asian Studies, Harvard University Press.

(1992) *Confucian Discourse and Chu Hsi's Ascendancy*, Honolulu: University of Hawaii Press.

Tjan, Tjoe Som (tr. 1973) *Po Hu T'ung – The Comprehensive Discussions in the White Tiger Hall*, vols. 1–2, Leiden: E. J. Brill, 1949. Reprinted by Hyperion Press, Westport, CT.

Tsunoda, Ryusaku (tr. 1951) *Japan in the Chinese Dynastic Histories: Later Han Through Ming Dynasties*, South Pasadena: P. D. and Ione Perkins.

Tsunoda, Ryusaku, de Bary, Wm. Theodore and Donald Keene (eds. 1958) *Sources of Japanese Tradition*, New York: Columbia University Press.

Tu, Wei-ming (1976) *Neo-Confucian Thought in Action – Wang Yang-Ming's Youth (1472–1509)*, University of California Press.

(1979) *Humanity and Self-Cultivation: Essays in Confucian Thought*, Berkeley: Asian Humanities Press.

(1981) 'The "Moral Universal" from the Perspectives of East Asian Thought', in *Philosophy East and West*, vol. 31, no. 2, pp. 259–67.

(1985) *Confucian Thought: Selfhood as Creative Transformation*, Albany: State University of New York Press.

(1989) *Centrality and Commonality: An Essay on Confucian Religiousness*, Albany: State University of New York Press.

(1991) 'A Confucian Perspective on the Rise of Industrial East Asia', in Silke Krieger and Rolf Trauzettel (eds.). *Confucianism and the Modernization of China*, Mainz: v. Hase & Koehler Verlang, pp. 29–41.

(1993a) *Way, Learning and Practices: Essays on the Confucian Intellectuals*, Albany: State University of New York Press.

(1993b) *Confucianism*, in Arvind Sharma (ed.), *Our Religions*, New York: HarperCollins Publishers, pp. 139–227.

(1996a) *Xiandai Jingshen yu Rujia Chuantong*. 现代精神与儒家傳統 (*Modern Spirits and the Confucian Tradition*), Taipei: Lianjing.

(ed. 1996b) *Confucian Traditions in East Asian Modernity: Moral Education and Economic Culture in Japan and the Four Mini-Dragons*, Cambridge, MA: Harvard University Press.

Tu, Wei-ming, Milan Hejtmanek and Alan Wachman (eds. 1992) *The Confucian World Observed: A Contemporary Discussion of Confucian Humanism in East Asia*, Honolulu: Institute of Culture and Communication, The East–West Centre.

Tucker, Mary Evelyn (1989) *Moral and Spiritual Cultivation in Japanese Neo-Confucianism: The Life and Thought of Kaibara Ekken 1630–1740*, Albany: State University of New York Press.

Twitchett, Denis (1976) *The Birth of the Chinese Meritocracy: Bureaucrats and Examinations in T'ang China*, London: The China Society Occasional Papers, no. 18.

Twitchett, Denis and Michael Loewe (eds. 1986) *The Cambridge History of China: Vol. 1: The Ch'in and the Han Empires 221 B.C. – A.D. 220*, Cambridge University Press.

Uno, Tetsuto (1957) *Zhongguo Jinshi Ruxue Shi* 中國近世儒學史 (*History of Modern Confucianism in China*), tr. by Ma Fuchen, Taipei: Zhonghua Wenhua Shiye Weiyuanhui.

Waley, Arthur (tr. 1937) *The Book of Songs*, Boston: Houghton.

(tr. 1938) *The Analects of Confucius*, London: Allen and Unwin.

Wallacker, Benjamin E. (1978) 'Han Confucianism and Confucius in Han', in *Ancient China: Studies in Early Civilization*, David T. Roy and Tsuen-hsuin Tsein (eds.), Hong Kong, pp. 215–28.

Waltham, Clae (ed. 1972) *Shu Ching Book of History* – a modernized edition of the translation of James Legge, London: George Allen and Unwin Ltd.

Wang Jiahua 王家驊 (1990) *Rujia Sixiang yu Riben Wenhua* 儒家思想与日本文化 (*Confucian Thought and Japanese Culture*), Hangzhou: Zhejiang Renmin Chubanshe.

Ware, James R. (1966) *Alchemy, Medicine, Religion in China of* A.D. *320: The Nei P'ien of Ko Hung (Pao-P'u Tzu)*, Cambridge, MA: M. I. T. Press.

Watson, Burton (tr. 1961) *Records of the Grand Historian of China*, vols. 1–2, New York and London: Columbia University Press.

(tr. 1963) *Mo Tzu: Basic Writings*, New York: Columbia University Press.

(tr. 1964) *Chuang Tzu – Basic Writings*, New York and London: Columbia University Press.

(tr. 1966) *Hsün Tzu: Basic Writings*, New York and London: Columbia University Press.

(tr. 1970) *Han Fei Tzu, Basic Writings*, New York: Columbia University Press.

(tr. 1989) *The Tso Chuan – Selections from China's Oldest Narrative History*, New York: Columbia University Press.

Watters, T. (1879) *Guide to the Tablets in a Temple of Confucius*, Shanghai: The American Presbyterian Mission Press.

Weber, Max (1963) *The Sociology of Religion*, Boston: Beacon Press.

(1968) *The Religion of China: Confucianism and Taoism*, New York: Free Press.

Wieger, Léon (1927) *A History of the Religious Beliefs and Philosophical Opinions in China*, tr. by E. T. C. Werner, Hsien Hsien Press.

Wilhelm, Richard (1931) *Confucius and Confucianism*, London: Kegan Paul, Trench, Trubner and Co.

(tr. 1967) *The I Ching or Book of Changes*, English translation by Cary F. Baynes, Arkana: Penguin Books.

Wood, Alan Thomas (1995) *Limits to Autocracy: From Sung Neo-Confucianism to a Doctrine of Political Rights in China*. Honolulu: The University of Hawaii Press.

Wright, A. F. (1960) *The Confucian Persuasion*, Stanford University Press.

(ed. 1959): *Confucianism and Chinese Civilisation*, Stanford University Press.

Wu, Pei-yi (1979) 'Self Examination and Confession of Sins in Traditional China', in *Harvard Journal of Asiatic Studies*, 1979, no. 39.1, pp. 5–38.

(1990) *The Confucian's Progress – Autobiographical Writings in Traditional China*, Princeton University Press.

Wu Zhihe 吳智和 (1994) *Mingdai de ruxue Jiaoguan*, 明代的儒學教官, Taipei: Xuesheng Shuju.

Xiong, Shili 熊十力 (1996) *Xiandai Xinruxue de Genji* (現代新儒學的根基) – *Xiong Shili Xinruxue Luzhu Jiyao* (Collection of the Major Works by Xiong Shili), ed. by Guo Qiyong, Beijing: Zhongguo Guangbo Dianshi Chubanshe.

Xu, Fuguan 徐復觀 (1969) *Zhongguo Renxinglun Shi* 中國人性論史, Taipei: Shangwu Yinshuguan.

Yamamoto, Schichihei (1992) *The Spirit of Japanese Capitalism*, New York: Madison Books.

Yan, Buke 閻步克 (1995) *Yueshi yu Ru zhi Wenhua Qiyuan* 樂師与儒之文化起源 ('Music Masters and the Cultural Origin of the Ru'), *Beijing University Academic Journal*, 1995, no. 5, pp. 46–54.

Yang, C. K. (1961) *Religion in Chinese Society*, University of California Press.

Yang, Cheng-pin (1986) *The Political Thoughts of Dr. Hu Shi*, Taipei: Bookman Books.

Yang, Hsien-Yi and Gladys Yang (tr. 1974) *Records of the Historian*, Hong Kong: The Commercial Press.

Yang, P. Key and Henderson, Gregory (1958–9) 'An Outline History of Korean Confucianism', in *Journal of Asian Studies*, 1958, no. 18.1, pp. 81–101, 1959, no. 18.2, pp. 259–76.

Yao, Xinzhong (1995) '*Jen*, Love and Universality – Three Arguments Concerning *Jen* in Confucianism', in *Asian Philosophy*, 1995, vol. 2, pp. 181–95.
 (1996a) *Confucianism and Christianity*, Brighton: Sussex Academic Press.
 (1996b) 'Self-Construction and Identity: The Confucian Self in Relation to some Western Perceptions', in *Asian Philosophy*, no. 3, pp. 179–95.

Yen, Chih-tui (1968) *Family Instructions for the Yen Family*, tr. by Teng Ssu-yu, Leiden: E. J. Brill.

Yoshio, Abe (1970) 'Development of Neo-Confucianism in Japan, Korea and China: A Comparative Study', in *Acta Asiatica*, 1970, no. 19, pp. 16–39.

Young, John D. (1983) *Confucianism and Christianity – The First Encounter*, Hong Kong University Press.

Yu, Chai-Shin (1977) *Korean and Asian Religious Tradition*, Toronto: Korean and Related Studies Press.

Yü, Yingshi 余英石 (1970) *Cong Songming Ruxue de Fazhan Lun Qingdai Sixiangshi* 從宋明儒學的發展論清代思想史, in *Zhongguo Xueren* 中國學人, September 1970, pp. 19–41.

Yun, Sa-soon (1996) 'Confucian Thought and Korean Culture', in *Korean Cultural Heritage*, vol. 2, *Thought and Religion*, Seoul: The Korean Foundation, pp. 108–13.

Zaehner, R. C. (ed. 1988) *The Concise Encyclopedia of Living Faiths*, London: Hutchinson and Co. Ltd, 1988.

Zhang Binlin 張炳麟 (1909) *Yuan Ru* 原儒 ('On the Origin of *Ru*'), *Guocui Xuebao*, 國粹學報 1909, no. 56. In *The Whole Collection of Guocui Xuebao*, Taipei, 1970, vol. 10, pp. 2604–8.

(1976) *Zhang Taiyan Shiwen Xuanzhu* 章太炎詩文選註, Shanghai Renmin Chubanshe.

Zhang Dainian 張岱年 (1982) *Zhongguo Zhexue Dagang*, 中國哲學大綱, Beijing: Zhongguo Shehui Kexue Chubanshe.

Zhang Guangzhi 張光直 (1983) *Zhongguo Qingtong Shidai* 中國青銅時代, Beijing: Sanlian Shudian.

Zhang Liwen 張立文 (1992)*Boshu Zhouyi Zhuyi* 帛書周易註譯, Zhengzhou: Zhongzhou Guji Chubanshe.

(1996) *Hehe Xue Gai Lun* 和合學概論, vols. 1–2, Beijing: Shoudu Shifan Daxue Chubanshe.

Zhong, Youmin (1985) *Xielingyun Lungao* 謝靈運論稿, Jinan: Qilu Shushe.

Zito, Angela and Tani E. Barlow (eds. 1994) *Body, Subject and Power in China*, Chicago and London: The University of Chicago Press.

Zücher, E. (1959) *The Buddhist Conquest of China*, Leiden: E. J. Brill.

Transliteration table

Pinyin spellings	Other systems including Korean and Japanese spellings	Chinese characters
	An Hyang	安恂
Anle Xiansheng		安樂先生
anle wo		安樂窩
badao		霸道
bagua xiangdang		八卦相盪
	bakufu	幕府
baihu tong		白虎通
bailu dong		白鹿洞
baijia		百家
Baopuzi	Pao P'u-tzu	抱朴子
benran zhi xing		本然之性
benxin		本心
boshi	po-shih	博士
	boshidô	武士道
	bumbu-funi	文武不二
buxiu		不朽
Cao Duan		曹端
chan	ch'an/zen	禪
changan		長安
chanjiao		禪教

Transliteration table

Pinyin spellings	Other systems including Korean and Japanese spellings	Chinese characters
Chen Duxiu		陳獨秀
Chen Liang		陳亮
Chen Ping		陳平
Chen Xianzhang		陳獻章
chenwei		讖緯
cheng	ch'eng	誠
Cheng (King)		成王
	Cheng Chung-ying	成中英
Cheng Hao		程顥
Cheng Yi		程頤
Cheng–Zhu	Ch'eng–Chu	程朱
	chondo-kyo	天道教
	Choi Chi-won	崔致遠
	Choi Chung	崔沖
	Choi Je-wu	崔濟愚
	Choi Si-hyong	崔時亨
	Chong Yak-yong	丁若鏞
chong you lun		崇有論
	chondochaek	天道策
Chu (State)		楚(國)
chuanxi lu		傳習彔
	chuko-ippon	忠孝一本
chun qiu		春秋
chunqiu fanlu yizheng		春秋繁露義正
chunqiu gongyang zhuan		春秋公羊傳
chunqiu zuozhuan zhu		春秋左傳注
	chu his su julyo	朱子書節要
	Chung Do-jun	鄭道傳
	Chung Mong-ju	鄭夢周
chushi hengyi		處士橫議
cun tianli mie renyu		存天理滅人欲
cun xin		存心
da	ta	大
dasi	ta ssu	大祀
	Dasan	茶山
datong	ta tung	大同

Pinyin spellings	Other systems including Korean and Japanese spellings	Chinese characters
daxue		大學
da yitong		大一統
da zhangfu		大丈夫
da zhuan		大傳
Dai De		戴德
Dai Sheng		戴聖
Dai Zhen		戴震
dao	tao	道
Dao De Jing	Tao Te Ching	道德經
dao wenxue		道問學
dao xin		道心
dao xue		道學
daqin si		大秦寺
datong shehui		大同社會
de	te	德
de		得
De Qing		德清
de xiansheng		德先生
di		地
di	ti	帝
diaomin fazui		吊民伐罪
Dong Zhongshu	Tung Chung-shu	董仲舒
dongxifang wenhua jiqi zhexue		東西方文化及其哲學
du jing		讀經
duan		端
dui		對
Dunhuang	Tun-huang	敦煌
duo		多
er ya		爾雅
fa		法
fajia		法家
fayi		法意
fanben		反本
Fan Zhen		范鎮
Fan Zhongyan	Fan Chung-yan	范仲淹

Transliteration table

Pinyin spellings	Other systems including Korean and Japanese spellings	Chinese characters
Fang Dongmei		方東美
Fang Keli		方克立
fang shi		方士
fanshen er qiu		返身而求
fawang		法王
fendou		奮鬥
feng		封
fo		佛
	Fung Yu-lan	馮友蘭
fugu pai		復古派
	Fukuzawa Yûkichi	福澤諭吉
fu jiao ziwang, zi buwan buxiao		父叫子亡, 子不亡不孝
	Fujiwara Seika	藤原惺窩
Fu Xi	Fu Hsi	伏羲
Fuxing Shu		復性書
fuci zixiao		父慈子孝
fuzi zhi dao		夫子之道
gangrou xiangmo		剛柔向沫
gao		誥
Gao Panlong	Kao P'an-lung	高攀龍
Gaozi	Kao Tzu	告子
Ge Hong	Ko Hung	葛洪
ge ming		革命
ge wu		格物
gen		艮
genghua		更化
	Godaigo (Emperor)	后醍醐 (天皇)
Gongyang Gao		公羊高
goumao ru		溝瞀儒
Gu Huan		顧歡
Gu Jiegang		顧頡剛
Gu Xiancheng		顧憲成
Gu Yanwu		顧炎武
guangjing pusa		光淨菩薩
guan xue		官學

Pinyin spellings	Other systems including Korean and Japanese spellings	Chinese characters
guan yi		冠義
Guanzi	Kuan Tzu	管子
gui	kwei	鬼
Guliang		穀梁
guo		國
guo jiao		國教
Guo Xiang		郭象
guo yu		國語
guozi jian	kukjiakam	國子監
Han (Dynasty)		漢(朝)
Han Fei		韓非
	Hakkyo Mobum	學校模範
Han Shu		漢書
Han Yu		韓愈
haoran zhi qi		浩然之氣
	Hayashi Razan	林羅山
he		和
he		龢
he		禾
he		合
He Lin		賀麟
heqin		和親
heshang		河殤
He Xinyin		何心隱
He Xiu		何休
He Yan		何晏
hehui zhu-lu		和會朱陸
he zhongsheng		和眾聲
Hong Xiuquan		洪秀全
Houji		后稷
Hu Hong		胡宏
Hu Shi		胡適
Hu Wufeng		胡五峰
hua		化
Huainan Zi	Huai Nan Tzu	淮南子
Huan Dui		桓碓

Transliteration table

Pinyin spellings	Other systems including Korean and Japanese spellings	Chinese characters
huangji jingshi		皇極經世
Huang–Lao		黃老
Huan Tan		桓譚
huangtian shangdi		皇天上帝
Huang Zongxi		黃宗羲
Hui Yuan		惠遠
hun		魂
hun yi		昏義
	Itô Jinsai	伊藤仁齊
ji		祭
jisi		祭祀
Ji Kang	Ch'i Kang	嵇康
jia		家
jiaji suiji, jiagou suigou		嫁雞隨雞嫁狗隨狗
jian ai		兼愛
jian ru		賤儒
jiao		教
jiazu zhuyi		家族主義
Jie		桀
jie yong ai ren		節用愛人
Jin (Dynasty)		晉(朝)
jingfa		經法
Jin Luxiang		金履祥
jing		經
jing		敬
jing		靜
jing jiao		景教
Jingjing		淨景
jing tian		敬天
jing xue	ching hsue	經學
jingzuo		靜坐
jinshi		進士
Jixia	Chi Hsia	稷下
jiyi		集義
	Jujahak	朱子學
	Junanô Kenpô	十七條憲法

Pinyin spellings	Other systems including Korean and Japanese spellings	Chinese characters
junzi		君子
junzi ru		君子儒
	Kaibara Ekken	貝原益宣
kaixin		開新
Kang Youwei		康有為
kaozheng xue		考證學
	Keian	桂庵
	kiho (school)	畿湖(學派)
	Kil Chae	吉再
	Ki Taesung	奇大升
	Kobong	高峰
	kogaku	古學
	Koguryo	高句麗
	kojiki	古事記
Kong Fuzi	K'ung Fu-tzu	孔夫子
kong jiao		孔教
Kong Qiu	K'ung Ch'iu	孔丘
kong tan		空談
Kong Zhongni		孔仲尼
Kongzi	K'ung-tzu	孔子
Kongjiao Hui		孔教會
kongjiao xueyuan		孔教學院
Kongzi Gaizhi Kao		孔子改制考
Kongzi Jiayu		孔子家語
kongzi miao		孔子廟
Kou Qianzhi		寇謙之
Kuang Yaming		匡亞明
	Kumazawa Banzan	熊澤蕃山
kun	k'un	坤
Laozi	Lao-tzu	老子
li		禮
li		理
Li Ao		李翺
Li Dazhao		李大釗
lihuai yuebeng		禮壞樂崩

Transliteration table

Pinyin spellings	Other systems including Korean and Japanese spellings	Chinese characters
Liji		禮記
lijiao		禮教
Li Si	Li Ssu	李斯
lixue		理學
Li Yong	Li Yung	李顒
liyue		禮樂
Liyun		禮運
Li Zhi	Li Chi	李贄
Li Zhizao		李之藻
Li Zhou	Li Chou	李周
Liang (Dynasty)		梁(朝)
Liang Qichao		梁繁超
liangneng		良能
Liang Suming		梁蕨冥
liang zhi		良知
Liao Ping		寥平
Lifu Chen	Ch'en Li-fu	陳立夫
Liji Jijie		禮記集解
lin		麟
Lin Yutang		林語堂
Lin Zhaoen	Lin Chao-en	林兆恩
Liu Bang	Liu Pang	劉邦
liu jing		六經
Liu Jishan		劉蕺山
Liu Shao		劉韶
Liu Shuxian	Liu Shu-hsien	劉述先
Liu Xiang		劉向
Liu Xin		劉歆
liu xue		六學
liu yi		六藝
Liu Yuxi		劉禹錫
Liu Zongzhou		劉宗周
Luo Congyan		羅從彥
Lu (state)		魯(國)
Lu Jiuyuan		陸九淵
Lu Xiujing		陸修靜
Lushi Chunqiu		呂氏春秋

Pinyin spellings	Other systems including Korean and Japanese spellings	Chinese characters
Lu-Wang		陸王
Lu Xiangshan		陸象山
Lü Zuqian		呂祖謙
Lunyu		論語
Luo Qinshun		羅欽順
luo xue		洛學
Ma Rong		馬融
Mao Zedong		毛澤東
Meng Ke		孟軻
Mengzi	Mencius	孟子
ming		命
Ming (emperor)		明(帝)
ming		明
Ming (Dynasty)		明(朝)
mingjia		名家
mingjiao		名教
mingjiao chuyu ziran		名教出於自然
mingjiao ji ziran		名教即自然
ming jiaohua		明教化
ming tang		明堂
ming xin		明心
mo		謨
Mo Di	Mo Ti	墨翟
	Motoda Eifu	元田永孚
moer shizhi		默而識之
Mouzi	Mou Tzu	牟子
Mou Zongsan		牟宗三
Mozi	Mo-tzu	墨子
	Nakae Tôju	中江藤樹
	Nanking	南京
neisheng		內聖
	Nihon Shoki	日本書記
	Nishi Amane	西周
	Nishimura Shigeki	西村茂樹
nuzi wucai jiu shi de		女子無才就是德

Transliteration table

Pinyin spellings	Other systems including Korean and Japanese spellings	Chinese characters
	Ogyû Sorai	狄生徂徠
	Ôjin (emperor)	應神(天皇)
	Oshio Chusai	大鹽中齊
Ouyang Xiu		歐陽修
	Paekche	百濟
	p'an-gong	泮宮
Pei Wei		裴頠
pinyin		拼音
po		魄
qi	ch'i	氣
Qi (state)	Ch'i	齊(國)
Qian Dehong		錢德洪
Qian Mu		錢穆
qianzi wen		千字文
qian	ch'ien	乾
Qin (Dynasty)	ch'in	秦(朝)
Qing (Dynasty)		清(朝)
qing		情
qingtan		清談
qiongli		窮理
Qi Song		契嵩
qiu fangxin		求放心
qizhi		氣質
qizhi zhi xing		氣質之性
quanzhen		全真
ren	jen	仁
ren	jen	人
renxin		人心
renzhe		仁者
renzhe renye		仁者人也
ren zheng		仁政
renfu tianshu		人副天數
renren		仁人
renren jie keyi wei Yao Shun		人人皆可以為堯舜

Pinyin spellings	Other systems including Korean and Japanese spellings	Chinese characters
renyu		人欲
rixin		日新
ru	ju	儒
Ruan Ji	Juan Chi	阮籍
ru dao wei yi		儒道為一
rujia		儒家
rujiao		儒教
rushang		儒商
ruhua xiyang wenhua		儒化西洋文化
rujia jingshen wei ti, xiyang wenhua wei yong		儒家精神為體, 西洋文化為用
rujia sixiang de xinkaizhang		儒家思想的新開展
rujiao ziben zhuyi		儒教資本主義
Rutong Pusa		儒童菩薩
ruxue		儒學
sai xiansheng		賽先生
	Sakuma Shôzan	佐久間象山
sancai		三才
sangang		三綱
sanji		三極
sanjiao		三教
sanyi		三一
sanyi jiao		三一教
sanjiao binxing		三教並行
sanjiao heliu		三教合流
sanjiao si		三教寺
sanjiao tang		三教堂
sanjiao xiansheng		三教先生
sanjiao yiti		三教一體
seng		僧
shan		禪
Shang (Dynasty)		商(朝)
Shangdi		上帝
Shang Shu		尚書
Shang Ju		商瞿

Transliteration table

Pinyin spellings	Other systems including Korean and Japanese spellings	Chinese characters
Shangjun Shu		商君書
Shang Yang		商鞅
shanren zhi dao		善人之道
shao		韶
	Shao-Chou	邵州
Shaolin		少林
Shao Yong	Shao Yung	邵雍
	Satô Issai	佐藤一齊
shen	shan	神
shendu		慎獨
sheng		聖
sheng		生
sheng sheng		生生
shengde		盛德
shengjiao		聖教
shengwang		聖王
shenren		神人
shenxin xingming		身心性命
shi		師
shi		誓
	Shibusawa Eiichi	澀澤榮一
shier zhe		十二哲
Shi Jing		詩經
Shiji		史記
shiyi zhi changji yi zhiyi		師夷之長技以制夷
	shinju-gôichi	神儒合一
	Shôtoku (Prince)	聖德(太子)
shu		書
shu		恕
shu shi		術士
shu yuan	sowon	書院
shuer buzuo		述而不作
Shun		舜
shun yinyang		順陰陽
	shushigaku	朱子學
si		祀
si		寺

Pinyin spellings	Other systems including Korean and Japanese spellings	Chinese characters
	Silla	新羅
	silhak	實學
sipei		四配
siwen		斯文
sixue		私學
Sima Qian	Ssu-ma Ch'ien	司馬遷
Sishu Zhangju Jizhu		四書章句集注
situ zhi guan		司徒之官
	So Kyong-dok	徐敬德
	Sohn Byong-hi	孫秉熙
Song (Dynasty)	Sung	宋(朝)
Song Lian		宋濂
Song-Ming	Sung-Ming	宋明
Song Shi		宋史
Song Shu		宋書
song xue		宋學
	Song Hon	成渾
	sôngnihak	性理學
	sonno-joi	尊王攘夷
su wang		素王
Sui (Dynasty)		隋(朝)
Sun Bin		孫臏
Sun Chuo		孫綽
	Sunghak Sipto	聖學十圖
Sun Zhongshan	Sun Yatsen	孫中山
tai		泰
taichang		太常
	Taigi-roku	大疑籙
taihe		太和
taiji		太極
Taijitu Shuo		太極圖説
tailao		太牢
Taiping Shangdi		太平上帝
taixu	tai hsü	太虛
Taixue	Tai Hsue	太學
Tao Hongjing		陶弘景

Transliteration table

Pinyin spellings	Other systems including Korean and Japanese spellings	Chinese characters
Tan Sitong		譚嗣同
Tang (Dynasty)		唐(朝)
Tang		湯
Tang Junyi		唐君毅
	Tenchi (Emperor)	天智(天皇)
ti		悌
ti		體
tian		天
tian busheng zhongni, wangu ru changye		天不生仲尼万古如常夜
tianli		天理
tianming		天命
tianchao		天朝
tianren ganying		天人感應
tianren heyi		天人合一
tianren xiangtong		天人相通
Tian Tai	Tendai	天台
tianxu		天序
Tianyan Lun		天演論
tianzhi		天秩
tiandi zhi xing		天地之性
tianxia		天下
tianxia yijia		天下一家
Tianzhu		天主
Tianzi		天子
	T'oegye	退溪
	Tokugawa Ieyasu	德川家泰
tong		同
	Tonghak	東學
	Tongkyong Daejon	東學大全
Tong Shu		通書
	toyo no dotoku, seiyo no gakugei	東方倫理西方科學
	Tu Wei-ming	杜維明
	Ugye	牛溪

Pinyin spellings	Other systems including Korean and Japanese spellings	Chinese characters
waiwang		外王
wanban jie xia pin,		萬般皆下品,
weiyou dushu gao		唯有讀書高
wanfa fencou, wuyue sanjiao zhijing		万法汾湊無越三教之境
Wang Bi	Wang Pi	王弼
wang (king)		王
Wang Chong		王充
Wang Chongyang		王重陽
wang dao		王道
Wang Daoyuan		王道淵
Wang Fuzi		王夫之
Wang Gen		王艮
wangguan		王官
Wang Ji		王畿
	Wang In (Wani)	王仁
wangmen houxue		王門後學
Wang Shouren		王守仁
Wang Yangming		王陽明
wei		為
Wei–Jin	Wei-Chin	魏晉
Wei Lue		魏略
weiren		為人
weiru		偽儒
weishi		唯識
wei tianming	wei t'ien-ming	畏天命
weiwo		為我
weixue		偽學
weiyan dayi		微言大義
Wei Yuan		魏源
Wen (King)		文(王)
wei zhongguo wenhua jinggao shijie renshi xuanyan		為中國文化敬告世界人士宣言
weiji		為己
weiren		為人

Transliteration table

Pinyin spellings	Other systems including Korean and Japanese spellings	Chinese characters
Wenchang Gong		文昌宮
wenhua yishi yu daode lixing		文化意識與道德理性
wen-miao		文廟
	Wing-tsit Chan	陳榮捷
Wu (King)		武(王)
wu		悟
wu		無
Wu (Emperor)		(漢)武(帝)
wuchang		五常
Wu Cheng		吳澄
wuji	wu-chi	無極
wujing		五經
wuwei		無為
Wu Qi		吳起
wuxing		五行
Xi Ming	Hsi Ming	西銘
xishi		西士
Xia	Hsia	夏
xian		賢
xiandai xin ruxue		現代新儒學
xiang		享
Xiang Xiu	Hsiang Hsiu	向秀
xiangfu jiaozi		相夫教子
Xiangshan Xianshen		象山先生
xianru		先儒
xianren		賢人
xiansheng miao		先聖廟
xian tianxia zhi you er you, hou tianxia zhi le er le		先天下之憂而憂, 後天下之樂而樂
xianwang zhi dao		先王之道
xian xian		先賢
xiao	hsiao	孝
xiaoren		小人
xiaoren ru		小人儒

Pinyin spellings	Other systems including Korean and Japanese spellings	Chinese characters
xiaoru		小儒
xiaosi		小祀
xiao xue	hsiao hsue	小學
Xie Lingyun		謝靈運
xin		信
xin	hsin	心
xin ji li		心即理
xin lixue		新理學
xin rujia		新儒家
xin songxue		新宋學
xin xinxue		新心學
xinxue		心學
xing	hsing	性
xing ji li		性即理
xingshen		省身
Xingsiu		行秀
Xinti yu Xingti		心体与性体
xinwang		新王
Xinya Xueyuan		新亞學院
Xiong Shili	Hsiung Shi-li	熊十力
xiushen		修身
xiuxin		修心
xu	hsü	虛
xu		需
Xu Fuguan		徐復觀
Xu Guangqi		徐光縈
Xu Heng	Hsü Heng	許衡
Xu Shen		許慎
xuan		玄
xuanjiao		玄教
xuanxue		玄學
xue		學
xuegong		學宮
Xue Xuan		薛瑄
xun		訓
Xun Qing		荀卿
Xunzi	Hsun Tzu	荀子

Transliteration table

Pinyin spellings	Other systems including Korean and Japanese spellings	Chinese characters
	Yamazaki Ansai	山崎闇齋
Yan Fu		嚴復
Yan Hui		顏回
	Yamaga Sokò	山鹿素行
yan yi		燕義
Yan Yuan		顏淵
yang		陽
Yang Rongguo		楊榮國
Yang Tingyun		楊廷筠
yangqi		養氣
yangsheng		養生
Yang Xiong		楊雄
Yang Zhu	Yang Chu	楊朱
Yao Shun		堯舜
yasheng		亞聖
yeqi		夜氣
Ye Shi		葉適
yi		義
yi		易
yi		一
	Yi (Dynasty)	李(朝)
Yi Baisha	I Pai-sha	易白沙
	Yi Hwang	李滉
	Yi I	李珥
	Yi Ik	李瀷
Yi Jing	I Ching	易經
yi ren		一人
yili sharen		以理殺人
yili xue		義理學
yili zhi tian		義理之天
yin		陰
Yin (Dynasty)		殷(朝)
yin–yang		陰陽
yinyue hediao		音樂和調
	Yi Saek	李穡
Yixia Lun		夷夏論
	Yômeigaku	陽明學

Pinyin spellings	Other systems including Korean and Japanese spellings	Chinese characters
yong		勇
yong		用
	Yongnam (school)	嶺南學派
	Yoshida Shôin	吉田松陰
you	yu	有
Yu		禹
Yudao Lun		喻道論
	Yu Hyang-won	柳聲遠
Yu Ji		虞集
	Yulgok	栗谷
Yu Yingshi	Yü Ying-shi	余英時
Yuan (Dynasty)		元(朝)
yuan fu		原富
yuan ru		原儒
yuan ru mo		原儒墨
Yuan Shikai	Yuan Shi-kai	袁世凱
yuan yi		元一
yue		樂
yue		侖
yue jing		樂經
yu tiandi wei yiti		與天地為一體
yue mingjiao ren ziran		越名教任自然
zai	tsai	災
zalan kongjia dian		砸爛孔家店
zaoming		造命
Zeng Shen	Tseng Shen	曾參
Zengzi	Tseng Tzu	曾子
zeng zufu		曾祖父
Zhan Roushui		湛若水
Zhang Binglin		章炳麟
Zhang Huang		章潢
zhangju		章句
Zhang Junmai	Carsun Chang	張君勱
Zhang Liwen		張立文
Zhang Xuecheng	Chang Hsue-cheng	章學誠
Zhang Zai	Chang Tsai	張載

Transliteration table

Pinyin spellings	Other systems including Korean and Japanese spellings	Chinese characters
Zhao		趙
Zhao Fu		趙復
Zhao Qi		趙岐
Zhaoqing		肇慶
zhao zhuo		照著
zhenyuan		真元
zheng		正
zheng meng		正蒙
zheng qiyi bumou qili, ming qidao buji qigong		正其義不謀其利, 明其道不計其功
Zheng Xuan	Cheng Hsuan	鄭玄
Zheng Yu		鄭玉
zhenru		真如
zhi	chih	直
zhi		智
zhiben		知本
zhi liangzhi		致良知
zhi qi		治氣
Zhi Xu		智旭
Zhi Yuan		智圓
zhi zhi		致知
zhi zhonghe		致中和
zhong		忠
zhong		中
zhonghe		中和
zhongyong	chung yung	中庸
Zhongdu		中都
Zhongguo Renwen Jingshen zhi Fazhan		中國人文精神之發展
Zhongni		仲尼
zhongsi		中祀
zhongti xiyong		中體西用
Zhou (Dynasty)	Chou	周(朝)
Zhou (the Duke)	Chou (the Duke)	周公
Zhou Dunyi		周敦頤
Zhou Yi		周易
Zhu Fuzi	Chu Fu-tzu	朱夫子

Pinyin spellings	Other systems including Korean and Japanese spellings	Chinese characters
Zhu Hong	Chu Hung	袾宏
Zhu Xi	Chu Hsi	朱熹
zhuan		傳
Zhuangzi	Chuang-tzu	莊子
zhuhou fangzi		諸候放恣
Zhuzi Jiali		朱子家禮
Zhuzi Jicheng		諸子集成
zi		子
zi bu		子部
zi bujiao, fu zhiguo		子不教父之過
Zi Gong		子貢
ziran		自然
Zisi	Tzu Ssu	子思
zixue	tzu hsue	子學
zhu renjun		助人君
zhulin qixian		竹林七賢
zong	tsung	宗
zong jiao	tsung chiao	宗教
Zou	Tsou	鄒
Zou Yan	Tsou Yan	鄒衍
zu		祖
zun dexing		尊德性
zuo		作
Zuo Zhuang	Tso Chuang	左傳

Index

Index